Ricardo and the History of Japanese Economic Thought

T0298617

David Ricardo's theories were introduced in fragments in Japan after the Meiji restoration of 1868, and his work came into prominence late in comparison to other major thinkers figuring in the history of economic thought.

The book seeks to analyse the studies in Japan from the year 1920 to the end of the 1930s—during the time before the outbreak of the Second World War, when even the study of classical economics became difficult. The book covers different aspects of his works and contains elements which may be interesting to foreign and even Japanese readers today without necessarily coming under the influence of Marx's reading. It presents works on Ricardo that are at present, wholly unknown to the Ricardo scholars and more generally to the historians of economic thought outside Japan.

This book is an essential read on the history of economic thought in Japan.

Susumu Takenaga is a Professor of Economics at Daito Bunka University, Japan. He has co-edited a book with Yuji Sato, *Ricardo on Money and Finance: A bicentenary reappraisal*, which was also published by Routledge.

Routledge Studies in the History of Economics

For a full list of titles in this series, please visit www.routledge.com

Ricardo and the History of Japanese Economic Thought

A selection of Ricardo studies in Japan during the interwar period

Edited by Susumu Takenaga

Routledge
Taylor & Francis Group

LONDON AND NEW YORK

First published 2016 by Routledge

2 Park Square, Milton Park, Abingdon, Oxfordshire OX14 4RN
52 Vanderbilt Avenue, New York, NY 10017

*Routledge is an imprint of the Taylor & Francis Group,
an informa business*

First issued in paperback 2019

British Library Cataloguing in Publication Data
A catalogue record for this book is available from the British Library

Library of Congress Cataloging-in-Publication Data
Ricardo and the History of Japanese Economic Thought :
   A selection of Ricardo studies in Japan during the interwar
   period / edited by Susumu Takenaga.
      pages cm
   Includes bibliographical references and index.
  1. Ricardo, David, 1772–1823.   2. Economics—Japan—
History—20th century.   I. Takenaga, Susumu, editor.
   HB103.R5R535 2015
   330.15′30952—dc23
   2015031444

ISBN: 978-1-138-85361-4 (hbk)
ISBN: 978-0-367-35051-2 (pbk)

Typeset in Galliard
by Apex CoVantage, LLC

Contents

Illustrations

Editor's notes

Chapters from 1 to 6 are editor's translations from the original Japanese texts, which have undergone a native English language correction.

Though this is an edited collection, there is no list of contributors of all the six chapters as they are by scholars whose careers belong to the interwar period. Refer to the Introduction for the presentation of each of them.

Quotations from Ricardo made by the authors of these chapters were from the editions available at the times of their writing, but the editor has collated them for check and correction with the texts included in *The Works and Correspondence of David Ricardo*, edited by Piero Sraffa, Cambridge University Press, 1951–1955, by adding in square-brackets the corresponding volume and page numbers such as [I/51]. These texts of Ricardo are now published online by Liberty Fund, freely available for academic purposes.

The same applies to the quotations from Marx. The editor has done the same in making use of the new MEGA (Marx Engels Gesamtausgabe) edition and has referred to the English translation of *Marx/Engels Collected Works* (MECW) published from Progress Publishers (Moscow) in collaboration with Lawrence and Wishart (London), 1975–2005 without raising any copyright issue, since this book contains no single quotation from Marx over and above 300 words.

The same also applies for the quotations from the secondary literature in the six chapters, originally published before the War. In editing this book, the editor has tried to give updated bibliographical data with page numbers in square brackets, as far as there exist new editions, more readily available for the present day reader.

The quotations from non-English (mainly German and Japanese) literature have been translated into English by the editor, with the usual language correction process.

The editor is grateful for the financial support granted from The Japanese Society for the History of Economic Thought (JSHET).

Introduction

Ricardo studies in Japan during the interwar period

Susumu Takenaga

1. Foreword

This book is a collection of English translations of a small number of writings selected from the research works on Ricardo carried out in Japan during the interwar period, which have remained unknown in other countries because of the language barrier. These documents may serve as a witness to the history of Ricardo studies in Japan, and as they present research performed in the historical contexts particular to Japan during a time reaching back nearly a century, they may still be of interest today to Ricardo scholars in particular and historians of economic thought in general, both inside and outside Japan. This introduction contains some preliminary explanations by the editor: 1) the reason for selecting the interwar period out of the long history of Ricardo studies in Japan, which began in the latter half of the 19th century and has continued to the present day, 2) the historical context forming the background to the writings collected in this book, and the positions, roles and individual careers of each author within that context, and 3) the features and significance of their works, now translated for the first time into English for publication.

The Tokugawa Shogunate pursued a policy of isolationism during most of the Edo period, for more than two hundred years from the 17th to the mid-19th century, throughout the period when the Western world was undergoing modernization and the modern history of political economy was taking shape. As a result, the Japanese, cut off from all other countries except Holland and China, knew nothing about European economic thought of the time, except through a narrow channel of Dutch literature. After the Meiji Restoration of 1868 and the opening up as a result of the external pressure symbolized by the 'Black Ships of Perry', Japan followed a path of rapid modernization in an attempt to catch up with the advanced Western countries. To modernize, Japan had to adopt everything from these countries, starting with their advanced scientific and military technologies. Naturally, economics (or economic thought) was no exception to this. From the early Meiji era, economic works were imported one after another from Western countries and were read, studied and translated by a small number of intellectuals of the time, not yet called 'economists'.

It was as part of this movement, which started at the beginning of the Meiji era, that Ricardo's work entered Japan and was introduced into Japanese intellectual circles. Up to the present time, there have been very few research works on the dissemination and introduction into Japan of Ricardo's economic thought, in particular covering the period prior to the Second World War. To the editor's knowledge, only the following three are available: Mazane, 1962, 1965 (the latter was subsequently reprinted in Sugihara, 1972) and Izumo, Sato, 2014. In his works, Mazane meticulously scrutinizes Ricardo studies from the beginning of Meiji era to the end of the interwar period, following the author's own criteria of periodization, to evaluate and historically situate the representative research works. The paper by Izumo and Sato, a chapter in the collection of articles on the international dissemination of Ricardo's economics, is mainly for readers outside Japan and presents the long history of Ricardo studies in Japan, spanning about one and a half centuries, divided by the two authors into two periods: before and after the Second World War. The objectives of these valuable studies largely overlap those of this Introduction, which owes much to them. As for the history of the introduction and reception of Western economics in general (including that of Ricardo) in Japan since the Meiji era, this Introduction draws no less on the following works: Mizuta, 1988; Morris-Suzuki, 1989; Sugihara, Tanaka, 1998, and Nishizawa, 2012.

2. The dissemination of Western economics in modern Japan and the introduction of Ricardo

i) *The influx of liberal Anglo-American economics after the Meiji restoration*

The dissemination of Western economics in Japan, from the early Meiji era onwards, began with the translation into Japanese of economic literature written in European languages (by intellectuals conversant with these languages). During the Edo era, the only European literature that the Japanese had been allowed to import and read was Dutch. For this reason, Dutch still predominated in the translation and presentation of foreign economic literature even in the early Meiji era, when the influx of literature in other European languages began. Most of the Dutch economic works translated into Japanese at this time were either retranslations of originals written in English or French, or else vulgarizations by Dutch scholars of economic works of English or French origin. But this situation changed rapidly a few years after the Meiji restoration, and the indirect translation and presentation via Dutch of works in other languages was discontinued, as a result of which the translations of literature from England and America began to predominate (Nishizawa, 2012: 307). This Anglo-American literature was more or less in line with the liberal tradition of English classical political economy since Adam Smith. Yukichi FUKUZAWA (1835–1901), Enlightenment thinker in the Meiji era and founder of the present-day Keio University, played an important role in the introduction of Anglo-American economics into Japan. He visited the United States as a member of diplomatic missions before and after the Meiji restoration, and brought back a number of economics books, to use as textbooks for his teaching activities and for translation by his students. The translation and presentation of a number of Anglo-American liberal economic works may have been helpful to the Enlightenment movement promoted by some intellectuals and politicians in the 1870s (the centre of which was 'Meirokusha' (the 'Meiji 6 Society') founded in the 6th year of Meiji (1873), of which Fukuzawa was a co-founder and 'Meiroku Zasshi' (Meiji 6 Journal) was the organ). These translations may also have been helpful to 'Jiyū Minken Undō (the Freedom and People's Rights Movement)', which campaigned for the institutional establishment of Japan as a modern nation state, with a view to enhancing its status with respect to the advanced Western countries (above all through the establishment of a constitution and parliament), in order to abolish the unfair trade treaties concluded with some of them before the Meiji restoration, and thereby obtain tariff autonomy.

However, most of the economic literature translated into Japanese at that time did not involve the original texts written by the classical political economists, but easily understandable commentaries written for the purposes of popular diffusion. It was through such commentaries that the names, works and theories of the classical political economists, Adam Smith to begin with, came to be known to Japanese readers. Among such popular commentaries, the most widely read in Japan at that time was *Political Economy for Beginners*, Macmillan, 1870, 1876 (4th ed.) by Millicent Garrett Fawcett (Mizuta, 1988: 12; Nishizawa, 2012: 308). After its first Japanese translation in 1873, this book was published several times by different translators up until 1905, towards the end of the Meiji era. This phenomenon probably reveals something about the level at which the introducers, translators and readers of foreign economic literature in Japan understood economics in the early Meiji era, dawn of the introduction of Western economics.

In contrast, it was only after the 1880s, when the trend in the modernization of Japan was already changing, that the translation of classical writings began to appear. According to 'Western Economics Books Translated into Japanese, 1867–1912' [from the year previous to the 1st year of Meiji till the year of transition to the Taishō era], included as 'Appendix 2' at the end of Sugiyama and Mizuta, 1988, only two works by classical political economists were translated during this period, namely Adam Smith, *An Inquiry into the Nature and Causes of the Wealth of Nations*, 1776 (translated by Eisaku ISHIKAWA and Seisaku SAGA, Keizaizasshi Publisher, 1883–1888 in 12 fascicles) and John Stuart Mill, *Principles of Political Economy*, 1848 (translated by Tadasu HAYASHI, Shigetaka SUZUKI, Eirandō Publisher, 1875–1885, in 27 fascicles). Some parts of Thomas Robert Malthus' *Principles of Population*, 1798 had already been translated in 1876 (by Sadamasu ŌSHIMA), but his economic writings were not translated during the Meiji era. For a long time, Malthus was known in Japan exclusively as a population theorist, and this overshadowed his existence as a political economist. His *Principles of political economy* was only translated into Japanese in the 9th year of Shōwa (1934), probably in relation to the centenary of its author's death (by Hideo YOSHIDA, Shōhakukan Publisher). But when it comes to Ricardo, neither his name nor his work appears in the above list. In other words, none of his works were translated into Japanese during the Meiji era. However, this does not mean that the existence of Ricardo in the history of English political economy remained unknown in Meiji Japan.

Japanese economic literature prior to the end of the 19th century (during the first half of the Meiji era) consisted for the most part of commentaries by Japanese writers replicating Western commentaries or textbooks for the needs of economics lectures in the high schools and colleges newly established after 1890. In this literature, Ricardo was presented from descriptions in foreign manuals of the history of economic thought containing fragmentary treatments of his theory (Mazane, 1962: 108). However, such mentions of Ricardo were not based on the study of Ricardo's texts by the Japanese writers themselves, but only on paraphrases of the descriptions found in the foreign secondary literature. According to Mazane, 1962, out of all the theoretical topics in Ricardo's writings, it was his theory of ground rent that was the preferred subject of fragmentary presentation. Although Japan was in the process of rapid modernisation after the Meiji restoration, the overwhelming majority of the active population was still working as peasants. Under the landowner regime established by the 1873 land tax reform of the Meiji government, these peasants were subjected to very high rates of ground rent and extremely hard living conditions. Social questions in Japan at that time were concerned mainly with the situation of the rural population as peasants. This historical context may well explain why particular attention was paid to the theory of ground rent in the economic thought of Ricardo, who was thus treated as if he was a theorist of ground rent. But as the capitalist economy began to develop fully in Japan at the turn of century, between the Sino-Japanese and Russo-Japanese Wars (the late Meiji era), the focus of social questions shifted from the relations between landowner and peasant to those between capital and wage labour. It was against the background of this evolution of Japanese society towards the turn of century that attention shifted away from the theory of ground rent onto the theory of wages in Ricardo's economic thought (Mazane, 1962: 127). But whether the focus was on the theory of ground rent or that of wages, the economic theory of Ricardo in the Japanese economic literature of the time was only fragmentarily understood via the secondary literature of the West that was then available.

The fact that Ricardo's works were not translated during the first half of the Meiji era (unlike certain original texts of English classical political economy, representative examples of which were given above) seems to be closely related to the international position of Japan, hurriedly modernizing in an effort to catch up with Western countries. In his economic writings, Ricardo affirmed that industrial capital represented the general interest of society in England, at a time when it had completed the industrial revolution and was establishing its position as 'factory of the world' in advance of the other European countries.

One can easily imagine that this economic theory of the most advanced country would be of little interest to the broad mass of Japanese readers, including politicians and businesspeople confronted with problems of a very different nature. On the contrary, to the Japanese leaders of the time, seeking to catch up with the Western countries under slogans such as 'Shokusan Kōgyō' (increase in production and founding of industries) or 'Fukoku Kyōkei' (rich country, strong army), *The Wealth of Nations* of Smith appeared to offer the appropriate theoretical weapons for pushing forward with their purposes, although this is an obvious misunderstanding of Smith. For this reason, *The Wealth of Nations* was repeatedly translated and published after the 1880s as it had been before, and became well known to general readers during the Meiji era. But all the Japanese translations of that time were entitled 'Fukokuron (Enriching Nations)', failing to convey the message of the original title correctly. This can be considered as circumstantial evidence of the manner in which Smith was received in Japan during the beginning of its modernization. It was only from the 1920s that this work by Smith came to be translated with the title of 'Kokufuron', much nearer to the meaning of its original title. Not only Smith's work, but Western economics in general was selectively introduced into Japan at the beginning of the Meiji era according to the preoccupations of those for whom it was destined, i.e., Japanese intellectuals and politicians and more largely the general readership. Western economics was therefore freely interpreted for the pleasure of those who received it. In such a context, the writings of Ricardo as characterized above had little possibility of being accepted. At the most, Ricardo's theory was presented only indirectly and fragmentarily in commentaries or textbooks reproducing Western secondary literature.

ii) *The shift from liberal Anglo-American economics to the economics of the German historical school*

In Japan during the 1870s, with the rise of the Jiyū Minken Undō (Freedom and People's Rights Movement) which campaigned for the establishment of a constitution and an elected legislature, there existed a relatively liberal atmosphere tending towards the institutional arrangement of Japan as a modern nation state. In various regions, a number of projects for constitutions were drafted on private initiatives. But the government, with its bureaucracy placed under the direct command of the Emperor, did not take these movements into consideration, seeking rather to oppress them. For example, 'Zanbōritsu (the Defamation Law)' was promulgated in 1875, and 'Meiroku Zasshi (the Meiji 6 Journal)' was obliged to suspend publication only two years after it had started. And in 1880, 'Shūkaijōrei (Public Assembly Ordinance)' was promulgated, regulating the freedom of assembly and association. At the same time, following an imperial order of 1876 requiring a constitution to be drafted, the government began studies for preparing such a constitution. Various different projects were proposed, of which the main point of conflict was related to fundamental issues of the Meiji state such as the duty of the Emperor to observe the constitution, or the competence of the parliament. The opposition between Hirofumi ITŌ (1841–1909), who insisted on the prerogative of the Emperor, and Shigenobu ŌKUMA (1838–1922), who proposed a more liberal constitution, came to the surface, and this led to the ouster of Ōkuma from the government with some of his advisers from Keiō University (the 1881 political crisis).

The following year, Itō visited Berlin and Vienna to study constitution. He attended university lectures on political science and sought advice from jurists such as Lorenz von Stein and detailed explanations of the German Imperial Constitution (Verfassung des Deutschen Reiches). After a process of adjustment in the government based on the draft constitution prepared by Itō himself after returning to Japan in 1883, the Imperial Japanese Constitution, modelled on the Constitution of the German Empire established by Bismarck in 1871, was promulgated in 1889 and enforced in 1890. At the same time, the Imperial Parliament was inaugurated in 1890. Thus, little more than 20 years after the Meiji restoration, Japan attained the institutional arrangement of a modern nation state, based not on the English but on the German model of state institutions, with the prerogative of the Emperor and limited powers of the parliament. Having accomplished national unification in 1871 (4th year of Meiji), the latecomer Germany was at that time achieving remarkable economic development under state hegemony, becoming a serious rival to the first industrial nations, England and France. Needless to say, Germany served as a suitable model for the modernisation of Japan, which was in a similar international position to Germany in many respects, despite large geographical and cultural differences as a country on the edge of Asia. Contrary to the period before 1880, the relative influence of Germany on Japanese culture and scholarship, compared to that of other Western countries, naturally increased after the political crisis of the early 1880s, and even more so after the promulgation of the Imperial Japanese Constitution. Of course the dissemination and introduction of economic thought was no exception to this.

Meanwhile, Ōkuma, banished from official position in the '1881 political crisis', was occupied with political activities with the aim of forming a party in preparation for the opening of parliament (within 10 years) promised by the government in 1881. During the same period, in 1882, he established the 'Tokyo Senmon Gakkō' (Tokyo Academy, now Waseda University), as a liberal private institution for research and education that kept its distance from the official higher education system. Together with 'Keiōgijuku' (now Keiō University) established at the end of the Edo era by Yukichi Fukuzawa, who was a contemporary of Ōkuma, Tokyo Senmon Gakko would play an important role in the development of liberal academism in Japan, different from that of the official higher education institutions, in particular imperial universities. On the other hand, the official higher education institutions placed under the direct auspices of the state were established at about the same time. The University of Tokyo, established in 1877, was reorganized as the Imperial University by the Imperial University Act of 1886 (and then renamed again as Tokyo Imperial University when Kyoto Imperial University was established in 1897). And the

Tokyo School of Commerce was established in 1884 (reorganized as the Higher School of Commerce in 1887 and now called Hitotsubashi University). Though not invested with the status of university, it did in fact function as a higher education establishment. These educational institutions other than the Imperial Universities were upgraded to universities by the University Act of 1919. It was after 1919, when a number of universities were established by the University Act, that the faculties of economics were set up in these universities as their independent specialized departments for economic research and teaching. Before that, economics had been taught in faculties of law, as it had been in certain universities in the Western countries. The establishment of faculties of economics in many of the Japanese universities, and above all in the Tokyo Imperial University, meant that both economics and social science became independent from political science (Staatswissenschaft).

To begin with, almost all the scientific disciplines studied and taught in the Western-style higher educational institutions that emerged in Japan at about the same time as the constitution and parliament had to resort to importation from the advanced Western countries. As an indispensable part of the importation of science, scholars were invited from these countries to carry out research and teaching in Japan. Foreign teachers gave lectures in the Imperial University of Tokyo and other universities and schools. They were called 'Oyatoi-gaikokujin (employed foreigners)', and were offered salaries equal to or even higher than those they were paid in their countries of origin, which amounted to several times more than their Japanese colleagues were paid, at a time when there was still a considerable economic gap between the Western countries and Japan. And in most cases, their lectures for Japanese students were conducted not in Japanese but in the languages of their respective native countries: English, German, French, etc. For the students, such lectures were occasions for practising foreign languages as well as learning specialized sciences. The foreign teachers, conveying in their own languages the sciences and thoughts of the advanced countries not yet enrooted in Japan to Japanese students with an uncertain command of foreign languages just learnt in school, may have held greater authority in the eyes of these students than their Japanese teachers.

The American Ernest Fenollosa, a philosophy and sociology graduate from Harvard University, was the first such foreign teacher to give lectures in Japan. He arrived in 1878 to teach political economy and philosophy at the University of Tokyo, before it was reorganized as the Imperial University by the Imperial University Act of 1886. The contents of his economics lectures were on the whole along the lines of Anglo-American economics (Mizuta, 1988: 31–2). In contrast, the two foreign teachers invited to Tokyo Imperial University during the period around the passage from the Taisho era to the Shōwa era (in the 1920s) were Emil Lederer (from 1923 to 1925), an Austromarxist, professor of Heidelberg University and research director of Hyōe ŌUCHI (1888–1980) when the latter studied in Germany, and Alfred Amonn (from 1926 to 1929), an Austrian who had been teaching at the Deutsche Universität in Prague. In addition, Eijirō KAWAI, then assistant professor at Tokyo Imperial University, invited Schumpeter to come and teach there, but the offer was eventually declined. All of these teachers were from Germany or German-speaking countries, suggesting that at that time, the faculty of economics of Tokyo Imperial University had more affinity with the German economic profession, close to Marxian economics.

With the organisation and expansion of higher education establishments taking place in the context of the institutional arrangement of Japan as a modern nation state, during the period around the 20th year of Meiji (1887), many textbooks were published for lecturing purposes. Naturally, economics, including the history of economic thought, was no exception to this. But many of these textbooks were not written by the researchers in charge of lectures, based on studies of the primary resources in the history of economic thought, but were translations of the textbooks already published in Western countries, or at best their Japanese adaptations rearranged for the convenience of each case. At the same time, the translation of classical works in the history of economic thought continued. Before the 1880s, most of these translations were from the English literature, and those from the German literature represented a small number of exceptions, but after 1881 the German literature grew in importance. Translations from German literature, including works published in Austria, came to account for half of the economic literature translated in 1889 (Nishizawa, 2012: 307, Izumo, Sato, 2014: 214). And subsequently, this tendency continued.

This does not mean, however, that the translations from English literature were overwhelmed by those from German literature and disappeared, or that they lost their importance, as in the case of the translations from Dutch literature after 1874. Along with the German literature, the English literature maintained its significance in the research and teaching of economics in Japan. One could say, on the whole, that the economics of German origin was valued in imperial universities and related official establishments, which were strongly interested in Germany during and after that period, attaching importance to the German language taught to promising young students and sending them to study in Germany for their future political, academic or bureaucratic careers, while the Anglo–American liberal economics was valued, as it had been before the 1880s, in the private universities and in official higher education establishments other than imperial universities, which attached importance to research and teaching of liberal tendencies. In Japan, where economics was strongly characterized as an imported science, such differences in the 'origins of importation' led almost straightforwardly to differences in the methods of research and teaching of economics in the universities of each category, and although it became less pronounced, this situation continued until later times. The same also applies to some representative examples of the introduction of Ricardo's economics during the interwar period, as we will see later in this Introduction.

Among the many translations from the German economic literature published in Japan in and after the 1880s, those from the original works considered even today as classical in the history of economic thought are the following (from Sugiyama, in Hiroshi Mizuta, 1988: 297; the translations are ordered according to the year of publication of the original work): Friedrich List, *Das nationale System der politischen Oekonomie*, 1841 (translated by Sadamasu Ōshima, 1889, in two volumes); Wilhelm Georg Friedrich Roscher, *System der Volkswirtschaft II*, 1860 (2. Aufl.) (translated by Sumizō SEKI, Teijirō HIRATSUKA, Germanist Association, 1886–1889, in five fascicles); Wilhelm Georg Friedrich Roscher, *System der Volkswirtschaft III*, 1881 (translated by Tōsuke HIRATA et al., Kokkō Publisher, 1896, in two volumes); Werner Sombart, *Sozialismus und soziale Bewegung im neunzehnten Jahrhundert*, 1896 (translated by Masao KANBE, Japan Economic Publisher, 1903); Adolf Wagner, *Lehr- und Handbuch der politischen Ökonomie*, Hauptabteilung 4: *Finanzwissenschaft*, 4 Bände, 1877–1901 (in Ministry of Agriculture and Commerce, 1895, translated by Yoshio TAKIMOTO, Dōbunkan Publisher, 1904); Adolf Wagner, *Ibid.* Hauptabteilung 1: *Grundlegung der politischen Oekonomie*, Tl.1: 'Grundlagen der Volkswirtschaft', 1883 (translated and commented by Hajime KAWAKAMI, Dōbunkan Publisher, 1906), and Adolf Wagner, *Agrar- und Industriestaat. Eine Auseinendersetzung mit den Nationalsozialen und mit Professor L. Brentano über die Kehrseite des Industriestaats und zur Rechtfertigung agrarischen Zollschutzes*, 1901 (translated by Hajime SEKI and Tokuzō FUKUDA, Ōkurashoten Publisher, 1902).

It is worth noting that Tokuzō Fukuda and Hajime Kawakami appear as the translators of the two works by Wagner at the end of this list. Their studies on Ricardo are to be included in this collection. After the 1880s, the interval between the year of publication of the original work and that of the Japanese translation gradually narrowed. Already at the beginning of the 20th century, the academic situation in Europe and the United States seems to have been known in Japan almost immediately.

The above list contains original works by economists from the old and new generations of the German historical school from List to Sombart, showing the important presence of this school in the Western economics imported into Japan during and after the 1880s. This may also have contributed to the rise of protectionism in Japan. In 1890, Sadamasu Ōshima, journalist and translator of List, founded the 'National Economic Society' with some of his companions. This was the first economic society in Japan, and its aim was to win over public opinion for their demands based on the principles contained in the work of List (Sugihara, 1988: 243–5; Morris-Suzuki, 1989: 61). Japan had been deprived of tariff autonomy by the unequal treaties concluded before the Meiji restoration, and it had to wait until 1911, the end of the Meiji era, before it could finally recover this autonomy by concluding equal treaties with its Western trade partners.

Modern capitalism was established in Japan through the industrial revolution around the turn of the 20th century, between the Sino–Japanese and Russo–Japanese Wars. As a result of these two wars, which served to demonstrate its military and economic force, Japan was recognized by the Western powers as a member of the advanced countries and admitted to their 'imperialist club'. This capitalist development was achieved within a short period of time, under state initiative, just as in the case of Germany immediately before Japan. And as in Germany, which served as the model for Japan, various contradictions accompanied the development of capitalism in Japan at that time (rapid expansion of towns with slums on their peripheries, extremely severe conditions of labour, low wages, rising unemployment, etc.). Consequently, European socialist ideas, already known from much earlier times, turned into real political movements in connection with labour organisations. In Germany, confronted with this situation, the Society for Social Policy (Verein für Socialpolitik) was established as early as 1872, the year after the foundation of the German Empire. This society assembled a wide range of German scholars around the economists of the German (new) historical school. And in response to the various social questions, starting with labour problems, raised by rapid capitalist development of the economy, the Society deployed activities of so-called *Kathedersozialisten* ("academic socialists"), discussing how to implement social reforms within the framework of capitalism, against both laissez-faire and socialism, formulating policy recommendations for the state to intervene in terms of regulation and support. From the end of the 19th century, Japan had to face similar situations, and probably under the influence of the economics of the German historical school, the Japanese Society for Social Policy was established in 1897, just after the Sino–Japanese War, along the lines of the German Society.

iii) *The foundation of the 'Society for Social Policy', its activities and disappearance*

The Society for Social Policy in Japan started its activities with a small workshop of members returning from studies in Germany at the end of the 19th century, influenced by the new historical school and *Kathedersozialisten* (Morris-Suzuki, 1989: 64–5). When the Society was established, the public security agency kept close watch on it for a time, because of the resemblance of Society's name to "socialism" and because some of its recommendations could be interpreted as socialistic (prohibition of child labour, legal recognition of trade unions, etc.), although its members shared the common view that social policy was different from socialism. But, as the aim of the Society was to prevent the existing social order from becoming unstable, by means of policy intervention by the state, it had to make efforts to demarcate itself from the socialism of the time in its deployment of social and political activities.

Because there were still no academic organizations in each specialized field of economics, participants from different fields assembled at the Society for Social Policy. At first it held regular meetings attended only by its members, to discuss the current social and economic problems, but in the 40th year of Meiji (1907), it started to hold an open annual conference to discuss the problems of the time and make policy recommendations to the government. The theme of the first such conference was 'factory acts', which had long been an open question for the Japanese government, becoming particularly topical after the Sino–Japanese War with the proposal of a new bill. The 'factory act' was actually passed four years after that, and the activities of the Society contributed to this enactment. The Society attained recognition not only in the narrow circle of researchers but also on a wider social scale. The members it attracted were not only economists from higher education institutions, but also journalists, businesspeople, bureaucrats and social activists, thus surpassing the framework of a simple academic corps. At the end of the Taishō era (beginning of the 1920s), a quarter of a century after its foundation, there were over 200 members, ten times more than the initial number. Thus it became an important society, incorporating not only diverse fields of economics but also related fields of social sciences in Japan.

But such an organization and style of activities gave rise to latent fissures in the Society. In addition, the differences in generations and longevity among the members increased with time, becoming so many factors of discordance within it. From the outset, the Society's admission of members of divergent tendencies left it vulnerable to inner conflicts between left and right about how to conceive of social policy and how to distance the Society from socialism. The series of evolutions within and outside Japan during the first half of the Taishō era (mid- and late-1910s) such as the First World War, the Russian Revolution, and 'Kome Sōdō (the rice riots)' in Japan, together with the diffusion of Marxism, inevitably brought to the surface the existing conflicts in the Society for Social Policy.

The central figures in what was then the younger generation of the Society were Tokuzō Fukuda (1874–1930) and Hajime Kawakami (1987–1946), who both wrote Ricardo studies that are to be included in this collection. Although he had studied in Germany under the direction of Lujo Brentano, Fukuda, a graduate of Tokyo Higher School of Commerce (now Hitotsubashi University), familiar with Marshall's work and of liberal tendency, took a position in the Society that was distinct from both the left and right—a middle-of-the-road position, so to say. Furthermore, Kawakami had not yet clearly adopted Marxism as his own position during the 1910s, when he was active in the Society. But when the opinions of the members were divided about the question of whether the Society should participate in the 'Kyōchōkai (Cooperation Society)', founded in 1919 for the purposes of studying and promoting cooperation between employers and workers by a partnership of government officials, businesspersons and researchers, both Fukuda and Kawakami were for non-participation, contesting the pro-participation position adopted by the old leaders of the Society, regarded as rightists. And when, in the same year, the 'Ohara Institute for Social Research' (now called the 'Ohara Institute for Social Research, Hosei University' and located in Tokyo as an affiliated establishment of Hosei University) was established in Osaka by the Ohara financial clique as part of its social works, important leftist members of the Society from the newly-established (in 1919) faculty of economics of the Imperial University of Tokyo (Iwasaburō Takano, Tatsuo Morito, and Hyōe Ōuchi) left the Society to join the Institute. Such behaviour by these leading figures of the Society, ranging from founding members to members from the younger generation, plunged it into confusion and paralyzed its activities. With the 18th annual conference in Osaka in 1924, the year after the Kantō earthquake, the Society ceased de facto its activities and fell into dormancy. In this way, the first national multidisciplinary society of the social sciences centred on economics in Japan became non-existent. In its place, the 'Socio-Economic History Society' was founded in 1930 and the 'Japanese Economic Association' in 1934. And a society with the same Japanese name (with a small but symbolic difference in English), the 'Society for the Study of Social Policy', was founded after the Second World War, in 1950. However, although it shares the same Japanese name and officially succeeded the pre-War Society, this new Society differs fundamentally from the old one in both its membership and the nature of its activities. It is rather one of the ordinary scholarly bodies now called 'Academic Societies'. The Society for Social Policy, which lasted for a quarter of century from the end of the Meiji era until the end of the Taishō era, was a very particular entity in the history of social sciences of modern Japan.

Viewing the above process as a whole, the dormancy (or more precisely, dissolution) of the Society for Social Policy can be considered as a result of the rapid penetration of Marxism and its growing influence in Japan from around the year 1920. It is also possible to consider that the Society for Social Policy was de facto divided into two factions: 'the right', which was absorbed into the 'Kyōchōkai (Cooperation Society)', and 'the left', which joined the Ohara Institute for Social Research, and the researchers belonging to imperial universities and other related schools strongly influenced by Marxism. During the 1920s, the Ohara Institute published both empirical studies on the social and labour problems in Japan and theoretical studies on Marxism, including translations of the works of Marx and Engels. And in the faculties of economics (newly established in 1919 or immediately afterwards) of Tokyo Imperial University and other related universities, a number of economists conducted theoretical and empirical studies from the standpoint of Marxist economics. Marxism (here, the economic theory of Marx in particular) was science and thought of German origin, written in German like the economics of the historical school. Its reception was not difficult for the Japanese intellectuals who had been educated in higher schools or universities. And for many competent young men sent abroad for study with official grants, Germany was a preferred destination. It is hardly surprising that some of these elite intellectuals read Marxist literature, including the works of Marx, and inclined towards Marxism, given the situation in the world and in Japan at that time.

It was in this intellectual environment that Japanese economists came to address the classical works of David Ricardo. Unlike the early Meiji period, when Ricardo was indirectly and fragmentarily introduced through secondary literature, the economic theory of Ricardo was now examined in relation to Marx's theory of capitalist economy. Hence Ricardo was not considered in direct relation to the current problems in Japan; the sole object of examination was his system of abstract theory. The serious research on Ricardo from the 1920s was overwhelmingly carried out by scholars of imperial universities (explicitly or implicitly) in close relation to and inseparably from research on Marx. Here, Ricardo's theory was regarded as an origin or a shadow of Marx's theory. But this was not the only approach to Ricardo developed during this period. For economists of the private universities like Waseda or Keiō, with a persistent liberal tradition, unlike the imperial universities and non-imperial official universities such as the Tokyo Higher School of Commerce (upgraded to Tokyo University of Commerce in 1919 by the University Act), Anglo–American liberal economics since Adam Smith retained its importance during the period of dominance of the German historical school. Here, Ricardo was received mainly in the later historical context of English economics, more precisely in relation to J.S. Mill and Marshall (and their interpretations of Ricardo). For this reason, they did not take up particular theoretical topics contained in the economics of Ricardo in relation to the concrete problems Japan was facing at that time, but they studied the historical progress of the theory as a whole and its systematic character. On the whole, Ricardo's thought came to Japan in the later years of the Taishō era through two distinct intellectual routes with two different aspects, although there existed a degree of interplay between them.

The representative of the first stream was Hajime Kawakami, mentioned above as a translator of Sombart and one of the main members of the Society for Social Policy. Tsuneo HORI (1896–1981) and Kōjirō MORI (1895–1962) began their studies of Ricardo under the direction and influence of Kawakami and both of them achieved remarkable results in the 1920s. Though not directly related to Kawakami et al., Chōgoro MAIDE (1891–1961) was equally active during the interwar period as an imperial university researcher. The representative of the second stream was Tokuzō Fukuda, also mentioned above as a translator of Sombart and one of the main members of the Society for Social Policy, like Kawakami. Though the research works of Fukuda to be translated and presented in this collection were written shortly before the First World War, they can be included in the interwar studies insofar as they anticipate the characteristics of the post-1920 Ricardo studies as described above. Shinzō KOIZUMI (1888–1966) carried out his studies of Ricardo as a disciple and under the influence of Fukuda, and he proposed his own particular interpretation of Ricardo in opposition to the other four imperial university researchers. Some of the results of the research by these six scholars, with characteristics specific to each of them, will be presented in this collection. The translation and presentation of these works will show the main achievements of Ricardo studies in interwar Japan, with their levels, particularities and problems.

3. The reception of Ricardo's work in Japan

i) How Ricardo was recognized by Japanese economists

As we have seen above from several perspectives, the introduction of Ricardo into Japan was very late, compared with the other figures of English classical political economy or their epigones in 19th century America. Not only was Ricardo introduced late, but he also attracted much less attention from Japanese economists than Smith and Malthus throughout the entire history of economic research in Japan.

After its first full translation in the 1880s, with the Japanese title 'Fukokuron (enriching nations)', Smith's work *The Wealth of Nations* was repeatedly translated, and his name was widely known from early times. In 1923, the year in which the Kantō earthquake occurred on the 1st September, the Japanese economics profession was busy commemorating the bicentenary of Smith's birth. In one of the commemorative meetings, Fukuda delivered an address entitled 'Adam Smith as a fighter for welfare economics'. And in January 1924, Kyoto Imperial University published a special issue of Keizai Ronsō, its house organ, entitled 'commemorative issue for the bicentenary of Adam Smith's birth'. Although the year 1923 was also the centenary of Ricardo's death, there is no record of similar commemorative events for him. Before and after 1917, the centenary of the publication of the first edition of *Principles of Political Economy and Taxation*, Ricardo's chief work, his works and documents related to the bullion controversy were published in England and America by E. Cannan, E.C.K. Gonner, T.E. Gregory and J.H. Hollander, but at that time the economics of Ricardo was not yet well-known in Japan.

As noted above, Malthus's *Principles of Population* was translated as early as in 1876, and his *Principles of Political Economy* was translated in 1934, the centenary of his death. Two years after that, the original English text of his *Principles* was reprinted (*Principles of political economy: considered with a view to their practical application*, by T. R. Malthus, Tokyo series of reprints of rare economic works, v.1, International Economic Circle: Kyo Bun Kwan, 1936). This was also the year in which Keynes's *General Theory* was first published. Keynes lauded this reprint of Malthus as a 'praiseworthy enterprise' in his short preface to the Japanese edition written in the same year. But similar reprints of Ricardo's works were never published in Japan, either then or later. In 1915, the Jurisprudence Society of Kyoto Imperial University held a 'commemorative meeting for the 150th anniversary of the birth of Malthus', and in the following year, its house organ *Keizai Ronsō* published a special issue for the commemoration of Malthus. Moreover, in 1934, on the occasion of the centenary of his death, the 'Journal of Imperial University' of Tokyo Imperial University published (on page six of its issue of 20th October) a 'Special column for the centenary of the death of Malthus', to which four economists (Chōgoroō Maide, Hyōe Ōuchi, Itsurō Sakisaka [1897–1985] and Hideo Yoshida [1906–1953], all well-known in Japan up to the present day) contributed articles. In particular, Maide, occupied with Ricardo studies, pointed out at the end of his article that in 1923, the centenary of Ricardo's death, 'there was almost no enterprise for commemorating it', in contrast to the case of Malthus. Addressing in detail the problems of population and poverty accompanying industrialisation and urbanisation, and arguing in favour of protectionism in international trade, Malthus was considered to be more relevant than Ricardo to the problems arising from the process of modernisation that was taking place in Japan at that time.

The fact that Ricardo was rather overshadowed by other more popular figures in the history of economic thought, such as Smith and Marx, did not change very much, even after the Second World War. In 1967, the centenary of the publication of the first volume of *Capital*, and in 1976, the bicentenary of the publication of *The Wealth of Nations*, the Japanese Society for the History of Economic Thought edited and published two commemorative collections of articles, entitled respectively 'Making of *Capital*' and 'Making of *The Wealth of Nations*' (both published by Iwanami Shoten). A line-up of leading Japanese researchers in their respective fields contributed to each of these collections, while in the number 10 of the 'Annual Bulletin of the Society for the History of Economic Thought' published in 1972, the bicentenary of Ricardo's birth, Kōji NAKAMURA published a survey entitled 'Ricardo studies', together with a similar text by Tadashi HAYASAKA entitled 'Studies in modern economics – a hundred years of modern economics', and Tsuneo Hori published a memorandum of his career as a researcher entitled '50 years of my Ricardo studies in retrospect'. It was probably in relation to the bicentenary of the birth of Ricardo that these two researchers, among the representative Ricardo scholars of their time, contributed their articles on Ricardo to the same issue of the Bulletin, but the number 10 itself was neither a commemorative nor a special issue. However, the theme of the plenary session of the 36th annual conference of the JSHET held in November of that year was the 'Ricardo Symposium'. The two articles on Ricardo in the Annual Bulletin and the main theme of the Annual Conference seem to have been naturally chosen to commemorate the year 1972, the bicentenary of Ricardo's birth. As far as Ricardo is concerned, this was the first commemorative enterprise since the Meiji era in the history of economic thought in Japan.

It follows from the above that from the 4th year of Meiji (1872), when it is not certain that even the name of Ricardo was known in Japan, till the bicentenary of his birth nearly 30 years after the Second World War, nothing was done to commemorate him in any of the landmark years relating to his birth or death, or to the publication of his important works. Now the two bicentenaries of the publication of *Principles* and of the death of its author are approaching. How will the Japanese (and world) academic circles address the next landmark year?

ii) *Methods of research and selection of subjects*

As seen above, Ricardo studies in the interwar period proceeded inseparably from the rapid penetration of Marx's influence into the Japanese academic circles of the time. Because of this, Marx's treatment of Ricardo seems to have largely influenced, explicitly or implicitly, the importance that Ricardo scholars attached to specific problems in Ricardo's theory or their selection. The detailed examinations by Marx of Ricardo's theories of value, profit and ground rent in *Theories of surplus value*, edited and published as Volume 4 of *Capital* by K. Kautsky at the beginning of the 20th century, were taken as criteria for either the positive evaluation of these theories or a critical and negative attitude towards them based on Marx's criticism. Ricardo's theory of wages was studied in relation to the theory of surplus value (exploitation) directly following the theory of commodity and money in Volume 1 of *Capital*, and its place in the history of economic theory was determined according to its distance from Marx. As for Ricardo's theory of money, apart from his criticism of Ricardo's understanding of the 'essence of money' in the first chapters of *Capital*, Marx only examined it once, in the brief historical survey 'C. Theories of the medium of circulation and of money' at the end of chapter 2 ('Money or Simple Circulation') of *A Contribution to the critique of political economy, part one* (1859), where he criticized 'Ricardo's quantity theory of money' as proposed in the pamphlet *The high price of bullion, a proof of the depreciation of bank notes* (1810–11). And in this brief survey, out of all Ricardo's writings on money and finance, Marx only considered *High Price* (and even then, only part of it). All his other works (*Reply to Mr. Bosanquet's practical observations on the report of the bullion committee* (1811), *Proposals for an economical and secure currency* (1816), chapter 27 of *Principles* ('On currency and banks'), *Plan for the establishment of a national bank* (1823)) were neglected. Marx never mentioned Ricardo's theory of international trade expounded in chapter 7 ('On foreign trade') of *Principles* or his theory of taxation presented in chapter 8 ('On taxes') and in the following chapters. However, this may be explained by Marx's plan for the 'Critique of Political Economy'. *Capital* and its manuscripts only contained the very beginning part of this plan, from which these subjects had to be excluded.

On the whole, under the influence of this treatment by Marx, the subjects of Ricardo studies in and after the 1920s (and after the Second World War) were overwhelmingly concentrated on the 'theory of value and distribution'. As for the theory of money and finance, the almost exclusive aim of a small number of research works was, after Marx, to highlight the inconsistency and contradiction between Ricardo's quantity theory of money and his theory of value in *High Price* (a representative example of such research in the interwar period is provided by Suenaga, 1934). The other writings Ricardo produced during his short career as an economist (listed above) were hardly taken into consideration. Although a Japanese translation of quality including almost all the main monetary writings of Ricardo was published in 1931 (see below; it seems that even in English there were, at that time, no such publications of comparable quality in terms of scrupulous text critique and comprehensiveness), no subsequent research works undertook any comprehensive study of Ricardo's theory of money, taking all of these writings into account. This is in striking contrast to the situation during the first half of the Meiji era, before about 1890, when the theories of international trade and money and finance were among the preferred topics in the indirect and fragmentary presentations of Ricardo's theory, as seen above, although most of them were entirely insufficient or at times beside the point. A number of studies were carried out in the fields not considered by Marx, in the interwar period after 1920, but they were not in the framework of systematic research with the aim of situating Ricardo in the history of economic thought and understanding his theory as a whole (these systematic studies were all focused on the 'theory of value and distribution', the main subject of Ricardo studies before the Second World War, and all the documents included in this collection belong to this category), and they only appeared in the form of one-off journal articles (for details see Mazane, 1965: 32–48). Furthermore, many of the authors of the articles of this kind were not specialists of the history of economic thought, but of other fields of economics, and some of them were quite far-removed from Marxist economics. The particularity of Koizumi's systematic Ricardo study can be appreciated in this context. He carried it out just like Hori, Mori and Maide, contemporarily with them but from an opposite standpoint, in taking up various subjects not limited to the 'theory of value and distribution' in his series of articles on Ricardo published during the first half of the 1920s and in his work included in this collection, the last product of his Ricardo studies.

iii) *Translations of Ricardo's writings and related literature*

The study of economic theory in Japan after the Meiji restoration was totally reliant on the importation of economics from the advanced Western countries, written in European languages. Much energy had to be spent on deciphering the economic literature in foreign languages and transferring it into Japanese. The work of translation therefore occupied an important place in research activities. The translation of the essential foreign literature into Japanese as a fundamental resource was the precondition for further research, and conversely, the extent of the translation was an indicator of progress in the research on the original resources. Let us now see how far this preliminary process was taken during the interwar period, preceding the production of research results in the strict sense of the term, by examining the situation as regards the translation of Ricardo, Marx and the main secondary literature of the Western countries.

a) *Selected list of translations of the writings of Ricardo himself, covering all the works of Ricardo translated during the interwar period*

Partial translation of *Principles* by Tsuneo Hori, with a foreword by Hajime Kawakami, Iwanami Shoten, 1921. Actually a co-translation by both of them. The first Japanese translation of Ricardo's own writing.

> Entire translation of *Principles* by Shinzō Koizumi, Iwanami Shoten, 1928.
> Entire translation of *Principles* (variorum edition) by Tsuneo Hori, Kōbundō, 1928.

Ricardo Kahei Ginkō Ronshyū (Collection of Ricardo's writings on money and banking), edited and translated by Shigeo OBATA, Dōbunkan, 1931. Included in this translation are the following five texts by Ricardo:

1 *Three letters on the price of Gold, contributed to the Morning Chronicle in August–November, 1809. A reprint of economic tracts*, edited by J.H. Hollander, with Introduction and Notes by J.H. Hollander, Baltimore 1903.

2   *The high price of bullion, a proof of the depreciation of bank notes, 4th ed., corrected, to which is added an appendix, containing observations on some passages in an article in the Edinburgh Review, on the depreciation of paper currency; also suggestions for securing to the public a currency as invariable as gold, with a very moderate supply of the metal*, London 1811.
3   *Reply to Mr. Bosanquet's practical observations on the report of the bullion committee*, London 1811.
4   *Proposals for an economical and secure currency; with observations on the profits of the Bank of England, as they regard the public and the proprietors of bank stock*, 2nd ed. London 1816.
5   *Plan for the establishment of a national bank*, London 1824.

Apart from item 1, all of the above were translated directly from the original text. Obata, the translator, subjected the editions of McCulloch and Gonner (see below) to a rigorous text critique by collating them with the original texts. He confirmed the editorial errors in McCulloch's edition that had been indicated by J.H. Hollander, the editor of item 1. From his own search, he also listed the minor editorial faults in McCulloch's edition. And on the basis of this search, he confirmed that Gonner's edition, published more than half a century later, faithfully reproduced the errors contained in McCulloch's edition (and added further new errors to the old edition), which led Obata to infer that Gonner's edition was not compiled directly from the original texts, but from McCulloch's edition. Furthermore, since McCulloch's edition omits item 1 and Gonner's edition omits item 5, the collection of monetary writings of Ricardo edited by Obata was probably the best possible one for that time, in terms of comprehensiveness and the text critique, even though it was a publication of Japanese translations. If it did not include chapter 27 of *Principles* ('On currency and banks'), this may have been because it is not an independent work by Ricardo, and also because the entire translation of *Principles* had just been published by two specialists, Koizumi and Hori. However, as the theory of money and banking was not one of the principal themes of Ricardo studies in and also after the interwar period, this collection of translated writings seems unfortunately not to have been sufficiently used for subsequent research.

> *Ricardo Nōgyō Hogo Seisaku Hihan—Chidai Ron—(Ricardo's criticism of the policy of protection of agriculture – theory of ground rent)*, translated by Kazushi ŌKAWA, Iwanami Shoten, 1938. Entire translations of *An Essay on the influence of a low price of corn on the profits of stock and on protection to agriculture*, from McCulloch's *Works of David Ricardo*.
> *Letters of David Ricardo to Thomas Robert Malthus*, in two volumes, translated by Tadashi NAKANO, Iwanami Shoten, 1942–43, translation on J. Bonar's edition (1887).

The above are Japanese translations of Ricardo's works. Without translations, naturally, the researchers studied Ricardo in English. The following is a list of the principal English editions of Ricardo's works available for research during the interwar period.

> *The works of David Ricardo, Esq., M.P.: with a notice of the life and writings of the author,* edited by J.R. McCulloch, John Murray, 1846.
>
> *Letters of David Ricardo to Thomas Robert Malthus 1810–1823,* edited by James Bonar, Clarendon Press, 1887.
>
> *Principles of political economy and taxation, edited with introductory essay, notes, and appendices,* by E.C.K. Gonner, George Bell and Sons, 1891.
>
> *Letters of David Ricardo to John Ramsay McCulloch, 1816–1823,* edited with introduction and annotations by J.H. Hollander, pub. for the American Economic Association by Macmillan, 1895.
>
> *Letters of David Ricardo to Hutches Trower and others, 1811–1823,* edited by James Bonar and J.H. Hollander, Clarendon Press, 1899.
>
> *Economic Essays by David Ricardo,* edited with introductory essay and notes by E.C.K. Gonner, G. Bell, 1923 (reprinted by Routledge, 2013).
>
> *Notes on Malthus' 'Principles of political economy',* edited with an introduction and notes by Jacob H. Hollander and T.E. Gregory, Johns Hopkins Press, Humphrey Milford, Oxford University Press, 1928.

b) Translations of writings by Marx

The translations of documents relating to Marx and Marxism, which had a profound impact on Ricardo studies, were published successively from the year 1919. Below are listed some of the translations of Marx's main economic writings, which appear to have had a relatively large number of readers.

> Entire translation of *Capital,* published as part of the *Works of Marx.* Volumes 1 and 2 were published in three fascicles, Volume 3 in four fascicles. Publication began in 1920 and was completed in 1924, translated by Motoyuki TAKAHATA, Daitōkaku-Adachisha.
>
> *Wage labour and capital,* and *Wages, price and profit,* translated by Hajime Kawakami, Kōbundō, 1921.
>
> *Contribution to a critique of political economy,* as part of the *Works of Marx,* translated by Manabu SANO, Daitōkaku, 1923.
>
> Entire translation of *Theories of surplus value,* translated by Tatsuo MORITO, Samezō KURUMA and others. Published in the form of pamphlets by Ōhara Institute for Social Research, in fascicles from 1925 to 1930. Independent publication of the translation of Itsurō Sakisaka and others, Kaizōsha, 1936.

c) Translations of Western research works on Ricardo

> Lastly, let us see which Western research works, often mentioned and referred to in Japanese studies of Ricardo, were translated during the interwar

period. They are listed in order of the publication dates of the Japanese translations.

Karl Diehl, *Sozialwissenschaftliche Erläuterungen zu David Ricardo's Grundgesetzen der Volkswirtschaft und Besteuerung*, W. Engelmann, 1905, 2., neu verfasste Aufl., Teil 1, Teil 2 (translated by Juntarō WASHINO, Adachisha, 1925).

Edwin Cannan, *A history of the theories of production and distribution in English political economy from 1776 to 1848*, Percival, 1893, 1894, 2nd edition with two additional sections, 1903 P.S. King & Son, 3rd edition, 1917, P.S. King (translated by Ichirō WATANABE, Shūhōkaku, 1926).

Alfred Amonn, *Ricardo als Begründer der theoretischen Nationalökonomie : eine Einführung in sein Hauptwerk und zugleich in die Grundprobleme der nationalökonomischen Theorie, zur hundertjährigen Wiederkehr seines Todestages (11. September 1823)*, G. Fischer, 1924 (translated by Isamu ABE and Masao TAKAHASHI, Meizensha, 1928).

Heinrich Dietzel, *Vom Lehrwert der Wertlehre und vom Grundfehler der Marxschen Verteilungslehre*, A. Deichert, 1921 (translated by Shinichi WATANABE, Nihonhyōronsha, 1933).

Jacob Harry Hollander, *David Ricardo: a centenary estimate*, John Hopkins Press, 1914 (translated by Hideo YAMASHITA, Yūhikaku, 1941).

The above list shows that a major part of the research works on Ricardo, an English classical political economist, translated into Japanese at that time were written in German. Incidentally, when the Japanese translation of Amonn's work appeared, he was in charge of lectures in the faculty of economics of Tokyo Imperial University (see above).

In economic research, especially theoretical research, the further back we look from the present time towards the early Meiji era, the more importance was attached to the translation of foreign literature. The translations listed above in three categories were published nearly 100 years ago. They can be regarded as a helpful indicator of the state of Ricardo studies at the time. But there is another circumstance that must be taken into account concerning the translation into Japanese. As a latecomer, Japan had to carry out its modernisation in a much shorter time-span than the other advanced countries. This means that Japanese society, its human relations and more generally its culture underwent repeated, profound transmutations over a short period of time. The language (here we are only concerned with the written language) was also exposed to continual changes. Because of this particularity in the process of modernisation that started in the Meiji era, Japanese economists, obliged to devote a significant part of their research and teaching activities to translation work, faced the following difficulty concerning the language of translation they created.

Along with the short-term changes in society, the Japanese language used for translation also continued to evolve. Today, for every generation, it is not easy to read the texts written in Meiji more than a hundred years ago. Special training and culture are required to understand them sufficiently. And at present, more than half a century after the end of the Second World War, comparison between Japanese texts written before and after the War brings to light clear differences. Furthermore, but to a lesser degree, the language has continued to change since the War. This means that, at least up until now, the obsolescence of language (in terms of the notation—forms and usages of characters—diction and syntax of sentences) has been rapid in Japan, so that different contemporaneous generations encounter varying degrees of difficulty in communicating between themselves in writing. For example, a good number of teachers have probably observed that their students must surmount a feeling of incongruity about the Japanese language of their textbooks before they can understand the contents, if the authors belong to an older generation, even if they are not yet in retirement. This means that even if the translations are estimated to be relatively good at the time of their appearance, they cannot be of practical use for very long, and after a certain time new translations are required.

Specialised researchers can of course read the old translations, if they are prepared to make the necessary effort. But even in such cases, if they understand the foreign language in which the work was first written, it is often better to read the original text than to struggle with the translation in outdated Japanese. All of the translated literature listed above falls into this class. In other words, they hardly conserve any utility as research material today. The classical works of Marx and Ricardo have since been repeatedly translated, so that they can now be read in relatively new translations. On the other hand, the research works listed in c) were only translated once during the early Shōwa period, and their translations are therefore of little use at present. In contrast, until the publication of a new translation of the *Principles* of Ricardo (Ricardo, David, *Des principes de l'économie politique et de l'impôt, édition anglaise de 1821*, translated by Cécile Soudan et al., GF-Flammarion, Paris, 1992), a revised edition of the translation made by F.S. Constâncio in 1819 continued to circulate in France during about one and a half centuries (though its various faults were pointed out). This would be inconceivable in Japan. In any case, the Japanese translations of foreign literature can generally be considered relatively short-lived. The currently available Japanese translations of Ricardo's works made after the Second World War are for the most part more than 40 years old, so their renewal will be required in the near future, if the economics of Ricardo is not to perish in Japan.

The first difficulty to overcome when translating Ricardo literature into Japanese (or, more generally, when writing about Ricardo in Japanese) is to determine how to notate the very name "Ricardo" in Japanese. It is always difficult to express the pronunciations of proper nouns (including names of people) notated in a foreign language with characters used in Japanese (usually 'katakanas' today). As for the figures in the history of economic thought, Smith and Marx are examples of cases in which the notation in Japanese is considered relatively easy. On the contrary, Ricardo is a good example of those foreign names whose notation in 'katakanas' is very difficult (or essentially impossible). His first and second names have probably been written in more than 10 different ways between the Meiji era and today. There is a tendency to converge on a few notations and their conventionalization over time; nevertheless there is no single fixed notation even now.

4. The systematic introduction of Ricardo's work and its promoters

In this section, the careers and works of each of the six economists mentioned at the end of the section 2 will be presented in turn, focusing on their Ricardo studies. The order of presentation is based on the period in which each of them was occupied with Ricardo studies. The present book, a collection of Ricardo studies in Japan during the interwar period, contains two exceptional cases. Firstly, Fukuda wrote his main articles on Ricardo at the beginning of the 20th century, before the First World War (from the end of Meiji to the beginning of Taishō era), but his approach to Ricardo anticipated that of the research conducted after 1920 (see below for details). As his approach was a historical forerunner of the later period, his works will come first in our presentation. Secondly, Hori, who began his Ricardo studies in 1920, continued them for a considerable time after the Second World War. This later work was a prolongation of his interwar research, and it conserved most of the characteristics of his earlier work (see below for details). It is therefore reasonable not to divide the works of this single researcher, Hori, into two parts, but to treat them together, as products of the interwar period during and after the 1920s. On the other hand, Fukuda, Kawakami and Koizumi were, in various fields in and out of academic circles, involved in a wide range of activities that cannot always be included with those of Ricardo researchers or historians of economic thought in the narrow sense of the term, and they left a lasting impact after their deaths. Even now, between 50 and nearly 100 years later, articles and books on their works and activities are still being published. What will be mentioned in the following presentation is only a minor part of their achievements, concerning their Ricardo studies. In particular, although Fukuda and Kawakami played an important role in the introduction of Ricardo into Japan early in the 20th century, only a small part in their academic careers was directly related to Ricardo.

i) *Tokuzō FUKUDA (1874–1930)*

Source: The photo is offered with permission from Hitotsubashi University Library.

Fukuda took up the post of lecturer at the Higher School of Commerce (now Hitotsubashi University) in 1896, the year he graduated from this school. By order of the Ministry of Education, he studied in Germany for three years from 1897, mainly under the direction of Lujo Brentano, a proponent of the new historical school, then professor at the University of Munich. He obtained a doctoral degree from the same university in 1900. His doctoral thesis *Die Gesellschaftliche und Wirtschaftliche Entwickelung in Japan (The social and economic development in Japan)* was published in Germany in the same year. Immediately after returning to Japan in the same year, he was nominated professor at the aforementioned school.

For a young new lecturer to be promoted professor in this way on returning from studies in a Western country was a typical pattern common to many Japanese university teachers before the Second World War. The other five writers presented below were promoted to the post of professor in exactly the same way. Fukuda was placed on administrative leave because of his opposition to the administrator of the aforementioned school (renamed Tokyo Higher School of Commerce in 1902 with the establishment of Kōbe Higher School of Commerce (now Kōbe University)). However, he obtained a post of professor at Keiōgijuku University in 1905, through the intermediary of his acquaintances, and remained there until 1918. In 1918 he was reinstated to the post of professor at Tokyo Higher School of Commerce, and after the promotion of the School to Tokyo University of Commerce in 1920 by the University Act, he became professor there.

From his undergraduate years, Fukuda had been familiarised with the economics of Marshall and the German historical school. Fukuda's lectures at the Higher School of Commerce after returning from his studies in Germany were based on the lectures by Brentano that he had attended there (Nishizawa, 2012: 312–3). In addition, he translated and published with Hajime Seki, his colleague (who later became mayor of Osaka), a work that Brentano had published with Wagner soon after Fukuda's return from Germany (see Section 2. ii) above). But his first important book *Lectures on Economics*, written for his lectures at Keiōgijuku University and published soon after he transferred to Keiōgijuku (Ōkurashoten, 1907), consisted of commentaries on the main parts of Marshall's *Principles of economics*, with his own supplements. After graduating from Keiōgijuku University in 1910, Koizumi became a lecturer there, recommended by Fukuda who directed his undergraduate studies. Koizumi began to study the history of economic thought, including Ricardo, under the influence of Fukuda (see below).

This book by Fukuda was revised and reprinted several times while he was professor at Keiōgijuku University. And as for the original work by Marshall, after his restoration to the Tokyo Higher School of Commerce, Fukuda got Kinnosuke ŌTSUKA, his first disciple, to translate and publish it, himself revising the translated text. Fukuda studied and wrote on many different branches of the history of economic thought, but Marshall invariably occupied the central place in his preoccupations. Fukuda's interpretation of Ricardo was naturally strongly influenced by that of Marshall. The three main research works Fukuda produced, to be translated and presented in this collection, were all written when he was teaching at Keiōgijuku University. In this respect, Koizumi could be said to have succeeded to the Ricardo studies of Fukuda in Keiōgijuku.

Fukuda took a position opposed to the Marxism and socialism that gained influence in Japan after the Russian revolution, but on the other hand he was also a liberal thinker, not only agreeing with and defending their free scientific research but also actively helping them. He himself translated and published writings by Engels. It is to be noted in this respect that the first entire Japanese edition of the three volumes of *Capital* published during the first half of the

1920s (see Section iii, List c of this Introduction) was translated by Motoyuki Takahata, an indirect disciple of Fukuda, on his suggestion. Fukuda himself added the notes of reviewers to some parts of this translation.

Now, the Society for Social Policy in Japan was founded at about the same time as Fukuda became a lecturer in his alma mater, at the end of the 19th century. But it was only after his return from studying in Germany under Brentano, economist of the new German historical school and member of the *Kathedersozialisten* ('academic socialists') that he began his activities in the Society as one of the principal members of the younger generation. He engaged in debates with many scholars in and outside the Society. Particularly with Kawakami, another of the Society's principal members from the younger generation, Fukuda repeated debates on varied subjects for a long time, from the beginning of the 20th century when they came into contact until the end of the 1920s, just before his death. The debates between them got particularly heated from about 1920, when Kawakami began to commit himself to Marxism. Although Fukuda opposed Kawakami on the subject of Marxism, when Kawakami left the post of professor at Kyoto Imperial University in April 1928, Fukuda immediately published an article in the newspaper Tokyo-Asahi entitled *Hue Hukazaruni Odoru ('We did not play the pipe for you, but you did dance')* (a play on 'we played the pipe for you, but you did not dance', from Matthew 11:17, New Testament—the mother of Fukuda had been a Christian). In this article he fiercely criticised the actions of the president of Kyoto Imperial University, who had obliged Kawakami to resign by advising him to quit the university for his alleged 'questionable behaviour', linked to the suspicion of political agitation of his students. He also challenged the infringement on the freedom of scientific research and the self-government of the university, and defended Kawakami.

The economic writings of Fukuda are included in the 23 volumes of his *Complete Works* (Dōbunkan, 1925–29) edited and published during his lifetime. About these enormous achievements on diverse subjects, Mazane wrote: 'the great intellectual competence of Fukuda made the fields of his economics extremely wide-ranging, but at the same time it caused uncertainty about what his specialized fields were. His writings were not only numerous but very difficult to ascertain, as they underwent retouches, revisions and deletions every time he re-edited them' (Mazane, 1962: 152). His studies in the history of economic thought, including Ricardo, make up just one of these numerous fields. He was probably the first in Japan to establish the style of research in the history of economic thought based on the classical texts. Today this is matter of course, but it was epoch-making in Japan, a latecomer to scientific research, which had not yet attained this minimum level in the late Meiji era. And this greatly contributed to the improvement of the level of research after him. He tried for the first time to place Ricardo in the context of the history of economic thought, based on his own direct study of the original works of Ricardo and without recourse to contemporary secondary Western literature. The Ricardo studies he carried out were not specialized or systematic, but he created one of the essential preconditions in the history of Japanese studies of the history of economic thought.

Furthermore, while he was professor at Tokyo Higher School of Commerce and later at Tokyo University of Commerce after 1918, Fukuda taught a number of disciples who were to produce many remarkable scientific works in economics and the adjacent social sciences, such as Kiichirō SŌDA, Kaname AKAMATSU, Kinnnosuke ŌTSUKA, Nobuyuki ŌKUMA, Zenya TAKASHIMA, Eiichi SUGI-MOTO, Ichirō NAKAYAMA and Yūzō YAMADA (who belong to the generations of grandfathers or great grandfathers of the researchers active today), and he himself was to reign at the summit of the academic circle called the 'Hitot-subashi Academy'.

ii) *Hajime KAWAKAMI (1879–1946)*

Source: The photo is a reproduction of Kawaka-mi's photo included in his book, *Keizaigaku Taikō* (Outline of Political Economy), published in 1928.

Kawakami, who played an important role in introducing Marxist economics into Japan at about the same time as Fukuda was active (after the mid-Taishō era), was also a significant figure in the history of the introduction of Ricardo's economics into Japan, like Fukuda.

From his time as a student at the Law School of Tokyo Imperial University, he was influenced by the humanism of Christianity and deeply interested in social questions such as the gap between rich and poor, which was widening in Japan at that time in the midst of the industrial revolution. He was to become Marxist in later years, but his humanist approach remained unchanged throughout his life. This was an important factor in eliciting esteem for his writings from many people, whether or not they were Marxists. He graduated from Imperial University in 1902 and then worked in various jobs, including university lecturer and journalist. After becoming a lecturer at Kyoto Imperial University in 1908, he devoted the next 20 years to research and teaching in the university. He was a member of what was then the only national academic organisation, the Society for Social Policy (established in 1897), engaged at that time in animated activities involving open annual conferences for debating current social and political problems. With Fukuda, five years his senior, he became one of the most important younger members in the Society, but he left it on the occasion of the internal conflict in 1919 provoked by its relations with labour movement organizations, etc. (see above).

In 1913, a year before the breakout of the First World War, he went to study in Europe. He took the chair of professor at Kyoto Imperial University immediately after returning in 1915, as was the custom at that time. In 1916 he published a series of articles in the newspaper Osaka Asahi entitled *Binbō Monogatari (Pauper Tales)*, which he published as a book in the following year.

This book that Kawakami wrote before he became Marxist became a bestseller. Not only did this book suddenly make its author famous, but it was also to be the most important in his life. Even today, the name of Kawakami remains synonymous with this book in Japan. In it, he depicted and denounced the reality of many people's poverty, aggravated by the rapid industrialization of Japan. But his analysis was not based on Marxian economic theory. From his particular humanistic standpoint, he required the rich to refrain from luxury in order to reduce the gap between the rich and the poor and solve the problem of poverty. Economists and socialists including Fukuda and Toshihiko SAKAI made many critical comments of this reasoning.

The name of Smith appears in *Pauper Tales*, but there is no mention of Ricardo. Kawakami only began to pay attention to Ricardo in relation to his Marx studies, and he only undertook the serious study of Marx's economic theory during the period after the book's publication. He was engaged in translating the economic writings of Marx (*Wage labour and capital*; *Wages, price and profit*; *Capital*; *A contribution to the critique of political economy*) after 1920. The first Japanese translation of Ricardo's work was carried out by Tsuneo Hori, who had just begun his study of Ricardo under Kawakami's direction. It was published in 1921, in fact with Kawakami as co-translator (see Section iii, List a of this Introduction). At the same time, drawing on Marx's economic theory, he repeatedly wrote and rewrote textbooks for his university lectures on the subject matters he was in charge of (the principles of economics and the history of economic thought). Almost all of his economic writings during the 1920s were produced by such a process. Through these energetic writing activities, Kawakami played an enormous role in propagating Marxist economics or Marxism in Japan during the 1920s. The final achievement in these works was *Keizaigaku Taikō (Outline of political economy)* (Kaizōsha, 1928), which integrated principles of political economy and the history of economic thought and was published after his retirement from the post of professor at Kyoto Imperial University in April 1928. This book can be considered to assemble Kawakami's final conclusions as Marxist economist and Marxist historian of economic thought. Part of the preface of this book, in which the author talks about the course and aim of his study of economics and the history of economic thought, will be translated and presented in this collection.

Kawakami, who had worked for a while as a newspaper reporter after graduating from university, was also remarkably active as a journalist at the same time as translating and writing research works. In 1919, he founded his own magazine, *Shakai Mondai Kenkyū (Studies on social questions)*, in which various social questions were discussed. At the time of its foundation he was still the humanist of *Pauper Tales* rather than Marxist, but after he made his commitment to Marxism in 1920, this magazine came to serve as an important Marxist stronghold for debating current and theoretical problems. Lasting for more than 10 years, until 1930, it gradually obtained a wide readership and played a very important role in fostering many young Marxists.

For Kawakami himself, Ricardo was certainly a significant figure in the history of English classical political economy, but still more important in relation to Marx. Although Kawakami did attach some importance to Ricardo's economics, he only treated it as part of his work on the history of economic thought written as manuals for his university teaching; he never took it up as a subject of his own specialized research. His role in the introduction of Ricardo into Japan consisted rather in suggesting specialized studies of Ricardo to his disciples Hori and Mori, and in helping them both to achieve significant results. It was after 1920, when Kawakami began to appear as a Marxist economist, that they began specialized studies and translations of Ricardo under his direction. It is possible that Kawakami envisaged a sort of scientific division of labour in entrusting to his disciples the specialized studies of Ricardo, while he himself concentrated on Marx studies, with some recognition of the importance of Ricardo. In fact, the section on Ricardo in his 1928 book *Outline of political economy* is based on the research work published by Mori in 1926 rather than his own studies (see below). Section 2 on Ricardo in Chapter 3 ('Malthus and Ricardo') of Part 2 ('Development of capitalist economics') summarises Ricardo's life and works in as few as 30 pages and gives a cursory description of the main points of the theory contained in *Principles*. In particular, most of the passage relating to the theory of value draws on the specialized research work of Mori (as Kawakami himself points out in a note on page 693). Since this Section 2 does not present Kawakami's own specific viewpoint, it will not be included in the texts translated and presented in the present book.

He was removed in 1928 from Kyoto Imperial University for his Marxist behaviour (see above). At that moment he approached the Communist Party of Japan and from 1932 entered into clandestine activities as a party member. He was arrested and imprisoned in 1933, and released from prison in 1937. After that he retired from all public activity, continued writing his autobiography, etc. and died in 1946. Some of his writings were translated into Chinese and are said to have influenced Mao Zedong. In Japan, his name has long been remembered, particularly by leftists and the Communist Party of Japan, and he was even quasi-idolised. In the University of Kyoto where Kawakami taught for 20 years, the 'Festival of Kawakami' was celebrated each year until 1982, more than 35 years after his death, to commemorate the time when he taught there.

His life as a whole is not so much that of an economist or communist but of a philanthropist, a humanist thinker, and his relations with Marxian economics and Marxism and his activities as a member of the Communist party can be considered transitory episodes in his life as a thinker. After his death, just a year after the end of the Second World War, he naturally continued to be highly esteemed as the pre-War introducer and propagator of Marxist economics, but if writings about the life and thought of Kawakami have never ceased to appear in Japan up to the present day, it may be because he remains fascinating as a thinker far beyond his relation with Marxism. Incidentally, research works on him have also been published outside Japan, for example: Reiner Schrader,

Kawakami Hajime (1879–1946): der Weg eines japanischen Wirtschaftswissen- schaftlers zum Marxismus, Mitteilungen der Gesellschaft für Natur- und Völkerkunde Ostasiens, Bd. 63, 64, 1976, or Gail Lee Bernstein, *Japanese Marxist: A Portrait of Kawakami Hajime,* 1879–1946, Harvard University Press (Harvard East Asian Monographs), 1990.

iii) *Shinzō KOIZUMI (1888–1966)*

Shinzō Koizumi had a close relationship to Keiōgijuku University from his birth throughout his life. His father, Shinkichi, was a direct disciple of Yukichi Fukuzawa. On the eager recommendation of Fukuda, who recognised and highly esteemed the competence of Koizumi from his undergraduate years, he became a teacher at the aforementioned university on gradu- ating in 1910. Two years later he went to study in Europe, and stayed there from 1912 to 1916. Just like Fukuda and Kawakami, he was named professor immediately after his return. He lectured the eco- nomics of Ricardo in Keiōgijuku University while Fukuda was still teaching there. During the 10 years between Koizumi's entry into the university and his assumption of the chair of professor, Fukuda was a professor in the same university, and Koizumi started his researches under his direction. It was probably because of Fukuda's influ- ence that Koizumi got interested in the history of economic thought. From this time his position was based on liberalism, like Fukuda, and thoroughly opposed to Marxism, which was already gradually becoming known at that time. It is considered that one of the aims of Koizumi's economic research was to consolidate this position through the historical study of economics. Like Hori, he began systematic studies of the history of economic thought in about 1920. His ultimate objective was a theoretical criticism of Marxist economics. He studied Ricardo in order to pursue this criticism by returning to the his- torical origins of Marx's economic theory. And to lay the foundations for his critical examination of Marx, he first studied Rodbertus, considered to have proposed Marx's theories of surplus value and of ground rent before Marx himself.

Source: The photo is a repro- duction of Koizumi's photo published online by a free source.

According to Koizumi, Marx only reproduced on a larger scale the short- comings of Ricardo's theory, and the orthodox successors of Ricardo's eco- nomics were represented by J.S. Mill and Marshall in the liberal current of English economics. Koizumi was consistent in this view of the history of economics. However, unlike Fukuda, he was not interested in the German historical school. It was towards the end of the First World War that he returned from studies in Europe and began to publish the results of his research. At that time the cleavage in the Society for Social Policy came to the surface and the economics of the historical school began to lose its early impetus. After returning to Japan, he made his debut as a young researcher from the tribune at the annual conference of the Society (Ōuchi, 1970: 88) on the verge of its disruption. His relation with the Society was limited to this episode. At that time, the gap between Japan and the Western advanced countries was closing, and the foreign and domestic economic policies conventionally claimed by the historical school were losing actuality. It was probably because of this difference in their ages that the German historical school receded in the research interests of Koizumi, who inherited much from Fukuda.

Since before the Second World War, Koizumi has always been considered a representative of the critics of Marx in Japanese economic circles. But it was not an easy task. He criticized Marx in an altogether immanent way, acquiring beforehand a deep understanding on the subject to be critically examined by reading the original texts in European languages, a work that few could have done at the beginning of the 20th century when reliable translations of Marx's fundamental economic writings were not yet sufficiently available. From this position he fiercely debated in periodicals, particularly on the fundamental problems of Marx's theory of value, with Kawakami, who was then publishing articles and books on Ricardo and Marx, and with Tamizō KUSHIDA, a disciple of Kawakami. These debates highlighted their names and works and drew the attention of the general public to Marx. However, the pattern of the debates in Japan was essentially no more than a repeat of those held in Europe a little earlier, at the turn of the century, and these debates did not produce any positive results. On the criticism that Koizumi based on Böhm-Bawerk, Kawakami and Kushida retorted with anti-critical arguments advanced by Rudolf Hilferding. It was only in the course of the debates about Japanese capitalism, about ten years later, that the researchers on Marxist economics in Japan began to produce truly creative results of their own, based on the reality of Japanese capitalism.

As in the case of Hori, who started his Ricardo studies at about the same time, Koizumi pursued two inseparable and simultaneous objectives in his Ricardo studies: to present a 'correct and just' interpretation of Ricardo's theory, and to translate Ricardo's texts 'correctly and justly' into Japanese and present them to Japanese readers. While Hori first published a partial translation of *Principles* under the direction of Kawakami and later an entire translation, over which he took considerable time, Koizumi first published successively the partial translations of *Principles* in the review of Keiōgijuku University *Mitagattai Zasshi (Keiō economic studies)* and then published them as a book (see Section iii, List a, Items 1 and 2). And in 1929, the year after the publication of their respective entire translations of *Principles*, both Hori and Koizumi published the results of their research carried out over nearly 10 years (Hori, *Ricardo no Kachiron oyobi sono Hihanshi [Theory of value of Ricardo and history of its critiques]*, Iwanami Shoten; Koizumi, *Ricardo Kenkyū [Ricardo studies]*, Tettō Shoin). Hori's translation work finally resulted in the Japanese version of Volume 1 of *Works* by Sraffa, published in 1972 after several revisions of his earlier translation, and this final translation of his is still in use today. On the other hand, Koizumi's translation of *Principles* was available in the paperback collection of Iwanami Shoten for nearly 60 years, from 1928 until 1987, with partial revision in 1952 for renewal of the text in accordance with the new notations of Japanese adopted after the Second World War. In 1987, *Principles* in the paperback series of Iwanami was replaced by the translation by Takuya HATORI and Yoshiki YOSHIZAWA, leading Ricardo scholars in Japan after the War, and this new edition is currently available and in use. Because of this translation work, Koizumi has also long been remembered as the translator of the chief work of Ricardo.

However, research in the history of economic thought in the strict sense was only one short stage in Koizumi's career as researcher and thinker. He continued publishing many articles and books between the end of the 1910s and his death in 1966 (his complete works, published soon after his death, are made up of 26 volumes and 28 books), but *Adam Smith, Malthus, Ricardo, Seitōha Keizaigaku Kenkyū (Adam Smith, Malthus, Ricardo, studies of the orthodox economics)* (Iwanami Shoten, 1934) was the last of his works directly related to the history of economic thought. This book may be said to be the ultimate accomplishment of his studies in this field. So his career as a historian of economic thought only lasted about 10 years, between his 30s and 40s, and after that he never returned to the field. In 1950, the Society for the History of Economic Thought (SHET) was founded in Japan. Of the six researchers whose works are discussed in this Introduction, four (Hori, Koizumi, Mori and Maide) were alive at that time. Of these four, Hori and Maide were among the six promoters of its foundation, and the names of Hori, Maide and Mori figured in the list of its initial members (about 120 in number). Hence, only Koizumi had no relation with the Society from its foundation after the Second World War.

Koizumi, professor at Keiōgijuku University from 1916, became its president in 1933 and remained in the post until 1947. During this time he was nominated as a member of the Imperial Academy. In 1949 he became the tutor of Crown Prince Akihito (the present Emperor of Japan, then 16 years old) and taught him the duties of an emperor for the new age. After the Second World War he continued manifold writing activities and was widely known as an ideologue of anti-socialism and conservatism. Among others, his *Kyōsan Shugi Hihan no Jōshiki (Common sense of the criticism of communism)*, published in 1949, quickly became a bestseller during this period when symptoms of the Cold War were spreading through the world and the labour movement was rising in Japan. It was repeatedly reprinted and finally included in 1976 in the collection of academic paperbacks of Kōdansha. During the Cold War period, he occupied a solid position as an ideologue of Western liberalism, and was praised and blamed by the two opposing camps. After his death, Keiō University established the 'Koizumi fund' to celebrate his achievements. This fund continues to finance the 'Koizumi memorial lecture' to this day.

iv) Tsuneo HORI (1896–1981)

Source: Photo provided by the compilation office of the history of Kwansei Gakuin in Kwansei Gakuin.

a) Research in the 1920s and its particularities

In 1920 Tsuneo Hori graduated from the newly established faculty of economics at Kyoto Imperial University and entered the graduate school, to study the history of economic thought, particularly Marx and Ricardo, under the direction of Kawakami. In the year of his entrance to the graduate school he published in *Keizai Ronsō* a series of five articles based on his graduation thesis, entitled 'Fundamental propositions of the labour theory of value of Marx' and 'Ricardo and Marx in the theory of value'. Though this was the only time Hori published articles on Marx, it is clear that his study of Ricardo was preceded from the outset by his study of Marx, and presupposed it. Today, these articles cannot be said to contain any original views deserving particular attention, but they do show the competence of the young Hori as a beginner who hunted out a wide range of literature in foreign languages (notably German) available at that time and who endeavoured to decipher and analyse on his own the original texts of Ricardo and the voluminous *Theorien über den Mehrwert (Theories of surplus-value)*, not yet translated into Japanese, not to mention the unavailability of preceding researches in Japan. In particular, the latter series of articles are considered to represent 'the first article in history of the substantial introduction of Ricardo into Japan', and 'the first research on Ricardo founded on *Theories of surplus value*, to become mainstream in Japan' (Mazane, 1965: 8). In the following year, 1921, he published a partial translation of *Principles*, mainly focused on the section on 'principles of political economy', carried out on Kawakami's initiative (see Section iii, List a of this Introduction). He was nominated as assistant professor at Tōhoku Imperial University in 1922. He went to Europe to study by order of the Ministry of Education for two years from 1923 to 1925, residing mainly in London. There he spent most of the time transcribing manuscripts in the British Museum and buying works from second-hand booksellers in London with his own money and his faculty's budget. On returning to Japan, he was promoted to professor. The Ricardo studies Hori carried out during the 1920s with this two-year stay abroad were integrated into the *Theory of value of Ricardo and history of its critiques*, his first monograph, published in 1929.

This book is composed of two parts: 'Book I: The theory of value and the theory of price', and 'Book II: The theory of wages'. The last chapter of each book presents a 'History of critiques' on that particular subject. Apart from the fact that Hori took up 'the theory of wages' and 'the theory of value' as one of the central themes in the economic theory of Ricardo (on the significance of this treatment, see below), it is these chapters on the 'History of critiques' that distinguish this work from the other works on Ricardo published during the interwar period by the Japanese researchers presented in this Introduction. The two 'Histories of critiques' occupy as much as two thirds of the total number of pages, so that quantitatively they may be considered the central parts of this work, rather than appendices (on the contrary, only one third is allotted to an examination of Ricardo's actual theories of value and wages, which should have been the main subjects). The most remarkable characteristic of the 'Histories of critiques' is, as the author himself said long afterwards, 'that they treated rather obscure figures, secondary so to say, or minors playing the role of intermediaries between the majors', this was 'an experiment with few similar antecedents' (Hori, 1973: 13). Concretely, among these 'minors' submitted to critical examination are: J. Mill, McCulloch, De Quincey, Torrens, Ramsay, Malthus, Bailey and Marx in the first Book, and J. Mill, West, Ramsay, J.S. Mill, Samuel Read, Senior, McCulloch and Marx in the second. This list includes figures who were already widely known in their times and who cannot always be called minor, in particular Marx, who appears at the end of both books and is considered to have brought Ricardo's theory to fruition. Hori's 'Histories of critiques' can therefore be described as a history of diverse discussions that were finally and definitively brought by Marx to the 'solution': the 'overcoming' of the 'shortcomings' and 'questionable points' in Ricardo's theory.

But, for many of these 'secondary' authors, even if their names were known through the secondary literature, the contents of their original texts were probably presented to Japanese researchers for the first time in this work by Hori. Herein lies its most important contribution to the Japanese academic circles of the time. Hori was able to write these 'Histories of critiques' of such significance thanks to the second-hand books he had bought in London (most of which were classical works in the history of English economic thought) and brought back to Japan. In his book review published in the magazine *Kaizō* in July of the year of publication of Hori's work, Fukuda praised it highly, as follows: 'I cannot but feel myself blessed with this work which convincingly proves that the economic research of Japan does not always walk in the footsteps of the West. [. . .] I profoundly wish that the author would translate this book into a foreign language to make it known to the world academic circles'. At a time when third-hand publications reproducing secondary literature by Western historians of economic thought like Cannan, Diehl, Böhm or J.H. Hollander, then considered as first-class authorities, were not at all rare, Hori's 'Histories of critiques' could certainly be esteemed as a distinguished work. And it stimulated the interest of Japanese researchers in the so-called 'minor' figures in the history of economics (Samuel Bailey, for example), whose writings came to be studied and translated later. It thus contributed to a deeper understanding of the theories and thoughts of 'major' authors like Smith, Ricardo, Malthus and Marx. Today, however, these research works of Hori are probably no more than objects of historical interest.

As mentioned above, this work is made up of two parts: 'Book I: The theory of value and the theory of price', and 'Book II: The theory of wages'. This book on Ricardo's theory of value was composed in such a way because the author considered the theory of wages to be closely related to the theory of value. On this point, Hori wrote in the 'Preface': 'In the Ricardian school, wages are discussed as 'value or price of labour (power)'. And since, because of this, the derivation of wages, profits and rent from value—in other words, the distribution of value—can be explained, it would be highly proper to treat the theory of wages together with the theory of value in general, as the precondition for the theories of profits and rent, and independently from these theories'. However, in the first chapters of Ricardo's *Principles*, what follows immediately the theory of value is the theory of rent, followed by the theory of wages, and the theory of profits comes last. In short, wages are placed between the other two categories of distribution, rent and profits. Therefore, at least from the point of view of the order of subjects in Ricardo's *Principles*, the theory of wages is not closely related to the theory of value as a precondition for explaining rent and profits. Hori attached such importance to the theory of wages because from the outset, he adopted the theory of Marx as the frame of reference for his study of Ricardo.

In *Capital*, the theory of surplus value (i.e., of capitalist exploitation) directly follows the theory of commodity (value) and the theory of money. The explanation of the origin of surplus value necessarily presupposes that of the particularities of labour power as a commodity and the determination of its value, i.e., wages (see the chapter on 'the transformation of money into capital' and the chapter on 'the labour process and the process of producing surplus value', placed just before the explanation of the production of surplus value). Although he did not discuss wages as a category of income along with profits and rent in Volume 1 of *Capital*, Marx had to write about the determination of wages insofar as necessary for developing the theory of surplus value. And in the part on wages, in concluding the theory of surplus value, he talks about the transformation of the value of labour power into the price of labour (wages) as its phenomenal form.

It seems that Hori gave the theory of wages a particular place in his studies of Ricardo's theory of value because he wanted to base his consideration of Ricardo's theory on the theoretical composition of *Capital* (which moves from the theory of value to the theory of surplus value). Though he never explicitly mentioned *Capital* and its theoretical composition with respect to the place of the theory of wages in Ricardo, he was consistent in attaching particular importance to the theory of wages from his first monograph of 1929 right through to *Riron Keizaigaku no Seiritsu* (*Establishment of theoretical economics*) (Minerva Shobō, 1958), the ultimate summation of his Ricardo studies published 30 years later. Repeated, detailed examination of the theory of wages was a notable characteristic of all Hori's Ricardo studies, beginning with his graduation thesis that took Marx as its point of departure (for a detailed presentation of this thesis and the significance of Hori's special treatment of the theory of wages, see Tanaka, 1991: 29).

b) Career after the 1930s; post-War research as a continuation of his pre-War research

Of the six researchers presented in this Introduction, Hori, who had already produced important results in his Ricardo studies during the interwar period, was the only one to continue activities of significance for the history of research on Ricardo until after the War. Of the other five, Koizumi, Mori and Maide were still active after the War, but Koizumi and Mori had already ceased to study the history of economic thought and Maide, while remaining in that field after the War, did not produce any results beyond those he had obtained before the War, which will be presented later in this Introduction. Not only was Hori active in academic research, but he also assumed several important posts in academic societies and institutions. He resigned from the professorship of Tōhoku Imperial University, his first academic position, in 1932, and in the same year he became professor at Ōsaka University of Commerce (renamed Ōsaka City University after the War), where he remained until 1948. After that he held the post of professor at Kwansei Gakuin University until his retirement in 1966, at the age of 70. From 1955 until his retirement, he was president of this university. He was decorated and nominated to membership of The Japan Academy at the time of his retirement. And in 1950, when the Society for the History of Economic Thought was founded in Japan, he was chosen as a member of the permanent executive committee, and held the position of president of this society for 10 years from 1958 to 1968.

The most representative research work on Ricardo that Hori published after the War was the *Establishment of theoretical economics – theory of value and theory of distribution of Ricardo* (1958, see above). In 1938, just before the outbreak of the Second World War, he had published *Keizai Genron (Principles of economics)* (Kawade Shobō), a book with the same title as his translation of *Principles* of Ricardo. Below the title on the front cover, the two names of Ricardo and Hori are juxtaposed without specifying the author or translator. It appears as if this book was half translation and half research work. He republished it 10 years later with minor revisions under the new title *Ricardo Keizai Genron Kaisetsu (Commentary on Ricardo's principles of economics)* (Hori Shoten, 1948). The *Works* of Ricardo edited by Sraffa began to be published just after that date. And in 1958, Hori published a second revised edition of the 1948 book, seeking to incorporate the results of the new edition of Ricardo's writings. The title of this third revised edition was altered, with the addition of a subtitle 'theory of value and theory of distribution of Ricardo', announcing explicitly that the book did not treat the whole of Ricardo's economic theory, but only his 'theories of value and distribution'. In keeping with this, the treatment of topics such as international trade, money and finance, and taxation are extremely simplified compared with the former editions. This book was written for general readers and students, drawing on the research work (1929) and commentary (1938) published before the War. It was conceived primarily as a commentary on Ricardo's *Principles*, but also contains the author's own interpretations of some important topics debated among specialists on Ricardo. Because of its process of composition, this book naturally concentrates on 'the theory of value and distribution' and devotes only the last one chapter to the other domains of Ricardo's economic theory, which are given an extremely brief and cursory explanation. And in the area of 'the theory of value and distribution', not only is disproportionate weight allotted to the theory of wages, but also an important supplement is added to the previous version, to such an extent that the chapter on wages is far longer than all the others.

All of these traits stem from the time when Hori began his Ricardo studies under the direction of Kawakami at the beginning of the 1920s. And although this book was published more than 10 years after the War, the references given in it are all drawn from the 1920s or even earlier. No mention is made of more recent literature, in particular concerning Japanese and foreign research works published after the War. The only things that are newly added and used are a number of documents and materials included in the *Works* of Sraffa. This book gives the impression that its author has only drawn on the accumulated results of his own past works, without seeking to revise and develop his own past research in the light of new developments. Therefore, this work published after the War in 1958 (in a sense the summation of Hori's Ricardo studies) can be regarded as a part or continuation of his pre-War Ricardo studies, rather than post-War. It is treated thus in this Introduction. That is why the part on the theory of wages (chapter 4) of his 1958 book has been selected from among his many writings for translation and presentation in the present collection.

c) Sraffa impact I

One of the main reasons why Hori published the above work in 1958 may be that the *Works* by Sraffa had just been completed. Hori began to translate the *Principles* at the start of his career as a Ricardo scholar, intending to produce a variorum edition of his Japanese translation that did not exist at the time in English, and he could achieve this intention to some extent in 1928. So for Hori, the publication of a new edition of *Principles* edited by Sraffa with an impeccable comparison of the three successive original editions might oblige him to review his previous research (Hori, 1973: 11). Not only the *Principles* but also the new materials made available for the first time in Sraffa's edition (manuscripts and letters, particularly from other persons to Ricardo) may have made him feel the need to revise his earlier research. It is certainly possible to say that in many regards, the Ricardo studies that Hori made after the publication of Sraffa's edition incorporate its results. However, Hori showed no reaction to the particular, meticulous and scrupulous interpretations contained in the extensive introduction Sraffa prefixed to Volume 1 of the *Works*. The impact of the *Works* on Hori was limited to the fact that many new materials were published in it and that Sraffa had performed admirable editorial work on Ricardo's writings. In particular, Hori said nothing about the 'corn ratio theory', which was to become a subject of lasting, animated debates both in Japan and internationally. This was an original interpretation of Ricardo which probably appeared extremely new (or novel) to the researchers of every country at that time. Since Hori's book was published two years before Sraffa's chief work *Production of commodities by means of commodities*, based on the idea of the economic surplus measured in physical terms as exemplified by the corn ratio, it is possible that Hori did not recognize the importance of this particular interpretation of Ricardo's theory that Sraffa presented in his introduction to Volume 1 of the *Works*.

The main scientific achievements of Sraffa in his lifetime can be summarised in the following three points. 1) The editing and publication of the works of Ricardo. 2) An original interpretation of Ricardo's economic theory, particularly his 'theory of value and distribution' (introduction to Volume 1 of the *Works*). 3) His chief work of 1960, developing a positive theory based on points 1 and 2. As explained above, Hori only recognised and valued the first of these three points. This approach to Sraffa's work has been widely shared in Japan by many Ricardo scholars after Hori. There is not one who does not highly esteem Sraffa's *Works*. However, with regard to his 'corn ratio' interpretation, a number of researchers, starting with Takuya Hatori (1922–2012) who was for a long time the leading figure in Ricardo studies in Japan after the War, criticised it or called it into question, mainly on the basis of philological examinations of Ricardo's texts. But these criticisms of Sraffa have remained within the framework of exegetic contests on the subject of Ricardo, never going so far as to examine critically Sraffa's actual idea of measuring the surplus by a physical term (the corn ratio) instead of labour value. For Ricardo scholars, such examinations would have been beyond the scope of their work. It was therefore out of question that Sraffa's 'corn ratio' interpretation should be taken up together with his chief work that systematically developed this idea. For many Ricardo scholars in Japan, this work of Sraffa was not within the scope of their research and probably very difficult to understand.

However, in contrast to this reception among Ricardo researchers, Sraffa's work was translated into Japanese by Izumi HISHIYAMA and Hiroshi YAMASHITA in 1962, only two years after its original publication (in 1956, Hishiyama had also translated Sraffa's two articles of 1925 and 1926, publishing them together as a book entitled *Keizaigaku ni okeru Koten to Gendai: Shin Kotenha no Kentō to Dokusen Riron no Tenkai [Classics and contemporaries in economics: examinations of the neo-classical school and development of the theory of monopoly]*). Hishiyama (1923–2007) was known in Japan as a researcher in classical economics, but he was also considered as a researcher of 20th century economics, like the Cambridge school including Post-Keynesians and Wicksell, who appeared after Marx but with almost no relation to him. For a considerable time after the War, all the economics that appeared after the latter half of the 19th century and that was not directly or indirectly connected with Marx was categorised in Japan as 'modern economics', (with contemptuous and accusing connotation, without any distinction between neo-classicals, Keynes, Schumpeter, etc.) in opposition to Marxist economics. Although such a view has now greatly declined in popularity, it still partly persists. Therefore, researchers like Hishiyama were apt to be regarded as somewhat alien to the narrow circle of Ricardo scholars in Japan, many of whom had Marxist economics as their common intellectual background until the latter half of the 20th century. For this reason, since Sraffa's chief work had no direct relation to the textual studies of Ricardo, and was regarded as part of the 'modern economics' of the 20th century, it has only been discussed on the fringes of academic circles by a few of the researchers of 'modern economics'.

Up to the present time, when Ricardo is the subject of research in the history of economic thought, Sraffa's interpretation has never exercised a positive influence on Ricardo studies, although sometimes it has been critically examined. In this respect, Ricardo studies carried out in Japan after the War have been very different from those carried out by the European researchers known as 'Neo-Ricardians', especially those belonging to the generations who started their activities in the 1960s and 70s. However, since the question is beyond the scope of this Introduction, which aims to present Ricardo studies in Japan before the War, we can do no more than point it out briefly, leaving detailed discussion to another occasion, concerning Ricardo studies after the War.

d) Sraffa impact II

Hori knew about the editorial process and the plan for publication of the *Works* through his correspondence with Sraffa from relatively early on, when the latter started preparation of the *Works*. Publication of the *Works* actually began in 1951, and Hori asked for and obtained permission from Sraffa to translate them into Japanese in 1953, in the middle of their publication (Hori, 1973: 18). Two years later, in 1955, when the publication of *Works* was completed, except for Volume 11 (indices), he organized the 'publication committee of the Japanese edition of *Works and correspondence of David Ricardo*' and made a plan for their translation and publication. The committee was composed of the following six members: Shigeki Suenaga (1908–1977), Kōichirō SUZUKI (1910–1983), Tadashi Nakano (1912–1985), Toshirō SUGIMOTO (1913–2011), Yoshirō TAMANOI (1818–1885) and Tsuneo Hori (1896–1981). The five members other than Hori belonged to the generation below him, but they were all from 25 to 37 years old at the end of the War. So their elementary training and the first phase of their activities as researchers belonged to the pre-War period. The translation of the *Works* can be regarded on the whole as an enterprise planned by researchers of the pre-War period, including Hori himself.

However, it took more than 10 years from then for the work of translation and publication to be actually realized. During the period from 1969 to 1975, nine volumes, all except for Volumes 5 and 11, were translated and published by Yūshōdō. Volume 5 was published in 1987 and the final installment, Volume 11, in 1999, when all the volumes of Sraffa's *Works* had been translated into Japanese. Therefore, except for the last two volumes, almost the whole of the *Works* was translated into Japanese in the space of a few years between the end of the 1960s and the beginning of the 1970s, which might be called an 'exceptional undertaking' without parallel elsewhere in the world, in view of the speed of its realisation and its timing. Needless to say, the accomplishment of this large enterprise of translation was of great benefit for the following generations of researchers after the War, and it provided a favourable context for promoting Ricardo studies in Japan. Every volume was translated by one of the six members of the translation committee. Almost all of them died before 1985, a few years after the end of the enterprise. In this sense, the translation and publication of *Works* could be said to be the 'final accomplishment' in the Ricardo studies of the pre-War generations, although it was realised around the year 1970, a quarter of century after the end of the War.

The same could be said for Hori. Hori accepted the translation of Volume 1, probably the most important, containing the *Principles*. The fulfillment of this translation is considered, together with *Establishment of theoretical economics* published 10 years before, to be the culmination of the work Hori aimed at from the start of his career as a Ricardo scholar in 1920. This is not specific to Hori, but one of the major patterns of research in the history of economic thought in Japan, observed in the past and still observed today to a lesser degree, aiming to present a 'correct and immanent understanding' of the principal writings of one particular figure in the Western history of economic thought and at the same time to translate them accurately.

v) Kōjirō MORI (1895–1962)

Source: The photo is a reproduction of Mori's photo included in the collection of papers published in 1958 in commemoration of his 60th anniversary.

After graduating from the faculty of economics of Kyoto Imperial University in 1922, Kōjirō Mori entered the graduate school and became a lecturer at the same university two years later. During that time he studied mainly under the direction of Kawakami. In 1928 he was nominated as assistant professor in the faculty of law and letters at Kyūshū Imperial University. In 1931 he went to study in the West and assumed the post of professor immediately after his return in 1933, remaining in this post until his retirement in 1958. Five years after the end of the War, in 1950, when the Society for the Study of Social Policy was established on the initiative of Kazuo ŌKŌCHI (1905–1984), professor in the faculty of economics at Tokyo University, in succession to the former Society for Social Policy which remained dormant after the Kantō earthquake, Mori was one of the promoters of its foundation. And when, in the same year, the Society for the

History of Economic Thought was established by Hori and others, he figured
in the list of its initial members.

Mori began his Ricardo studies at Kyoto Imperial University under the
direction of Kawakami. Also under Kawakami, Hori had already begun his
studies a little earlier than Mori, who pursued the work as if trying to catch
up with Hori (and Koizumi, who was then steadily publishing articles on
Ricardo at the same time as, and in competition with, Hori). From 1924,
Mori, the latecomer, published the results of his studies in *Keizai Ronsō* at
a faster rate than Hori and Koizumi. In his study of Ricardo's economics,
he set out to estimate the historical significance of Ricardo's theory and
to criticise it with reference to *Capital* and *Theories of surplus value* of Marx,
just like Kawakami, his teacher, and Hori. In the above articles he chose
Ricardo's theories of value and wages as the central theme of his study and
discussed them in detail, as in the case of Hori. This seems to be because of
the strong connection between the theory of value and the theory of surplus
value in Marx's theory. On the other hand, since his doctoral thesis on the
theme of social policy submitted in 1925, he was also interested in social
policy as well as the history of economic thought. His interest in the theory
of wages and the theory of value appears to have been related to this research
career.

Mori published the results of the Ricardo studies (or studies of the history
of economic thought including Ricardo) that he had started in 1924 in two
books, namely *Ricardo Kachiron no Kenkyū (Study of the theory of value of
Ricardo)* (Iwanami Shoten, 1926) and *Rōchin Gakusetsu no Shiteki Hatten
(Historical development of the doctrines on wages)* (Kōbundō, 1928), a little
earlier than his precursors Hori and Koizumi. These monographs can be
regarded as discussing independently, in two separate books, the same two
themes that Hori treated in the first and second halves of his *Theory of value
of Ricardo and history of its critiques* published in 1929. However, the latter is
a historical study of the theories of wages, as indicated by its title, rather than
a specialized study of Ricardo's economics like the book by Hori. In Mori's
work, Ricardo's theory is certainly in the foreground, but only insofar as it is
one stage in the history of the theories of wages. In this sense, Mori's book
is somewhat of a different character to that of Hori, which really is a research
work specialized in Ricardo's economics. Mori's book of 1926 'won a reputa-
tion of the highest level among the Ricardo studies of the time, including those
of Hori and Koizumi' (Mazane, 1965: 17).

As mentioned above, Mori took up the post of assistant professor in the
faculty of law and letters at Kyūshū Imperial University in 1928, the year of
publication of his second book. Because of his teaching obligations, he abandoned his study of Ricardo and of the history of economic thought in general
after this year, focusing exclusively on research into social policy issues. It was
only during a few years that Mori's research activities, which had produced
epoch-making results in Ricardo studies before the War, were closely related to
the history of economic thought and Ricardo.

vi) *Chōgorō MAIDE (1891–1961)*

Source: The photo is a reproduction of Maide's photo included in the collection of papers published in 1952 in commemoration of his 60th anniversary.

Chōgorō Maide graduated in 1917 from the politics section of the faculty of law at Tokyo Imperial University. After receiving a special scholarship, he was nominated to assistant professor responsible for the history of economic thought in the faculty of economics when it was established in 1919. He began his specialised research in the history of economic thought in this year, but he went abroad to study in 1920, staying mainly in Germany until 1922. He became professor just after returning in 1923 and remained in this post until his retirement in 1952. After retiring from Tokyo University, he became professor at the private university Gakushuin, where he was occupied with teaching and research until the end of his life (the year of his retirement from this university). In the faculty of economics at the Imperial University of Tokyo before and during the War, a considerable number of professors, assistant professors and others were de facto dismissed from their posts (most were reinstated after the War), in the tidal wave of the time oppressing the freedom of scientific research and thinking, involving incidents such as the Morito affair (1919), the incident of the Popular Front (1937), the scientific purge of Hiraga (1939), etc. Those dismissed were above all academics studying Marx and subjects directly or indirectly related to Marx, and finally even those who were simply considered liberals. Because of the theme of his research and the nature of his writings, Maide could have naturally become the subject of such treatment during this period. But he was one of the exceptional few members who were never dismissed from or left the university. Immediately after the War, he played a central role in the faculty in campaigning for the reinstatement of staff members deprived of their posts by pressure from the military during the War and for reconstruction of the faculty of economics of Tokyo University after the War, including those who were thus reinstated (Ōuchi, 1970: 352–4).

On returning from his studies in Germany in 1922, Maide brought into the newly established faculty of economics the knowledge of Marxist economics that he had acquired directly from original texts like *Capital* as well as a lot of Marxist literature he had bought in Germany, taking advantage of the inflation there. Thus, he was the first to play an important role in propagating an interest in Marxist economics among the junior members of the faculty (Ōuchi, 1970: 193–4). Young researchers like Moritarō YAMADA (1897–1980) and Hiromi ARISAWA (1896–1988), who would later become known as eminent Marxist economists, were his assistants at that time. Yamada later became the cult figure of the 'Koza School' in the debates on Japanese capitalism in the 1930s, and the first article he published as a Marxist economist ('Contradictions and their surmounting in the theory of value', *Keizaigaku Ronshu*, vol.4, no.4, 1925) was written during this period. The slightly older Hyōe Ōuchi (1888–1980), who became assistant professor in the same year as Maide, said in retrospect that Maide gave him the opportunity to study Marxist economics seriously during their concurrent stay in Berlin and after their return to Japan (Ōuchi, 1970: 96). Maide thus played a considerable role in strengthening the influence of Marxist economics in the newly established faculty of economics at the beginning of the 1920s. The faculties of economics at Tokyo Imperial University and at Kyoto Imperial University, where Kawakami was teaching, became one of the strongholds of the Japanese Marxist economics of the time and exercised a profound influence on intellectuals, students and society in general. Needless to say, since Marxism was then rapidly spreading both in and outside Japanese academic circles, the role played by Maide must be considered within the context of this movement as a whole. For Maide, in any case, Marx came before Ricardo, and his study of Ricardo was from the outset unthinkable without its relation with Marx.

Maide's systematic research in the history of economic thought, including Ricardo, began in 1924, when he started lecturing on the history of economic thought, and it was developed over a long period in the lectures he repeated every year. And his research seems to have been entirely directed towards carrying out his professional duties (lectures and research for lectures) in the faculty he belonged to. This research style of his never changed, throughout his career. Because of this, he published relatively few books and articles; moreover, many of them had similar titles or themes. The 'Preface' of *Keizaigakushi Gaiyō Jō Kan (Summary of the history of economic thought, part I)* (Iwanami Shoten, 1937), begins thus: 'This book is part of my lecture notes on the history of economic thought in Tokyo Imperial University, published for the convenience of the auditors'. This book can be seen as a provisional summation of the results of the research he carried out in this way. His publications after this book were few in number, and in general they were more or less simply a re-run of his previous writings. Therefore, in order to understand the outlines of his Ricardo studies, it is probably sufficient to take up chapter 5 ('David Ricardo') of this book and his article 'Compendium of Ricardo's theory of distribution' (*Keizaigaku Ronshu*, vol.3, no.3, 1924), based on the notes of his first lectures delivered more than 10 years before the book and marking the starting point of his research in the history of economic thought. As Marx was the point of departure for Maide's economic research, it was quite natural for him to adopt Marx's work *Theories of surplus value*, in his article published in 1924, as the most important point of reference for his research in the history of economic thought. However, that was not all. Exceptionally for a study written in the interwar period, and particularly its early phase, in relation to the global theoretical plan of Ricardo's *Principles*, he took up *An essay on the influence of a low price of corn on the profits of stock*, edited and published in the previous year 1923 by Gonner (in Gonner, 1923, above, pp. 223–56, hereafter *Essay* for short), in order to compare the theory of profits contained in this *Essay* with that expounded in the *Principles* (he did the same in his later book with Ricardo's theory of profits).

Summary of the history of economic thought, part I is composed of seven chapters and treats the historical period from mercantilism to J.S. Mill. Ricardo is discussed in chapter 5, entitled 'David Ricardo'. According to Mazane, 1965, the composition of the whole book is substantially the same as the notes of the first lectures Maide delivered in 1923, meaning that his research was conducted inseparably from his university lectures, and he was consistent in this from the beginning. Moreover, he took a long time to achieve this final result. As far as we can tell from the existing records of his publications, he applied himself almost exclusively to this one task during the whole of this period and beyond (six years after the publication of this work, Maide, 1943 was published by Iwanami Shoten as a sort of by-product of his research in the history of economic thought). Since the 1937 book was called *Part I*, a *Part II* may have been planned, but it never actually appeared.

Part I covers the history of economics from 'Mercantilism' (chapter 1) to 'J.S. Mill' (chapter 7). *Part II* was probably intended to deal with economic thought after the time of J.S. Mill. But in the general atmosphere after 1937, on the eve of the War, it was in fact impossible to publish *Part II*, which was to include the socialist thoughts of Marx and others. Furthermore, in chapter 5 of *Part I*, which treats Ricardo particularly in relation to Marx, even in the passages which are evidently based on the theory and thought of Marx, his name is not explicitly mentioned (the same is also true for the index), and the use of terms specific to Marxist economics (exploitation, surplus value, etc.) is kept to the strict minimum. Many of the Japanese researchers in classical economics, who were gradually pursuing their research in the 'dark age' between the latter half of the 1930s and the Second World War, when Marxism was 'state-prohibited thought', were obliged to edit their books and articles in this way. And instead of continuing to publish their research works in this way, many of them preferred to apply themselves to translating the primary literature in the history of economic thought that had not yet been translated into Japanese. Indeed, a considerable number of classical works, including minor ones, were translated for the first time around the year 1940.

In *Summary of theoretical economics*, published in 1943, i.e. six years after *Summary of the history of economic thought, part I*, Maide wrote that the economic theory of Marx is 'an error by and large' (Maide, 1943: 51). He adopted a position whereby he recognised the benefits of enterprise deriving from the personal aptitudes of the capitalist, hence rejecting the labour theory of value. This was not compatible with his position as a Marxist economist, nor with the interpretation of Ricardo he had proposed in *Summary of the history of economic thought, part I*, nor with the position he was to take with regard to Ricardo and Marx in a small number of writings after the War. Hyōe Ōuchi, while highly praising this book on the whole, considered this position to be a 'drawback' (Ōuchi, 1970: 298) and attributed its provenance to the economics of Schumpeter, who was in vogue in the economics profession during the Second World War instead of Marx, and was also from German-speaking origins. Whether this evaluation is appropriate or not, this book may show how 'Marxist economics' sought to survive by escaping from oppression under the military dictatorship.

After the War, Maide only published one research article. This was *Marx to Ricardo—Chidai Ron, Kachiron oyobi Chikusekiron wo Chūshin toshite (Marx and Ricardo: their theories of ground rent, value and accumulation)*, published in 1954 in the house organ of Gakushūin University, where he became professor after retiring from Tokyo University in 1952 at the age of 60. In Japanese universities, it was customary for newly employed teaching staff to contribute at least one article to the house organ of the faculty soon after assuming their post (as a salutation to their colleagues, as it were). This article was probably written by Maide for such a purpose. But it only repeats the substance of the research he had carried out in his younger years, before the War, and does not contain the results of any new research carried out specifically for the purposes of this article, of which Mazane says that it is 'to be described as the embers of an old authority' (Mazane, 1965: 31). *Keizai Gakushi (History of economic thought)* (Kōbundō, 1955) was the only new book published by Maide after his retirement. It was co-authored with Masahiko YOKOYAMA (1917–1986), successor to the post of Maide (Yokoyama was a staff member of Tokyo University from 1946 until his retirement in 1978, lecturing on the history of economic thought long after Maide had retired. He fostered a number of Marxist economists and historians of economic thought who were [and some of them still are] active in Japan after the War, but he could not appoint his successor after his retirement from Tokyo University, where there have been no tenured teaching staff of the history of economic thought in the faculty of economics for more than 30 years). Chapters 6 to 8 seem to correspond to the contents of *Summary of the history of economic thought, part II*, planned before the War but finally unpublished. According to the 'Afterword' signed by Maide and Yokoyama, the first five chapters of this book were a summary by Yokoyama of Maide's pre-War work. Chapter 6 on socialist economics between Ricardo and Marx and chapter 7 on Marxist economics were written by Yokoyama. The last chapter (chapter 8) deals with the German historical school.

Considering the scientific career of Maide as a whole, his Ricardo studies were certainly of a 'durably adhesive type' (Mazane, 1965: 15), achieving a well-developed result in reciprocation with the lectures he gave in the faculty for more than 10 years. But he must be said to belong to a rather short-lived class of researcher. Once he had finished writing a thorough history of economic thought including Ricardo, he never attempted any new developments in his research, and after his mid-40s he spent more than 20 years of his career as a researcher, corresponding to the extremely difficult period of the Second World War and the subsequent post-war years of confusion, without producing anything of substance.

5. From the Ricardo studies of the interwar period: research works to be included in this collection

i) Tokuzō FUKUDA (Three articles written between the end of Meiji era and the beginning of Taishō era—around the year 1910)

'Ricardo no Chidai Riron yori Marx e' ('From the theory of ground rent of Ricardo to Marx') (Résumé of the conference 'Chidai Shinron' ['New theory of ground rent'], held on the 16th May 1908 in Chūō University)

From what Fukuda writes in this article, one obtains a glimpse of how Ricardo and Marx were recognized in Japan at the end of Meiji era. The theme of this article is the theory of ground rent developed in the economic thoughts of Ricardo and Marx, who already belonged to the past at that time. This article shows Fukuda to be fairly well informed about the evolution and currents of Western economics up to his time. In characterising their economic theories, he attached importance to the fact that Ricardo and Marx were both of Jewish origin. Particularly with Ricardo, Fukuda tried to connect his theories of free trade and ground rent with his Jewish character. However, for Japanese readers and researchers, the Jewish question was a very unfamiliar and alien one, and Fukuda also treated it in this way. On the other hand, he sought to find a connection between Ricardo and Marx in the fact that Ricardo's theory of ground rent has implications of a socialist tendency, opposing the interests of the landowner class to those of the society as a whole. This interpretation is quite contrary to the one subsequently advanced by Kawakami, to the effect that Ricardo defends the landowner class in his theory of ground rent. But Fukuda wanted to see a relation of succession or progression between Ricardo and Marx, in that Marx called land ownership into question, while Ricardo did not go so far.

'Kachi no Genin to Shakudo to ni kansuru Malthus to Ricardo to no Ronsō' ('Debate between Malthus and Ricardo concerning the cause and measure of value') (Initially published in *Kokumin Keizaizasshi [Review of National Economy]*, Kōbe Higher School of Commerce [now Kōbe University], 1912)

In this article Fukuda considered the overall outline of the history of economic thought as streams bifurcating from the source of Smith. The opposition between Malthus and Ricardo in the theory of value contains problems that remained unsolved 100 years later. Fukuda emphasized the importance of historical research going back to the origin. This stance on research was only affirmed by Fukuda during this period, which initiated research in the proper sense of the term. It is symbolic that this article appeared in the year that Meiji ended and Taishō began. Every time he made quotations, for both Malthus and Ricardo, Fukuda collated the editions of the original texts with more or less rigour. Following the vicissitudes in the text of Ricardo's *Principles* between the first and third editions, and referring to the letters to Malthus, McCulloch and Trower edited and published by Bonar and J.H. Hollander at the end of the 19th century, Fukuda argued that Ricardo, starting from the labour theory of value, approached the cost of production theory of value *à la* J.S. Mill. He seems to have accepted the validity of Marshall's interpretation of Ricardo. At that time, the article by Hollander, the prototype of his 1914 book, had been already published. And for Malthus too, Fukuda compared the first and second editions of the *Principles* and noted the differences between them. He drew attention to the distinction between the cause and the measure of value in the *Definitions* of 1827 and in the second edition of *Principles*, published posthumously in 1836. According to Fukuda, both Smith and Ricardo, as well as Malthus in earlier times, confused these two things. It was J.S. Mill who followed through the inclination towards cost theory of Ricardo's later years and established the cost theory of value. Fukuda argued that the utility theory arose as an antithesis to this evolution, and the comparison between these two becomes the theme in the latter half of this article. He discussed the difference between the reception of Ricardo and Malthus as economists in posterity, affirming that unlike Ricardo, Malthus was not given sufficient attention as an economist. One reason for this was that he became too famous as a demographer, but it was also because Malthus often changed his mind and his sentences were not easy to understand. Lastly, quoting the metaphor of the 'two blades of the scissors', he lauded Marshall's arguments for integrating the utility theory of value and the cost theory of value (*Principles of economics*, Book V 'General relations of demand, supply and value', chapter 3 'Equilibrium of normal demand and supply'). But Fukuda kept his distance from the eclectic doctrine and ultimately rejected both the reconciliatory solution between utility and cost and the utility theory itself, and he concluded his article by inquiring how this problem should then be addressed.

'Ricardo Keizai Genron no Chūshin Mondai' ('Central problems of Principles of political economy *of Ricardo')* (initially published in *Kokumin Keizaizasshi,* Kōbe Higher School of Commerce, 1913)

In this paper, Fukuda took an entirely different approach from that of the reception of Ricardo in the Meiji era, by considering his chief work as a system of theories and seeking to determine its core. And he found the core of Ricardo's *Principles* in the issue of distribution as the application of the fundamental principle of value. The theory of value does not have meaning or importance in itself, but only as the cornerstone of the theory of distribution. According to Fukuda, the point of the theory of value that Ricardo proposed at the very beginning of *Principles* is that value is exclusively determined in the process of production, so that the process of distribution (in particular the level of wages and its rise or fall) has no relation to the determination of value. This interpretation goes one step further than the simple determination of value by the quantity of labour. Overlooking the independence of value determination from distribution necessarily leads to an erroneous understanding of the theory of ground rent, he added. In making this statement, he was probably mindful of the unilateral treatment of Ricardo's theory of ground rent, quite frequently taken up in Japan until then separately from his economic theory as a whole. Fukuda wanted to make clear the inappropriateness of this treatment by going back to the theory of value. Therein lay the novelty of this article for that time. Fukuda produced pioneering results on the fundamental character of Ricardo's economics and its significance in the history of economic thought during the transition period from Meiji to Taishō. This was probably because for a Japanese researcher of the time, he had widely read in Western economic literature and had excellent knowledge about the long-term trends of economics.

In contrast to the importance of production in the determination of value in Ricardo's theory, his theory of production in itself was very simple and clear, without substantial content that could become the subject of detailed discussion. This was the fundamental cause of the misunderstanding about the importance of production in Ricardo's theory, according to Fukuda. He discussed the differences in the application of the primary principle in the latter half of chapter 1 (on changes in value and the measure of value) and in chapters 2 to 6. For him, this constituted the body of economic theory. The economics of Ricardo is nothing other than 'a study of the operation of the basic principle of value in the process of distribution (and exchange)'.

(For the translation of the above three articles, we used the texts reproduced in *Keizaigaku Kenkyū, Kō Hen [Economic studies, latter part]*, 1920, Dōbunkan.)

ii) Hajime KAWAKAMI (extract from *'Preface'* to *Keizaigaku Taikō [Outlines of political economy]*, Kaizōsha, 1928)

This book is composed of two parts ('Anatomy of capitalist society' and 'Development of capitalist political economy'), each of which is based on Kawakami's notes for the lectures on the principles of political economy and the history of economics that he delivered in Kyoto Imperial University until April of the year of publication of this book. Ricardo only appears in the second section of chapter 3 of the second part of the book. The lack of importance attached to Ricardo in this book, which can be considered the summation of Kawakami's economic research, is symbolic of the place of Ricardo in his research as a whole. If Kawakami nevertheless played an important role in the rise of Ricardo studies in Japan from the end of Taishō to Shōwa era, it was largely because of the overwhelming influence of his studies of Marxist economics at that time. Ricardo was read and studied along with Marx, as the most important historical source of Marx—his shadow, in a manner of speaking. Kawakami himself never made Ricardo the subject of his specialised studies, but he almost certainly considered Ricardo to be one of the most important figures in studying Marx. Because of this, at the beginning of the 1920s when he became ever more committed to the theory of Marx, he directed his disciples in Kyoto Imperial University to conduct specialised studies on Ricardo (in his place, as it were), and taught representative Ricardo scholars of the time like Tsuneo Hori and Kōjirō Mori, who are both presented in this Introduction. So the role Kawakami played in the progress of Ricardo studies in Japan before the War was not so much due to his own research works, but to his indirect role as a mentor. Consequently, in the present collection, this book, the 'summation' of Kawakami's research in both economic theory and the history of economic thought, will be represented not by the section in which he discusses Ricardo directly, but by passages taken from the Preface where he relates the process leading to this 'summation'. This extract concisely shows the personality of Kawakami as scholar and thinker, the progress of his studies with the development of his thoughts, and his conception of the significance of his research in economic theory and the history of economic thought. This provides an insight into the intellectual framework underlying the work of the disciples who undertook Ricardo studies under his direction.

iii) **Shinzō KOIZUMI (***'David Ricardo no Keizaigaku'*** [***'Economics of David Ricardo'***], extract from Book III of** ***Adam Smith, Malthus and Ricardo, Sietōha Keizaigaku Kenkyū [Adam Smith, Malthus and Ricardo, studies of the orthodox economics]***, Iwanami Shoten, 1934)**

Like Hori, Koizumi carried out his Ricardo studies intensively during the 1920s. While Hori endeavoured, following Kawakami, to evaluate Ricardo's texts and determine his place in the history of economic thought by the yardstick of Marx's theory (in particular *Theories of surplus value*, which had not yet been translated at the time), Koizumi, profoundly influenced by the scientific research of Fukuda, pursued his Ricardo studies with the aim of returning to the original source ('original sin') of Marx's thought in order to criticise him. Koizumi's first subject of study was the German economist Rodbertus, who was said to have developed some important aspects of Marx's economic theory from Ricardo (the theory of surplus value and the theory of absolute rent, for example) before Marx did. Koizumi intended to use the results of this first research for his Ricardo studies. As in the case of Hori, Koizumi's Ricardo studies also consisted in translating the text of his main subject of research, the *Principles*, into Japanese. He first published successive partial translations in the review of Keiōgijuku University, *Keiō Economic Studies*. These were then published as one work in the paperback collection of Iwanami Shoten in 1928. In addition to this translation, he published *Ricardo studies* in 1929 (Tettō Shoin), collecting the articles he had written during the 1920s. Thus, Hori and Koizumi synthesised the final results of their research works in the same way and at the same time.

One can consider that Koizumi's Ricardo study substantially ended with the above. The text presented in this collection is a largely extended and developed version of the commentary he added to the re-edition of his above-mentioned translation of *Principles*, published by Iwanami Shoten in 1930 as a title in the 'Collection of classics of political economy'. It was not written as a specialised article but as a commentary on Ricardo for general readers, but it incorporates the results and arguments of the Ricardo studies Koizumi had carried out in the 1920s. Leaving aside the parts containing biographical and bibliographical descriptions, we translate and present mainly the parts closely related to his 1920s studies. Below are commentaries about these extracts.

He starts by describing the debates about the rising price of bullion and the Corn Laws as the current topics that motivated Ricardo to study economic problems. Concerning the price of bullion in particular, the writings in which Ricardo discussed the monetary and financial problems of the time, from his debut as economist to the last years of his life, are almost exhaustively presented to show that 'the currency problem had a special connection with his life as an economist'. One of the remarkable differences between Koizumi's Ricardo studies and those of the other researchers (especially Hori, Mori and Maide) is the diversity of the subjects he treats (all except for taxation and international trade). In particular, he was the only researcher apart from Suenaga, 1934 to treat Ricardo's theory of money and finance as an independent research theme. This was exceptional for Ricardo studies of the time, probably because the above-named researchers other than Koizumi, together with many of the other Ricardo researchers of the time, adopted the theory of Marx as their frame of reference.

While making a detailed critical examination of Ricardo's 'theory of value and distribution', Marx never discussed as a whole all the monetary and financial writings that Ricardo produced during his career as an economist. One exceptional case in which Marx mentioned Ricardo's arguments about currency problems was a historical sketch in the supplement added at the end of chapter 2 of *A Contribution to the critique of political economy*, entitled 'C. Theories of the medium of circulation and of money'. In this sketch he makes critical comments about Ricardo's theory of the value of money based on his reading of part of *The high price of bullion*. But these comments do not seem to be based on a proper understanding of Ricardo's arguments in this pamphlet. Moreover, Marx never examined Ricardo's later monetary writings in relation to this pamphlet. The above-mentioned article by Suenaga is, in a different sense to that of Koizumu, one of a small number of research works on Ricardo's monetary theory published before the War. Its overall tone is critical of the contradictions in Ricardo's currency theory, along the lines of Marx's argument in the above-mentioned supplement, which seems to end up denying the importance of studying Ricardo in money and finance. In the Ricardo studies conducted in Japan under the overwhelming influence of Marx, this treatment (or rather neglect) of Ricardo's theory of money was predominant not only in this period, but for a long time after the War. In this context, the only researchers who undertook research on this theory (or on the bullion debates in general) were the minority who did not take

Marx's theory as their point of reference (or who took an anti-Marxist position). In this sense, Koizumi's presentation and examination of Ricardo's monetary theory deserves attention, along with the translation by Obata in 1931 (see above).

As for the theories of value and distribution, Koizumi did not regard the theory of value as the precondition or basis for the theory of distribution, unlike the other researchers of his time who took Marx's theory as their yardstick, like Hori, Mori and Maide. He argued, on the contrary, analysing the theories of value in *Essay* and *Principles*, that the theory of distribution (particularly of profits) forms the basis for the theory of value. In other words, Ricardo's theory of value depends on the presupposition of profits. Koizumi pointed out that in Ricardo, profits (furthermore those at a certain average rate) and the inverse relation between wages and profits, are posited as a presupposition for the theory of value without any prior explanation.

Already in his Ricardo studies that began in the early 1920s, emphasising the significance of the changes in the determination of value by the quantity of labour bestowed that Ricardo admitted for various reasons in the latter half of the first chapter of *Principles*, Koizumi asserted that already in Ricardo, orthodox economics had adopted the principle that value is determined by the cost of production rather than labour bestowed. Hence, according to Koizumi, the evolution of the theory of value in the history of orthodox English political economy in the 19th century from Ricardo to Marshall (Koizumi attaches importance to Senior, J.S. Mill, Cairnes, Jevons and Marshall) was a process in which the cost theory originally contained as the essential element in Ricardo's theory came to the foreground, displacing the labour theory of value.

As for the new marginal utility theory of value proposed at the time of the so-called 'marginal revolution' of the 1870s, Koizumi sought to comprehend it as a more general theory comprising both labour theory and cost theory as its special cases, extending the theory of exchange to cover every kind of good that could become its object. According to Koizumi, therefore, the utility theory of value was neither opposed to nor incompatible with cost theory. The theory advanced by Jevons and others did not bring about a revolutionary change in classical theory, but only removed the special conditions imposed on it (thus enriching the scope of objects covered by it) and observed the phenomena of exchange more carefully. Consequently, its innovativeness had been overestimated. In thus highlighting the aspect of the classical theory of value that Marx had treated rather negatively, Koizumi espoused the interpretation that Ricardo's theory of value was a cost theory. In contrast, from this viewpoint of Koizumi, Marx's theory of value must be considered as having 'failed by diverging from Ricardo' in reproducing on a larger scale the inessential aspect of Ricardo's theory, rather than as being its orthodox successor.

(For the translation, we used the text reproduced in Volume 5 of *Koizumi Shinzō Zenshū* [*The complete works of Shinzōo Koizumi*], Bungei Shunjū, 1968).

iv) Tsuneo HORI (*'Rōchin Ron'* [*'Theory of wages'*], chapter IV
of *Riron Keizaigaku no Seiritsu—Ricardo no Kachiron
to Bunpairon* [*Establishment of theoretical economics—
Ricardo's theory of value and theory of distribution*],
Kōbundō, 1958)

This work by Hori is not in the form of a specialised article, but one chapter
in his above-mentioned book, commentaries on the theory of wages developed
in chapter 5 of Ricardo's *Principles*. However, its contents are not just summary
explanations; they are of a specialised nature, advancing the author's own interpretations of problems such as the relation between Ricardo's theory of wages
and the theory of wage funds or the iron law of wages (these were the topics
of debates from the 1920s when Ricardo started to be studied seriously), the
relation between natural and market wages, and the differences between Malthus
and Ricardo in their applications of the principles of population to the theory
of wages, etc. It is a largely extended and modified version of the corresponding
chapter of Hori's *Principles of economics* published in 1938, prototype of the
above book. The chapter on the theory of wages was expanded and modified
far more than the other chapters. This chapter differs from the others in its
character as research rather than commentary, and it occupies a disproportion-
ately large place, giving the impression of an imbalance. This may be a result
of the particular emphasis the author laid on the study of the theories of wages
and value since his first monograph *Theory of value of Ricardo and history of its
critiques* (for the probable reasons for this, see above). This one chapter of his
book, the result of the Ricardo studies Hori pursued from the pre-War period,
is therefore presented here separate from the other chapters.

Following Smith, Ricardo thought that although the market price for commodities is determined by the prevailing relation between supply and demand,
changes in this relation will lead the market price to converge in the long
run and on average with the natural price, ensuring an equal profit for every
industry. In the case of general commodities, the market price gravitates
around the natural price, with the result that the latter functions as the focus
of the former. However, in the case of 'labour' as a special commodity,
Ricardo did not conceive the relation between its natural price (wages) and
its market price (wages) in the same way, the former marking the lower limit
below which the latter cannot fall for very long, according to Hori. In his
'Introduction' to *Principles*, Sraffa showed that Ricardo separated the text of
chapter 4 (on the relation between the natural price and the market price)
from the text of chapter 5 (on wages), which had originally been part of the
same chapter, just before publication (Ricardo, 1951: xxvi). According to
Hori, Ricardo took this measure because he had noticed the difference between
general commodities and the commodity 'labour' in terms of the relation
between the natural price and the market price. So the natural wages that
function as the lower limit of market wages do not exist as a fixed norm, but
change with the conditions of society.

Since the level of natural wages is determined by the prices of the articles consumed for the subsistence and reproduction of the workers, it might be said in principle that every kind of consumption good likely to be consumed by them is related to this level. But Ricardo considered convenience and luxury goods to be of negligible importance in this respect, and for him it was in fact only the necessities, in particular the most important of them, the staple food, i.e. bread, or corn as its raw material, that determine the level of natural wages. It is easy to imagine the kind of life that would be allowed to workers by the natural price of labour in the classical political economy, including Ricardo. One can then appreciate the soundness of Hori's interpretation, in which the natural price is not the central point of up-and-down movements in the market price, but the lower limit, below which the market price cannot fall for very long.

The one factor that causes wages to fluctuate is the demand for the commodity 'labour', which depends on the amount of capital. In chapter 31 (on machinery) that was added to the third edition, the demand for labour does not depend on the total amount of capital, but only on the circulating capital. However, in chapter 5 (on wages), Ricardo continued to affirm that the total amount of capital invested determines the demand for labour, so that the variations in the former are wholly reflected in those of the latter. Hori pointed out that the view of Ricardo has thus become ambiguous. Ricardo appears to have been unmindful of this discrepancy in his writings.

In any case, as the money paid to workers in the form of wages increases with the accumulation of capital, we can consider Ricardo's theory of wages to be of a different nature to the wage fund theory. Today, the question of the relation between these two theories is largely overlooked, but in the Ricardo studies of the pre-War period it was a contentious issue for a time, and in Hori's work it was also an important question. Hori denied that Ricardo's theory of wages had the character of a wage fund theory, while considering that it coincided with Lassalle's iron law of wages. A rise in market wages favours an increase in the consumption of food and hence in the number of workers, rather than a rise in their living standards, and it is this mechanism that finally brings market wages back to the level of natural wages, spent for the most part on food, besides the staple food (effect of the principle of population). Ricardo hoped that workers might improve their living standards, thus raising the natural wage level, rather than persist in their conventional lifestyle, thus increasing the population, when the increase in capital exceeds that of the population and raises the market wages in a 'progressing society'. However, he believed that in reality, Malthus' principle of population operates with overwhelming force, and so he was pessimistic about the increase in natural wages, which would remain close to the subsistence level. Although obliged to recognise as most unlikely, Ricardo hoped that the increase in wages could be maintained, by encouraging workers to improve their living standards, but not by exhorting them to control their population. In this sense, he may be said to have shown more flexible thinking in applying the principle of population to the movement of wages.

v) Kōjirō MORI (extract from *Ricardo Kachiron no Kenkyū [Study on the theory of value of Ricardo]*, Iwanami Shoten, 1926)

Here we present extracts from this work of a little over 500 pages. This is a research work specialised in Ricardo's theory of value, in which it is unique among the Ricardo studies of the time. It discusses exhaustively the problems related to Ricardo's theory of value and contains arguments that would not be worth taking into account in the light of the current state of research. In this collection, we extract several parts of this book which can still lay claim to some originality today, to show some of the particularities of Mori's Ricardo studies and of those in Japan in the 1920s.

Although this book is a specialised study on the subject of Ricardo's theory of value, Mori did not aim to examine the abstract theory of value in itself, as presented at the beginning of *Principles*. The significance of the theory of value is recognised only insofar as it forms the basis for elucidating the laws that regulate the distribution of the national product to the three classes, which Ricardo himself described as 'the principal problem in Political Economy' (Ricardo, 1951: 5). Following Ricardo, Mori also emphasised the significance of this point in his study of the theory of value. Marx, who was the reference point for Mori in his Ricardo studies, emphasised the inseparability of production and distribution in '(2) The general relation of production to distribution, exchange, and consumption' in the *Introduction (Einleitung)* to *Grundrisse*, and called Ricardo, who regarded distribution as the principal problem of political economy, 'the economist of production *par excellence*' (Marx, 1976: 33). In view of the structure of the three volumes of *Capital*, it is evident that Marx would consider production and distribution to be inseparable in capitalism. In conformity with these views of Marx, in the Ricardo studies that took Marx as their frame of reference, it may have been believed that when Ricardo addressed the question of distribution, he also presupposed the theory of value on which he based his theory of production (of surplus value in Marx). Indeed, research works discussing 'Ricardo's theory of surplus value' were produced both before and after the War. However, Mori argues that Ricardo did not develop the theory of production, and therefore that production and distribution are not aggregated in his theory. In reading Ricardo's text in his own way, on this important question relative to the essential character of Ricardo's economics, Mori proposed a different view to that of Marx, who exercised a strong influence on him. Though he was interested in Ricardo through the influence of Marx, Mori did not simply draw on Marx but developed his own interpretation directly from Ricardo's text. The style shown here characterises a certain part of the research in the history of economic thought in Japan existing up to the present time. However, this is not to deny that Mori's Ricardo studies were on the whole, like those of Hori, under the influence of Marx. In Mori too, the keynote runs as follows: Marx brought Ricardo's theory to fruition, and the significance of Ricardo in the history of economic thought is to be measured by his distance from Marx.

The economic research carried out from Meiji era was almost without exception focused on theories of Western origin, and the point of departure was always to decipher and translate correctly the original texts written in European languages. And it was the secondary research literature, equally of Western origin (see Section iii, List c of this Introduction), that served as a supplementary resource for accomplishing these tasks. Economic research in Japan generally remained at this stage and did not progress beyond it. It was not at all rare that among the books and articles Japanese researchers published as their own, some were actually mere translations of works by foreign writers, or at best a paraphrase of them in Japanese (see Nishizawa, 2012: 313, for an astonishing example of this). Even these publications could have a certain significance inside Japan by propagating the knowledge of and interest in Western economics among general readers without direct access to foreign literature. Of course they would have had little significance if they had been translated into European languages and sent abroad. This may be a sort of fate imposed during a certain period on the economics of modern Japan, because of the need to start by introducing the original sources from abroad. A similar situation persisted for a long time after the War, though to a lesser extent. It was the originality of Tokuzō Fukuda, who began energetic writing activities from the late Meiji era (at the turn of the 20th century), that played an important role in changing this situation. Fukuda nurtured a number of talents in Keiō and Hitotsubashi Universities, and through their efforts he helped to gradually draw Japanese economic research out of its initial stage. In the Ricardo studies of the interwar period, Western research works, as 'authorities', still exercised a profound influence on the interpretation of Ricardo's texts, and 'Ricardo studies' that could not go beyond the level of their followers were not rare in Japan (in his above-mentioned review of Hori's book, written in 1929, a year before his death, Fukuda lamented this situation and welcomed the exception made by Hori's research).

At the end of his book to be included in this collection, Mori provides a list of references that is 18 pages long. Here, one can see how far and in what editions he consulted the primary literature of Ricardo and others, and which Japanese and foreign research works he made use of in producing this book. The list is extensive not because of the number of references, but because Mori adds brief comments to many of them. From these comments one can see how Mori approached the primary and secondary literature. Incidentally, the only Japanese literature mentioned in this list are the works of Koizumi, Hori, Kawakami and Maide (which are all included in this collection). Among the writers listed as 'authorities' on Ricardo studies in the West, the important researchers often referred to by Mori and his contemporaries are Gonner, Cannan, J.H. Hollander and Diehl, and one can probably also add Marshall, Dietzel and Amonn. In saying that 'the interpretations of these scholars appear to be generally recognised today in academic circles', Mori was describing the situation of the time, when these interpretations were widely accepted among Japanese researchers. However, he added immediately, 'I am sceptical whether these interpretations and critiques really transfer correctly the true meaning of Ricardo's theory of value'. In this way, he openly distanced himself some-what from the secondary literature of the West, often referred to in the Japanese academic circles of the time as reliable 'authorities', refusing to accept them uncritically. Together with the substantial divergence from Marx mentioned above, this stance with regard to the secondary research literature by presti-gious Western writers may be worthy of 'the period of full-fledged introduction or establishment of Ricardo' (Mazane, 1965: 5).

vi) Chōgorō MAIDE (*'David Ricardo'*, chapter 5 of *Keizaigakaushi Gaiyō, Jō Kan [Summary of the history of economic thought, part I]*, Iwanami Shoten, 1937)

The work by Maide to be presented in the following is one chapter of a text-book written for his university lectures. Since Ricardo was the main theme of his research leading up to this work, this chapter is the longest of the seven chapters in the book. Comparing this chapter with his first research article, entitled 'Compendium of Ricardo's theory of distribution' (*Keizaigaku Ronshu*, vol.3, no.3), written in 1924 and based on the Ricardo content of his first lectures on the history of economic thought, it is clear that this chapter is closely connected with the research Maide conducted up until 1937. His first article was composed of six sections, while this chapter has seven, including a new one, 'Theory of foreign trade', inserted just before the 'Conclusion'. The titles of all the other sections remain the same, and their contents are comparable on a case-by-case basis. This does not mean, however, that the chapter on Ricardo in his 1937 book was a simple reproduction of the article published more than 10 years before. Although the general framework was the same in terms of the choice of subjects and the structure, many passages throughout the chapter were modified, and the results of his article 'Ricardo's theory of machinery' (ibid., vol.5, no.3), published in 1926, were incorporated as part of the 'Con-clusion'. These points show concretely the characteristics of his Ricardo studies as mentioned above in our brief description of Maide's career as a researcher.

Like his contemporaries Hori and Mori, Maide pursued his Ricardo studies from the early 1920s with reference to the economic writings of Marx, and firstly *Theories of surplus value*. Their interpretations of Ricardo were severely limited by Marx's treatment and evaluation of Ricardo. Of the various different aspects of Ricardo's economic theory, those that Marx considered important were also taken up by these three scholars as the main subjects of their research, and the others tended to be taken lightly or neglected. It would be fair to say that the subjects were selected in this way for all of their Ricardo studies. This also applies to the summation of Maide's Ricardo studies, represented by chapter 5 of this book (also described as 'the pinnacle in the general introduction of Ricardo before the War', Mazane, 1965: 25). If the economics of Ricardo is treated in one chapter of a textbook on the history of economic thought, it should give a general presentation of the whole of his economics, including its historical evaluation. But in each section of this chapter, Maide only takes up the subjects of the first seven chapters of *Principles*, including the 'theory of foreign trade' mentioned above ('theoretical part'), i.e. 'the theory of value and distribution'. Only cursory mention is made of the theories of taxation, money and finance, despite the fact that they all occupy an important place in the economics of Ricardo. Moreover, these brief mentions do not go beyond the level of a simple repetition of the critical assessment of part of Ricardo's theory of money, made by Marx in *A Contribution to the critique of political economy* and based on a misunderstanding of Ricardo's work. In a specialised study of certain specific aspects of Ricardo's economics, the aspects not directly related to the subject of the study must be omitted. This bears no reflection on the evaluation of the aspects that have been omitted. But if a similar procedure is adopted in a general compendium about the economics of Ricardo such as this chapter of a textbook, it is possible that the selection of subjects is directly connected to the relative evaluation of the different aspects of Ricardo's economic theory. This procedure may have exercised a non-negligible influence on Ricardo studies in Japan, including those undertaken after the War—all the more so if Maide's work won the esteem of academic circles in pre-War Japan as suggested by Mazane's comment above.

The Ricardo studies carried out by Hori and Mori during the 1920s adopted Marx's theory as their frame of reference, and they were characterised as research in the history of economic theory whose main aim was to compare Ricardo with Marx, or more precisely to measure the distance between the two. Maide, on the other hand, in the 'Preface' of his book, emphatically required that the history of economic thought should examine theories by placing them in a wider historical context: 'in research in the history of economic thought, one should not only consider the economic doctrines or theories; it is more important to understand them as the results of each epoch, and hence of a stage in the general historical process leading finally to the present time'. In his review article 'Two studies on the theory of value' (*ibid.*, vol.5, no.4, 1926), which includes a review of Mori's *Study on the theory of value of Ricardo*, 1926, Maide, while highly praising Mori's study on the whole, pointed out that Mori 'leaves a point still to be desired to some extent', and asked, 'can we not hope for the description of the historical background of the doctrines to be a little more meticulous?' Every chapter in Maide's book seems to embody this requirement of his. But in chapter 5 on Ricardo, which is to be translated and presented in this collection, matters which seem to be indispensable for understanding Ricardo's economics, such as the historical background or the reactions of other economists, are embedded in the examination of 'the theory of value and distribution', the central theme of this chapter, and recede into the background. This may be because he considered the explanations in the preceding chapter on Malthus to be applicable to this chapter on Ricardo. In any case, despite the fact that Maide called for a style of study of the history of economic thought rather different from that of Hori and Mori, his treatment of Ricardo in chapter 5 produced what can, on the whole, be described as a study of the history of economic theories, just like Hori and Mori.

In his 1937 book as well as in his article of 1924, Maide attached importance to *Essay* Ricardo wrote before *Principles*, indicating that his study of Ricardo was not always entirely confined by the framework of Marx's treatment of Ricardo. Comparing these two works by Ricardo, he showed that Ricardo had already anticipated, in the pamphlet preceding his chief work, what he subsequently developed in a more systematic way: the configuration of the relations of interest between the three classes in modern capitalism and the long-term dynamics of these relations in the process of capital accumulation. But he did not pay any particular attention to the problems contained in *Essay* relative to the interpretation advanced by Sraffa in later years, such as the measurement of surplus by a physical term or the undeveloped labour theory of value.

As far as we can tell from MEW (Marx Engels Werke), Marx only mentioned Ricardo's *Essay* once in his principal economic writings: he quoted a short passage without adding any comment in Volume 2 of *Theories of surplus value*, in the context of his critical examination of Ricardo's theory of ground rent. He left no other mention or examination of this pamphlet by Ricardo. As explained above, Japanese researchers must have known *Essay* from relatively early on, but of all the Ricardo scholars of the pre-War period presented in this collection, apart from Maide, only Koizumi, the opponent of Marxism, examined the text of *Essay* in relation to *Principles* (see above).

In any case, according to Maide, the conflict of interest between classes over distribution in modern capitalism as conceived by Ricardo in *Principles* and *Essay* turns on the relation between the landowners, benefiting from an increase in ground rent made possible by the rise in agricultural product prices, and the capitalists, incurring a fall in profits as the reverse side of this process. In between these two opposing classes, the workers certainly obtain higher wages with the rise in corn prices. But this only compensates for their increasing living costs, leaving real wages unchanged. Indeed, if the increase in wages tends to fall short of the rise in living costs, their real wages will fall and the workers will, like the capitalists, be victims of the rise in ground rent. Therefore, Maide argues, the workers are in a similar position to the capitalists; they are passively concerned with the change in the relation of distribution that occurs with the process of accumulation. If the 'inverse relation between wages and profits' in Ricardo is of this nature, that does not necessarily imply an inverse or opposing relation between the interests of the two classes who obtain these two kinds of revenue. Unlike Marx, who considered that capitalist production turned on the relation of opposition between wage labour and capital, Ricardo did not consider the level of real wages to be the subject of conflict between them. Nor did he believe that the level of profit was determined as a result of exploitation in the labour process. He considered that a certain profit rate (varying inversely with wages) was given from the outset. Maide emphasises these points both in this chapter and in his first article of 1924. This actually highlights a view of class relations in modern capitalism that is specific to Ricardo and different from that of *Capital*, where Marx developed the theory of surplus value from the theory of value through the introduction of labour power as a commodity.

As mentioned above, the examination of the 'theory of value and distribution' in this chapter concludes with 'the theory of foreign trade'. In the Ricardo studies carried out in the field of the history of economic thought during the interwar period, under the influence of Marx's theory of the capitalist economy, it was extremely rare for chapter 7 of *Principles* to be taken up as a subject of research. This was not limited to the pre-War period. For a long time after the War, Ricardo's theory of foreign trade never counted among the major themes of research in the Marxist economic profession in Japan. The reason is the same as for the theory of money and finance: Marx did not take up this theme in his writings. According to his plan for the 'critique of political economy', in principle Marx always abstracted away from external economic relations in *Capital* (Book 1, first edition, 1867) and in all the manuscripts for the following books, covering only the first part of the plan. In this sense, Maide's examination of Ricardo's theory of foreign trade is remarkable. As for chapter 7 of *Principles*, the 'principle of comparative advantage' is one of the subjects most frequently discussed since J.S. Mill, but Maide makes no mention of this 'principle'. On the whole, he adopts a very critical position towards Ricardo's theory of foreign trade. Maide rejected the idea of specific conditions that differ from domestic economic relations, which Ricardo posited as the precondition for his theory of international trade, such as the limited movement of capital between countries or the inapplicability of the labour theory of value to international trade, and he attributed these conditions either to a historical constraint on Ricardo imposed merely by the 'immaturity of international credit organisations' or simply to 'absurdity'. Against Malthus, who contended that the expansion of exports is an effective measure for preventing a decline in the rate of profit, Ricardo upheld that foreign trade has no influence on the rate of profit. Maide criticised this assertion by Ricardo, arguing that it contradicted another assertion he made in the debates on the Corn Laws, to the effect that the free importation of cheap food (and raw materials) would be an effective means for preventing a decline in the rate of profit. Whether or not each of these arguments put forward by Maide is correct, it is certain that his presentation and examination of Ricardo's theory of foreign trade in this chapter are unique.

References

(As the Ricardo studies made in Japan during the interwar period are given in 'References' in Izumo, Sato, 2014: 232–5, the list given below does not include them. Moreover, the classical works in the history of economic thought, by Ricardo and others, mentioned in this Introduction are not included in the list below, except for those which are quoted above.)

Keitarō Amamo (1962), *Bibliography of the Classical Economics, Volume 2, Part 3, David Ricardo*, The Science Council of Japan, Division of Economics, Commerce & Business Administration, Economic Series No.30

Tsuneo Hori (1973), '50 years of Ricardo study in retrospect', *Keizaigaku Ronkyū* (Economic association of Kwansei Gakuin University), vol.26, no.4

Masashi Izumo, Shigemasa Sato (2014), 'The reception of Ricardo in Japan', in Gilbert Faccarello, Masashi Izumo (eds.), *The Reception of David Ricardo in Continental Europe and Japan*, Routledge

Chōgorō Maide (1943), *Riron Keizaigaku Gaiyō (Summary of theoretical economics)*, Iwanami Shoten

Karl Marx (1976), *Ökonomische Manuskripte 1857/58*, Marx Engels Gesamtausgabe (MEGA②, II/1·1), Dietz Verlag, Berlin

Kazuo Mazane (1962), 'Meiji oyobi Taishō Zenki ni okeru Ricardo Dōnyū Shi' ('History of Ricardo introduction in the Meiji era and in the first half of the Taishō era'), *Keizaigaku Nenpō* (Faculty of economics of Osaka City University), vol.16

Kazuo Mazane (1965), 'Taishō Kōki yori Senzen madeno Ricardo Dōnyūshi' ('History of Ricardo introduction from the latter half of the Taishō era to the War'), *ibid.*, vol.23

Hiroshi Mizuta (1988), 'Historical introduction', in Chuhei Sugiyama, Hiroshi Mizuta (eds.), *Enlightenment and Beyond: Political Economy comes to Japan*, University of Tokyo Press

Tamotzu Nishizawa (2012), 'The emergence of the economic science in Japan and the evolution of the textbooks 1860s–1930s', in Massimo M. Angello, Marco E.L. Guidi (eds.), *The Economic Reader: Textbooks, manuals and the dissemination of the economic sciences during the nineteenth and early twentieth centuries*, Routledge

Hyōe Ōuchi (1970), *Keizaigaku 50 Nen (Jō, Ge) (50 years of economic study, I.II)*, University of Tokyo Press

David Ricardo (1951), 'Principles of political economy and taxation', *The Works and Correspondence of David Ricardo*, edited by Piero Sraffa, vol.1, Cambridge

Shigeki Suenaga (1934), 'Ricardo no Kaheiron' ['Theory of money of Ricardo'], *Kenkyu Nenpō Keizaigaku I (Annual bulletin, Economics I)*, Tōhoku Imperial University

Shirō Sugihara (ed.) (1972), *Kindai Nihon no Keizaishisō—Kotenha Keizaigaku Dōnyū Katei o Chūshin toshite [Economic thoughts in modern Japan – centring on the introduction of the classical economics]*, Minerva Shobō

Shiro Sugihara (1988), 'Economists in journalism: liberalism, nationalism and their variants', in Chūhei Sugiyama, Hiroshi Mizuta (eds.), *Enlightenment and Beyond: Political Economy comes to Japan*, University of Tokyo Press

Shiro Sugihara, Toshihiro Tanaka (eds.) (1998), *Economic Thought and Modernization in Japan*, Edward Elgar

Tessa Morris-Suzuki (1989), *A History of Japanese Economic Thought*, Routledge

Toshihiro Tanaka (1991), 'Hori Tsuneo Hakushi no Ricardo Kenkyū' ['Ricardo study of Dr. Tsuneo Hori'], in *Hori Tsuneo Hakushi to sono Keizaigakushi Kenkyū [Dr. Tsuneo Hori and his Study in the History of Economic Thought]*, Genbunsha, chapter 2

1 Ricardo in the history of economic thought

(Three articles written from the end of Meiji era to the beginning of Taishō era – circa 1910)

Tokuzō Fukuda

1. From Ricardo's theory of rent to that of Marx

The word 'rent' is used in everyday life in a sense altogether different from that in economics. In the latter usage, it is linked to three further terms: 1. wages, 2. interest, and 3. entrepreneurial profit. These four items (rent, wage, interest and entrepreneurial profit) are elements of the economic theory of distribution. However, it is only rent that is treated in a very particular way. The primary reason for this lies in Ricardo's use of the term. He was an English economist, with so keen a mind that he can be said to be the founder of economics. He advanced a theory of rent that was subsequently named after him; once published, it was accepted by the majority of economists, although there was some criticism. His theory of rent made use of the term in a way distinct from the meaning ordinarily associated with the word. This initiated a definition of rent peculiar to economics, as part of a theory of distribution in which wages, interest and profits were used in a more everyday sense, and this situation prevailed until very recently. Two major and different tendencies have emerged: first, a tendency to treat wages, interest and profit of enterprise in the same way that rent has been treated; second, a tendency to cease treating rent in any specific sense, treating it instead as an ordinary word, analogous to the treatment of wages, interest and profits. This may, I think, be by far the most important current problem of pure economic theory. If economics is to progress further, then it will have to begin with the theory of rent.

According to the conventional account, the production of wealth prior to distribution requires four agents: 1. the landlord, 2. the capitalist, 3. the labourer, and 4. the entrepreneur. These four agents effect production, and the wealth thus produced is divided among them. The part received by the landlord is called rent, that received by the capitalist interest, that by the labourer wage, and that by the entrepreneur entrepreneurial profit. In this process of distribution only rent is treated differently to the other three, being deducted at the end of the process. Some American economists seek to extend this particular treatment to the other three, which are to be treated in the same way as rent. Mr. Clark, Professor of Columbia University, celebrated for his erudition and

extremely clear thinking, has proposed this approach, and he has been supported
in this by a number of scholars. Austrian scholars represent another tendency
that proceeds in the opposite direction. In Austria economics has made rapid
progress recently, prominent economists emerging with new doctrines. Among
them Böhm-Bawerk, who was finance minister for some time, is a redoubtable
opponent. He claims that the special treatment with regard to rent should be
abandoned, treating it like the other three terms. Clark and Böhm-Bawerk have
recently engaged in a significant debate. Many of the English and French scholars
continue to follow the conventional doctrine, agreeing with neither Clark nor
Böhm-Bawerk, with some exceptions. A conflict has consequently arisen between
these supporters of the conventional doctrine and a faction of (socialist) scholars
that attacks it. Among the latter, the most sharp-witted and widely read is Marx
in Germany. The conflict arose because Marx integrated the theory of rent into
his economic doctrine; Ricardo became the adversary of Marx. Curiously both
were Jewish. The Jews are humiliated everywhere in Europe, but they are eco-
nomically very powerful, especially in banking and business. Nonetheless, we
find on close investigation a number of Jews among those economists who are
the most admired for their thinking. Marx and Ricardo are remarkable examples
of this phenomenon, so much so that we would incline to think that the theory
of rent is owed to some kind of Jewish thinking, although I am in no position
to judge, but simply remark upon it. I suppose that few parts of economic
theory are as interesting, and this has become the basis of the entire doctrine
of Marx. There is a fundamental difference between England in Ricardo's day
and England as it is today. Today we have an England of free trade, although
some elements of protectionism have been reintroduced, while on the whole
remaining in the framework of free trade. In Ricardo's time, by contrast, protectionism largely prevailed, especially with regard to very high tariffs on corn
to prevent its import. It was in such an era that Ricardo published his works.
Witnessing the harmful effects of this protectionism, in direct opposition to this
he advocated free trade. Moreover, we must take into account the fact that he
was Jewish. A race leading a cosmopolitan and rootless life throughout Europe,
the Jews made no national distinctions from the outset. This point is also particularly clear in Marx. We also need to take account of his social position.
Ricardo was not educated as a scholar; his economics was learned later in his
life, after he had made money as a broker in the stock exchange. It was therefore
quite natural that Ricardo, with this racial background and his experience as a
broker, became indignant about the prohibition of corn imports. This indigna-
tion was expressed clearly in his general doctrine, and also in his theory of rent,
which is opposed to the landowner, concluding that *rent is not a part of the
cost of production.* Wages, interest and entrepreneurial profit are all payments
for human labour, but rent is not. Though initially limited, it increases with
the gradual increase in population. The price of land rises and rent increases,
so that rent is never a payment for the work of particular persons. By prohibiting the importation of corn more will have to be produced domestically, requiring
in turn more land. This makes landowners rich. The happier the landowners

are, the more the social progress is obstructed. In other words, the wealthier the landowners are, the less wealthy are people of other classes; and so landowners are enemies of social progress. Marx adopted this proposition and extended it to his own theory. In extending Ricardo's doctrine one must necessarily arrive at a socialist conclusion with respect to the theory of rent. Ricardo himself did not develop his doctrine to that point, which is why Marx appeared soon after the death of Ricardo. There were many other economists in the intervening period, orthodox economists on the one hand and 'Ricardian socialists' on the other.

2. The debate between Malthus and Ricardo on the cause and the measure of value

i) *Labour expended or labour commanded?*

Labour expended or labour commanded? Malthus and Ricardo held fundamentally different opinions on this question; one hundred years ago they engaged in continuing debate throughout their life as scholars. The streams of thought flowing from the work of Adam Smith became divided, and the division continues up to the present. This is cause for concern. Even today the problem has not yet resolved, rather it seems to have become more complicated. So to re-examine exactly what Malthus and Ricardo said can never be a fruitless task. Malthus wrote: 'Adam Smith, in his chapter on the real and nominal price of commodities, in which he considers labour as an universal and accurate measure of value, has introduced some confusion into his inquiry by not adhering strictly to the same mode of applying the labour which he proposes for a measure. Sometimes he speaks of the value of a commodity as being measured ['determined' in the first edition] by the quantity of labour which its production has cost, and sometimes by the quantity of labour which it will command in exchange'. These sentences appear in both the first and the second editions of Malthus's *Principles of Political Economy*, while the following passage can be found only in the second edition. (See the first sentences of Section 4 of chapter 2 in the first edition [p. 85], the seventh paragraph of Section 4 of the same chapter in the second edition [p. 84]). 'It is in the latter sense, however, in which he applies it much the most frequently, and on which he evidently lays the chief stress. "The value of any commodity," he says, "to the person who possesses it, and who means not to use or consume it himself, but to exchange it for other commodities, is equal to the quantity of labour which it enables him to purchase or command. Labour, therefore, is the real measure of the exchangeable value of all commodities".[Smith's sentences quoted by Fukuda in English] Other expressions in the same chapter apply labour as a measure of value in the same way; [. . .] It would not then be worthwhile to inquire how far labour may be considered as a measure of value, when applied in the way which Adam Smith has practically rejected (meaning labour expended [phrase inserted by Fukuda]) in reference to the more advanced stages of society, if this mode of applying it had not been adopted by some distinguished modern writers as the foundation of a new theory of value'. (p. 85 in the second edition)

It is of course Ricardo who is called to be among the 'distinguished modern writers'. In fact Ricardo writes the following in *Principles of Political Economy and Taxation*:

> Adam Smith, who so accurately defined the original source of exchangeable value, and who was bound in consistency to maintain, that all things became more or less valuable in proportion as more or less labour was bestowed on their production, has himself erected another standard measure of value, and speaks of things being more or less valuable, in proportion as they will exchange for more or less of this standard measure [. . .]; not the quantity of labour bestowed on the production of any object, but the quantity which it can command in the market: as if these were two equivalent expressions.

If this were true, 'either might accurately measure the variations of other things: but they are not equal' (Page 6 in the first edition, no alteration in the third edition [Fukuda quotes from *The Works* edited and published by McCulloch in 1846 and gives the page numbers for this edition. We add the volume and page numbers in the Sraffa edition, indicated e.g. I/13–4, ditto infra]). Ricardo continues as follows:

> It cannot then be correct, to say with Adam Smith, "that as labour may sometimes purchase a greater, and sometimes a smaller quantity of goods, it is their value which varies, not that of the labour which purchases them;" [. . .] but it is correct to say [. . .] "that the proportion between the quantities of labour necessary for acquiring different objects seems to be the only circumstance which can afford any rule for exchanging them for one another" [Smith's sentences quoted by Fukuda in English]; or in other words, that it is the comparative quantity of commodities which labour will produce, that determines their present or past relative value, and not the comparative quantities of commodities, which are given to the labourer in exchange for his labour.
>
> [I/16–7, emphasis added. Pages 10–11 in the first edition, the same text appearing in the third edition.]

Put simply, the above means that the comparative value of one commodity with another depends solely on the process of production using labour, and not on the amount distributed as wages.

Ricardo is not always coherent in maintaining his doctrine that labour is value. Although there are not many textual modifications between the first and the third edition of *Principles*, there are non-trivial substantive differences. Moreover, his letters to Malthus, McCulloch and Hutches Trower [published toward the end of the nineteenth century by Bonar and J. H. Hollander: see

Introduction, p. 19] show that he did not cease thinking about this problem, gradually changing his mind to the approach to the production cost theory of value which he bequeathed to posterity via John Stuart Mill. Nevertheless, there was almost no change in his argument endorsing the labour expended theory and rejecting the idea of a labour commanded theory; and he eventually and reluctantly concluded that an invariable measure of value does not exist. He lamented this in a letter to Malthus, saying that 'We both have failed' [quoted in English] (letter of 15th August 1823, IX/352). For Malthus however circumstances were different. There are major differences between the first edition (1820) and the second edition (1836) of his *Principles of Political Economy*, although not so great as between the first and second editions of his *Essay on the Principle of Population*. Regarding the passage quoted above, while in the first edition of Malthus's *Principles* the title of Section 4 was 'Of the labour which a commodity *has cost*', in the second edition it was modified to 'Of the labour which *has been employed* on a commodity' [these two titles quoted in English, in the original the titles of both editions are entirely italicised]. And the first edition lacks the paragraph quoted above beginning with 'however' [pp. 61–2 above]; instead we find there the following sentences [following two quotations from Malthus are from original English texts]:

These two measures are essentially different; and, though certainly neither of them can come under the description of a *standard*, one of them is a very much more useful and accurate *measure* of value than the other.
    When we consider the degree in which labour is fitted to be a *measure* of value in the first sense used by Adam Smith, that is, in reference to the quantity of labour which a commodity has cost in its production, we shall find it radically defective.
                    [Emphasis by Fukuda. Page 85 in the first edition]

And on page 87 Malthus writes:

I cannot, therefore, agree either with Adam Smith or Mr. Ricardo in thinking that, "in that rude state of society which precedes both the accumulation of capital and the appropriation of land, the proportion between the quantities of labour necessary for acquiring different objects seems to be the only circumstance which can afford any rule for exchanging them for one another."
                                    [cf. I/13]

What attracts our attention here is the fact that, in the letter to Malthus of 15th August 1823 sent from Gatcombe Park, hence only 26 days before his death, Ricardo mentions this problem and writes: 'The difference between us is this, you say a commodity is dear because it will command a great quantity of labour, I say it is only dear when a great quantity has been bestowed on its production. In India a commodity may be produced with 20 days labour and may command 30 days labour. In England it may be produced by 25 days labour and command only 29. According to you this commodity is dearer in India, according to me it is dearer in England' [IX/348]. Bonar writes in his Introduction that the letters sent from Malthus to Ricardo can no longer be traced, so we cannot know what the response to this letter was. Ricardo was continuing his debates with Malthus unaware of his imminent death; something that allows us to sense the degree of his zeal for truth, while we can also see that this problem continued to preoccupy him. He returned to the same problem in his last letter to Malthus on 31st August. He had concluded the letter of the 15th by writing that 'I am just now warm in the subject, and cannot do better than disburden myself on paper' [IX/352, quoted in English], which explains why he wrote this last letter. He wrote there that: 'I have only a few words more to say on the subject of value, and I have done. You cannot avail yourself of the argument that a foot may measure the variable height of a man, altho' the variable height of a man cannot truly measure the foot, because you have agreed that under certain circumstances the man's height is not variable, and it is to those circumstances that I always refer' [IX/380]. And he concludes this letter with the following words: 'And now, my dear Malthus, I have done. Like other disputants after much discussion we each retain our own opinions. These discussions however never influence our friendship; I should not like you more than I do if you agreed in opinion with me' [IX/382, quoted in English]. He died on 11th September 1823. Malthus survived for another 11 years and continued thinking about this problem. Four years after the death of Ricardo he published *Definitions in Political Economy*, presenting his new ideas about the theory of value, which had always been in opposition to those of Ricardo. *Definitions* is indispensable for an understanding of the changes in Malthus's thinking. He could not convince himself, and thought about the matter again and again. He attempted to prepare a new edition of his *Principles* making use of the results of his later studies, applying himself intensively to this task. However, he died in 1834 before he could finally complete the work. Fortunately the new edition was published as the second edition after his death by his two friends, so that we are aware of his final ideas about this problem. In this second edition Malthus *newly* inserted the following extremely notable passage as a footnote, at the beginning of Section 4 of chapter 2:

> The labour worked up in a commodity is the principal CAUSE of its value, but it will appear in this chapter that it is not a *measure* of it. The labour which a commodity will command is NOT the CAUSE of its value, but it will appear in the next chapter to be the *measure* of it.
> [Footnote to page 83 in the second edition (words in capitals are italics in the original and emphases in italics are by Fukuda)]

Ricardo as well as Adam Smith did not distinguish between the cause and the measure of value, arguing only that labour was value. They spoke sometimes of labour as a 'source', a 'foundation' or a 'circumstance', at other times as a 'measure' or 'standard measure', and often used the word 'determine' [some words in quotation marks above are written in English]. While in the first edition Malthus was also very ambiguous on this matter, in the second edition he came to regard the *cause* and the *measure* as quite different things. In this way for him, as for Ricardo, labour as the cause of value is 'labour expended'; but for the measure he adopted a position opposite to that of Ricardo, arriving at the conclusion that it should be '*labour commanded*'. In the following we quote some introductory paragraphs from Ricardo's chapter on value, showing that he does not distinguish the *cause* and the *measure* at all. [all the following quotations from Ricardo and J.S. Mill are from the original English texts]

> Utility then is not the measure of exchangeable value, although it is absolutely essential to it.
>
> [I/11]

This sentence appears to mean that the primary cause giving rise to value is utility, which cannot however be considered to be the measure.

In the next paragraph he writes:

> Possessing utility, commodities derive their exchangeable value from two sources; from their scarcity, and from the quantity of labour required to obtain them.

Here Ricardo seems to recognise utility as the common cause of value, and recognise scarcity and labour expended as its direct cause.

But since he says that 'there are some commodities the value of which is determined by their scarcity alone' [I/12], he seems to regard labour as a cause in the sense that it determines value. Thus, in the debate with Malthus, labour as a cause of value was scarcely mentioned, and the discussion centred exclusively on labour as a measure, particularly as an invariable measure. The question was evidently whether 'labour expended' should be considered the measure of value.

John Stuart Mill says about this:

> [T]he idea of a measure of value must not be confounded with the idea of the regulator, or determining principle, of value. [. . .] To confound these two ideas would be much the same thing as to overlook the distinction between thermometer and the fire.
>
> [John Stuart Mill, *Principles of Political Economy:*
> *with some of their applications to social philosophy*,
> edited with an introduction by Sir W. J. Ashley, p. 568]

Mill himself made the following concluding remarks on the theory of value:

> The value of a thing means the quantity of some other thing, or of things in general, which it exchanges for [. . .] The temporary or Market Value of a thing depends on the demand and supply [. . .] Besides their temporary

value, things have also a permanent, or, as it may be called, a Natural Value; [. . .] The natural value of some things is a scarcity value; but most things naturally exchange for one another in the ratio of their cost of production, or at what may be termed their Cost Value.

Principles of Political Economy, p. 478

Thus the cost value is said to be the cost value of the 'most costly portion'. Some of the costs of production are permanent and general, others are temporary. The former include wages and profits on capital, the latter taxes and costs caused by scarcity, in general 'things which admit of indefinite increase', and which 'naturally and permanently exchange for each other according to the comparative amount of wages which must be paid for producing them, and the comparative amount of profits which must be obtained by the capitalists who pay those wages' [*Principles of Political Economy*, p. 479]. Therefore there is no distinction in Mill between 'labour expended' and 'labour commanded', and capital is also 'expended', like labour. The theory regarding labour as value is extended to become a production cost theory of value. Here economics as a theory of cost was firmly established; and we must recognise this to be very similar to the position at which Ricardo arrived during the last few years of his life. Economics as a utility theory appeared to be an alternative to, the opposite of, a cost theory founded in this way.

Since the notion that something was 'expended' had a central place, it was natural that this doctrine would sooner or later end up as a cost theory. But it is quite secondary whether labour alone is to be regarded as something 'expended', or whether the employment of capital and also consumption should be included in this. Whether rent is something 'expended' is a tertiary issue. While Mill tried to solve the problem at the secondary level, the economics of today is seeking to resolve the issue at the tertiary level. The fundamental problem is whether the option between 'expended' or 'commanded' has been altogether neglected since Mill. It is not at all surprising that economics has advanced a good deal as cost theory by disregarding its other aspects. From the point of view of Malthus, it would have been a matter for lifelong regret that he had not continued discussion of this fundamental problem while Ricardo was alive, seeking a point of agreement with him. In the collection of letters edited by Bonar [mentioned above] can be found a commemoration by Malthus that was published in the January 1837 issue of the *Edinburgh Review*:

I never loved anybody out of my family so much. Our interchange of opinions was so unreserved, and the object after which we were both enquiring was so entirely the truth and nothing else, that I cannot but think we sooner or later must have agreed.

[*Letters of David Ricardo to Thomas Robert Malthus 1810–1823*, edited by James Bonar, Clarendon Press, Oxford, 1887, p. 240]

This could well be not only a eulogy to his departed friend, but also testimony to Malthus's own firm faith. He thought it possible that by pursuing discussion he might convince Ricardo of his own view. However, he not only failed to gain agreement from Ricardo; he also failed to gain the support of posterity. Only Ricardo's doctrine, the view of his adversary, enjoyed wide diffusion, and his 'labour commanded' theory has remained in total obscurity up until today. Malthus, the Professor of Political Economy at East India College, lacked the kind of support from disciples that Ricardo, originally a stockjobber, had from McCulloch and later from John Stuart Mill. There was a good reason for this difference. While Ricardo was constant in his views, occasionally Malthus altered his opinions. His theory of population also underwent repeated changes. This was particularly notable in the case of his theory of value. Ricardo's doctrine is easy to understand at first view, but at first reading Malthus is not that clear. The former was readily accepted, while the latter was ignored. In addition, Malthus became famous for his theory of population, so that his *Principles of Political Economy* and theory of value were overshadowed by the prestige of the former. Ricardo's theory of value found many readers, since it is placed in the *Principles* where it attracts the attention of the reader, together with the theory of rent. But the theory of value in Malthus's *Principles* was neglected, and hardly read. Such cases are not rare in our world. However, it is not so easy to weigh the gain and the loss of this for our discipline.

ii) The theory of cost and utility theory

The theory of cost (Kostenlehre) considers cost value (Kostenwerte) to be the central idea of economics. According to Mill, the idea of value is not necessarily the central point of economics, since many economic factors can be discussed without it. On the other hand, he also says that his definition of value means the quantity of the commodity to be obtained in exchange; hence he does not seem to understand economics purely as a theory of cost. But it was he who firmly established economics as a theory of costs. Not only Mill, but also many of those who subsequently accepted his theory and paraphrased it, cannot necessarily be united under the banner of a theory of cost; nevertheless, all of them are cost theorists. Since cost theory originates in the labour expended arguments, it is not wrong to say that Ricardo is the father of economics as a theory of costs.

The direct opposite of cost theory is utility theory (Nutzenlehre or Genußlehre). Menger and Jevons advanced the idea of economics as a theory of utility in the same year (1871). Jevons writes: 'When at length a true system of Economics comes to be established, it will be seen that able but wrong-headed man, David Ricardo, shunted the car of Economic Science on to a wrong line—a line, however, on which it was further urged towards confusion by his equally able but wrong-headed admirer, John Stuart Mill. There were economists, such as Malthus and Senior, who had a far better comprehension of the true doctrines, but they were driven out of the field by the unity and influence of the Ricardo-Mill School'. The final sentences of the 'Preface to the Second Edition' [W. Stanley Jevons, *The Theory of Political Economy, with notes and an extension of the bibliography of mathematical economic writings by H. Stanley Jevons*, Macmillan and Co., Limited, St. Martins Street, London, 1924, pp. Ii–Iii. Quotation from the original English text.]. In fact, Mill emphasised the conception of something that was 'expended', and he also extended and defined the meaning of 'expended'. On this one point Jevons is not wrong in what he writes in the 'Preface' to the second edition of his *Theory of political economy*. He tried to revive the forgotten and abandoned legacy of Malthus (and of Senior), to take it in a different direction. He treated utility as the sole cause of value, and its determinant. In this sense Menger did the same as Jevons.

One cannot deny that taking cost as the central concept of value, hence of economics, is deeply embedded in our scientific thinking. This is evident by the growing number of publications devoted to this issue in recent years. Professor Fuchs represents this tendency most eloquently, writing that he felt the need to attach more importance to what had no recompense (Das Unentgeltliche) in his introduction to Sōda's new book [Kiichirō Sōda, *Die logische Natur der Wirtschafts-gesetze*, mit einem Vorwort des Herausgebers (Karl Johannes Fuchs), Stuttgart, Verlag von Ferdinand Enke, 1911, S. VI]. It is well known that Fuchs defines concepts in economics on the basis of 'satisfaction of desires by means of material goods'. But this new doctrine, advancing the idea of what goes without recompense, cannot but bring about some changes to his doctrine. Although it at first appears to be a good move to limit economic goods to those with materiality, our real life relates to the immaterial services (Dienstleistungen) of others, and these are almost the equivalent of material goods. To limit our attention only to material things would be to banish from economic theory all those things that make up half of economic phenomena, which would be extremely inadequate. In particular, by following the doctrine according to which 'value is the standard explaining why a good is a good', many difficulties must arise in trying to explain the labour of others endowed with value. Agreeing with Fuchs, I once adopted materiality as the standard of economic goods, but then later abandoned it. And so I sympathise with his words quoted above. Disappointed with the materiality as a standard, I thus conceived the unrecompensed as its substitute, just like Fuchs.

Contact with Oppenheimer's doctrine was for me something like a ray of light. Oppenheimer says that what is important is not economic desires, but the economic satisfaction of desires. He states that the meaning of what he calls 'economic' lies in the need to 'make expenditures on costs'. I gave the same explanation in the first part of my textbook, and only after came across Oppen-heimer's doctrine. Neither value nor good can be defined in economics. It is only when they become economic that economic argument begins. Therefore the fundamental concept of economics is neither desire, nor value, nor good, but only the economic, and nothing else. To understand this, what is 'material' may certainly be very useful, but is in fact extremely inadequate. The 'unrec-ompensed' is far more suitable.

However, on further reflection this is not only not a new discovery, but is in fact nothing other than a revival of the labour expended theory of value. Of course, in comparison to the doctrines of Ricardo and Mill, the theory of the unrecompensed, or sacrifice of the present, is much more sophisticated and refined. From this we become aware of our remaining uncertainty about the fundamental concept of the economic, occupying a place not so distant from Malthus and Ricardo, while feeling at ease 100 years after their time (and although this does not necessarily apply to the new doctrine of Mr. Sōda, I put this point aside for now). Of course Mr. Kawakami, emphatically pointing out the inadequacy of marginal utility theory, has come very close to the idea of 'sacrifice' or of 'cost'. Cost or utility? We are always somewhere between these two extremes. A majority of today's scholars have worked out a convenient way of solving this puzzle. According to them, both cost and utility govern value, but which of them is predominant depends on circumstances. They explain that for beliebig vermehrbare Güter (goods that can be multiplied at will) the (marginal) utility is the maximum of value, and the cost (of production) is its minimum; and that for nicht beliebig vermehrbare Güter (Monopolgüter) (goods that cannot be multiplied at will [monopoly goods]), situated somewhere between these two extremes depending on given circumstances, only utility governs value, irrespective of cost.

Seligman's explanation of 'One buyer, one seller' etc., though apparently very careful, is in fact only a plausible paraphrase of the above reasoning. We can find there no explanation of how the actual price is determined. I wonder if one does not already make an error in speaking of something like beliebig vermehrbare etc. What can be increased without cost is not something that economics deals with. If you do not say 'mit dem Kostenaufwand vermehrbar, mit dem Kostenaufwand nicht vermehrbar' (replicable with the expenditure of costs, not replicable with the expenditure of cost), there will be no meaning. Or even if its meaning is not wrong, the above explanation can be said to explain nothing. It is a 'truism'. Is this not something that we might know from common sense, not needing to bother with the study of economics? Whether or not Seligman has become aware of this, he says that cost and utility amount to the same thing, hence value can be expressed 'in terms either of social utility or of social cost' [Edwin R. A. Seligman, *Principles of Economics with special reference to American conditions*, Longmans, Green, and Co., New York, London and Bombay, 1905, p. 201]. This is a quite interesting explanation, but it can be very much doubted that it corresponds with the facts. It is already questionable that anything like 'social cost' or 'social utility' exists. Cost is necessarily something that someone provides concretely, utility must be what a living person feels. There is no cost, no utility in what we call society. Even if in assuming the existence of an average man, an economic man, this 'man' must necessarily be human, and society cannot become a 'man' in any respect. A supposition should not always be rejected, but it is of no use at all if not related to something concrete.

Marshall, Dietzel and more recently Lexis are not so obscure as the writers noted above. They have tried to make a clear connection to cost and utility, apparently with great success. The suggestive chapter on Value and Utility in Marshall [Book III, chapter VI] can be read as many times as you wish. Reading this chapter together with Lexis, I feel myself approaching the right solution. When I read Schumpeter, Oppenheimer, Amonn, Clark etc. with these ideas in mind, I am seized with the feeling that I have really understood something.

However, eclecticism is always eclecticism, confusion is nothing other than confusion. Marshall makes interesting use of comparison with a pair of scissors. He compares cost and utility to a pair of scissors, and says that you cannot cut anything without both blades, although sometimes one scissor blade remains stationary while the other moves, and sometimes both move. Ancient people asked themselves which made the sound, the bell or the hammer. But I cannot help asking myself whether the problem of value is comparable to cutting with scissors or hitting a bell with a hammer. To say that there can be various outcomes is certainly possible. But if a question about a fundamental concept of a science can be answered in such a trivial manner, I cannot but wonder what may be the use of science.

When a cow drinks water, it becomes milk; when a snake drinks water, it becomes poison. [Buddhist proverb, meaning that a unique truth can have very different interpretations, effects.] Desire can or cannot become economic, value can or cannot become economic, a good can or cannot become economic. What we should study is not the water in itself, but how it becomes milk or poison. Meinong is quite right when he makes fun of the Austrian School by saying that 'kaum wird jemand meinen, der Tatsache des Wertes durch ausschließliche Berufung auf die intellektuelle Seite der menschlichen Natur Rechnung tragen zu können. [. . .] Es wird wohl in erster Linie Aufgabe der psychologischen Untersuchung sein, dieser Möglichkeit nachzugehen' (Hardly anyone will think it possible to think about the fact of value by relying exclusively on the intellectual aspect of human nature. [. . .] Certainly the pursuit of this possibility will first of all be a task for psychological research.)' [Alexius Meinong, Psychologisch-ethische Untersuchungen zur Werth-theorie, Graz, 1894, S.4]. Some economists consequently abandon their discipline to try and solve this problem as 'dilettante' psychologists, logicians or philosophers. But, if they direct themselves to the study of water while always leaving unaddressed milk and poison, then economics will finally lose its raison d'être. We want to know what water is, but we want to know even more what milk and poison are. Economics as utility theory may become merely applied psychology via marginal utility theory, but this was originally an idea planted by others, and I have no right to consider the flowers that blossomed from this. Before the blossoming we already had complaints. It seems to be pointless to switch to utility theory because we have wearied of cost theory. Though the latter may be superficial, it is after all a small idea planted by myself in my own field, and it is consequential in its own way. It is best to cherish the flower planted and grown by myself, even if it is poor and scrubby, rather than be attracted by a flower inspiring exorbitant hopes, but which is in fact trivial. Mr. Sōda makes fun of me in his *Antikritik*, saying that he will continue to follow my work to see how I will relate the unrecompense theory to the theory of money. This is probably because he does not recognize what I was doing. On the other hand, if Prof. Kawakami's attack on marginal utility found enthusiastic support from Mr. Terao etc., the Beweggrund (motive) seems to be here, whether conscious or not.

We are now standing at the crossroads: to advance along the road of cost, or to take the route of utility. The 'sphinx' of value looms nearer with this enigma. Without a solution to this enigma we cannot advance. Does the theory of surplus value not indicate to us the way we should take, without keeping to the road of cost, or diverting on to the road of utility? Do not Malthus's 'labour commanded' and Gossen's two laws point the way for us? Does not Thompson's 'surplus or additional value', later made use of by Marx, lay a foundation for our study? These are the themes I am going to study further.

3. The central problem of Ricardo's *Principles*

Ricardo placed at the centre of his *Principles* the *problem of distribution*, which he treated as an application of his fundamental law of value. And it was exactly *this application of value to the process of distribution* that had the greatest influence on posterity. In other words, it was nothing other than what Malthus called 'value as distributor of income' in the first edition of his *Principles*. Ricardo's economic theory is presented almost entirely in the first six chapters of his *Principles*, the remainder containing only variations dealing in a fragmentary way with various problems. Hence we will examine here these six chapters.

He first determines the essence of value by saying that

> the value of a commodity or the quantity of any other commodity for which it will exchange, depends on the relative quantity of the labour which is necessary for its production, and not on the greater or less compensation which is paid for that labour.

> Page 1 of the third edition of *Principles*
> [I/11, quoted in English]

This is what was later called the labour theory of value, introducing the fundamental proposition that anything that requires more labour has more value, and vice versa. But when the doctrine of Ricardo is described in the books about economics, it is often only this one point that is noticed, ignoring the fact that the above theorem contains a second and more important point. At the same time as affirming that 'the value [. . .] depends on the relative quantity of the labour which is necessary for its production', he also emphasised that it does 'not [depend] on the greater or less compensation which is paid for that labour'. For his theory as a whole, it is this negative statement which is far more important. Ricardo did not merely intend to define value as determined by the quantity of labour, but emphasise that the determination of value does not depend on the amount paid in wages, but more or less on the quantity of labour actually expended. In other words, the determination of value has no relation to the process of distribution, but takes place solely in the process of production. Therefore he wants to say that the quantity of labour actually employed in production and the amount of wages paid out for this labour are not necessarily correlated, their relation can vary: sometimes a lower wage is paid for more labour, sometimes a higher wage is paid for less labour.

Therefore he does not recognise the existence of what is called Verteilende Gerechtigkeit (distributive justice), and maintains that the determination of value has nothing to do with this. Hence, for him, the determination of value is not related to the process of distribution, but is exclusively related to the process of production. This is an indispensable point and not to be missed if we are to understand his true intention. It must be said that it is a great pity that later scholars focused on the question of whether it is justifiable to make labour the sole determinant of value, seemingly forgetting the existence of this far more important problem. Indeed, because of this serious error the other parts of his doctrine seem to be largely misunderstood or even misused; in particular, the real message of his theory of rent appears not to have been understood at all. Having now established this fundamental proposition, to further consolidate his negative affirmation Ricardo repeatedly makes this point and creates a section called 'Labour of different qualities differently rewarded. This no cause of variation in the relative value of commodities' (*Principles of Political Economy*, p. 15 [I/20, quoted in English]). Then he writes: 'as the inquiry to which I wish to draw the reader's attention, relates to the effect of the variations in the *relative value* of commodities, and not in their *absolute value*, it will be of little importance to examine into the comparative degree of estimation in which the different kinds of human labour are held. We may fairly conclude, that whatever inequality there might originally have been in them, whatever the ingenuity, skill, or time necessary for the acquirement of one species of manual dexterity more than another, it continues nearly the same from one generation to another; or at least, that the variation is very inconsiderable from year to year' [emphases added by Fukuda. Ricardo, *Principles*, p. 25. Error for 15, I/21–2].

Ricardo thus discussed the essence of value only in relation to the process of production, disregarding the process of distribution. He established in this way the fundamental principle: the quantity of labour required for the production of a commodity governs the value of that commodity. He therefore vehemently objected to Malthus's argument founded upon 'labour commanded'. This was because Malthus maintained that it was not the process of production that determined value, but primarily the process of exchange. According to Malthus, the value of a commodity is determined when it is brought to the market for exchange, by the quantity of the labour of others it can obtain in exchange. It may at first sight seem to be a flagrant contradiction that value came to be discussed primarily in terms of exchange in economics, given that only Ricardo's theory prevailed and that of Malthus more or less disappeared. However, if we consider the texts Ricardo wrote after he established his fundamental principle, we can see how this came about. For Ricardo, the problem of production is so simple that it needs no kind of economic theory; it was enough to explain the fundamental proposition, that value is determined by the quantity of labour expended in production. This fundamental principle was so simple and so clear that nothing need elaboration in the theory of production, other than its significance.

The starting point for economic theory is not so much this fundamental proposition, but rather the way it is used. Economic theory must have as its object of research the fact that, in real economic life, this fundamental proposition is not a rule, but something that creates various anomalies. There is no point in wasting purposeless words on the fundamental proposition itself. There are other problems of production alongside this fundamental proposition. This is why Ricardo emphatically claims that the issue concerns only the change in the relative value of a commodity, not its absolute value. In other words, the object of economic investigation is not to establish what value is in essence, but how one might make use of it. We can summarise as follows. Ricardo maintains as above that, though different kinds of labour are naturally remunerated to different degrees, this difference in remuneration is not the cause of variation in the relative value of commodities. He goes on to argue that the labour expended does not only involve what is actually directly necessary for the production of the commodity itself, but also includes labour expended for the production of tools and machines auxiliary to labour. The fundamental reason why the principle of the determination of value by the quantity of labour expended for production creates various anomalies in real economic life is that the labour in question is composed not only of direct labour actually worked up in that commodity, but also of labour expended in the past. Capital, accumulated past labour, is among the elements expended for production, in addition to current labour. This presents to economic analysis the problem to be investigated.

This is why Ricardo entitled Section 4 of the first chapter of his *Principles* as follows: 'The principle that the quantity of labour bestowed on the production of commodities regulates their relative value, considerably modified by the employment of machinery and other fixed and durable capital'. [Ricardo, *Principles*, p. 25. I/30, quoted in English]. Adam Smith also thought that the determinant of value was labour, but he imposed an important condition restricting this proposition to 'that early and rude state of society which precedes both the accumulation of capital and the appropriation of land [quoted in English]', and denied its validity for present-day society where there is accumulated capital and the appropriation of land. By contrast, Ricardo maintained that this principle remains valid when profit of capital and rent of land are paid. He did however think that the degree of influence they can exert on value varied. This, he thought, was the subject matter of economics. In that part of the first chapter beginning with Section 4 he studies the differences in the application of the above principle brought about by the differences in proportion between the two sorts of capital, between fixed and circulating capital, as well as by the variation in the value of money. The following five chapters deal with: the theory of rent (chapter 2), the theory of rent of mines (chapter 3), the natural and market price (chapter 4), wages (chapter 5), profits (chapter 6); here he discusses the differences in the application of the above principle, constituting the core of his economic theory. In other words, economics is for Ricardo nothing other than the study of how the fundamental principle of value works through the process of distribution (and exchange). Because of this he writes at the beginning of the Preface to *Principles* that:

> the produce of the earth—all that is derived from its surface by the united application of labour, machinery, and capital, is divided among three classes of the community; namely, the proprietor of the land, the owner of the stock or capital necessary for its cultivation, and the labourers by whose industry it is cultivated.
>
> But in different stages of society, the proportions of the whole produce of the earth which will be allotted to each of these classes, under the names of rent, profit, and wages, will be essentially different; depending mainly on the actual fertility of the soil, on the accumulation of capital and population, and on the skill, ingenuity, and instruments employed in agriculture.
>
> To determine the laws which regulate this distribution, is the principal problem in Political Economy: much as the science has been improved by the writings of Turgot, Stuart, Smith, Say, Sismondi, and others, they afford very little satisfactory information respecting the natural course of rent, profit, and wages.
>
> Pages 1–2 in the Preface [I/5]

It can be said that Ricardo considered that the subject of economic study was the investigation of reasons why, in contemporary economic life, the law of the distribution of income among the different classes does not always correspond to the proportion in which each class has participated in production, and the value that each of them receives is not proportional to the value of the whole product. Here we see the fundamental difference between Malthus and Ricardo. Because of this Ricardo objected to Malthus's argument relating to 'labour commanded', advancing instead the notion of 'labour expended'. The quotation above is not intended as a criticism to Ricardo's theory. I wanted only to make clear the core of Ricardo's economic theory. It is well know that there is a tripartite division in economics. Although Say stressed the importance of this trichotomy and contributed to its diffusion, Ricardo *dealt only with distribution as his subject*, as seen above. And in spite of this trichotomy and the apparent segmentation of economics, the orientation that Ricardo established still governs economic theory today. However, this cannot always be attributed solely to a lack of competence on the part of the scholars after him, that they lacked originality and only followed the mainstream. Given that the ultimate foundation of economics was heavily marked by Ricardo, this must have inhibited development on the part of later economists. In Ricardo's words, the subject of economic theory is relative, not absolute, value. He placed at the beginning of his book the grand principle that labour is value. He maintained that the process of distribution should be dealt with by deducing everything from this principle. Of course, present-day scholars unanimously condemn Ricardo's mode of argument, which I also reject. However, additions to the theory of production by later scholars do not go beyond the theory of the components of production; or rather, not even beyond the idea that the components of production increase. The law of diminishing returns, maybe the most general law of this approach, is originally not a problem proper to economics (the same goes for the theory of population). The theory of capital likewise does not for the most part go beyond the level of common sense. It is hardly wrong to say that the proper domain that economics can legitimately claim as its own goes no further than that which Ricardo discussed in the first six chapters of his *Principles*. I do not know whether this humble opinion of mine is ultimately right or wrong.

2 From my career of economic research

(Extract from the Preface to
Outlines of political economy,
Kaizōsha, 1928)

Hajime Kawakami

The 'Anatomy of capitalist society', the first part of this book, began as notes for lectures given at the faculty of economics in Kyoto Imperial University during the academic year April 1927 to March 1928. I taught there for 20 years, making a point of writing new lecture notes every year. Even for those parts I did not rewrite, I found myself unable to deliver an interesting lecture if the ink on the pages in my notebook had faded. In recent years, however, I found that I needed to make only small changes. Repeating almost the same lecture each year made me increasingly uncomfortable; but I was then given the opportunity to resign from my post. I gladly seized this opportunity to quit the lecture room for the quiet of my own study. I no longer had to write new lecture notes on the same subject. Instead, I wanted to make good use of this unique opportunity to extend my studies into other fields. Before doing so, however, I decided to revise my last lecture notes and publish them. [. . .]

Some explanation is called for. First of all, it is obvious that the initial section, while written for lectures on the principles of economics, is in fact almost a running commentary on Marx's *Capital*. Many may think the idea curious, but for me Marx's *Capital* presents the principles of economics in the best way possible; and so when lecturing on the principles of economics I cannot do anything other than rely entirely on *Capital*. Some may say, 'even if that is the case, you concentrate too much on Marx'. But there are not two truths, and if the doctrine of Marx represents the truth, our research must proceed on the foundations that he laid. According to the method of research and form of exposition adopted by Marx, the content of Book One of *Capital* is focussed exclusively upon the process of production. The process of circulation is there put to one side and dealt with in Book Two, which is focussed exclusively on the process of circulation (hence in turn excluding the process of production). Book Three then deals with the whole process, as a unity of these processes of production and circulation. The same can be said about Book One: there the narrative must necessarily follow the order commodity – money – capital. Anyone who thinks that this order could simply be reversed has not properly understood Marx's method. My lectures had to reflect the structure of *Capital* point by point. Of course, the writings of various scholars working in the field of bourgeois economics advance a variety of systems. We have a book on the principles of economics written by one person, and another by someone else. They differ in order of exposition as well as in content. As an independent scholar, an author would be ashamed if his book was not different in some way from the others. However, if a science is to be worthy of its name, the work done by scholars in that field must be unified as one system. It is only in this way that cooperation between the studies of different scholars becomes possible, making it possible to realise the development of the science. The reader can prove this to himself by looking at the situation in the natural sciences or in medicine. Within the camp of Marxism, all study must rest upon the foundation laid by Marx. The groundwork is so orderly, and so solidly constructed, that it can admit of no significant reconstruction. And it is primarily for this reason that my lectures expounding the elements of economics have become a virtual commentary on *Capital*.

[. . .]

On the other hand, although my last lectures, published here, are almost entirely a paraphrase of Marx's theory, it was not originally so. The lectures previous to this one, and also those I delivered two years ago, have all been printed and sold without my permission. It is thus evident that my lectures systematically approach and conclude with comment upon Marx's theory. Hence I did not begin in blind obedience to Marx. I started instead from a non-Marxist economics, the kind that we now reject and call bourgeois or vulgar economics. In fact, in the lectures of 1916–1917 on the theory of distribution and entitled 'Particular problems in economics', I dealt only with the doctrines of Böhm-Bawerk, Taussig, Clark, Carver, Fischer, and Commons among others, hardly mentioning Marx. Incidentally, in the 1923–1924 lecture notes on the principles of economics the introduction is made up of two sections: 'what is economics?' and 'what is wealth?', while the main section is composed of three parts: 1. production, 2. exchange, 3. distribution. The first part, for example, is further subdivided into five chapters: 1. production and labour, 2. socialisation of labour, 3. means of production, 4. reproduction, 5. productive forces and social organisation. One need only glance at these notes to see clear differences in their systematic character and content compared with what I publish here, these earlier lectures being still far removed from Marx. In short, I began from bourgeois economics, and while seeking the Promised Land I approached Marx step by step, finally adopting the polar opposite of my initial starting point. It took me 20 years at Kyoto University to effect this transformation, and the time that this took demonstrates how fatuitous I have been. At the same time, this could serve as a defence against those who might say that my present position represents an uncritical and blind obedience to the doctrine of Marx. My complete acceptance of Marx's doctrine arose only very gradually, after a long period of hesitation and eclecticism; indeed, so long as to be worthy of scorn. All the same, since I arrived at this point only after lengthy reflection and study, I would now go willingly to the stake for my scientific convictions.

The 'Development of capitalist economics', the second part of this book, is a somewhat revised version of my *Historical development of capitalist economics*, published in August 1824. [. . .] The important changes consist in the following additions: some paragraphs in the Introduction, and on the labour theories of value of Adam Smith and of David Ricardo in the second and third chapters.

This material was created by arranging the materials for studying the history of economic thought (mainly involving English economists) that I had collected over the course of several years preceding publication, and is formed by the main sections of the lectures on the history of economic thought I was giving in the university at that time. [. . .]

From autumn 1898 to summer 1902 I was a student in Tokyo Imperial University, and it was during this time that I first read the Bible. I was very much struck by the way that altruism was a central teaching. Since then, the problems of egoism and altruism have never ceased to preoccupy me. In December 1905, three years after graduating from the university, I voluntarily embraced the Mugaen [meaning literally 'self-renunciation garden'] inaugurated by Shōshin Itō, who was at the time preaching 'self-renouncing love'; I abandoned every professional position that I then held. My action was intended to resolve a problem that I had nursed for a long time, but it was not a decision taken in an impulsive moment. In the autumn of 1908, three years later, I came to teach at Kyoto Imperial University and up to the spring of this year I have been here for almost 20 years. Looking back, the studies that I completed during the first 10 years or so in the domain of the history of economic thought always centred on this older problem: the relation between egoism and altruism. For this reason, my earlier work, the *Historical development of capitalist economics*, begins with Mandeville's affirmation of egoism, and concludes with Ruskin disclaiming it. My work was to be a history of moral thought reflected in the domain of economics, rather than a more straightforward history of economic thought. Rightly or wrongly, it appears to have come together as a coherent unity. While Adam Smith's and David Ricardo's theories of value were omitted from the previous work, and only added when the text was reprinted, that was a reflection of the plan to which I was working at that time. However, by adding these new sections I feel that I have rather disturbed the previous coherence.

As a description of historical changes in thought endorsing altruistic activities— a description of the historical process of the rise, development and demise of such thought and ultimately its replacement by an opposite—this earlier work may still retain a certain value. What I there call the approbation of egoistic activities is essentially approbation of the egoistic activities of capitalists. In the period of transition from feudal to capitalist society—in the period during which feudal society collapsed and capitalist society developed from its ruins—the bourgeoisie merely represented the developing productive forces of human labour. At that time they were endowed with a revolutionary mission, and in realising this mission history had to guarantee them a freedom to act without constraint. The coining of the phrase 'private vices, public benefits' as a protest against feudal moral thinking was nothing but a reflection of a human ideology of the transformation of the material conditions of human life. This idea developed along with the development of capitalist production, and will now wither in the period of its collapse. My previous efforts might still be of some value in detailing the process of this change.

Now we are in the second revolutionary period, where the proletariat is going to take up the role of representing the development of the productive forces of human labour, displacing the bourgeoisie. The historical mission of revolutionising the social form has already shifted from the bourgeoisie to the proletariat. In addition, every action on the part of the proletariat is physically and morally constrained. As regards the moral treatment of their activities, the strikes and acts of sabotage characterising the proletarian struggle are all condemned on moral grounds. However, just as the idea of 'private vices, public benefits' emerged at the beginning of the 18th century, in the society in which we today live there must emerge, and is actually emerging, the idea that 'the struggle of the working class in the interest of their class is a struggle in the interests of humanity as a whole'. In a class society, public benefit must necessarily be realised through the realisation of private benefit.

To sum up, the second part of this book describes one part of the historical development of bourgeois economics, while its first part expounds proletarian economics, the successor of a historical process. It may be somewhat presumptuous to call this book *Outlines of political economy*, but I have sought to have grasped these outlines as far as is possible with the limited resources available to me.

3 Ricardo as apogee of the orthodox economics

(From 'Part III: Political economy of David Ricardo' in *Adam Smith, Malthus, Ricardo – studies of orthodox economics*, Iwanami Shoten, 1934)

Shinzō Koizumi

Rise in the price of bullion and Ricardo's participation in the currency controversy

Ricardo made his debut with an anonymous contribution entitled 'The Price of Gold' to the newspaper *Morning Chronicle* of the 29th August 1809. It is not by chance that the subject of the first article by Ricardo, a stockbroker familiar with the affairs of the stock and financial markets, was the currency problem of the time. He was inspired to write this article by the rise in the price of bullion vis-a-vis banknotes over-issued in an inconvertible regime and the phenomenon of adverse quotations of foreign exchange. In 1797, four years after the outbreak of the war with France in 1793, the Government suspended the convertibility of Bank of England notes, by an Order of the Privy Council of the 26th February, for fear of specie drain. The Order was subsequently ratified in Parliament on the 3rd May by the Bank Restriction Act. Though the Bank was thus exempted from its duty of conversion, it did not over-issue notes for a long time. But in 1808, when speculation fever (allegedly caused by the opening of commerce with South America) erupted in the English economy and prices rose, the Bank of England relaxed somewhat its accommodation policy, partly because it could not raise its discount rate, fixed by the Usury Laws in force, and partly because it was itself infected with this fever. As a result, the balance of its issue rose from 17,467,170*l*. in November 1808 to 18,646,880*l*. in May 1809, and then to 19,811,330*l*. in August of the same year. And the market price of gold bullion rose continually from 1806 to 1808. While its mint price remained at 3*l*. 17*s*. 10.5*d*. per ounce, in 1809 its market price fluctuated between 4*l*. 9*s*. and 4*l*. 12*s*. At 4*l*. 10*s*., it exceeded the mint price by as much as 15.5%. At the same time, the foreign exchange with continental countries became adverse to England. During the latter half of 1808 and the first quarter of 1809, the exchange vis-a-vis Hamburg and Amsterdam was quoted from 16 to 20% below par, and it fell further vis-a-vis Paris (Paper Pound of 1797–1821. *A Reprint of Bullion Report*. With an Introduction by Edwin Cannan, 1919, pp. VII–XXI).

In the face of this anomaly, Ricardo explained its cause and proposed relieving measures. He wrote this article without intending to make it public, but on the advice from Perry, president of the aforementioned *Morning Chronicle*, he finally consented to publish it 'not without some reluctance' (*Three Letters on the Price of Gold by David Ricardo*, edited by Hollander, Baltimore, 1903. [quoted from 'Editor's introduction', p. 3]). Such was the debut of Ricardo as an economist.

Ricardo explained the rise in the price of gold bullion by the rise in the issue of Bank of England notes caused by the suspension of convertibility, hence with the fall in its value. He first pointed out that it was after the enactment of the Bank Restriction Act that the price of gold bullion per ounce rose to 4*l.*, 4*l.* 10*s.* and finally to 4*l.* 13*s.* And afterwards he affirmed that 'whilst the Bank pays its notes in specie, there can never be any great difference between the mint and market-prices of gold' [III/15. For all the quotations from Ricardo, only the volume and page numbers of Sraffa's edition will be indicated.]. Another index demonstrating the fall in the value of banknotes is the adverse quotations of foreign exchange. As a rule, the exchange can neither fall below par with the transfer cost of gold, nor rise over that point. This is the natural limit for the variation of foreign exchange. If nevertheless the actual exchange far exceeds this limit, it is because the merchants are obliged to buy adversely-quoted bills of exchange in order to pay their foreign debts, instead of exporting gold abroad. To do the latter it would be necessary to convert the banknotes in their possession into gold not at the official rate of 3*l.* 17*s.* 10.5*d.* per ounce but at the current market rate of 4*l.* 13*s.* But Ricardo did not argue for an immediate resumption of the convertibility of banknotes. He affirmed that the difference in value between gold and banknotes should be resolved by reducing the amount of its issue. 'Let the Bank be enjoined by Parliament gradually to withdraw to the amount of two or three millions of their notes from circulation, without obliging them, in the first instance, to pay in specie, and we should very soon find that the market price of gold would fall to its mint price of 3*l.* 17*s.* 10.5*d.*, that every commodity would experience a similar reduction; and that the exchange with foreign countries would be confined within the limits above mentioned" [III/21].

One of a number of refutations of this contribution from Ricardo was the anonymous contribution entitled 'A Friend of Bank Notes but no Bank Director' [III/22], also published in the *Morning Chronicle* on the 14th September. In response to this, Ricardo again made a contribution on the 20th, this time signed R. The second contribution of the anonymous critic in response to this appeared in the newspaper on the 30th October, to which Ricardo answered with his third contribution published on the 23rd November. With this the debate in the newspaper ended.

Subsequently, Ricardo 'thought proper to republish his sentiments on this question in a form more calculated to bring it to fair discussion' [III/51] and wrote a pamphlet entitled *The High Price of Bullion, a Proof of the Depreciation of Bank Notes*, which was to be his first published book. The publication was in 1810, with 'Introduction' dated from the 1st December 1809. In this pamphlet, explaining the international distribution of gold and silver and the value of currency, he further argued that the variation in the quantity of currency should not be judged by the rate of interest, and that gold is the standard measure of value in England. Since it was originally the article *A Friend of Bank Notes* which affirmed that the rate of interest should be taken as the criterion for judging the excess or shortage of currency, and that silver is the standard measure of value, the form of Ricardo's first independent publication can be said to owe something to the above-mentioned debate in the newspaper. The anonymous adversary with whom Ricardo debated thus, not knowing who he was, turned out to be his friend Hutches Trower, with whom he was already acquainted at that time, or presumed to be (*Letters to Trower*, pp. VI–VII and Appendix).

The contention in *The High Price of Bullion* is of the same tenor as in the newspaper contributions. To speak of a rise in the price of bullion lacks precision. The variation in value is actually in the banknotes. The fall in their value is due to their over-issue, which is in turn due to the Bank of England being exempted from the duty of converting the banknotes it issues. Therefore, the way to get rid of all these evils is 'that the Bank should gradually decrease the amount of their notes in circulation until they shall have rendered the remainder of equal value with the coins which they represent, or, in other words, till the prices of gold and silver bullion shall be brought down to their mint price' [III/94].

The High Price of Bullion immediately prompted the action of Francis Horner, member of the House of Commons. On the 19th February, on his motion, the House appointed the Select Committee 'to enquire into the Cause of the High Price of Gold Bullion, and to take into consideration the State of the Circulating Medium, and of the Exchanges between Great Britain and Foreign Parts' [III/352]. This was the so-called Bullion Committee.

The tenor of the Report the Committee submitted to the House on the 8th June was substantially the same as what Ricardo had affirmed. The Report attributed the cause of the rise in the price of bullion to the over-issue of inconvertible banknotes, and stated that 'a portion at least' of the adverse exchange 'must have resulted not from the state of trade, but from a change in the relative value of our domestic currency', and affirmed that after all 'no sufficient remedy for the present, or security for the future, can be pointed out, except the Repeal of the Law which suspends the Cash Payments of the Bank of England' (The Paper Pound of 1797–1821, pp. 32, 68). Horner, one of the authors of this Report, wrote himself that the great merit of the Report is 'that it declares, in very plain and pointed terms, both the true doctrine and the existence of a great evil growing out of the neglect of that doctrine' (Cannan's introduction, p. XXII). Though not mentioned here, 'the true doctrine' is that of Ricardo. Hence, criticism of the Bullion Report became criticism of Ricardo. Therefore, in response to Charles Bosanquet's *Practical Observations on the Report of the Bullion Committee*, 1810, attacking the Report, Ricardo wrote *Reply to Mr. Bosanquet's Practical Observations on the Report of the Bullion Committee*, 1811.

Ricardo responded point by point to Bosanquet's criticism and affirmed that 'to conclude, Mr. Bosanquet is persuaded that much evil will ensue from the resumption of cash payments, and he cannot anticipate any improvement in the course of exchange, or any fall in the price of bullion from a reduction of the circulation, unless our imports are diminished and our exports increased', but to him 'it appears perfectly clear, that a reduction of Bank notes would lower the price of bullion and improve the exchange, without in the least disturbing the regularity of our present exports and imports' (Ricardo, *Reply*, ch. IX. [III/245]).

Incidentally, according to a recent discovery, not only did Ricardo contradict Bosanquet, but he had already praised the Bullion Report and made public a writing defending the Report against its critics. These articles were all contributions to the *Morning Chronicle*, published respectively on the 6th, 18th and 24th of September 1810. In the first of them, in praise of the Report, he wrote that 'the Bullion Committee has most ably illustrated the principles upon which a paper currency should be regulated' [III/133], and in the other two articles he defended the Report against the attacks from Sinclair and Randle Jackson respectively. These three contributions, not previously recorded by anyone, have recently been discovered and published by J. H. Hollander, a Ricardo scholar (*Minor Papers on the Currency Question 1809–1823, by David Ricardo [Three letters to the Morning Chronicle on the Bullion Report*, 1810, III/131–153]).

Ricardo's theory of currency was further developed in *Proposals for an Economical and Secure Currency; With Observations on the Profits of the Bank of England, as they regard the Public and the Proprietors of Bank Stock*, 1816. His proposal consists in the idea that the conversion of paper currency must be done not in specie but in bullion, in order to secure both the interest of using paper currency instead of specie and the interest of maintaining the equivalence of currency to the standard metal. He wrote:

> To secure the public against any other variations in the value of the currency than those to which the standard itself is subject, and, at the same time, to carry on the circulation with a medium the least expensive, is to attain the most perfect state to which a currency can be brought, and we should possess all these advantages by subjecting the Bank to the delivery of uncoined gold or silver at the mint standard and price, in exchange for their notes, instead of the delivery of guineas; by which means paper would never fall below the value of bullion without being followed by a reduction of its quantity. To prevent the rise of paper above the value of bullion, the Bank should be also obliged to give their paper in exchange for standard gold at the price of 3*l*. 17*s*. per ounce. Not to give too much trouble to the Bank, the quantity of gold to be demanded in exchange for paper at the mint price of 3*l*. 17*s*. 10.5*d*., or the quantity to be sold to the Bank at 3*l*. 17*s*., should never be less than twenty ounces.
>
> (sec. IV [IV/66])

This work first appeared in the Appendix to the fourth edition of *The High Price of Bullion*. And since this Appendix was written for the purpose of responding to Malthus' criticism in the *Edinburgh Review*, Malthus also stimulated

Ricardo's work in this respect (Hollander, p. 49). From 1810 to 1814, Ricardo was engaged in recurrent epistolary debates with Malthus on the currency and exchange problems.

The theory of currency and bank in chapter 27 of *Principles*, his masterpiece, is a summary with some revisions of the theory of money proposed in the works mentioned above. What I call 'some revisions' refers to his application of the cost theory of value, the pivot of *Principles*, to the value of money metal. He wrote: 'gold and silver, like all other commodities, are valuable only in proportion to the quantity of labour necessary to produce them, and bring them to market'. If gold is fifteen times dearer than silver, it is because fifteen times the quantity of labour is necessary to obtain the same quantity of gold as silver [I/352]. However, Ricardo acknowledged that the value of money as money is not always bound to the value of gold or silver, its material. If the state does not levy any seigniorage in minting, the coin will be equivalent to any other pieces of the same metal of the same weight and fineness, but when the state does impose seigniorage, the value of money will exceed that of bullion by the amount of this seigniorage. However, since this amount is not necessarily in proportion to the quantity of labour necessary for the minting, the value of money can easily deviate from the value of gold or silver that is based on the quantity of labour bestowed. It is only by limiting its quantity that the value of money can thus rise above the value of gold or silver. On this point he wrote as follows: 'While the State alone coins, there can be no limit to this charge of seigniorage; for by limiting the quantity of coin, it can be raised to any conceivable value' [I/353]. This theory also explains why the paper currency, a mere script, can circulate. 'Though it [paper currency] has no intrinsic value, yet, by limiting its quantity, its value in exchange is as great as an equal denomination of coin, or of bullion in that coin' [I/353]. In extending this logic, the conversion of paper currency into specie is not always necessary for maintaining its value. The only necessity is that its quantity be suitably regulated. But in the light of experience, unlimited issuing power of paper currency is necessarily abused, so that the imposition of convertibility is the most appropriate way of securing the limitation [I/353–4, 356].

From what we have said above, it is evident that Ricardo is a proponent of the quantity theory of money. And he did not in the least change this position throughout his career as an economist. He repeatedly expressed his opinion in different words. Let us quote some examples. He stated that:

> If our circulating medium has been augmented a fifth, till that fifth be withdrawn the prices of gold and commodities will remain as they are. Increase the quantity of notes, they will rise still higher; but withdraw the fifth, [. . .] and gold and every other commodity will find its just level, and [. . .] the representative of an ounce of gold, or 3*l*. 17*s*. 10.5*d*. in banknotes will always purchase an ounce of gold.
>
> (*Three Letters*, p. 18 [Three Contributions to the *Morning Chronicle*, III/25])

He also wrote:

> There can exist no depreciation of money but from excess; however debased a coinage may become it will preserve its mint value, [. . .] provided it be not in too great abundance.
>
> (*Reply to Mr. Bosanquet*, p. 95 [III/224–5])

Elsewhere, he said that:

> All commodities cannot rise at the same time without an addition to the quantity of money.
>
> [I/105]

He also asserted that: 'quantity regulate[s] the value of everything'. This is true of every commodity, 'and more, perhaps, of currency, than of anything else' (Speech to the House of Commons on the 12th June 1822 [V/209]).

Retired to his estate in Gatcombe Park during the recess of the House in 1823, Ricardo wrote *Plan for the Establishment of a National Bank* in his leisure time. But as he died of sickness in the autumn of this year, the *Plan* was published in the following year as a posthumous manuscript. In this last writing, Ricardo made a rigorous distinction between the businesses of issuing and lending money and emphasised that these two should not necessarily be implemented by the same organ (*The Works of Ricardo*, edited by McCulloch, 1846, p. 503 [IV/276]). Already, in *Proposals for an Economical and Secure Currency*, Ricardo had advocated for the nationalisation of this kind of business, arguing that the gain from issuing paper money should not be attached to a private interest. Now in this manuscript he detailed concretely how to realise this idea. Making his debut with the *Price of Gold*, Ricardo described the plan for a national bank in his last, posthumously published work. The currency problem was inseparable from his whole life as an economist.

The Corn Laws debate and Ricardo's theory of distribution

However, Ricardo was not interested solely in the currency problem for very long. In the Preface to *Principles*, he affirmed that the whole produce of the earth is divided between the landlord, the capitalist and the labourer under the names of rent, profit and wages, and that 'to determine the laws which regulate this distribution, is the principal problem in Political Economy' [I/5]. The essential of these laws of distribution was already given in *An Essay on the Influence of a Low Price of Corn on the Profits of Stock*, 1815. Ricardo was inspired to this pamphlet by the debate on the amendment of the Corn Laws between 1813 and 1815.

Till the end of the 18th century England, as a leading agricultural country, could export its corn to foreign countries. But with its rapid population growth, exports ceased around the turn of the century, and on the contrary it gradually became a corn-importing country. Malthus too, in a pamphlet published in 1800, wrote that 'it is a fact now generally acknowledged [. . .] that of late years, even in the best seasons, we have not grown corn sufficient for our own consumption; whereas, twenty years ago, we were in the constant habit of exporting grain to a very considerable amount' (*An Investigation of the Cause of the Present High Price of Provisions*, 1800, p. 26). Hence, it naturally became a subject of discussion whether to adopt as national policy the supply of cheap corn dependent on foreign countries.

The debate on the Corn Laws began with the report on the corn trade of the Select Committee of the House of Commons published on the 11th May 1813, and the speech of Sir Henry Parnell, president of the Committee, delivered to the House on the 15th June, expounding the need to amend the Corn Laws in force. These Laws had been amended in 1804, imposing a prohibitively heavy duty on imported corn when the domestic price was lower than 63*s.* per quarter. The members of the Committee arrived at the conclusion that the minimum price for imposing the duty should be raised above 63*s.*, saying that in this way, the English people 'would procure a sufficient supply from their own land and at the same time the corn price would fall'. When this Select Committee was appointed, the price of corn was far above the minimum for imposing the duty (106*s.* 5*d.* in 1810, 95*s.* 3*d.* in 1811, 126*s.* 6*d.* in 1812, and above 116*s.* during the first half of 1813). It would be a too hasty judgement to say that the appointment of the Committee was made on the proposal of representatives of the landlord class, worried about the fall in the price of corn. However, after the beginning of discussion about this problem, an extraordinary rich harvest was followed by a rapid fall in corn prices (73*s.* 6*d.* in December), and both landlords and tenant farmers fell into difficulties, so that an amendment of the Corn Laws was strongly required. The landlords were accustomed to the high prices they enjoyed every year and often enclosed common land in anticipation of such prices. They paid above-standard prices to till the land. They spent much money in their everyday lives. Tenant farmers also invested capital in land in anticipation of similar situations and renewed their tenancy contracts with high rates of rent. Therefore it was quite natural that they now panicked at the sudden fall in price.

On the other hand, public opinion against amendment of the Corn Laws was also on the rise. At the beginning of 1814, 130 petitions 'on the Corn Laws' and 170 petitions 'against the bill' were filed. The petition of Newcastle went so far as to say 'the bestial efforts of those who try to pass the bill, to raise the corn price, in order to diffuse distress and devastation among the manufacturers and labourers and so to deprive our country of the Providence'. In the meantime, the corn price did not appear to recover, and the distress of the agricultural class seemed to reach an extreme. In February 1815, the House placed the problem of amendment of the Corn Laws as the first item on the agenda because of its urgency, and the bill of the Under-Secretary of Commerce stipulating a total prohibition of the importation of corn, flour and meat till the price of corn rose to 80*s*. obtained agreement from the majority of the Members. Despite a number of petitions from various rural areas and a protest movement of citizens outside the House, debate in the Commons was closed on the 10th March and the bill passed in the House of Lords on the 20th.

Such was the entire process about the problem of amending the Corn Laws between 1813 and 1815.

In view of the problem of the Corn Laws, Malthus said that 'it is the duty of those who have any means to contributing to the public stock of knowledge, not only to do so, but to do it at the time when it is most likely to be useful', and just after that, in January 1815, he published the part on rent from his lecture notes written for Haileybury College as a pamphlet entitled *An Inquiry into the Nature and Progress of Rent, and the Principles by which it is Regulated*. And at about the same time he wrote two pamphlets entitled respectively, *Observations on the Effects of the Corn Laws, and of a Rise or Fall in the Price of Corn on the Agriculture and General Wealth of the Country* (1814), and *The General Grounds of an Opinion on the Policy of Restricting the Importation of Foreign Corn; intended as an Appendix to 'Observations on the Corn Laws'* (1815).

Sir Edward West also wrote, under the pseudonym of A Fellow of University College, Oxford, an *Essay on the Application of Capital to Land, with Observations Shewing the Impolicy of any Great Restriction of the Importation of Corn, and that the Bounty of 1688 did not Lower the Price of it* (1815).

Colonel Torrens wrote *An Essay on the External Corn Trade; containing an Inquiry into the General Principles of that Important Branch of Traffic; an Examination of the Exceptions to which these Principles are liable; and a Comparative Statement of the Effects which Restrictions on Importation and Free Intercourse are calculated to produce upon Subsistence, Commerce, and Revenue* (1815).

And Ricardo also published, between February and March, *An Essay on the Influence of a Low Price of Corn on the Profits of Stock; Shewing the Inexpediency of Restrictions on Importation: with Remarks on Mr. Malthus' two Last Publications: 'An Inquiry into the Nature and Progress of Rent', and 'The Grounds of an Opinion on the Policy of Restricting the Importation of Foreign Corn'* [hereinafter referred to as *Essay*].

Ricardo only knew of the works of West and Torrens after publishing his pamphlet (*Letters to Malthus*, pp. 63, 65 [the 9th and 12th of March 1815, VI/179, 185]), but he wrote it after considerable discussion with Malthus. We know from the collection of Ricardo's letters that in 1814, he and Malthus abandoned the 'old problem' of currency and foreign exchange to debate the subject of the influence of the tariff on corn. In this debate, Ricardo repeatedly affirmed that the restriction on corn importation would lead to a rise in its price and this rise would lead to a rise in wages, which would reduce profit. This argument will ultimately result in another assertion, that profit is determined by the difficulty of producing food.

In contrast, Malthus' opinion was as follows: the rate of profit in agriculture regulates that in other industries, which in its turn regulates the former. Cheap food is certainly a cause of rising profit, but there exist other causes. For example, if a new market is discovered and a greater quantity of foreign goods than before is obtained in exchange for our domestic products, profit will rise and interest will equally rise (*Letters to Trower*, p. 5 [the 8th March 1815, VI/103–4]).

In the course of repeated discussions with Malthus, Ricardo became increasingly convinced of his opinion. Among his letters to Malthus conserved today, in all the eight letters from the 26th June 1814 to the 13th January of the following year, he discussed the same problem and repeatedly affirmed the same opinion. He wrote as follows: 'I never was more convinced of any proposition in Political Economy than that restrictions on importation of corn in an importing country have a tendency to lower profits' (p. 35 [the 26th June 1814, VI/109]). As for the route through which the accumulation of capital leads to the fall in the rate of profit, he stated that: 'a rise in the price of raw produce may be occasioned by a gradual accumulation of capital which by creating new demands for labour may give a stimulus to population and consequently promote the cultivation or improvement of inferior lands, – but this will not cause profits to rise but to fall, because not only will the rate of wages rise, but more labourers will be employed without affording a proportional return of raw produce' (p. 47–8 [the 23rd October 1814, VI/146]). And further: 'accumulation of capital has a tendency to lower profits. Why? Because every accumulation is attended with increased difficulty in obtaining food, unless it is accompanied with improvements in agriculture. [. . .] If with every accumulation of capital we could tack a piece of fresh fertile land to our Island, profits would never fall' (p. 52 [the 18th December 1814, VI/162]).

In the above quotations from his letters we can recognise the early germ of the whole of Ricardo's theory of distribution, which presupposes first of all the adoption of the principle of population. I have already said that he praised Malthus' theory of population. 'New demands for labour' and the rise of wages 'may give a stimulus to population'. But what about the productive force of food of the land for nourishing this increased population?

In speaking about the law of diminishing return we recall the name of Sir Edward West, a contemporary of Ricardo. In the above mentioned pamphlet he said that

> The principle is simply this, that in the progress of the improvement of cultivation the raising of rude produce becomes progressively more expensive, or, in other words, the ratio of the net produce of land to its gross produce is continually diminishing

and that

> the additional work bestowed upon land must be expended either in bringing fresh land into cultivation, or in cultivating more highly that already in tillage. [. . .] And the very fact that in the progress of society new land is brought into cultivation proves that additional work cannot be bestowed with the same advantage as before on the old land.

(pp. 2, 10)

But, independently of West, Ricardo recognised the law of diminishing return from land as an evidence. In the absence of progress in agriculture or of import of foreign corn, the price of corn necessarily rises with the rising population. It rises because less fertile lands must be cultivated, because the yield does not increase in proportion to the additional capital invested on the land already cultivated. He therefore supposed that as human beings tend to proliferate to the maximum allowed by their material means, they will inhabit land with productivity that decreases with the progress of cultivation. It would be an underestimation of the significance of the principle of population for the scholar or for orthodox economic theory to say that 'this [classical] system would remain as what it is, even if the principle of population were omitted from it' (J. Schumpeter, Epochen der Dogmen- und Methodengeschichte. *Grundriss der Sozialökonomik*, Bd.I. 1914. S.77. [Joseph Schumpeter, *Economic Doctrine and Method, an historical sketch*, translated by R. Aris, George Allen and Unwin Limited, London, 1954, p. 111]). Of course, this must be deemed a pointless judgement.

In addition, although Ricardo did not mention it explicitly, he took the law of the average rate of return in general, and the law of the average rate of profit in particular, as the key to his theory of distribution. Ricardo himself and the bankers, bill brokers and stock-jobbers with whom he was in constant contact in his professional life were all competing for yield, however little it might be. He inferred the psychology of the labourer, capitalist and landlord in general from the behaviour of the London citizens he met every day. Every capitalist and every labourer will necessarily move toward a sector yielding higher reward. As a result, the wage rate and profit rate would be naturally averaged. When he said that the profit of agricultural capital regulates every other rate of profit, it was because he recognised this law of averaging. Why does the agricultural rate of profit regulate the other rates of profit? It is because Ricardo thought that the capital movement from a sector with lower profit to another sector with higher profit would average it, when there were wide differences in profit between agriculture and the other sectors. Now, if there already exists an average rate of profit between these sectors, the profit of capital in the same agricultural sector should naturally level out, regardless of the fertility of the soil it is used to cultivate. Capital accumulation stimulates population growth, which pushes cultivation toward land under worse conditions, and the cultivation of these lands means an increase in the difficulty of food production, leading to a fall in the rate of profit. But if the agricultural rate of profit must be uniform regardless of the fertility of land, a question arises: what will become of the difference between the profit obtained by those who cultivate fertile lands and the lower profit from less fertile lands, and who will obtain this difference? According to Ricardo, it becomes rent. He wrote as follows: 'rents are always withdrawn from the profits of stock', and 'rents are in no case a creation of wealth, they are always a part of the wealth already created, and are enjoyed necessarily, [. . .] at the expense of the profits of stock' (*Letters to Malthus*, p. 59 [the 6th February 1815, VI/173]). Hence, according to Ricardo, rent fills the gap made by the fall in profit, and with the fall in profit it erodes more and more the area originally occupied by profit. Therefore the theory of profit cannot be complete without presupposing the theory of rent. Each is the reverse side of the other.

In his method of research, Ricardo stands in notable contrast to Malthus. Ricardo once compared Malthus with himself in their attitudes of argumentation and accused the latter of attaching too much importance to the practical details to defend his method of abstract reasoning, regardless of those details. Thus he wrote:

> If I am too theoretical, which I really believe is the case, – you I think are too practical. There are so many combinations, – so many operating causes in Political Economy, that there is great danger in appealing to experience in favour of a particular doctrine, unless we are sure that all the causes of variation are seen and their effects duly estimated.
>
> (*Letters to Malthus*, p. 96 [the 7th October 1815, VI/295])

He also wrote:

> Our differences may in some respects, I think, be ascribed to your consider-ing my book [*Principles*] as more practical than I intended it to be. My object was to elucidate principles, and to do this I imagined strong cases that I might shew the operation of those principles.
>
> (pp. 166–167 [the 4th May 1820, VIII/184])

This difference between the attitudes of these two thinkers was evident to everyone. For example, Torrens, their contemporary, commentated this point in saying that

> If Mr. Ricardo generalises too much, Mr. Malthus generalises too little. If the former occasionally erects his principles without waiting to base them upon a sufficiently extensive induction from particulars, the latter is so occupied with particulars, that he neglects that inductive process which extends individual experience throughout the infinitude of things, and imparts to human knowledge the character of science.
>
> (Torrens, *Production of Wealth*, pp. IV–V [1821])

In thus continuing with his abstract reasoning, Ricardo gave as axioms, so to say, the three laws of population growth, decreasing return from land and average profit. Nassau William Senior, economist after Ricardo, applied a deduc-tive and almost geometrical method to political economy. In his *Political Economy*, 1850, he enumerated the following four fundamental propositions of political economy: 1. everyone seeks to obtain additional wealth with the least possible sacrifice; 2. the world population, i.e., the number of people inhabiting the world, is limited solely by moral or physical evils, or by worries about insufficiency of the wealth habitually required of individuals in each class of inhabitants; 3. the force of labour and the other instruments of production can be infinitely augmented by using their products as a further means of production; and 4. if agricultural technology remains constant, additional labour bestowed on a certain area yields in most cases a harvest less than proportional, in other words, though the total harvest increases with labour bestowed, the increase in harvest will not be proportional to the increase in labour. These propositions should be regarded as a clarification of Ricardo's theoretical pre-suppositions in a slightly different form.

In the *Essay*, Ricardo's theory of rent, which constituted a rather minor subject in the letters, is explained in detail. As for the essence of rent, there existed a theory of rent in Adam Smith, and in Anderson, contemporary with Smith, we can find some elements hinting at Ricardo of later times (James Anderson, *An Inquiry into the Nature of Corn Laws etc.*, 1777). However, it is not these works of his predecessors which motivated Ricardo to give attention to the theory of rent, but, as we have seen above, the current problem he observed directly of the amendment of the Corn Laws.

The rent is according to him 'the remuneration given to the landlord for the use of the original and inherent power of the land' (*Works*, p. 375 n. [IV/18]). The rent in this sense is, according to Ricardo, made up of the surplus remaining after subtracting the cost of production from the total value of land product. It is then natural that

> Whenever, then, the usual and ordinary rate of the profits of agricultural stock, and all the outgoings belonging to the cultivation of land, are together equal to the value of the whole produce, there can be no rent. And when the whole produce is only equal in value to the outgoings necessary to cultivation, there can neither be rent nor profit.
>
> (*Works*, p. 371 [IV/10])

Let us assume, for example, that in a new country with abundant fertile land, a man invests on land an amount of capital equivalent to 200 quarters of corn, of which one half consists in fixed capital like buildings and machines, and the other half in circulating capital. And if after compensating for both of these parts there still remain products equivalent to the value of 100 quarters of corn, the net profit for the owner of the capital will be 100 over 200, i.e. 50%. The rate of interest determined in this way will also fix the profit of commercial and manufacturing capitals, since capital will move from one to another if there are differences in profit rates between them. If the increase in capital and population makes it necessary to cultivate worse lands with respect to their locations or fertilities, the cost of production (of cultivation, and of transport) will increase. If this increase is equivalent to the value of 10 quarters of corn, the value of capital invested on the new land with a view to obtaining the same harvest as before will be 110, so that the profit of capital will fall to 90 over 210, i.e. from 50% to 43%. Then the profit obtained from the cultivation of better land will be divided to become profit and rent. In this case, 86 quarters will be the profit and the remaining 14 quarters the rent. In the case where capital and population further increase and even worse lands come into cultivation, needless to say, the profit will fall even more and the rent will increase by as much. In extending the cultivation to worse lands, 'rent would rise on the land previously cultivated, and precisely in the same degree would profits fall' (p. 373 [IV/14]). If, instead of cultivating new, worse lands, additional capital is invested on the land already cultivated, the result will be the same (p. 374 [IV/14]).

But the doctrine thus affirming that rent is not the creation of wealth or revenue but arises from eroding profit is incompatible with Malthus' idea that the rent is a surplus due to a gift of providence. Although Ricardo acknowledged that Malthus' theory of rent contains 'original ideas, – which are useful' [IV/15] and pays some respect to it, he emphasised that Malthus was in error on one point mentioned above. Malthus recognised the following three points as giving rise to rent: 1. the land has a surplus productive power over and above nourishing its cultivator; 2. it is in the nature of the necessities of life that they create demand for themselves; and 3. fertile land is comparatively scarce. Out of these three, he attached particular importance to the first two (*The Nature and Progress of Rent*, p. 17 [Rev. T. R. Malthus, *An Inquiry into the Nature and Progress of Rent, and the Principles by which it is regulated*, London, 1815]). Malthus did so because he wanted to defend rent against the doctrine that it arises from the harmful monopoly of land. Thus, he insisted that rent is never 'merely a transfer of value, advantageous only to the land lords, and proportionately injurious to the consumers', but that it is 'a clear indication of a most inestimable quality in the soil, which God has bestowed on man – the quality of being able to maintain more persons than are necessary to work it', a 'bountiful gift of Providence' (pp. 16, 17). It may have been under the influence of the Physiocrats that Adam Smith said that 'in agriculture too, nature labours along with man; and though her labour costs no expense, its produce has its value, as well as that of the most expensive workmen' (*Wealth of Nations*. Edited by E. Cannan, vol. I, p. 343 [Adam Smith, *An Inquiry into the Nature and Causes of the Wealth of Nations*, Clarendon Press, Oxford, 1976, I. p. 363]). This thought was followed by Malthus and is expressed in the sentences quoted above. Ricardo's theory of rent represented a rupture with Physiocracy.

At the same time, this theory of rent is a negation of Adam Smith's doctrine on the relation between price and rent. Though developing different theories in different places, in his theory of price he says that rent is a component part of price, so that a rise in rent causes a rise in price. But according to Ricardo, just like the other general commodities, 'the difficulty or facility of their production [of agricultural products] will ultimately regulate their exchangeable value' [I/20]. Hence, the price of corn will rise when the cultivation of worse lands becomes necessary. The rent from a land is nothing other than the difference between the net product of this land (surplus in the total yield remaining after the subtraction of wages) and that of the last cultivated land. As the net product of the last cultivated land constitutes the profit of capital, this land gives rise solely to profit and leaves no rent, and therefore causes no rise in the price of corn, while for Adam Smith the rent is a component part of price (*Wealth of Nations*, vol. I, pp. 51–2, 57, 59 [Smith, 1976, pp. 61–8, 72–5]) and the land allotted to the production of food necessarily yields a surplus constituting rent in addition to wages and profit (pp. 147–8 [Smith, 1976, p. 162–4]). For Ricardo's theory, therefore, both of these doctrines of Adam Smith must be inacceptable. In the *Essay*, Ricardo did not yet treat Adam Smith critically, but here it is already evident that Ricardo's theory of rent will naturally overturn the essential parts of Smith's theory of rent.

If rent is not a creation of new revenue but only a part of revenue already created, the conclusion will be drawn that the interests of the landlord conflict with the interests of the other classes. 'His [landlord's] situation is never so prosperous, as when food is scarce and dear: whereas, all other persons are greatly benefited by procuring food cheap' (*Works*, p. 378 [IV/21]). But Ricardo was not opposed to the fact that with the development of society, rent naturally rises and profit falls. He called into question artificial means such as the Corn Laws that unjustifiably favour the interests of the landlord. But it is undeniable that in so doing, Ricardo tended unintentionally to identify the interests of the capitalist class directly with those of the society itself. If Ricardo regarded cheap corn as desirable, it is because of its effect in decreasing wages. Therefore, in the long run, the interests of the labourer can be said to have almost no relation to the difficulty or facility of food production. Then what Ricardo considers as the interests of society as a whole, in opposition to those of the landlord, finally turns out to be nothing other than the interests of the capitalist class. Why, then, should their interests be favoured over those of the landlord? In *Essay* he gives almost no explanation of this point, as if he took it as a self-evident fact not requiring any demonstration, except a few words suggesting that the prosperity of this class would lead to capital accumulation and hence to an encouragement of productive industries. But in view of his observations on other occasions, it is clear that he considered high profit as the first stimulus to promoting the wealth of the nation, or as its first symptom. For example, in a passage of his later work *On Protection to Agriculture*, 1822, with respect to the opinion of a member of the House approving low profit, he wrote as follows:

> The very contrary, I imagine, is the truth. A low rate of interest is a symptom of a great accumulation of capital; but it is also a symptom of a low rate of profits, and of an advancement to a stationary state; at which the wealth and resources of a country will not admit of increase. As all savings are made from profits, as a country is most happy when it is in a rapidly progressive state, profits and interest cannot be too high. It would be a poor consolation indeed to a country for low profits and low interest, that

landlords were enabled to raise money on mortgage with diminished sacrifices. Nothing contributes so much to the prosperity and happiness of a country as high profits.

(*Works*, p. 474. [IV/234–5])

Judging by this, he may not be exempt from the criticism that he estimated the interests of the whole society from the viewpoint of a stock-jobber.

In opposition to Ricardo who promoted the free import of corn, Malthus argued for its restriction. The latter, in his *Observations on the Effects of the Corn Laws*, published in 1814, first introduced fairly the pros and cons on the restriction of corn importation, and in *Grounds* published in the following year, while making clear the attitudes of both sides, he affirmed the appropriateness of a temporary tax on imported corn to compensate for the artificially lowered value of the currency. This difference in their opinion is grounded on the views each of them held about the symptoms of the progress of national wealth or prosperity. While Ricardo saw them in high profit, as we have seen, for Malthus they consisted in the rising rent. This is a natural observation from the point of view that rent is due to the power of land to produce surplus. And from this position, it is also natural that the improvement in agricultural production benefits the landlord, because of 'the connection of the interests of the landlord and of the state' (Malthus, *Political Economy*, 1st ed. p. 217). Therefore Malthus criticised Ricardo's assertion that the interests of the landlord are incompatible with those of consumers and manufacturers (*Pol. Econ.*, ch. III, VIII, XI).

But for his part, Ricardo endeavoured to explain that he was not necessarily hostile toward the class of landlords, so that on this point his opinion did not differ from that of Malthus. Thus, he wrote:

Improvements in agriculture were in their immediate effects injurious to the landlord, and beneficial to consumers, but ultimately when population increased, the advantage of the improvement was transferred to the landlord,

and

Mr. Malthus is not justified by anything I have said in pointing me out as the enemy of landlords, or as holding any less favorable opinion of them, than of any other class of the community.

(*Notes on Malthus*, p. 51 [II/118–9])

Leaving aside for the moment the question of whether Ricardo himself was hostile toward landlords, it is undeniable that rent and profit stood in opposite relation to each other in his theory of distribution. The rise in the productive power of land with improvements in agriculture will increase the profit and reduce the rent. When the rise in profit accelerates accumulation, which in turn raises wages and so causes the population to grow, the rent will certainly rise again. But this rise takes place to the detriment of profit. A simultaneous rise in the rates of both profit and rent can never durably take place in his theory.

On the principles of political economy and taxation

Critical comments on the *Essay* made by some of his friends induced Ricardo to write *Principles*.

In his letter to Jean Baptiste Say of the 18th August 1815, Ricardo says that his *Essay* was not understood by some because he did not enter into sufficient detail in explaining his views, and that James Mill 'wishes me to write it over again more at large' [VI/249] (In his autobiography, Stuart Mill says of this book that it 'never would have been published or written, but for the entreaty and strong encouragement of my father' [John Stuart Mill, *Autobiography*, Longmans, Green, Reader, and Dyer, 1873, p. 27]). Soon, Ricardo decided to write in pursuit of this advice. In his letters to Malthus in spring 1816, he lamented the fact that his business affairs often interrupted the writing (his letters of the 24th April and of the 28th May 1816 [VII/28, 36]). He was not good at composition. In learning, he overcame this difficulty. In his letter of the 9th March 1817 he wrote that 'I have no misgivings about the doctrines themselves' [VII/140]. Thus, the printing was already begun in February. The last part of the manuscript seems to have been handed over to the printer at the end of March (*Letters to Malthus*, pp. 132, 134 [VII/143–5]). *On the Principles of Political Economy and Taxation* was published in the following month.

The publisher was John Murray. The body of text was printed in 589 pages of demy octavo, a layout with not many characters per page, with an additional four pages of Preface and 13 pages of Index.

Viewing its exterior form, it is evident that this work was not written and published with systematic preparation and sufficient elaboration. It would not necessarily be an exaggeration to say that Ricardo seems to have written down his ideas as they came into his mind. The disorder in exposition may be seen in the disposition of related subjects like 'value', 'natural price and market price', 'value and riches, their distinctive properties', 'comparative value of gold, corn and labour in rich and in poor countries' and 'influence of demand and supply on prices' in various dispersed places in the work, respectively in chapters 1, 4, 18, 26, 28 [The chapter numbers refer to the first edition. Ditto, infra.]. In the same way, the theory of rent is explained in chapters 2 and 3, as well as in chapter 22 on Adam Smith's theory of rent and in chapter 29 on Malthus' theory of rent, and so on. Profit is explained in chapter 5, and the effects of accumulation on profits and interest in chapter 19. And while the subject matter from chapters 8 to 16 is taxation, there is also a discussion on the taxes paid by the producer between chapter 26 on the comparative value of gold, corn and labour in rich and in poor countries, and chapter 28 on the influence of demand and supply on prices.

As we will see below, not a few scholars have therefore tried to re-organise the *Principles* to make it follow a more logical order. (According to what Ricardo himself wrote to Malthus, he first wrote his ideas down on paper as they came to mind, and after that he made comments on Smith, Say, Buchanan etc. when he found divergences of opinion from them in referring to their works. *Letters to Malthus*, p. 125 [VII/115]). As for the insufficiency of elaboration, the lack of rigour in wording and terminology has been often pointed out by scholars. Although we shall not dwell on the question here, the simple fact that chapter 5 and chapter 8 both appear twice in the book is already revealing enough (this was corrected in the second edition).

The *Principles* of Ricardo, renowned as the most eminent theorist among the economists of all times, is a work with such defects in form.

What, then, about its contents? As we have seen above, for Ricardo, the principal problem in political economy was to establish a theory of distribution. And on this point his opinion was already fixed in writing the *Essay*. Subsequently, as far as we know, he never encountered any kind of doubt. Ricardo continued to debate with Malthus in their correspondence but only repeated his doctrine in affirming as follows: 'profits I think depend on wages', and 'profits will rise when wages fall, and as one of the main causes of the fall of wages is cheap food and necessities, it is *probable* that with facility of production, or cheap food and necessities, profits would rise' (pp. 120, 121 [the 5th and the 11th October 1816, VII/72, 78, italics in the original]). He affirmed that 'rent is not a creation but a transfer of wealth. It is the necessary consequence of rent being the effect and not the cause of high price' (p. 128 [the 24th January 1817, VII/120]). The sole difference between the theory of distribution explained in *Principles* and that explained in *Essay* or in letters is that of detail.

The only new thing to trouble the mind of Ricardo in writing *Principles* was the theory of value. Concerning this problem, he realised that he would not be able to maintain the doctrine he had held before, and so he had to rethink it. Thus, in his letter to Malthus of the 5th October 1816, he confessed: 'I have been very much impeded by the question of price and value, my former ideas on those points not being correct. My present view may be equally faulty, for it leads to conclusions at variance with all my preconceived opinions. I shall continue to work, if only for my own satisfaction, till I have given my theory a consistent form' (*Letters to Malthus*, p. 120 [the 5th October 1816, VII/71–2]).

The result of this 'work' is the theory of value in chapter 1 of *Principles*.

Ricardo's theory of value

Ricardo's theory of value started from Adam Smith. Following Smith, Ricardo also distinguished the value in use – i.e., the utility – and the value in exchange – i.e., the purchasing power of one thing over another. For a thing to have a value in exchange, of course it must have utility. But in fact the utility and the value in exchange do not necessarily correspond. Therefore, the former cannot be the measure of the latter.

Ricardo divided commodities into two large classes: those which cannot be increased in disposable quantity, and those which can be increased or decreased in quantity by human effort, and on the production of which unlimited competition is applied.

For the former, the source of value is their scarcity. Antiques, rare books, antique coins, wines of a special quality produced in a limited quantity: – the value of all these things can be explained by scarcity. But day-to-day goods belong for the most part to the latter class. The value of this class is determined by the quantity of labour bestowed on their production.

> In the early stages of society, the exchangeable value of these commodities, or the rule which determines how much of one shall be given in exchange for another, depends solely [the 3rd edition reads 'almost exclusively'] on the comparative quantity of labour expended on each.
>
> (*Principles*, 1st ed. p. 3 [I/12])

With an increase in the quantity of labour necessary to its production, the exchangeable value of this commodity rises, and with a decrease it falls.

However, the 'expended labour', 'realised labour', or 'necessary labour' Ricardo speaks of, includes not only the labour directly bestowed on the production of a thing but also the indirect labour bestowed on capital, i.e., on the instruments for production. For example, the labour expended on hunting a beaver also includes the quantity of labour expended on fabricating the weapons used. And the determination of value by the quantity of labour expended in this sense is independent from whether or not the same person is the user of the capital (machine, instrument, raw material etc.) and its owner, and from the proportions in which the product is divided between capitalist and labourer as profit and wages. This is because a higher or lower profit of capital or wages 'would operate equally' (p. 18 [I/24]) on every industry.

Adam Smith also recognised that in a primitive society, the labour expended on production was 'the only circumstance' determining the exchangeable value. But according to Smith, in a society after the appearance of land appropriation and capital accumulation, the exchangeable value of a commodity is determined by the sum of the average wages, average rent and average profit paid for labour, land and capital. And since the actual price turns around this sum as its centre of gravity, the best measure for ascertaining the value determined in this way is the quantity of labour exchanged with this commodity, i.e., the quantity of labour this commodity commands. Ricardo pointed out the incoherence in the doctrine of Smith in saying that 'it is the comparative quantity of commodities which labour will produce, that determines their present or past relative value, and not the comparative quantities of commodities, which are given to the labourer in exchange for his labour' (p. 11. [I/17]).

However, prior to the *Principles*, Ricardo had already advanced that the exchangeable value of a thing is determined by the quantity of labour necessary for its production. In a passage in the *Essay* he wrote: 'the exchange-able value of all commodities, rises as the difficulties of their production increase. If then new difficulties occur in the production of corn, from more labour being necessary, whilst no more labour is required to produce gold, silver, cloth, linen, &c. the exchangeable value of corn will necessarily rise, as compared with those things. On the contrary, facilities in the production of corn, or of any other commodity of whatever kind, which shall afford the same produce with less labour, will lower its exchangeable value. [. . .] Wher-ever competition can have its full effect, and the production of the commodity be not limited by nature, as in the case with some wines, the difficulty or facility of their production will ultimately regulate their exchangeable value' (*Works*, p. 377 [IV/19–20]).

This explanation coincides with the theory of value in the *Principles* described above. But, as we have seen, after the publication of the *Essay*, Ricardo encoun-tered difficulties with value and price, and acknowledged that his prior explana-tion had been erroneous (his letter of the 5th October 1816). There must therefore exist passages in the theory of *Principles* and in that of *Essay* that are mutually incompatible. And indeed there are. They can be found in the latter half of the chapter on the theory of value in *Principles*, where he recognises the influence of variations in wages on the exchangeable value of a commodity, in addition to variations in the quantity of labour expended on production. But variation in the exchangeable value of a commodity caused by variation in wages is limited to the case where there are differences in the relative proportions of fixed capital (non-consumable goods) and circulating capital (consumable goods) employed in the production of commodities, or in the durability of fixed capital. He wrote:

> Besides the alteration in the relative value of commodities, occasioned by more or less labour being required to produce them, they are also subject to fluctuations from a rise of wages, and consequent fall of profits, if the fixed capitals employed be either of unequal value, or of unequal duration.
>
> (p. 23 [I/53])

Thus, the exchangeable value of those commodities, on the production of which a relatively large fixed capital or a fixed capital of relatively high durability is employed, rises with the fall in wages – i.e., the rise in profit – in comparison with the other commodities. In Ricardo's own words,

> In proportion to the quantity and the durability of the fixed capital employed in any kind of production, the relative prices of those commodities on which such capital is employed, will vary inversely as wages; they will fall as wages rise.
>
> (p. 41 [I/62–3])

Ricardo wrote this latter part of his theory of value, fully conscious of its 'novelty'. Nevertheless, few critical comments were made on this account by contemporary scholars. Rather, they concentrated mainly on the proposition that the value of a commodity is determined by the quantity of labour expended on it. Most influential among them were probably Torrens and Malthus. In his contribution to a review ('Strictures on Mr. Ricardo's Doctrine respecting Exchangeable value', *The Edinburgh Magazine and Literally Miscellany*, October 1818), Torrens said that it was rather Ricardo who committed an error in extending to the civilised society the principle of determination of value by the cost of labour, which Smith had limited scrupulously and appropriately to the primitive society, and said that after all,

> Whenever capitals consist of different proportions of raw material and wages, – whenever the rate of wages happens to be higher in one business than in another, – whenever capitals are of different degrees of durability, – and whenever, being of equal durability, the expenditure for wages is different, – the value of the products will not be in proportion to the quantity of labour employed on them.
>
> (*Letters to McCulloch*, pp. 15–16 n.
> [*The Edinburgh Magazine*, October 1818, p. 337])

The criticism of Malthus is also based on a similar argument. He said that even in the first phase of society's development, labour was already not the sole element in the cost of production, because a new element called 'varying quickness of return' was also a necessary factor in determining value, totally independent from labour and operating of course in the civilised society too (*Political Economy*, 1st ed. 1920, p. 88). In short, according to him,

> The quantity of labour which a commodity has cost in its production, is neither a correct measure of relative value at the same time and at the same place, nor a measure of real value in exchange, as before defined, in different countries and at different periods.
>
> (pp. 107–108)

But these points raised by Torrens and Malthus had already been taken into consideration by Ricardo himself. In fact, he had already discussed the cases where the variation in value caused by the variation in wages is explained in terms of the differing durability of fixed capital. Hence, somewhat dissatisfied with the criticism of Torrens, he said in his letter to McCulloch of the 24th November 1818 that 'I have distinctly stated in my book, that value is not regulated solely by quantity of labour, when capitals are employed in production which are not equally durable' [VII/338].

Here we must examine the foundations of Ricardo's law of value.

First of all, why did Ricardo say that the exchangeable value is determined by the labour cost, only for those commodities whose quantity increased at will?

Ricardo gave attention above all to the permanent effects brought about by a cause and not to those directly and temporarily effectuated by it. He was not at all ignorant of the movements of price induced by demand, but this effect is temporary. According to the relation of demand and supply at a certain moment, the market price of a commodity may rise above its labour cost. But in the case of commodities whose quantity can be increased at will, their price will fall again through the increase in supply, while such an effect will not oper-ate on commodities of fixed quantity. Why then does the supply increase when the market price is superior to the labour cost? Because the producers of a commodity sold at a market price above its labour cost can get extraordinary profits, and this attracts capital from other sectors to the production of this commodity. In other words, when the rate of profit is levelled out, the com-modities are exchanged with each other in proportion to the quantities of labour bestowed on them. Ricardo wrote:

> It is then the desire, which every capitalist has, of diverting his funds from a less to a more profitable employment that prevents the market price of commodities from continuing for any length of time either much above, or much below their natural price. It is this competition which so adjusts the exchangeable value of commodities, that after paying the wages for the labour necessary to their production, and all other expenses required to put the capital employed in its original state of efficiency, the remaining value or over-plus will in each trade be in proportion to the value of the capital employed.
>
> (pp. 87–88 [I/91])

And it is the natural price of a commodity mentioned here that is the 'exchangeable value of a commodity or its purchasing power'. This means that the law of the average rate of profit, foundation of Ricardo's theory of distribu-tion, is also the foundation of his theory of value. It is precisely because of this law that the actual exchange rates between commodities cannot long deviate from their exchangeable values as determined by the quantities of labour bestowed.

But this explanation supposes that the same amount of capital always employs the same quantity of labour. If this supposition does not hold, there is no longer any reason why the exchangeable value (natural price) of a commodity, deter-mined by the quantity of 'labour bestowed', should be the centre to which the market price is attracted at each moment. If, for example, of two capitalists each investing 10,000*l.*, one invests most of his capital in machinery (fixed capital) and the other in paying wages (circulating capital) to employ labourers, and they sell their products at prices proportional to the respective quantities of labour, the former will obtain much less profit than the latter on the same 10,000*l.* of capital. Then, to equalise these unequal profits, capital will leave the less advantageous industry and flow into the more advantageous one. Such a flow of capital will only cease when equalisation in the rates of profit is attained through the changes in supply that cause prices to rise and fall. But at that moment, the relative value of the two commodities will naturally not be proportional to the labour bestowed in each sector. Therefore, once it is admitted that the same amount of capital does not necessarily employ or represent the same quantity of labour, it is impossible to consider the law of the average rate of profit as the foundation for the proposition that the quantity of labour determines value.

Ricardo was already aware of this difficulty. It is for this reason that in the second half of chapter one of *Principles*, he modified the principle of doctrine that he had advanced in the first half of the chapter. Confronted with the criticism of Torrens, Malthus etc., he came to attach more importance to this modification.

In our example above, we examined the result of averaging the rate of profit by supposing two entrepreneurs who invest the same amount of capital but represent different quantities of labour. Our result may possibly be refuted in the following way: the elements of fixed capital like machines, instruments etc. are all products of labour, so that everything bought by the capital is directly or indirectly labour, hence the quantity of labour represented by the same amount of capital cannot be different. But Ricardo did not think so. The machines and instruments are products of past labour. Time is required from the moment that labour is first expended for the production of a machine till the sale of a product fabricated and accomplished with this machine. There must be a certain recompense for this lapse of time. When employing direct labourers, this lapse of time does not exist or is short if it does exist. Then, in investing the same 10,000*l.* of capital, the quantity of labour that can be employed with this amount of wages and the quantity of labour invested in the past to make a machine that costs 10,000*l.* are not the same. The machine naturally contains less quantity of labour. In other words, Ricardo regarded the difference in the proportions of circulating and fixed capital in the total capital as the difference in time elapsing from the moment when the labour is first expended till its result is brought to market. Thus, he gradually attached importance to the influence that this element of time exerts on the exchangeable value of commodities. He came to state that the time required till the accomplishment of production is a determining cause of the value of commodities, along with the labour cost.

His letters to McCulloch of the 2nd May and the 13th June 1820 are often quoted. In them he wrote:

> After the best consideration that I can give to the subject, I think that there are two causes which occasion variations in the relative value of commodities – 1st the relative quantity of labour required to produce them, 2nd the relative times that must elapse before the result of such labour can be brought to market. All the questions of fixed capital come under the second rule.

(p. 65 [VIII/180])

and

> If I were to write the chapter on value again which is in my book, I should acknowledge that the relative value of commodities was regulated by two causes instead of by one, namely, by the relative quantity of labour necessary to produce the commodities in question, and by the rate of profit for the time that the capital remained dormant, and until the commodities were brought to market.
>
> (p. 71 [VIII/194])

In the meantime, the second edition of *Principles* appeared in 1819. The format is the same as the first edition. But the number of pages fell to 535 because the layout was a little denser. There were several revisions of contents: chapter 1 was divided into five sections with subtitles for each of them, and in addition to the corrections of some phrases, in consideration of the criticism by Torrens, new cases were given of 'the unequal rapidity with which it [capital] is returned to its employer' [part of the subtitle of the section 4 in the second edition (section 5 in the third edition), I/38]. Ricardo acknowledged here that of two commodities, the one requiring a comparatively longer time for completion of the cycle of capital will fall in relative value when wages rise and the profit falls. Thus he became generally more cautious in explaining his labour theory of value.

Ricardo's theory of value (continuation)

The third edition of *Principles* appeared in spring of 1821. The format remained the same as before, but the number of pages of the body of text was reduced to 521 because the layout was made even denser. Revisions of contents were made in a considerable number of places. In particular, the first chapter changed appearance in comparison with the former editions. In the 'Advertisement', he wrote that 'I have endeavoured to explain more fully than in the last [edition], my opinion on the difficult subject of Value, and for that purpose have made a few additions to the first chapter' [I/8]. Those who know his letters quoted above can nearly anticipate the nature of these 'additions'. Indeed, he there gives a further, more detailed explanation of the reason why the law of labour value must be modified on account of the use of fixed capital and the different speeds of the cycle of circulating capital. As for the correction of phrases, he became more careful in this edition. For example, he had said in the former editions that the exchangeable value of commodities depends on labour or solely on labour, but in the new edition he replaced 'solely' with 'almost exclusively' [I/12, 20].

The exchangeable value of commodities is not determined solely by the labour expended. Even if one of the two commodities contains twice the quantity of labour, the rate of exchange between them will not be one to two, if the time elapsed till the accomplishment of production and sale is not equal, or if the one requiring more labour also requires more time.

On account then of the different degrees of durability of their capitals, or, which is the same thing, on account of the time which must elapse before one set of commodities can be brought to market, they will be valuable, not exactly in proportion to the quantity of labour bestowed on them, – they will not be as two to one, but something more, to compensate for the greater length of time which must elapse before the most valuable can be brought to market.

[I/34]

In other words, Ricardo explained the difference between the exchangeable value of commodities and the wages for labour bestowed in terms of the recompense for the lapse of time. Therefore, we can say that the germ of the abstinence theory of interest can be discerned in Ricardo.

Ricardo already recognised the temporary influence of demand on the price. However, as regards the commodity whose production can be increased at will, the variation in demand is immediately followed by a variation in supply. So, he argued, in the long run the price comes to be regulated by the cost of production regulating the supply. He affirmed to Malthus as follows: 'I do not dispute either the influence of demand on the price of corn and on the price of all other things, but supply follows close at its heels, and soon takes the power of regulating price in his own hands, and in regulating it he is determined by cost of production' (*Letters to Malthus*, p. 197 [the 24th November 1820, VIII/302]). But, as we have seen above, this cost of production is not determined solely by the labour cost. Along with the quantity of labour necessary for the production, the time required till the accomplishment of production also plays a role in determining the value of products, and it is the recompense for this elapse of time that constitutes the difference between the value of products and the wages for the labour bestowed. This is the very profit. Therefore, he repeatedly emphasised that the so-called cost of production includes the profit. Let me quote here a few examples: 'Cost of production, in money, means the value of labour, as well as profits' (*Letters to Malthus*, p. 176 [the 9th October 1820, VIII/279]). 'If by cost Mr. Malthus means cost of production, he must include profits, as well as labour' (*Notes [on Malthus]*, p. 14 [II/34]). 'Mr. Malthus appears to think that it is a part of my doctrine, that the cost and value of a thing should be the same; – it is, if he means by cost, "cost of production" including profits' [I/47 n].

Since it is now evident that Ricardo accepted that the value of commodities does not vary solely with the variation in labour cost, but also with the time required till the accomplishment of production, or that profit can be an independent cause regulating the value, and that he came to attach more and more importance to this in the 'modifications' from the first to the third edition of *Principles*, it is apposite to agree with Karl Diehl, Ricardo scholar in Germany, that 'Ricardo gives in his theory of value not a labour theory of value but a production cost theory' (K. Diehl, *Sozialwissenschaftliche Erläuterungen zu David Ricardos Grundgesetzen der Volkswirtschaft und Besteuerung*, 1905, I. Teil, S. 44).

Gonner, a Ricardo researcher in England, is also opposed to viewing his doctrine as a labour theory of value. Ricardo had a tendency to write as if labour were the basis of value, but in perusing his work this turns out to be false. 'All he wanted to assert was the existence of a steady relationship between the amount of effort exerted in the production of commodities and their exchangeable value, that, in other words, they vary together' (*Principles*, edited by E. C. K. Gonner, P. XLI). Verryin Suart, Böhm-Bawerk, G. Cassel and others are unanimous in considering Ricardo as a theorist of production cost (Diehl, a. a. O., S. 49).

However, while thus recognising the time necessary till the accomplishment of production as a cause determining the exchangeable value along with the quantity of labour cost, as for the relative weight of these two factors, Ricardo attached much more importance to the labour cost. The effect of time or profit as a cause of exchangeable value is 'comparatively slight', of a different nature to the other cause. He wrote as follows:

> In estimating, then, the causes of the variations in the value of commodities, although it would be wrong wholly to omit the consideration of the effect produced by a rise or fall of labour, it would be equally incorrect to attach much importance to it.
>
> [I/36]

This is why Ricardo could write in a matter-of-course way, in the chapters other than that on the theory of value, as if the value of commodities was simply determined by the quantity of labour cost, because he had announced beforehand in the chapter on the theory of value that

> I shall consider all the great variations which take place in the relative value of commodities to be produced by the greater or less quantity of labour which may be required from time to time to produce them.
>
> [I/36–7]

As we have seen above, Ricardo's theory of value is established on the foundation of the law of the average rate of profit, and the need to modify the principle also arises from this. If, then, the rate of profit is not levelled out, what will become of the law of the exchangeable value of commodities? In such cases, the exchangeable value will be totally independent from cost. If an excess in the price of a commodity over its cost does not attract a concentration of capital on its production, thus increasing its supply and causing its price to fall, or if a fall in price below its cost does not chase capital out of that industry, thus decreasing its supply and increasing profit, we must admit that the exchangeable value of commodities is determined solely by demand and supply under no constraint of cost. Even if a product of quantity A of labour and a product of quantity A×100 of labour are exchanged with each other, there will be no agent at work to adjust this rate of exchange.

Did Ricardo take into consideration the cases in which the exchangeable value of commodities is not under a constraint of cost? He did. The commodities supplied in fixed quantity belong of course to this description, but even in the case of commodities whose production can be increased at will, the same applies to international commerce, he explained. This is only because capital cannot move freely among nations, and so the disparity in the rate of profit is not cancelled out.

Ricardo developed an example. England and Portugal are in trade. In England, the production of cloth requires the labour of 100 men for a year, while the production of wine requires 120 men. In Portugal, the production of cloth requires 90 men, and the production of wine 80 men. In such a situation, the cloth produced by the labour of 100 men in England will be exchanged with the wine produced by the labour of 80 men in Portugal, so that England will buy the wine, which would require the labour of 120 men in the absence of such a transaction, with the labour of only 100 men, and Portugal will buy the cloth, which would require the labour of 90 men, with the labour of only 80 men. Ricardo explains that in this way, both countries benefit equally from the trade. But the exchange of a product of the labour of 80 men for a product of the labour of 100 men contradicts the principle of his theory of value. Ricardo himself explained this as follows:

> The same rule which regulates the relative value of commodities in one country, does not regulate the relative value of the commodities exchanged between two or more countries.
>
> [I/133]

And he continued:

> The quantity of wine which she shall give in exchange for the cloth of England, is not determined by the respective quantities of labour devoted to the production of each, as it would be, if both commodities were manufactured in England, or both in Portugal.
>
> [I/134–5]

The reason for this is that the law of the average rate of profit does not operate between nations. Ricardo wrote:

> Thus England would give the produce of the labour of 100 men, for the produce of the labour of 80. Such an exchange could not take place between the individuals of the same country. The labour of 100 Englishmen cannot be given for that of 80 Englishmen, but the produce of the labour of 100 Englishmen may be given for the produce of the labour of 80 Portuguese, 60 Russians, or 120 East Indians. The difference in this respect, between a single country and many, is easily accounted for, by considering the

difficulty with which capital moves from one country to another, to seek a more profitable employment, and the activity with which it invariably passes from one province to another in the same country.

[I/135–6]

As we will see below, if the rate of profit does not level out, then not only the labour theory of value, but the general cost theory in the theory of value are invalidated. It then becomes necessary to explain the exchangeable value in terms of elements other than cost. In this respect, we can see an aspect in Ricardo's theory of international value that tends to abandon cost theory (J. Schumpeter, a. a. O., S. 84–5 [English version, *Economic Doctrine and Method, an historical sketch*, translated by R. Aris, George Allen & Unwin Limited, London, 1954, pp. 127–8]).

This theory of international trade or theory of international value is one of the most valuable elements in Ricardo's theory. Stuart Mill later said that among the doctrines of Ricardo, nothing can compare with this theory in that it gave to political economy 'a comparatively precise and scientific character' (J. S. Mill, *Essays on Some Unsettled Questions of Political Economy*, 1844, p. 1). Ricardo was preceded by Adam Smith in the theory of international trade. However, though Smith's theory was extremely convincing as an attack on the mercantile system and of great influence, his explanation was rather insufficient and imprecise as to the conditions necessary for trade to take place between countries, or the extent to which a country can benefit from international trade. According to Smith, the advantage a country can take of international trade consists in exporting its surplus products without domestic demand in exchange for importing something in demand. But, as Mill pointed out afterwards, the term 'surplus products' is misleading. First of all, why does a country produce surplus products? If international trade is not carried out, do these surplus products have to be thrown away in vain? Or were the capital and labour allotted to their production useless in the end? Not at all. If some articles are produced in a country over and above the requirements of its domestic consumption, they are not thus produced necessarily or inevitably, but because they have been selected as the least expensive way to procure something. If the country cannot export these articles, the importation in exchange for them will have to cease and the capital and labour employed for the production of these exports will have to be diverted to the production of the former imports themselves or of some substitutes for them. If this country has relied on foreign countries for these imports or their substitutes instead of producing them, it is of course because in so doing they could be obtained *less* expensively. We can see then the incorrectness of Smith's opinion that the benefit from foreign trade consists in selling useless articles in exchange for useful ones. The advantage that a country obtains from foreign trade consists in procuring *less* expensively something that it could produce if it wanted to, in exchange for something else (exports). Therefore, the benefit arises here from the difference in the cost of production between the imports and exports. And since foreign trade is not carried out if it is not mutually advantageous, there must in this case be a similar, but symmetrically opposite situation in the partner country, with regard to the difference in the cost of production. In extending this reasoning to clarify the conditions for foreign trade to be carried out and the benefits to be obtained by the trading countries, we have exactly the above-mentioned theory of comparative advantage.

The neologism 'comparative advantage' does not originate in Ricardo, but probably began with Stuart Mill in later years. As he wrote in his *Essays on Some Unsettled Questions of Political Economy*:

> It may be to our advantage to procure iron from Sweden in exchange for cottons, even although the mines of England as well as her manufactories should be more productive than those of Sweden; for if we have an advantage of one-half in cottons, and only an advantage of a quarter in iron, and could sell our cottons to Sweden at the price which Sweden must pay for them if she produced them herself, we should obtain our iron with an advantage of one-half, as well as our cottons. We may often, by trading with foreigners, obtain their commodities at a smaller expense of labour and capital than they cost to the foreigners themselves. The bargain is still advantageous to the foreigner, because the commodity which he receives in exchange, though it has cost us less, would have cost him more.
>
> [first part in *Essay I*, 1844, pp. 2–3]

What are the differences between the theory of domestic value and that of international value? As we have seen above, in international trade the rate of exchange does not coincide with the cost of production. If the law of the cost of production does not apply, just as Mill said, we 'must revert to a principle anterior to that of cost of production [. . .] namely, the principle of demand and supply' [1844, p. 8]. Exchange in the domestic market is not free from the law of supply and demand either. But domestic exchange is different in that a relation between supply and demand causing a rate of exchange inconsistent with the cost of production does not last long, even if it does emerge, because of the capital and labour flowing into the favourable production.

Theory of value and theory of distribution in Ricardo

As we have said above, Ricardo's theory of value can hold only on the supposition of an average rate of profit. How then is the level of this average rate of profit ever determined? Ricardo sought its ultimate explanation in the power of land to produce surplus.

If the harvest from the land can hardly nourish the cultivator himself, there will be no room for profit to arise. Only if a surplus remains after the subsistence is produced can profit exist. But if there are differences in the power of land to produce a surplus, according to their degree of fertility, then the profit of agricultural capital will be determined by the surplus-producing power of the worst (marginal) land actually in cultivation, since these differences in harvest must constitute rent. The rate of the surplus harvest on this marginal land to the agricultural capital thus determines the rate of agricultural profit, which in turn determines the rate of commercial and manufacturing profit in general through the free flow of capital. Therefore, when cultivation extends to further, less-fertile lands because of population growth, the surplus harvest and hence the general rate of profit diminishes. And if the cultivation progresses so far that the land producing no surplus above the subsistence for the cultivator has to be cultivated, the profit will disappear in both agriculture and manufacturing.

As we have seen above, Ricardo particularly and repeatedly emphasised that the productive power of land determines in this way the rate of agricultural profit, which in turn determines the general profit, as opposed to Malthus, who affirmed that the rate of commercial and manufacturing profit also can regulate the rate of agricultural profit. He summarised the difference of opinion between him and Malthus in writing to his friend Trower:

> When Capital increases in a country, and the means of employing Capital already exists, or increases, in the same proportion, the rate of interest and of profits will not fall. Interest rises only when the means of employment for Capital bears a greater proportion than before to the Capital itself, and falls when the Capital bears a greater proportion to the arena, as Mr. Malthus has called it, for its employment. On these points I believe we are all agreed, but I contend that the arena for the employment of new Capital cannot increase in any country in the same or greater proportion than the Capital itself, unless there be improvements in husbandry, – or new facilities be offered for the introduction of food from foreign countries; – that in short it is the profits of the farmer which regulate the profits of all other trades, – and as the profits of the farmer must necessarily decrease with every augmentation of Capital employed on the land, provided no improvements be at the same time made in husbandry, all other profits must diminish and therefore the rate of interest must fall.
>
> (pp. 4–5, [the 8th March 1814, VI/103–4])

Briefs, the German researcher of orthodox economics, may be said to have hit the bull's-eye when he emphasised the significance of land as the pivot of Ricardo's theory of distribution (Goetz Briefs, *Untersuchungen zur klassischen Nationalökonomie*, 1915, S. 67, 68. passim).

If the agricultural profit is determined by the productive power of land, and the general rate of profit is determined on the basis of this agricultural profit, and if the natural price of an article as Ricardo calls its exchangeable value includes this general profit as its component part, this raises the problem of priority between his theory of distribution and his theory of value, i.e. the problem of their respective places. In my view, the theory of distribution comes first, before the theory of value. Since Ricardo took determination of the laws of distribution to be the principal problem in economics, and since, in addition, he developed his theory of value in detail in the first chapter, the latter is conventionally understood as a foundation of the former. There are reasons for this interpretation, but closer consideration shows that his theory of value is insufficient to form the foundation of his theory of distribution. On the contrary, the latter itself serves as the presupposition for the former – whether or not Ricardo himself was aware of this.

First, as for the chronological order of their conception, Ricardo addressed the question of the theory of value only in writing the *Essay* published in 1815, while the essential of his theory of distribution had been already shown in the correspondence with Malthus on the problem of corn tariffs in the previous year. The theory of value is certainly included in *Essay*. But, prior to the passage 'the exchangeable value of all commodities, rises as the difficulties of their production increase. If then new difficulties occur in the production of corn, from more labour being necessary, whilst no more labour is required to produce gold, silver, cloth, linen, &c. the exchangeable value of corn will necessarily rise, as compared with those things' [IV/19], the theories of rent and profit have already been given. So, prior to the theory of value, the following points have already been explained: that the profit on capital is determined by the surplus in the yield on the marginal land, that rent arises on the lands already in cultivation and to the same degree as the fall in profit, as less fertile or unfavourably located lands are gradually drawn into cultivation, and that 'rent then is in all cases a portion of the profits previously obtained on the land. It is never a new creation of revenue' [I/18].

However, what Ricardo repeatedly and emphatically affirmed from the beginning of the debate on the Corn Laws is that profit is determined by wages: the higher the wages, the lower the profit and vice versa. Is this not an affirmation which cannot be valid unless it is based on the theory of value? First, if profit and wages move inversely, it is because Ricardo regards profit as a surplus remaining after subtracting the wages from something. What then is that *something*? If it is the value of the product, we have here a theory of profit founded on the theory of value. But to be able to explain profit in this way, the value of this something must be explained, regardless of and independently from the variations in the wages to be subtracted from it. If it is possible to affirm, for example, that the value of an article is determined by the quantity of labour expended on its production, and that the proportion of value actually obtained by the labourer in no way changes its magnitude, then the theory of value becomes an indispensable presupposition of the theory of profit.

Indeed, what Ricardo wrote at the beginning of the chapter on value in *Principles* can be taken in this sense. The value of each commodity is determined by the quantity of labour directly expended on it or indirectly expended through instruments of production. And this relation does not change, whether or not the user and the owner of the instruments of production are the same person, and in whatever proportions the product is distributed between its possessor and its user, i.e., between capitalist and labourer: 'Whether the profits of capital were greater or less, whether they were 50, 20, or 10 per cent or whether the wages of labour were high or low, they would operate equally on both employments' (quoted above [I/24]).

This can provisionally be said as long as differences in the durability of capital are ignored. But once these differences are taken into consideration, Ricardo could not but admit that the change in wages influences the value of commodities. How does the former influence the latter? As we have said above, the exchangeable values of commodities, produced with a relatively large fixed capital or a fixed capital of relatively greater durability, vis-a-vis other commodities not so produced 'will vary inversely as wages; they will fall as wages rise' [I/63]. Why then do their relative values rise and fall inversely to changes in wages? It is because the profit rises and falls inversely to wages. In saying 'a rise of wages, and consequent fall of profits' [I/53], Ricardo treated this relation between them as if it were self-evident, not requiring any explanation. He set up an example, in which the rate of exchange between the product of a hunter equipped with a fixed capital of 150*l.* (durable for 10 years) and a circulating capital of 50*l.*, and the product of a fisher equipped with a fixed capital of 50*l.* and a circulating capital of 150*l.*, changes from 100:218 to 100:233 when wages rise by 6%. He explained this by the fall of profit from 10% to 4% accompanying the rise in wages of 6% (*Principles*, 1st ed. pp. 31–33 [I/56–8]). Those who seek the foundation of Ricardo's theory of profit in his theory of value will discover here an explanation of the changes of value itself in terms of profit.

On the relation between value and wages, Ricardo said conclusively as follows: 'no commodities whatever are raised in absolute price, merely because wages rise [. . .] all commodities in the production of which fixed capital enters, not only do not rise with a rise of wages, but absolutely fall', and later: 'Commodities may be lowered in value in consequence of a real rise of wages, but they never can be raised from that cause' (*Principles*, first edition, pp. 41, 48 [I/63, 66]).

The fall in value of a commodity caused by a rise in wages is, viewed from the opposite side, nothing other than an equivalent rise in value of the second commodity that is exchanged with the first one. Why did Ricardo unilaterally emphasise this side of the fall in value, without mentioning the other side of the rise in value? On this, Hollander provides an interpretation. Previously, Ricardo had repeatedly emphasised that the rise in wages is the sole cause of the fall in profit. And in order to validate this doctrine, it was necessary for him to demonstrate that the capitalist cannot raise the selling price of a product to compensate for the rise in wages. According to Hollander ([ibid.], p. 60 [The author did not indicate the source name, but a similar discussion can be found on page 90 in J.H. Hollander's *David Ricardo, a centenary estimate*, The John Hopkins Press, Baltimore, 1910]), it is for this reason that Ricardo emphasised that not only does the value of an article not rise, but on the contrary it may fall because of the rise in wages. If this is the case, then Ricardo was preparing the foundation for his theory of profit by developing the theory of value. This interpretation may be right as a presumption of his intention. But the fact that the relative value of an article can fall because of a rise in wages does not serve logically as a preliminary to the theory of profit, at least in the case of Ricardo, since, for the purpose of explaining this fact, he presupposes the profit itself, which was to be demonstrated in the last place. If the products in the industry with a larger weight of fixed capital fall in relative value because of the rise in wages, it is because Ricardo thought that a rise in wages leads directly to a fall in profit, and he concluded that the fixed capital requiring a long time for investment decreases the relative value of commodities employing much fixed capital for production when the profit falls. Therefore it is not profit that is explained by value, but value that is explained by profit.

If Ricardo tried to arrive at the theory of profit in starting from the theory of value, he should be accused, as Amonn, the critic of Ricardo, also points out, of substituting what precisely requires to be explained for its explanation.

In the third edition of *Principles*, Ricardo gave the following example: A and B each employ 100 men for a year to build a machine, and C employs the same number of labourers for a year to cultivate corn. In the second year, A and B make use of the machines finished at the end of the first year to make cloth and cotton respectively, each employing a further 100 men, but C continues to produce corn, employing 100 men as in the first year. In taking into account only the bestowed labour, the sum of value of the machine and the cloth of A or of the machine and the cotton of B would be twice as large as the value of C's corn. But in fact it will be more than twice as much, because in the cotton or textile industries, the profit on their capital during the first year is added to the capital, while in husbandry no such thing takes place.

> On account then of the different degrees of durability of their capitals, or, which is the same thing, on account of the time which must elapse before one set of commodities can be brought to market, they will be valuable, not exactly in proportion to the quantity of labour bestowed on them, – they will not be as two to one, but something more, to compensate for the greater length of time which must elapse before the most valuable can be brought to market.
>
> [I/34]

Since Ricardo explained value in terms of profit in this way, the profit cannot be explained in terms of value. As Amonn says:

> In these examples, for the moment it is no question of a change in the value of labour and of its consequence, a change in the value of product. A *different* element is introduced, namely 'profit'. Here the 'profit' is hence called to be a cause of modification in the formation of exchangeable value of goods in accordance with the relation of the quantities of labour necessary for their production. But from where does the 'profit' come? *How* is it that 'the profit on the clothier's and cotton manufacturer's capital for

the first year has been added to their capitals [I/34]'? *Why* 'must' the producers obtain a profit? Was not the profit probably added to the cloth-ier's and cotton manufacturer's capitals just because they have wanted a higher value (for a different reason)? The profit *itself* can probably be explained only from the difference in value of the goods produced with or without capital, or, with more capital or less capital. In other words: this disparity in value and the profit – as the difference in value – represents one and the same thing. Therefore the whole argumentation goes around in circles or it begins from a *petitio principii*. Here again the phenomenon of profit is accepted solely from the factual experience. Thus the modifica-tion in the formation of exchangeable value he speaks of and asserts, the alleged deviation of the formation of exchangeable value from the originally advanced fundamental law, is explained with something which is in itself in need of explanation.

> (Alfred Amonn, *Ricardo als Begründer der theoretischen Nationalökonomie*, 1924, S. 43–44)

Hitherto I have tried to explain that Ricardo's theory of distribution existed prior to his theory of value, irrespective of the intention of Ricardo himself, so that his theory of value cannot serve as the basis for his theory of distribution. We must pay attention to the fact that Ricardo himself admitted in some cases that his theory of distribution held in advance of his theory of value. That is, in his letter to McCulloch of the 13th June 1820, after saying that the quantity of labour and time are the two causes determining value, he stated as follows:

> After all, the great questions of Rent, Wages, and Profits must be explained by the proportions in which the whole produce is divided between landlords, capitalists, and labourers, and which are *not essentially connected with the doctrine of value* [italics by Koizumi]. By getting rid of rent, which we may do on the corn produced with the capital last employed, and on all com-modities produced by labour in manufactures, the distribution between capitalist and labourer becomes a much more simple consideration. The greater the portion of the result of labour that is given to the labourer, the smaller must be the rate of profits, and vice versa. Now this portion must essentially depend on the facility of producing the necessities of the labourer – if the facility be great, a small proportion of any commodity, the result of capital and labour, will be sufficient to furnish the labourer with necessities, and consequently profits will be high.
>
> (*Letters to McCulloch*, p. 72 [VIII/194–5])

Ricardo's theory of distribution makes it clear that the harvest from the last cultivated land or from the capital last invested on land are distributed between the labourer and capitalist with no part remaining for the landowner, and hence draws the conclusion that the price of corn does not rise because the landowner obtains rent. Here too the theory of distribution precedes that of value. Oppenheimer is altogether right in saying that Ricardo's theory of value and price is the centre of his whole theory, but that 'his theory of value stands or fails with the theory of rent, its presupposition' (F. Oppenheimer, *David Ricardo's Grundrententheorie*, 1909, S. 110).

Development and stasis of the society

As we have already said, the whole of Ricardo's theory of distribution is based on the land, the population and the average of the rate of profit (or generally of return) arising from free competition.

The size of population determines the quantity of corn to be produced to feed it. This quantity determines how large an area of land to cultivate and how intensively. This determines in turn the productivity of the land situated on the margin of cultivation, and the profit is what remains after subtracting the wages from the yield of this marginal land. The wages are finally reduced to the subsistence of the labourer due to the working of the law of population. Free competition gives rise to an average rate of profit throughout agriculture, manufacture and commerce. After subtracting the sum of this average rate plus wages from the yield of land, the remnant comes into the hands of the landowners as rent. Commodities whose production can be increased at will are exchanged at their natural prices, made up of the sum of the wages of labour and the profit of capital used in their production. Such is the 'natural' state of distribution and exchange in Ricardo's theory.

This 'natural' state evolves with population growth. When the population grows, cultivation is extended to less productive lands. As the yield from the marginal land diminishes, the surplus remaining after subtracting the living cost of the labourer – i.e., the profit – also diminishes: the general rate of profit falls. The rent increases as much as the profit decreases. With the fall in profit, the value of products employing more fixed capital falls. According to Ricardo's illustration, the relative value of the agricultural products that employ less fixed capital than those of manufacturing industry rises, owing to two causes: an increase in labour bestowed and a fall in profit. Thus, a second 'natural' state is attained. With further population growth, the margin of cultivation extends further, the rate of profit falls further, rent increases further, and the relative value of agricultural products vis-a-vis the articles of manufacturing industry rises further. How far is this development to continue? When the margin of cultivation extends so far as finally to equalise its yield with the living cost of the labourer, profit will disappear and only the two sorts of income, wages and rent, will remain. Moreover, with the disappearance of profit, the different lengths of time from the execution of labour till the products are brought to market will no longer influence their value, so that every commodity, except for those under monopoly, will be exchanged solely in proportion to the labour bestowed.

If the population continues to grow, what will happen? Since the marginal land already produces hardly sufficient to feed the labourer himself, it is impossible to invest further capital on land to increase the corn production. Then the corn will become a monopolised commodity, which will be certainly sold at a monopoly price beyond the cost of production on the marginal land. And Ricardo said on a few occasions that, if the corn is bought and sold at a monopoly price, then the last part of capital invested on the margin of cultivation or on the marginal land will bring about rent. For example, he wrote as follows:

> The corn and raw produce of a country may, indeed, for a time sell at a monopoly price; but they can do so permanently only when no more capital can be profitably employed on the lands, and when, therefore, their produce cannot be increased. At such time, every portion of land in cultivation, and every portion of capital employed on the land will yield a rent, differing, indeed, in proportion to the difference in the return.
>
> [I/250–1]

But from Ricardo's position, can such cases really happen as something ordinary? In other words, the question is whether or not he recognised the absolute rent arising in the margin of cultivation, in addition to the differential rent based on the differing yields caused by differences in the fertility of the land (and by diminishing yields). In my opinion, although there certainly are phrases that suggest Ricardo admitted the possibility of absolute rent, such as those given above, these are in fact unconsidered formulations that are incompatible with Ricardo's theory as a whole. I believe that for Ricardo, it was impossible to recognise the emergence of any other rents than differential rent.

First of all, what is called a monopoly price of corn, giving rise to the absolute rent, can only appear if population growth does not cease when the cultivation of land has extended till the profit disappears. But is it ever possible for the population to grow still further in such cases? Ricardo thought that the population grows as far as the conditions of life allow of it, i.e., as long as wages (as the market price of labour) exceed living costs (as its natural price). When there exists a gap between the natural price of labour and wages, the population grows and wages fall. And if the speed of population growth is slower than the increase in the demand for labour, wages will remain above the subsistence cost, and so the population will continue to grow. However, though the demand for labour is determined by capital accumulation, it is prompted by the stimulus of profit. If the population growth draws less and less fertile lands into cultivation, the rate of profit will fall accordingly, which must diminish the desire to accumulate capital. And when profit disappears in this way, the accumulation of capital will naturally cease. Far from this, Ricardo stated that long before the profit becomes null, 'the very low rate of profits will have arrested all accumulation' [I/120]. And with the end of accumulation, the stimulus for population growth will also be lost, because with the end of accumulation, the population will catch up with the demand for labour and wages will necessarily fall to the level corresponding to the subsistence cost. Therefore, if the population continues to grow when land is cultivated up to the point where profit disappears, the corn will actually be sold at a monopoly price. The absolute rent must then arise. However, as we have said above, there will be no more stimulus for population growth in such a situation. Then, from Ricardo's position, it must be said that as a rule, the monopoly price of corn cannot last for long, and so the absolute rent cannot arise.

In Ricardo's explanation given above, the profit seems to be considered as a remuneration for accumulating capital. This means that the accumulation of capital is carried out under the stimulus of profit. Therefore, if the profit becomes null, the accumulation will naturally cease. He also stated that, even before becoming null, the accumulation will cease if profit falls below a certain level. But why must the accumulation cease when the profit falls below a certain rate? This can only be explained by the meaning of capital accumulation for the agents themselves: a certain kind of sacrifice. That is, if the accumulation ceases when the profit falls below a certain level, it must be considered as the result of weighing the sacrifice of accumulation against the expected remuneration. In other words, it is the result of comparing them to choose between enjoying the present consumption of the sum to be accumulated and the obtainment of this sum plus the profit (for one year, for example) at a certain date in the future (in one year). If people completely equate the enjoyment of present and future consumption, the accumulation will be made without any stimulus for profit. If people only accumulate under the stimulus of profit and if the fall in the rate of profit below a certain level leads them to stop accumulating, this shows that as a rule people attach more importance to present enjoyment than to future enjoyment in spending the same sum of money. And the degree to which the present is valued more highly appears in the rate of profit. A high rate indicates a lack of accumulated capital relative to its employment, and this relative lack of capital comes from the high value people attach, as a rule, to present enjoyment. In this way, the profit can be called a compensation for the postponement of enjoyment. Let us suppose there are two commodities, on which labour has been expended in the proportion of two to one. If the commodity on which more labour has been spent also requires a durable fixed capital or a longer time from the beginning of its production till it is brought to market, the values of these two commodities will not be in proportion to the quantity of labour expended on each of them. In other words, 'they will not be as two to one, but something more, to *compensate* for the *greater* length of time which must elapse before the most valuable can be brought to market' (quoted above [I/34, italics by Koizumi]). This increment in value may be understood as above.

On the other hand, Ricardo repeatedly explained that the rate of profit is determined by the power of land to produce surplus. How can this proposition be reconciled with the interpretation I have proposed above, to the effect that the rate of profit is determined by the degree to which people avoid putting off the enjoyment of consumption? In the case of Ricardo, there seems to be no particular difficulty. According to him, these two propositions amount to the same thing in the end, because it is the degree of capital accumulation that determines the marginal productivity of land. Let me enter into more detail. According to Ricardo, it is the degree of need for compensation for time or for postponing the enjoyment that determines the degree of capital accumulation, which in turn determines the demand for labour and hence the wages. The wages determine the increase or decrease in population, which determines the degree to which the land should be cultivated, which in turn determines the surplus yield, which determines finally the rate of profit. In this way, if nature and the production technology are assumed to be given, the rate of profit will fall with the progress of accumulation, and a time will come when there will be no more accumulation and therefore no more population growth.

Elsewhere, Ricardo defined a 'stationary state' (*Works*, p. 474 [IV/234]) as a state in which profit will disappear and the country will have attained the limit of augmentation of its capital and population. The effort for accumulating capital is a driving force of social evolution, but the ultimate point to which the principle of population and the law of diminishing returns from land will infallibly lead is this 'stationary state'. This is Ricardo's conclusion.

Briefs, mentioned above, recognises Ricardo's originality in his logical reasoning about the impasse of this capitalist form of economy, and compares him in this point with Marx. According to Briefs, Ricardo's contribution to economics consists in

> the thought of overcoming of the dominant capitalist form of economy, the idea that the capitalism transforms itself into a quite other economic organisation. [. . .] It is certain that Ricardo has not explicitly developed this thought, but it is enough that he suggested it (in those places where he admitted the possibility of absolute rent). With the given presuppositions he could have easily arrived at the conclusion. In Ricardo as well as in Marx the capitalist society develops according to its immanent laws; in Ricardo as well as in Marx develops the same process of accelerated accumulation, here in the form of surplus value absorbed by the capital, there in the form of absorption of a constantly larger part in the whole material product and value product by the tent; in Ricardo as well as in Marx the blind profit instinct of capital is the source of energy, spurring up to a point where the capitalist system becomes incompatible with its own preconditions. Here Marx considerably overpasses Ricardo. And the awareness which makes possible this overpassing is the thought that violence is an economic potential, the idea of class struggle. If Ricardo allows society to dash helplessly up to the point where the rent will have absorbed all the surplus, without finding from this irremediable future prospect any other escape than that of free trade with its still aggravating effects, Marx is more radical: 'Force is the midwife of every old society pregnant with a new one. It is itself an economic potential'.

(S.192–193)

This comment is worthy of attention. But between Ricardo and Marx there is still an important difference that is not pointed out here. While in Marx it is the conflict between productive power tending toward infinite development and the restrictive social institution that leads to this impasse, in Ricardo it is caused on the contrary by the decline in productive power. The restriction comes from nature (the land), and it is mankind (the population) that is restricted. The conflict is between man and nature. Hence, for Ricardo, the impasse is not of a particular form of society but of human society itself. For Marx, the impasse of capitalism is the precondition of the birth of a new society to be welcomed, while for Ricardo the impasse of the present society means a complete catastrophe, rendering impossible the deployment of a new phase. Ricardo foresaw the ending not of capitalism but of human society itself. Herein lies his pessimism. In view of this point, I believe that Oppenheimer is altogether right in considering Ricardo's anticipation of the coming impasse of accumulation itself, with the final disappearance of profit caused by the accumulation of capital, not as the ending of capitalism but as 'the end of the world', or 'the downfall of human society ('Götterdämmerung der menschlichen Gesellschaft')' (Oppenheimer, S. 75). And this conflict between nature and man manifests itself as the conflict of interest between individual and whole, between classes. Society as viewed by Ricardo was never a harmonious world led by an 'invisible hand' as viewed by Adam Smith. Therefore, in commenting on McCulloch who wrote in his lecture notes that 'the interests of individuals are never opposed to the interests of the public', Ricardo said that: 'in this I do not agree. In the case of machinery the interests of master and workmen are frequently opposed. Are the interests of landlords and those of the public always the same? I am sure you will not say so' (*Letters to McCulloch*, p. 136 [the 7th May 1822, IX/194]).

The application of machinery and other technical improvements can postpone the arrival of the 'stationary state'.

With the increase in yield of agricultural products as a result of the application of machinery etc., the rate of profit must rise, or at least remain stable. However, on the influence of the application of machinery, in a chapter on machinery (chapter 31) newly added in the third edition of *Principles*, Ricardo stated a different opinion from that which he had held before.

In admitting a part of human labour being made superfluous by the application of machinery, he had thought that there would ultimately be no quantitative change in the demand for labour before and after the application of machinery, since the labourers deprived of employment would easily find other employment elsewhere. In his view, if the increased production caused by the application of machinery in a branch of production is not accompanied by a corresponding demand for its products, some labourers would necessarily be dismissed, but the capital which had employed them would continue to exist: it would naturally be invested in the production of other commodities in demand [I/387]. In his letter to McCulloch of the 29th March 1820, in opposition to his opinion that 'the fixed capital invested in a machine, must always displace a considerably greater quantity of circulating capital, – for otherwise there could be no motive to its erection; and hence its first effect is to sink, rather than increase, the rate of wages', Ricardo said that 'the employment of machinery I think never diminishes the demand for labour' (*Letters to McCulloch*, p. 57 [VIII/171]). In view of this, the change in his opinion obviously came later. It presumably occurred under the influence of Barton's pamphlet *Observations on the Circumstances which influence the Condition of the Labouring Classes of Society* (John Barton, 1817). As we will see later, in this respect too there were certain relations between the change in Ricardo's opinion and Malthus' writing activities.

According to what Ricardo himself said, he changed his opinion because he became aware of the misunderstanding he had committed concerning the relation between the net revenue and the gross revenue of society. He had thought that an increase in the gross revenue of society would go along with its net revenue, and that the fund constituting the source of revenue for the landlord and capitalist and the fund for the revenue received by the labourer would therefore simultaneously increase. But now he recognised that the fund for the labourer could decrease at the same time as the fund for the landlord and capitalist was increasing. In his example, he considers a capitalist who is occupied simultaneously with agriculture and the production of necessities with a capital worth 20,000*l*., of which 7,000*l*. is invested on fixed capital (buildings, instruments etc.) and the remaining 13,000*l*. is used as circulating capital for employing labour. The rate of profit is assumed to be 10%, so the capitalist obtains 2,000*l*. per year. The capitalist begins production every year with foodstuffs and other necessities (i.e., circulating capital) worth 13,000*l*., sells his product to the labourers for 13,000*l*. during the year, and pays them the same amount of money as wages in the same period. In one year, the labourers produce foodstuffs and other necessities worth 15,000*l*., to be recovered by the capitalist, of which he disposes of 2,000*l*. as he wishes. In this case, the gross revenue of this year is 15,000*l*. and the net revenue is 2,000*l*. If, in the second year, he spends 13,000*l*. getting one half of the labourers to produce machinery and the other half foodstuffs and other necessities as in the first year, the result will be the annual production of machinery worth 7,500*l*. and of foodstuffs and other necessities equally worth 7,500*l*. In other words, he will have the same amount of capital as at the end of the first year. Because, in addition to these two amounts of value, he keeps a fixed capital worth 7,000*l*., making an overall total of 20,000*l*. of capital and 2,000*l*. of profit. If he puts aside this 2,000*l*. for his personal consumption, his circulating capital disposable for the next year will be only 5,500*l*. Therefore the labourers previously employed with 7,500*l*. will become wholly unnecessary. In this case, for the capitalist it is no problem how much the gross revenue will actually be, as long as he can obtain a profit of 2,000*l*. on the total capital with the aid of machinery while employing less labourers than before. But, as the power of feeding the population, of employing labour, is determined not by the net revenue of the country but always by its gross revenue, the diminution of the latter accompanying the adoption of machinery means the population will become excessive and the labourers will inevitably face difficulties [I/388–390]).

For this reason, Ricardo affirmed that the labourers' opinion that the use of machinery often goes against their interests is never 'founded on prejudice and error, but is conformable to the correct principles of political economy' [I/392]. He did not go so far as to say that the demand for labourers does not increase at all with the increase of capital, but he said that it does not increase in the same proportion.

The doctrine that machinery renders the labourers unnecessary was to be further developed and exaggerated later by Marx and was enhanced into the law of capitalist accumulation (chapter 23 of Book I of *Capital*). If the accumulation of capital maintains the same proportions of the part spent on wages (variable capital) and the part invested in machinery, instruments, raw material, buildings etc. (constant capital), i.e., with no alteration in the so-called organic composition of capital, the demand for labour will increase with accumulation and raise wages, but it is rare for capital accumulation to proceed without changes in its organic composition, because capitalists increase the constant capital invested in machinery and raw materials while decreasing the variable capital, for fear of being defeated in competition on the market. For this reason, the more capital is accumulated, the more the industrial reserve army of the unemployed increases. This is what Marx taught. Ricardo and Stuart Mill, his successor, sought to demonstrate that 'the invention and use of machinery can be accompanied with a diminution of gross revenue", but nothing more than this. However, Marx went further and said that the result of the adoption of machinery must necessarily be harmful for the labourers.

In contrast, Adam Smith before Ricardo did not question the influence of the adoption of machinery on the demand for labour. Though he divided capital into circulating and fixed capital, Smith always thought of these two kinds of capital as a whole, in particular when discussing the demand for labour. Hence, for Smith, the amount of capital directly determines the quantity of productive labour, so that in a country with faster progress of national wealth the condition of the labourer will also be better. And this was a natural conclusion Smith arrived at by observing merely manual work, cottage industry or at most manufacturing, in total ignorance of the development of the industrial revolution. Moreover, long after Smith, capital was often taken to mean wage capital, while overlooking fixed capital. According to certain researchers, this was because much attention was paid to agricultural capital during the time of rising corn prices, and in agriculture the use of machinery was nearly out of question. In any case, even Ricardo wrote 'labour, machinery, and capital etc.' [I/5] in the Preface to the first edition of *Principles*. This must of course be an error, but here too we may have a glimpse of the trend of the time (Cannan, *Theories of Production and Distribution*, p. 112).

It was only after the publication of the second edition of *Principles* that Ricardo changed his mind, taking into consideration the effects of the adoption of machinery. To our knowledge, this new view was announced for the first time in a passage contained in his comments on Malthus. In a passage in chapter 4 on the wages of labour of his *Principles of Political Economy*, discussing the demand for labour, Malthus mentioned the name of Barton and said that there were some affirming that 'the demand for labour can only be in proportion to the increase of the circulating, not the fixed capital'. While admitting that this opinion is not beside the point, he finally arrived at the optimistic conclusion that 'in general, therefore, there is little to fear that the introduction of fixed capital, as it is likely to take place in practice, will diminish the effective demand for labour; indeed it is to this source that we are to look for the main cause of its future increase' (pp. 261–264. [II/234, 239–240]). In opposition to this, Ricardo supported the doctrine of Barton. Thus, he said that 'the effective demand for labour must depend upon the increase of that part of capital, in which the wages of labour are paid' [II/234]. But 'the country, which is enriched only by the net income, and not by the gross income, will be equally powerful in both cases' [II/235]. And he continued: 'To the capitalist it can be of no importance whether his capital consists of fixed or of circulating capital, but it is of the greatest importance to those who live by the wages of labour. [. . .] If capital is realized in machinery, there will be little demand for an increased quantity of labour' [II/235–6]. Whether Ricardo already knew Barton at that time or only became aware of him through Malthus is a difficult question to settle (*Notes on Malthus*, pp. LXX, 124–135). And Ricardo's new theory of machinery has a certain correspondence to the modification he brought to the theory of value, equally in consideration of the effect of the adoption of machinery. And, as in the case of the theory of value, in the theory of machinery McCulloch complained to Ricardo, who himself corrected the doctrine he had previously taught to McCulloch. In his letter of response to McCulloch, Ricardo again detailed his new view with other examples, and affirmed that the adoption of machinery truly leads to the dismissal of some labourers, saying that 'I confess that these truths appear to me to be as demonstrable as any of the truths of geometry, and I am only astonished that I should so long have failed to see them' (*Letters to McCulloch*, p. 109 [the 18th June 1821, VIII/390]). Afterwards McCulloch came to recognise that 'the case supposed by Mr. Ricardo' about machinery was 'possible' (*Principles of Political Economy*, 1825, p. 188). [In fact McCulloch wrote here that 'the case supposed by Mr. Ricardo is barely possible'. He was still denying Ricardo's new theory of machinery. This is a misunderstanding by Koizumi.]

Incidentally, this shows us the character of Ricardo himself, who never ceased to pursue the truth, not contenting himself with already-available knowledge. As we have said above, Ricardo modified his theory of value in continuing debates with his critics until just before the day of his death from disease. He finally ended without being truly satisfied with his own doctrine.

Theory of the measure of value

Ricardo was a successful person renowned for his *Principles* published in 1817. He became extremely rich, was a Member of Parliament and achieved fame as a scholar. His *Principles* 'became the bible of utilitarianism' (Leslie Stephen), a new trend of thought at the time. In the House of Commons his speeches were attentively followed, as pronounced by the supreme authority on the currency problem. But meanwhile, he himself was never content with his own doctrine. Sceptical about the value of his theory of value, he finally arrived at a negative conclusion that something like an accurate measure of value cannot be found. We can have a glimpse of what was happening in his mind in those years by referring to *Notes on Malthus* as well as his letters to McCulloch and Malthus. On the one hand, to James Mill and McCulloch who affirmed that the value of commodities is determined by the labour bestowed and that alone, he emphasised that the time from the bestowing of labour till the sale of products also plays a role in the determination of value, but on the other hand, to Malthus who affirmed that the measure of value is the quantity of a commodity exchanged with labour, he said that it is rather the quantity of labour expended on production which is the better measure.

In 1822 (on the 19th March), in reading the manuscript of McCulloch's lecture notes that a third person showed him, Ricardo pointed out that the opinion of McCulloch was too simple and naive. The value of a commodity is not determined, he said, solely by the quantity of labour expended on production, as McCulloch claims.

Ricardo quotes the example of the conservation of wine and the planting of a tree. The wine increases its value during its long conservation, and an oak tree, initially planted by labour employed with 2*s.*, may become worth 100*l.* after a number of years. This increase in value cannot be explained by labour, he asserted. To this, McCulloch responded that, although no more labour is expended on the wine conserved for three years than on the wine conserved for one day, this increase in value caused by the lapse of time should be calculated by the accumulation that the same amount of capital would realise during the same time if spent on the employment of labour, and that, although the quantity of labour spent on the oak tree grown for 200 years is very little, its value should be calculated by the accumulation of capital the initially expended labour would give rise to during the same time (*Letters to Malthus*, p. 222 [the 13th July 1823, IX/303]). Ricardo responded as follows: 'I question the propriety of calling these accumulated profits by the name of labour, and of saying that the commodity so worth a hundred pounds was valuable in proportion to the quantity of labour bestowed upon it. The tree which originally cost 2*s.* for labour and becomes in after-time of the value of £100, has never strictly more than 2*s.* worth of labour employed on it' (*Letters to McCulloch*, p. 175. [the 21st August 1823, IX/358–9]).

Malthus argued at first that the measure of value should be constituted of the average of the values of corn and of labour (*Principles*, 1st ed. sec. VII [Chap. II, Sec. VII, *Of a Mean between Corn and Labour considered as a Measure of Real Value in Exchange*]), but afterwards, like Adam Smith, he came to consider the quantity of labour exchanged with a commodity – i.e., the 'labour commanded' – as the measure for the value of that commodity. 'Measure of the natural value of a commodity at any place and time' is 'the quantity of labour for which it will exchange at that place and time, when it is in its natural and ordinary state' (*Definitions in Political Economy*, 1827, p. 243). This opinion had already been stated in *The Measure of Value stated and illustrated etc.*, 1823, p. 23 n.) (p. 16).

Ricardo regarded this opinion of Malthus as erroneous, just as he had earlier considered the same opinion of Adam Smith as erroneous, and in his six long letters addressed to the former from the 29th April to the 31st August 1823 he repeatedly explained the reason. Briefly, the 'labour commanded' does not satisfy the necessary condition of being invariable in itself, a condition indispensable to a measure of things. If the population falls to three-quarters of the former level because of a plague, the value of labour rises in comparison to every other commodity. Then Malthus would not call this a rise in the value of labour, but a fall in the value of commodities, although there is no variation other than that in the supply of labour. For Ricardo this surely could not be right (*Letters to Trower*, p. 210. [the 24th July 1823, IX/319]).

What was then the opinion of Ricardo himself? In opposition to Malthus, he affirmed that a commodity is 'only dear when a great quantity has been bestowed on its production' [the 15th August 1823, IX/348], but he never thought this opinion to be impeccable. He merely said that the proposition of Malthus was more incomplete than his own. This is a natural consequence of Ricardo's abandoning the simple labour theory of value. He told McCulloch that 'value is compounded of two elements wages and profit mixed up in all imaginable proportions; it is in vain, therefore, to attempt to measure accurately, unless your measure agrees precisely in the proportions of wages and profits with the commodity measured' (p. 177 [the 21st August 1823, IX/361]). To Malthus, he wrote that 'the difficulty is respecting the varying proportions which go to labour and profits', and concerning the variations arising from variations in the proportion between labour and profit, he added that 'there has never been, and I think never will be any perfect measure of value' (p. 237 [the 15th August 1823, IX/352]). He said further that 'the question is about an invariable measure of value, [. . .] I have acknowledged that my measure is inaccurate, [. . .] but not because it would not do everything which you assert yours will do, but because I am not secure of its invariability'. The discussion finally ended without arriving at any settlement. 'These discussions however never influence our friendship; I should not like you more than I do if you agreed in opinion with me' (pp. 239, 240 [IX/381, 382. This sentence is also quoted by Fukuda, see above p. 64]). These were phrases Ricardo wrote 11 days before his death, i.e., on the 31st August.

The debates about the measure of value continued after the death of Ricardo. It was De Quincey, the 'Opium Eater', who appeared in defence of Ricardo. He rigorously distinguished between the 'ground' of value and its 'criterion'. He emphasised that the doctrine of Ricardo was to explain the former and had nothing to do with the latter, and that, since Malthus did not see this, his theory of the measure of value was inacceptable. He gives the thermometer as an example. It is the standard for measuring the temperature but not the cause of heat. Ricardo was in search of a measure in the sense of this *cause* and not a measure in the sense of a *standard*. And according to him the most important problem in economy consisted solely in the theory of the cause of value. He said that Malthus and others attached too much importance to the discovery of a measure of value (De Quincey, 'Malthus on the Measure of Value', 1823; 'Dialogues of Three Templars on Political Economy: Chiefly in Relation to the *Principles* of Mr. Ricardo', 1824. *The Collected Writings of T. De Quincey*, by D. Masson [Edinburgh, Adam and Charles Black, 1890], vol. IX).

Samuel Bailey, a critic of Ricardo, also distinguished between the measure and cause of value and said that the quantity of labour bestowed in a commodity cannot be confirmed or practically applied, and that a practicably inapplicable measure of value is worthless. Since he insisted at the same time on the relativity of the concept of value, he did not recognise the existence of a measure of value with an invariable value of its own, and therefore he did not approve Malthus' theory of the measure of value (*A Critical Dissertation on the Nature, Measure and Causes of Value; chiefly in reference to the writings of Mr. Ricardo and his followers*, 1825). Malthus did not finally change his mind, but afterwards came to distinguish the cause and measure of value and said that 'the labour worked up in a commodity is the principal CAUSE of its value, but [. . .] not a *measure* of it. The labour which a commodity will command is NOT the CAUSE of its value, but [. . .] the *measure* of it' (*Principles*, 2nd ed. p. 83 n.) [the words capitalised in the quotation are italics in original and the italics in the quotation are by Koizumi. Incidentally, these sentences of Malthus are quoted in the second article of Tokuzō Fukuda included in the first chapter of the present collection, cf. p. 64].

Value and supply and demand

Then what determines the value of commodities existing in a limited quantity or, even if they can be increased in quantity, produced without the working of free competition? On this point Ricardo said as follows: 'their value is wholly independent of the quantity of labour originally necessary to produce them, and varies with the varying wealth and inclinations of those who are desirous to possess them' [I/12].

To be determined by the wealth and inclinations of those who are desirous to possess means nothing other than to be determined by demand. Why then is the value of commodities whose quantity can be increased at will not determined by demand? It is because supply follows demand and does not allow a value that deviates from the cost of production to persist. Hence, he said as follows:

> It is the cost of production which must ultimately regulate the price of commodities, and not, as has been often said, the proportion between the supply and demand: the proportion between supply and demand may, indeed, for a time, affect the market value of a commodity, until it is

supplied in greater or less abundance, according as the demand may have increased or diminished; but this effect will be only of temporary duration.

[I/382]

Ricardo thought thus that supply would soon follow demand. Therefore, apart from the question of whether supply actually always follows demand, the determination of value by the proportion between supply and demand is never incompatible with its determination by the cost of production, contrary to what 'has been often said'. The determination of value by the cost of production means nothing other than that the cost of production alters the supply of a commodity so as to create finally a relation between demand and supply that tends to align its value with its cost of production. He says that a relation between them such as to form a value not corresponding to the cost of production does not last long, even if temporarily possible. Therefore, there is no problem in saying that it is the proportion between demand and supply that determines value in both cases. As long as the supply can be varied by human power, it increases or decreases till the value coincides with the cost of production. As for the latter, this is what can be said at the most. We can make out what Ricardo was really thinking for example from the following passages:

I do not say that the value of a commodity will always conform to its natural price without an additional supply, but I say that the cost of production regulates the supply, and therefore regulates the price. Or again Mr. Malthus says the demand compared to the supply regulates price, and the cost of producing the commodity regulates the supply. This is a dispute about words – whatever regulates the supply regulates the price.

(*Notes*, pp. 21, 118 [II/48–9, 225])

The law of the cost of production is to the law of supply and demand what the particular law is to the general principle. They are never incompatible with each other. Attaching too much importance to the place of the cost of production in the determination of value, Ricardo used formulations apt to be interpreted as if he considered the theory of demand and supply to be erroneous when criticising Malthus, Say, Buchanan, Lauderdale etc. (for example in chapter 30). This is not only unacceptable from our point of view, but indeed, rigorously speaking, it must also be inadmissible from the position of Ricardo himself.

Ricardo wrote as if there existed two sorts of commodities, the value of some being determined by the proportion between demand and supply and that of the others by the cost of production, or the value of some arising from scarcity and that of the others from labour. This is not a correct wording. The value of a commodity arises uniformly from scarcity, it is determined by the proportion between the demand and supply of it. To this we can add that there exist two sorts of commodities: for some the quantity of supply or scarcity can be controlled by human power, for the others they cannot be controlled. It is decidedly incorrect to oppose demand and supply against the cost of production, scarcity against labour. The determination of value by the cost of production cannot be explained without relying on the law of demand and supply. If labour is the source of value, it is ultimately because everything that is only produced by labour is scarce. If someone, erring on this point, misunderstands Ricardo as if he advanced labour as the source of value of commodities apart from scarcity, he should be accused of using unconsidered and hasty argumentation.

The following comments of H. Dietzel, defender of Ricardo, hit the bull's-eye: 'Though the formulae "utility and *scarcity*" and "utility and *bestowment of labour*" sound different, they are in fact *identical*, since, in the second formula, what is called "bestowment of labour" is actually only one of the two *causes* of "scarcity". Certain goods are *scarce*, because they *cannot* be increased by labour; they are Ricardo's "one kind of goods". Here he gives the cause of scarcity. Most of the goods are scarce, because, while being increasable, they are so only by labour. The cause of scarcity of these goods of "another kind" of Ricardo is that labour is a scarce means available in limited quantity. *Every* good, which costs *labour*, is *scarce*' (*Theoretische Socialökonomik*, S. 230). Amonn makes similar comments (Amonn, a. a. O., S. 106).

Senior also says substantially the same thing. According to him, if a thing has value, it is because 1. it has utility; 2. it is limited in supply; and 3. it is negotiable. The most important among these factors is the limitation of supply. If a thing seems to be valuable because of labour bestowed on it, it is in fact because the labour is limited in supply, hence because a thing in need of labour for its supply is limited in its supply by this need itself. However, 'any other cause limiting supply is just as efficient a cause of value in an article as the necessity of labour to its production'. And 'as limitation of supply is essential to the value of labour itself, to assume labour, and exclude limitation of supply, as the condition on which value depends, is not only to substitute a partial for a general cause, but pointedly to exclude the very cause which gives force to the cause assigned' (p. 24).

Theory of utility and theory of cost

As we have said above, the value of every commodity must be universally explained by the proportion between demand and supply. And as for the essence of demand itself, we must absolutely say that the demand for a thing arises from its power of satisfying our desire, i.e., from its utility. In moving back up from demand to utility, however, the explanation of value encounters the problem, which has long troubled scholars, of the discrepancy between utility and value or between value in use and value in exchange. Why is the exchangeable value of water zero or very small despite its use value being tremendous? Why is the exchangeable value of diamonds huge despite their utility being very small? This question was not answered by Ricardo either. But for a long time, it has been a cliché of scholars that the value or price is determined by the relation between demand and supply. Why then does the value of a thing fall because of an increase in its supply and rise because of a decrease in its supply?

At about the same time that Cairnes was placing restrictions on the sphere of application of Ricardo's theory of the cost of production, Stanley Jevons published the *Theory of Political Economy*, 1871, seeking to overthrow the doctrine of Ricardo and his epigones from the standpoint that value is founded entirely on utility.

The work of Jevons starts from the observation of a very banal fact of experience, that as a rule, human desire diminishes in strength according to the degree of satisfaction and ultimately disappears. If desire weakens with satisfaction, it is meaningless to wonder simply about the utility of a certain good irrespective of its available quantity. When speaking of the utility of a thing, is it before or after satisfaction of the desire for this thing? Depending on the answer to this question, there must be a large difference in the amount of utility. Jevons then distinguished between the total utility obtained from the whole of a certain quantity of good, and the utility of the final increment of a certain quantity of good, i.e., the final degree of utility. Man cannot subsist without water. The (total) utility of water is tremendous. But in our daily life we drink almost as much water as we want. Therefore its (final) utility is normally reduced to almost zero. And the proportion of exchange of one good with another is determined by this final utility. 'The ratio of exchange of any two commodities will be the reciprocal of the ratio of the final degrees of utility of the quantities of commodity available for consumption after the exchange is completed'. The fact that water has a tremendous use value and little or no exchangeable value is explained in this way.

Jevons wrote that he had arrived at a 'somewhat novel opinion that value depends entirely upon utility' [passage quoted also by Fukuda and Mori, cf. 67–8, 164]. He believed that this novel opinion was totally incompatible with the doctrine of Ricardo and his epigones. Then he described Ricardo as 'that able but wrong-headed man [who] shunted the car of Economic science on to a wrong line'. In deploring the fact that the valuable implications contained in the works of a number of original scholars fell into oblivion because they were not understood by representative scholars of the orthodox Ricardian school, he went so far as to say that 'under these circumstances it is a positive service to break the monotonous repetition of current questionable doctrines, even at the risk of new error' (4th ed. p. 277).

However, it is questionable whether the 'novel opinion' of Jevons is really so incompatible with the doctrine of Ricardo. I believe that this is not at all the case. The doctrine of Jevons is never as revolutionary as he himself believed it to be. He said:

> Prevailing opinions make labour rather than utility the origin of value; and there are even those who distinctly assert that labour is the cause of value. I show, on the contrary, that we have only to trace out carefully the natural laws of the variation of utility, as depending upon the quantity of commodity in our possession, in order to arrive at a satisfactory theory of exchange.

(p. 2)

However, as long as we do not concentrate too much on his unconsidered phrases, Ricardo never said that value arises from labour. He only said that, though the actual rate of exchange between commodities is determined by the relation between demand and supply, supply immediately follows demand in the case of commodities whose quantity can be increased by additional labour, so that the relation between demand and supply must necessarily proportion the rate of exchange to the relative labour expended. Jevons recognised that labour often appears to determine value, but he added that it does so 'only in an indirect manner, by varying the degree of utility of the commodity through an increase or limitation of the supply' (p. 2), and concerning the cost of production and value he wrote that:

> *Cost of production determines supply.*
> *Supply determines final degree of utility.*
> *Final degree of utility determines value.*

(p. 165)

However, from the position of Ricardo this is not at all inadmissible, regardless of how Ricardo himself understood it. In consequence, I must again emphasise that Jevons' theory of value was not a revolutionary new theory. It was advanced only by adding deliberate and meticulous considerations on the relation between variations in the supply of goods and the intensity of demand, a relation which was recognised as given in the conventional theory of value. Jevons' theory added more precision and depth to a certain aspect of the old theory of value. But his theory of value was not opposed to the existing one. It merely supplemented it. The determinant of the value of a commodity is always demand and supply or utility and scarcity. Labour or the cost of production only influences the value insofar as it regulates this supply or scarcity. The theory of utility is to the theory of the cost of production what the general is to the particular. Only in certain cases, the cost of production can measure value more clearly than utility.

Roughly the same can be said concerning the theories of the Austrian school founded by Carl Menger, with his followers like Friedrich von Wieser, Eugen von Böhm-Bawerk etc. and of the Lausanne school led by Léon Walras.

The final utility of Jevons approximately corresponds to the marginal utility (Grenznutzen) of Wieser. Menger defines value as the significance (Bedeutung) we attach to a thing by 'the importance of the least important of the satisfactions assured by the whole available quantity and achieved by any equal portion', and says that such a significance is assured by the sum of existing goods and is equal to the significance of 'this least important satisfaction' among the satisfactions of desire given by a particular unit of these goods (*Grundsätze der Volkswirtschaftslehre*, 1871, S. 108 [Carl Menger, *Principles of Economics*, translated by James Dingwall and Robert F. Hoselitz with an introduction by F. A. Hayek, New York University Press, 1981, p. 139]). This 'least important' satisfaction of desire can be replaced by the words 'marginal utility' without changing its meaning. Wieser expressed this idea in saying that 'the greater or lesser value is determined by the marginal utility' (*Über den Ursprung und die Hauptgesetze des wirtschaftlichen Wertes*, 1884. *Der natürliche Wert*, 1889).

Böhm-Bawerk, the most important promoter of the theory of marginal utility, divided value into subjective and objective value, following Neumann. Among the values classed as objective, he attached the most importance to the objective exchangeable value, i.e., the power of a good to be exchanged with a certain quantity of other goods, but this objective exchangeable value of a good can ultimately be explained by its subjective value. And Böhm also arrived at the same conclusion that 'the value of a good is determined by its greater or lesser marginal utility' (Grundzüge der Theorie des wirtschaftlichen Güterwertes; *Jahrb. f. Nationalök. u. Statistik.*, 1886. *Positive Theorie des Kapitales*, 1889). And the relation between cost and value in the Austrian school is the diametrical opposite of that in the orthodox school. According to the former, it is not the cost of production that determines the value of a product, it is rather the marginal utility of a product that determines the value of production goods. Jevons said, in the same way, that the value of labour must be determined by the value of its product, and never is the value of a product determined by the value of labour (p. 166).

From the above, we can propose the following:

The two opposite extremes among all commodities are, on the one hand, those of which the quantity in existence is absolutely limited, such as works of old masters and on the other, those which can be supplied proportionately to the quantity of demand. The value of the former can only be explained by the theory of utility. Though the value of the latter is also explained by the theory of utility, we can *go further* and say that the rate of exchange between commodities is proportionate to their respective costs of production. And between these two extremes there exist infinite degrees. The nearer a commodity approaches to the latter, the more its value is influenced by the cost of production, and the closer it comes to the former, the more it is independent from the influence of the cost of production. However, since the commodities whose supply can vary immediately with the variations in demand are in fact very few if not totally inexistent, much time is required for the influence of the cost of production on value to appear. According to Alfred Marshall, who accepted the compatibility between cost theory and utility theory, to try to determine the value entirely with cost or entirely with utility is just as irrational as to try to cut something with only one blade of a pair of scissors. He concluded as follows:

> As a general rule, the shorter the period which we are considering, the greater must be the share of our attention which is given to the influence of demand on value; and the longer the period, the more important will be the influence of cost of production on value.
>
> (A. Marshall, *Principles of Economics*,
> 5th ed. p. 350)

This is the present state at which Ricardo's theory of value, supplemented and modified, has arrived.

4 Ricardo's theory of wages

('Theory of wages', chapter IV
of *Establishment of theoretical
economics*, Kōbundō, 1958)

Tsuneo Hori

I

The first thing that should be pointed out is that in Chapter 5 ('On Wages'),
Ricardo mainly discussed wages as a fraction of wealth and not as a fraction of
value. Particularly on wages, he argues very scrupulously about wages as wealth
or use-value, in other words, about wages in an absolute and real meaning.
There may be various interpretations about why he adopted such an attitude.
In my opinion, the reasons are (1) that for the labourer the absolute amount
of wages (i.e., their amount as a fraction of wealth) actually has a far greater
importance than that of rent and profits for the landowner and capitalist, and
(2) that it is indispensable to establish beforehand a theory about the absolute
amount of either wages or profits and its variation, in order to elucidate their
reciprocal relation and its evolution, considering these two revenues as two
fractions of value, and for this it is practical to establish a theory about the
absolute amount of wages and its variation – profits being a residual revenue
(in Ricardo's words, a part of net revenue or net income)-, etc.

II

Ricardo regarded labour as a sort of commodity and discussed its value and
price. Here, the value of labour means the labour value of labour (power) (that
is, the value determined by the quantity of labour needed to produce the commodities consumed by the labourer), and the price of labour means the money
wages directly paid to the labourer. However, as the value of labour plays an
important role in the theory of value distribution to be discussed later, the
question in this chapter is exclusively about the price of labour, i.e. the money
wages, and we will treat wages as a fraction of wealth.

Ricardo begins Chapter 5 of *Principles* with the sentence: 'Labour, like all
other things which are purchased and sold, and which may be increased or
diminished in quantity, has its natural and its market price' (I/93). Here we
must remember that Chapter 4 ('On Natural Price and Market Price') was part
of Chapter 5 until the moment just before the first edition of *Principles* was
bound for distribution on the market.

This sentence indicates the different forms of the price of labour, i.e., of money wages. First he gives the natural price of labour or the natural wages, by which he means 'that price which is necessary to enable the labourers, one with another, to subsist and to perpetuate their race, without either increase or diminution' (I/93). There are two points to be noted in this definition. One concerns the phrase 'without either increase or diminution', the other the word 'necessary'.

Regarding the first point, there have been divergent interpretations of the phrase 'without either increase or diminution'. Does it mean the maintenance of a certain constant number of labourers, or the number of labourers at a particular moment remaining constant, or again the number of labourers maintained being sufficient to meet the demand for labour? These differences may seem to belong to a trivial problem, but they are of great relevance for understanding the whole of Ricardo's theory of wages, because, depending on which of these interpretations is adopted, his natural price of labour will be taken as a static or a dynamic concept. And these different judgments will also influence the interpretation of his market price of labour or market wages.

It seems to me that, if we take natural wages as meaning the price of labour necessary to support a certain constant labour population, it is evidently a static concept, and if we take it as meaning the price of labour necessary to support the labour population with an appropriate rate of growth demanded by the progress of society, it is evidently a dynamic concept. Moreover, if we take natural wages as meaning the price of labour necessary to support the labour population at a particular moment, it can be said to be either a dynamic or a static concept depending on how we take the meaning of this 'labour population at a particular moment', because if it means the labour population increasing or decreasing in response to the constantly changing demand for it, the wages necessary to support it must necessarily be considered only as dynamic, but if it means the labour population before our eyes, assumed to be constant without change, then wages must be only static. In any case, this last interpretation will reduce to one of the other two interpretations.

In my view, the natural price of labour or the natural wages of Ricardo should be interpreted as a dynamic concept, which best conveys his true intention because, as we will see later, he questions the evolution of wages (not only market but also natural wages) with the progress of society. In consequence, his phrase 'without either increase or diminution' should be understood as meaning the maintenance of the number of labourers in response to society's demand for labour. Incidentally, Ricardo's theory of wages is largely due to that of Torrens (see I/93, Sraffa's note). In his book *An Essay on the External Corn Trade, etc.*, Torrens regards the natural price of labour as 'necessary to support the labourer, and to enable him to rear such a family as may preserve, in the market, an undiminished supply of labour', and says subsequently that 'the labourer must, usually, obtain for his work, a sufficient quantity of those things, which the climate may render necessary to preserve himself, and such a family as may keep up the supply of labour to the demand, in healthful existence [i.e. the necessaries and enjoyments of life]' (Robert Torrens, *An Essay*, 1815, p. 62. The phrase in square brackets is an addition by Hori).

Next, on the second point: what does Ricardo substantially mean by the word 'necessary' in his phrase 'that price which is necessary to enable the labourers, one with another, to subsist and to perpetuate their race'? On this point there seems to have been no great difference of opinion. The commentators are almost unanimous in considering that he means the price of labour necessary to ensure for the labourer and his family, not their physiological subsistence (i.e. an absolutely constant, unchanging minimal subsistence), but a minimal subsistence that changes with time and place. This is because Ricardo's text contains clear phrases such as:

> The natural price of labour depends on the price of the food, necessaries, and conveniences required for the support of the labourer and his family.
> (I/93)

and:

> It is not to be understood that the natural price of labour, estimated even in food and necessaries, is absolutely fixed and constant. It varies at different times in the same country, and very materially differs in different countries. It essentially depends on the habits and customs of the people.
> (I/96–7)

Or again:

> those comforts which custom renders absolute necessaries [of the labourer].
> (I/94. The phrase in square brackets
> is an addition by Hori)

In summary, the necessaries for supporting the labourer and his family contain, according to Ricardo, not only the articles necessary for maintaining merely a physical subsistence but also the enjoyments and conveniences that 'custom renders absolute necessaries', which in addition must differ according to the cultural state of each nation. Besides, they guarantee only the minimum degree of life in a given country and at a given time, and nothing more than that, since, according to him, natural wages always means 'the necessary expenses of production' (I/348), i.e., the costs necessary to recover or reproduce the labour power, and hence no deductions can be made from them for taxes or savings[1] (I/347–8). For this reason, Karl Diel (1864–1943) says in his interpretation of Ricardo's natural wages that:

> Natural wages do not represent an amount which can be somehow determined like a quantity in the natural sciences, but have a social significance. Ricardo thinks of them as a minimum for existence which has become a

custom, so the wages must be sufficient for procuring the necessaries of life but not for collecting capital.

> (*Sozialwissenschaftliche Erläuterungen zu David Ricardos Grundgesetzen der Volkswirtschaft und Besteuerung.* 2Bde. 1906. II. Bd. 1922. S.4.)

In short, the necessaries of life indispensable for maintaining a certain necessary size of labour population in Ricardo's definition of the natural price of labour or natural wages does not refer to the absolute but to the relative necessaries of life.

However, we note the fact that, while including conveniences and enjoyments in his definition of natural wages, in addition to the necessaries (food, etc.), as indicated above, Ricardo did not always consider, when discussing the variation in natural wages, that the price fluctuations of every item of food and other necessaries and conveniences would necessarily exercise uniform influence on these wages. As this point will become clear below, when we examine his explanation of the variation in the natural wages, here we simply announce in advance that he concentrates on the price of food as the main determinant of the natural wages, almost entirely neglecting the prices of the other necessaries and conveniences, etc.

III

Next, Ricardo's market price of labour or market wages means 'the price which is really paid for it, from the natural operation of the proportion of the supply to the demand', the price of labour which 'is dear when it is scarce, and cheap when it is plentiful' (I/94). In this definition, we must note, first that the market price of labour is the price actually paid to the labourer, and second that it is determined by the relation between the supply and demand for labour.

Concerning the first point: as is already clear, while the natural price of labour in Ricardo is something ideal, its market price is a concrete concept, because it means the price attributed to labour as a commodity every time it is actually traded on the market. However, just as the market prices of other commodities are ultimately governed by their natural prices, this market price of labour is also regulated by its natural price. However, Ricardo never considered the natural price of labour as the central value of the market price of labour.[2] Later, we will see more clearly how this is so when treating the reciprocal relations between the natural and market prices of labour, but at any rate we must say that it is his particularity and merit as a theoretical economist that he did not content himself merely with the superficial explanation of every economic fact, but endeavoured to explain the circumstances governing and underlying these facts (i.e., the natural price of labour or natural wages, in the case of the price of labour actually determined on the market).

Next, on the second point: Ricardo says that the market wages, this factual price of labour, are determined by the relation between the supply and demand for labour, but we must examine what were for him the indicators of the magnitude of the supply and demand for labour. According to Ricardo, it is the population that shows the magnitude of the supply of labour, and the capital that shows the magnitude of the demand for it. For the former, 'under favourable circumstances, population may be doubled in twenty-five years' (I/98), while for the latter, 'in different stages of society, the accumulation of capital, or of the means of employing labour, is more or less rapid', and it 'must in all cases depend on the productive powers of labour' (I/98).

This is Ricardo's general explanation of the supply and demand for labour. But, putting aside for the moment the problem of population meaning the supply of labour, we need to examine his detailed explanations about capital meaning the demand for labour, because in his distinction between fixed and circulating capital (distinction he made following Smith but on a different criterion), the question may arise as to whether the capital serving as the indicator of the demand for labour is capital in general, including both fixed and circulating capital, or only the latter. At least in reading solely Chapter 5 of *Principles*, I think it possible to conclude that he considers the quantitative changes in capital in general as the cause governing the demand for labour. But he expresses a somewhat different opinion in Chapter 31 ('On Machinery'), newly added to the third edition of *Principles*. We will discuss this point later.

Incidentally, in Chapter 1 of *Principles*, Ricardo sometimes uses the term 'circulating capital' in the sense of the 'wages-capital' of Frank William Taussig (1859–1940) or the 'variable capital' of Karl Heinrich Marx. This applies to the following passages: 'in one trade very little capital may be employed as circulating capital, that is to say in the support of labour' (I/32) and: 'a shoemaker, whose capital is chiefly employed in the payment of wages, [. . .] is said to employ a large proportion of his capital as circulating capital' (I/31). Judging casually from these passages, it may seem that we should draw the conclusion that the cause governing the increase or decrease in the demand for labour must naturally be the circulating capital. However, these passages only show that: (1) wages are paid from the circulating capital, not the fixed capital, and that (2) the main, nay, the sole element of circulating capital is wages. They never indicate that the circulating capital is the cause governing the magnitude of the demand for labour.

The increased or decreased demand for labour may certainly appear after all in the form of changes in the circulating capital. However, it is one thing that it appears in such a form, it is quite another to say that it is the cause. Ricardo also understood this distinction. In Chapter 5 of *Principles*, just after mentioning 'the impulse, which an increased capital gives to a new demand for labour', he defines this capital as follows: 'capital is that part of the wealth of a country which is employed in production, and consists of food, clothing, tools, raw materials, machinery, &c. necessary to give effect to labour' (I/95), and continues a little after this that: 'in proportion to the increase of capital will be the increase in the demand for labour; in proportion to the work to be done will be the demand for those who are to do it' (I/95). He thus makes it clear that the cause of variation in the demand for labour is the variation, not of circulating capital, but of capital in general. In addition, in *An Essay on the Influence of a Low Price of Corn on the Profits of Stock* (hereafter *Essay* for short), he writes that 'as experience demonstrates that capital and population alternately take the lead, and wages in consequence are liberal or scanty' (IV/23), and that 'in the advancing state, it depends on whether the capital or the population advance, at the more rapid course' (IV/22–3), and in his letter to Malthus of the 8th May 1815 he writes that

> Till the population increases to the proportion which the increased capital can employ, wages will rise, and may absorb a larger portion of the whole produce. [. . .] In the case of great improvements in machinery, – capital is liberated for other employments and at the same time the labour necessary for those employments is also liberated, – so that no demand for additional labour will take place unless the increased production in consequence of the improvement should lead to further accumulation of capital, and then the effect on wages is to be ascribed to the accumulation of capital and not to the better employment of the same capital.
>
> (VI/226, 228)

Further, in relation to the meaning or scope of the idea that capital indicates the magnitude of the demand for labour, the following two points arise: (1) as we seen above, Ricardo revises his opinion somewhat in Chapter 31, and (2) the meaning of such phrases as 'the fund for the maintenance of labour' and 'the fund of employing labour', to be found in various places, needs to be clarified. We will discuss the first point later, here let us examine only the second point.

Many examples of phrases similar to 'the fund for the maintenance of labour' can be found in Chapter 16 (14 in the first edition) 'Taxes on Wages' and Chapter 9 (8 in the first edition) 'Taxes on Raw Produce'. In view of the explanations given there, it may be understood that this fund (1) is not a synonym for capital in general but is in proportion to this latter in its magnitude, and (2) is not, however, identical to the circulating capital itself. It may thus be that this fund is a kind of shadowy concept belonging to neither capital in general nor the circulating capital. In view of this point, we can suppose that Ricardo still remained a wages fund theorist. However, we find the following passage in 'Taxes on Raw Produce':

> A fall in the value of money, in consequence of an influx of the precious metals from the mines, or from the abuse of the privileges of banking, is another cause for the rise of the price of food; but it will make no alteration in the quantity produced. It leaves undisturbed too the number of labourers, as well as the demand for them; for there will be neither an increase nor a diminution of capital. The quantity of necessaries to be allotted to the labourer, depends on the comparative demand and supply of

necessaries, with the comparative demand and supply of labour; money being only the medium in which the quantity is expressed; and as neither of these is altered, the real reward of the labourer will not alter. Money wages will rise, but they will only enable him to furnish himself with the same quantity of necessaries as before.

(I/164)

On this passage, Taussig writes as follows: 'it would be difficult to find in the writings of the classic economists a more direct statement of a predetermined fund, all of which must go to the labourers' (*Wages and Capital. An Examination of the Wages Fund Doctrine*, 1896, Ed., [by Frank William Taussig, *Wages and capital; an examination of the wages fund doctrine*, D. Appleton, New York,] 1915, p. 178.) In the passage in question, Ricardo may appear to be an exponent of the wages fund theory, since he undoubtedly affirms the invariability of the quantity of necessaries or subsistence to be assigned to the labourer for a certain period of time, irrespective of any change in the value of money, because of the simultaneous existence of a certain quantity of necessaries or food and a certain number of labourers. But the necessaries or food Ricardo is talking about here does not mean only food as part of the circulating capital; it covers the necessaries or food in general existing in the country. Therefore it never means 'a predetermined fund, all of which must go to the labourers'. In other words, what Ricardo called 'the quantity of necessaries to be allotted to the labourer' does not mean the quantity of necessaries to be allotted to him, but the quantity he will be able to buy with the money wages paid to him. Because if the quantity of necessaries in question was understood as that to be allotted to the labourer, the following sentence, that this quantity 'depends on the comparative demand and supply of necessaries, with the comparative demand and supply of labour', would be superfluous.

Thus, Ricardo never asserts the wages fund doctrine.

IV

In the above, I believe that I have made clear the significance Ricardo attributed to natural and market wages respectively. Next, we must consider his view of their rise and fall. His discussion of this point begins toward the end of the first fifth of the chapter 'On Wages' (I/97). We notice at once that in the following he comes to use only the general term 'wages', abandoning the distinction between natural and market wages rigorously observed up to then. He says for example that, in the absence of variations in the value of money occasioned by monetary causes, 'wages are subject to a rise or fall from two causes: 1st. The supply and demand of labourers. 2dly. The price of the commodities on which the wages of labour are expended' (I/97). The first cause he gives here (i.e., the supply and demand of labourers), is nothing other than the cause governing market wages, as is clear from what we have seen above, and the second cause, (i.e., the prices of commodities on which the wages are to be expended), is nothing other than the cause governing natural wages. These are not at all two causes governing the same thing. I can hardly understand why Ricardo adopts such an attitude here. Be that as it may, since a clear distinction can certainly be made, in the explanation he gives subsequently, between the content concerning the rise and fall in natural wages and that concerning the rise and fall in market wages, in spite of his ambiguous treatment, we will maintain the distinction between them. Let us begin with the rise and fall in natural wages.

As we have seen above, according to Ricardo, natural wages means the money wages necessary for purchasing the food and other necessaries, conveniences and enjoyments that custom has made indispensable for the life of the labourer. Therefore the natural price must necessarily undergo a corresponding variation when any one of these commodities changes in price. However, as we have mentioned above, in discussing the rise and fall in natural wages, he does not put food, other necessaries, conveniences and enjoyments on an equal footing: the price variation of each of them exercises a different influence on natural wages. For example, just after explaining that 'the natural price of labour depends on the price of the food, necessaries, and conveniences required for the support of the labourer and his family' (I/93, see above), he first excludes the 'conveniences', in writing that 'with a rise in the price of food and necessaries, the natural price of labour will rise; with the fall in their price, the natural price of labour will fall' (I/93). In the chapter 'On Profits', he writes that 'wages [depend] on the price of necessaries, and the price of necessaries chiefly on the price of food, because all other requisites may be increased almost without limit' (I/119), and in the pamphlet *On Protection to Agriculture* (1822) he writes: 'Corn being one of the chief articles on which the wages of labour are expended, its value, to a great degree, regulates wages. Labour itself is subject to a fluctuation of value, in the same manner as every thing which is the subject of demand and supply, but it is also particularly affected by the price of the necessaries of the labourer; and corn, as I have already observed, is amongst the principal of those necessaries' (IV/236). These passages testify that he considers the rise and fall of the price of food or corn as the principal cause of the rise and fall in natural wages. Of course, with these words, he does not withdraw his premise that the substance of natural wages consists in 'food, necessaries, and conveniences' that custom has rendered necessary for the labourer, but his reasoning actually almost completely neglects the price variations of necessaries and conveniences other than food as determinants of natural wages. If he had intended to recognize that natural wages are also governed by the price variations of necessaries and conveniences other than food, as he recognized the tendency for the price of these articles to fall progressively with the progress of society,[3] he would have made explicit, by contrasting this effect with the other effect of the gradual rise in the price of food, the fact that these two contradictory tendencies would cancel out in a certain degree the unilateral movement in the natural wages. In other words, he would have positively admitted that, in spite of the rise in the price of food with the progress of society, the tendency of natural wages to rise would be attenuated to a certain extent by the fall in price of necessaries and conveniences other than food.

Here, we know that Ricardo did not exclude the influence of price variations of the necessaries and conveniences other than food on the variation of natural wages merely for the sake of simplifying his line of reasoning, hence that his natural wages are, in spite of their formal definition, determined by the price of food for the labourer as their standard, and therefore that his discussion about the variation in natural wages is focused on the variation in the price of food.

Then which tendency will natural wages have: to rise or to fall? Ricardo answers this question as follows: 'with the progress of society the natural price of labour has always a tendency to rise, because one of the principal commodities by which its natural price is regulated [i.e. food (note by Hori)], has a tendency to become dearer, from the greater difficulty of producing it' (I/93). And the 'progress of society' he speaks of here means directly the increase in wealth and population.

He writes in *Essay* that:

> The price of corn, and of all other raw produce, has been invariably observed to rise as a nation became wealthy, and was obliged to have recourse to poorer lands for the production of part of its food.
>
> (IV/19)

And in the chapter 'On Wages' of *Principles* he writes that:

> As population increases, these necessaries [meaning mainly agricultural products (note by Hori)] will be constantly rising in price, because more labour will be necessary to produce them.
>
> (I/101)

or again:

> It appears, then, that the same cause which raises rent, namely, the increasing difficulty of providing an additional quantity of food with the same proportional quantity of labour, will also raise wages; and therefore if money be of an unvarying value, both rent and wages will have a tendency to rise with the progress of wealth and population.
>
> (I/102)

From these words of Ricardo, it seems evident that by the 'progress of society', he meant the 'increase in wealth and population'. Therefore he intended to say that, as the demand for food increases, the price of corn (governed by the law of diminishing returns) rises with the progress of society. In other words, with the increase in wealth and population, natural wages, regulated mainly by the price of corn, also tend to rise.

Of course, he did not think that the price of food would always necessarily rise with the progress of society. He recognised that 'as the improvements in agriculture, the discovery of new markets, whence provisions may be imported, may for a time counteract the tendency to a rise in the price of necessaries, and may even occasion their natural price to fall, so will the same causes produce the correspondent effects on the natural price of labour' (I/93). However, as we can see from this passage, though the improvements in agriculture and the importation of corn might counteract the rise in natural wages or even lower them, it is only temporarily. He never changed his intention to assert the long-term tendency of natural wages to rise with the progress of society. However, since this concept of 'temporary' is only relative, it may mean some years or even decades in certain cases. Particularly, considering that Ricardo was a partisan of free trade in corn, it is possible that he would admit, under the advent of free trade, the possibility for the corn price in England – and hence English natural wages – to remain constant or even fall for a considerably long time. In short, the concept of 'temporary' may mean at the most an indefinite period of resistance against the long-term trend of the progress of society, i.e., the increase in wealth and population.

I have made clear above Ricardo's doctrine, according to which natural wages are governed mainly by the price of corn (food), which ultimately rises with the increase of wealth and population in a country, so that natural wages constantly have a tendency to rise, over the long run. This doctrine is habitually called the parallel theory (Paralleltheorie) of Ricardo. But some commentators say that he advanced a contrary theory (Konträrtheorie) in opposition to this parallel theory (see K. Diehl, *Erläuterungen* [see above], II. Bd. S.86ff.). As, in my view, this contrary theory relates mainly to the tendency of what he calls the market price of labour or market wages to rise or fall, I am going to explain this in the next section, before presenting my interpretation of the relation between these two theories (parallel and contrary theory, or the tendencies of natural and market wages to rise or fall).

V

In order to examine Ricardo's point of view on the variations of market wages, we should refer at the same time to his explanation about the distinction between money wages and real wages. The reason for this is as follows: as far as I understand the meaning of Ricardo's natural wages, they rise or fall in accordance with the rise or fall in the price of commodities consumed by the labourer, in particular corn, with a natural connotation that he receives his necessary consumption goods – to be called, so to say, the natural real wages-, so that here we have no need to distinguish between money wages and real wages. On the contrary, when it comes to discussing market wages, since they are determined by the relation between the supply and demand of labour regardless of the prices of the commodities consumed by the labourer, we will naturally have to think about the cases in which the real wages received by the labourer fall at the same time as the money wages he receives rise, through the relation between demand and supply, if the prices of the commodities he consumes rise to a greater degree.

Now, according to Ricardo, since market wages are governed by the proportion between what represents the demand for labour (i.e., capital) and what represents the supply of labour (i.e., the population), they rise or fall according to this proportion. He seems to give two apparently contradictory explanations of how the proportion between capital and population evolves 'with the progress of society'. Let us quote his words for the purpose of their comparison:

(1) 'In the natural advance of society, the wages of labour will have a tendency to fall, as far as they are regulated by supply and demand; for the supply of labourers will continue to increase at the same rate, whilst the demand for them will increase at a slower rate. If, for instance, wages were regulated by a yearly increase of capital, at the rate of 2 per cent., they would fall when it accumulated only at the rate of 1½ per cent. They would fall still lower when it increased only at the rate of 1, or ½ per cent., and would continue to do so until the [increase of (annotation by Hori)] capital became stationary, when wages also would become stationary, and be only sufficient to keep up the numbers of the actual population.

(I/101)

(2) 'Notwithstanding the tendency of wages to conform to their natural rate, their market rate may, in an improving society, for an indefinite period, be constantly above it; for no sooner may the impulse, which an increased capital gives to a new demand for labour be obeyed, than another increase of capital may produce the same effect; and thus, if the increase of capital be gradual and constant, the demand for labour may give a continued stimulus to an increase of people.

[. . .]

Capital may increase in quantity at the same time that its value rises. An addition may be made to the food and clothing of a country, at the same time that more labour may be required to produce the additional quantity than before; in that case not only the quantity, but the value of capital will rise.

Or capital may increase without its value increasing, and even while its value is actually diminishing; not only may an addition be made to the food and clothing of a country, but the addition may be made by the aid of machinery, without any increase, and even with an absolute diminution in the proportional quantity of labour required to produce them. The quantity of capital may increase, while neither the whole together, nor any part of it singly, will have greater value than before, but may actually have a less.

> [. . .] in both cases the market rate of wages will rise, for in proportion
> to the increase of capital will be the increase in the demand for labour;
> in proportion to the work to be done will be the demand for those
> who are to do it.
> In both cases too the market price of labour will rise above its natural
> price [. . .].
>
> [. . .]
>
> Thus, then, with every improvement of society, with every increase in its
> capital, the market wages of labour will rise
>
> (I/94–6)

That is, Ricardo explains in quotation (1) that market wages tend to fall with
the progress of society, while in quotation (2) he explains that they tend to rise,
thus leaving us a little uncertain about which he really means. However, if we
examine his reasoning in more detail, we will find it not always necessary to
remain perplexed. Because, as we have seen above, he attaches two different
elements to the concept of 'progress of society': 'increase in wealth or capital'
and 'increase in population', and considers the cases in which these two evolve
at different speeds, to distinguish the different results. In other words, the results
attained with the 'progress of society' will differ according to whether or not
the rate of increase of the population is faster than that of capital. And Ricardo's
theory of demand and supply predicts both the fall and the rise in market wages.
The above quotation (1) explains the former case, while (2) explains the latter.
From what perspective can these cases be verified? In his explanation, if we
compare the rates of growth of capital and population over the long run, the
former tends to be left behind the latter, so that market wages can be said to
tend constantly to fall. But comparing them over a relatively short time, we can
say that they tend to rise for that time span, as we actually observe capital often
growing faster than the population. In fact, as if testifying to this, he says in the
case (1) not merely 'with the progress of society' but 'in the natural advance of
society', and in the case (2) 'for an indefinite period'. Ricardo thus adopted the
contrary theory, as far as market wages are concerned.

The above is an analytical explanation of Ricardo's doctrine on the tendencies
of the evolution of market wages. As pointed out at the beginning of this section, in considering this kind of wages, we must in particular distinguish between
money wages and real wages (i.e., the quantity of commodities that can be
bought with the money wages).

According to Ricardo, market wages are determined by the relation of population to capital, which is 'that part of the wealth of a country which is employed
in production, and consists of food, clothing, tools, raw materials, machinery, &c.
necessary to give effect to labour' (I/95, see above). But, as in the quotation (2)
given at the beginning of this section, with the increase in the quantity of capital,
its value may increase (first case) or remain stable or even decrease (second case).

According to Ricardo, market wages will rise in both cases, but in the first case, as the price of food and necessaries also rises, their purchase 'will absorb a large portion of his increased wages', meaning that real wages will not rise so much. Hence, 'the situation of the labourer will be improved, but not much improved' (I/96). In the second case, on the contrary, since the labourer 'will receive increased money wages, without having to pay any increased price, and perhaps even a diminished price for the commodities which he and his family consume', real wages will remain high until the population has greatly increased, and therefore 'the condition of the labourer will be very greatly improved' (I/96).

The above is Ricardo's explanation of the influence of the increase in capital on money wages and real wages, mainly in the cases in which this increase proceeds independently of the population. Next we must examine his doctrine concerning the case of a rise in the price of necessaries under the pressure of population. He says that with the increase in population, the prices of various commodities on which wages are spent, in particular corn, will necessarily rise, and 'if, then, the money [market (note by Hori)] wages of labour should fall, [. . .] the labourer would be doubly affected, and would be soon totally deprived of subsistence' (I/101). Therefore money wages will rise, 'but they would not rise sufficiently to enable the labourer to purchase as many comforts and necessaries as he did before the rise in the price of those commodities' (I/101–2). Now suppose that, when the price of corn was 4*l.* per quarter, the labourer earned 24*l.* (i.e., the equivalent of six quarters), but that when the price rises to 5*l.* per quarter, he earns 25*l.* (i.e., the equivalent of five quarters). Then money wages have risen by 1*l.*, but with this sum of wages 'he would be unable to furnish himself with the same quantity of corn and other commodities, which he had before consumed in his family [i.e., the same amount of real wages as before (note by Hori)]' (I/102).

The condition of the labourer in the case of a rise in the price of corn can be understood most clearly by comparing it with that of the landowner in the same case. Ricardo writes as follows:

> There is this essential difference between the rise of rent and the rise of wages. The rise in the money value of rent is accompanied by an increased share of the produce; not only is the landlord's money rent greater, but his corn rent also; he will have more corn, and each defined measure of that corn will exchange for a greater quantity of all other goods which have not been raised in value. The fate of the labourer will be less happy; he will receive more money wages, it is true, but his corn wages will be reduced; and not only his command of corn, but his general condition will be deteriorated, by his finding it more difficult to maintain the market rate of wages above their natural rate. While the price of corn rises 10 per cent., wages will always rise less than 10 per cent., but rent will always rise more; the condition of the labourer will generally decline, and that of the landlord will always be improved.
>
> (I/102–3)

In summary, since wages at their natural rate (i.e. the natural price of labour) mean that the money wages received by the labourer are sufficient to purchase the commodities necessary for the subsistence of himself and his family, in this case there is no need to distinguish between money wages and real wages, but on the contrary, since the market price of labour means the money wages actually paid to the labourer, which cannot always purchase or command the same quantity of commodities even if their amount remains the same, his condition can improve or worsen depending on the actual price of the commodities he buys.

Ricardo's position is thus that: (1) though market wages rise with the increase in capital, a large and continual rise in real wages (i.e., a large improvement in the condition of the labourer) cannot be expected if the value of capital itself rises at the same time, and (2) the rise in the price of necessaries, especially food, that occurs in particular with the growth of the population, reduces real wages to a greater extent than the rise in money wages, thus worsening the condition of the labourer.

VI

In the previous sections IV and V, I have explained Ricardo's doctrines on natural wages and market wages respectively. The next question is about what connection or relation Ricardo recognized between the two.

The answer to this question ultimately reduces to the simple proposition that 'however much the market price of labour may deviate from its natural price, it has, like commodities, a tendency to conform to it' (I/94). But in fact this apparently simple proposition contains various problems, of which the most important are: (1) whether Ricardo's natural wages are to be obtained by averaging market wages, (2) what are the forces driving market wages to conform to natural wages, and (3) in what relation his theory of wages stands to the so-called iron law of wages. I will consider them one by one in this and the following two sections [VI, VII, VIII].

The first problem is whether Ricardo's natural wages are to be obtained by averaging market wages. Up to the present day, a number of scholars have answered this question positively. For example, after presenting Ricardo's doctrine to the effect that it is the growth of population that drives market wages to conform to natural wages (which is a 'customary subsistence minimum' according to his understanding), Diehl writes: 'so for him [Ricardo (note by Hori)] the movement of population is the great regulator of wages: the ultimate cause explaining why wages never stand over and above a certain average amount for a long time' (Diehl, *Erläuterungen* [see above], II. Bd. S.5.), and Schrey, in agreement with Diehl on his treatment of Ricardo's theory of wages, says that 'the average wages, i.e., the natural wages, are determined according to the so-called subsistence minimum' (M. Schrey, *Kritische Dogmengeschichte des Ehernen Lohngesetzes*, [G. Fischer,] 1913, S.19.).

But such an interpretation seems to be erroneous, due to insufficient examination of Ricardo's doctrine. If such was the view of Ricardo, firstly he would have had no need to distinguish between natural and market wages, to take the trouble to attribute a different definition to the former, secondly he would have considered as nearly the same the degree to which market wages fluctuate in each direction, above and below natural wages, and thirdly he would not have thought it possible for market wages to stay above or below natural wages for an indefinite period of time. However, he took the opposite attitude on all three of these points. We have already examined the first of these points, i.e., his explanation of the fundamental distinction between natural and market wages. Therefore, we will now discuss his explanation of the second and third points, i.e., how market wages deviate above and below from natural wages. He says as follows:

> It is when the market price of labour exceeds its natural price, that the condition of the labourer is flourishing and happy, that he has it in his power to command a greater proportion of the necessaries and enjoyments of life, and therefore to rear a healthy and numerous family. When, however, by the encouragement which high wages give to the increase of population, the number of labourers is increased, wages again fall to their natural price, and indeed from a re-action sometimes fall below it.
>
> When the market price of labour is below its natural price, the condition of the labourers is most wretched: then poverty deprives them of those comforts which custom renders absolute necessaries. It is only after their privations have reduced their number, or the demand for labour has increased, that the market price of labour will rise to its natural price, and that the labourer will have the moderate comforts which the natural rate of wages will afford.
>
> (I/94)

From this passage it is evident that Ricardo judges of the worse or better condition of the labourer from the position of market wages with respect to natural wages. But it is equally clear that he did not attach the same weight to the deviations of market wages above and below natural wages, the former being the rule and the latter the exception. In interpreting Ricardo's view of natural wages, Cannan says correctly that 'instead of being an average rate above and below which market wages are continually fluctuating, they are a minimum below which market wages cannot continue for any length of time, though they may exceed it for an indefinite period' (E. Cannan, *A History of the Theories of Production and Distribution* [*in English Political Economy from 1776 to 1848*, third edition, London, P. S. King & Son, Ltd, 1922,] p. 248). But, as Ricardo says in the above quotation, 'when the market price of labour is below its natural price', the former can only attain the level of the latter when the labour population has diminished or the demand for labour (capital) has increased. And as this requires a considerable length of time, Cannan seems to me to go a little too far in considering natural wages as 'a minimum below which market wages cannot continue for any length of time'. Therefore, as I have said above, it would be a more exact interpretation of Ricardo to consider that for him, market wages are as a rule above natural wages and exceptionally below them. As quoted above, he says that 'notwithstanding the tendency of wages to conform to their natural rate, their market rate may, in an improving society, for an indefinite period, be constantly above it' (I/94–5, see above), and after affirming that the condition of the labourer will greatly improve when the amount of capital increases while its value remains constant or even falls, he adds that 'it will not be till after a great addition has been made to the population, that the market price of labour will again sink to its then low and reduced natural price' (I/96). These words clearly show that he considered as normal the state in which market wages are above natural wages.

But Ricardo makes these arguments under the supposition of a 'progressive society'. As the increase of capital ordinarily precedes that of population in such a society, market wages remain continuously above natural wages 'for an indefinite period', he explains. Then a question may arise about the relation between market wages and natural wages in a 'stationary society' or 'declining society'. In a sense this is a reasonable question, recalling Smith who distinguished between and considered the progressive, stationary and declining states of society respectively. However, first, Ricardo described the evolution of every society with similar adjectives such as 'progressive' or 'in progress' without recourse to this threefold classification of the state of society, at least when discussing wages, and second, he only said that market wages would gradually fall to the level of natural wages, and exceptionally below them, in Smith's 'declining state of society'.

As regards the first point, needless to say that Ricardo saw in market wages surpassing natural wages (i.e., in the rate of growth of capital above that of population) a phenomenon of the 'progressive society'. But, as in the quotation above, he did not forget to add an adverbial phrase 'in the natural advance of society' when he spoke of the general tendency that 'the wages of labour will have a tendency to fall, as far as they are regulated by supply and demand'. Ricardo then affirms that market wages, whether rising or remaining continuously above the natural wages or again declining, represent equally a phenomenon of the progressive society. This may seem to be a contradiction, to which a counter-argument can be raised. However, as we have already said, in using words like progress, progressive or advance, he meant generally the faster growth of population and/or wealth (hence capital), and in his view, both the case in which the growth of capital is predominant over that of population and the contrary case fall into the category of 'progressive'. Therefore the above possible counter-argument does not apply to Ricardo. Moreover, he did not enumerate these two possible cases arbitrarily or incoherently. His explanation is altogether in line with historical development as he conceived it: as the normal state of a progressive society, the time during which the growth of capital dominates that of the population lasts for an indefinite period, and subsequently a period arrives when the growth of the population dominates that of capital. Therefore, market wages are higher than natural wages during the first period, but they gradually fall to the level of the latter or at times even below it.

Let us now examine the second point, namely that Ricardo recognizes only exceptionally the cases in which market wages fall below natural wages. After recommending that 'in all countries the labouring classes should have a taste for comforts and enjoyments' (I/100), in other words, that natural wages should be enhanced (we will have occasion to discuss this policy later), as the best means to prevent overpopulation when 'population presses against the means of subsistence' (I/99), he says as follows:

> In those countries, where the labouring classes have the fewest wants, and are contented with the cheapest food, the people are exposed to the greatest vicissitudes and miseries. They have no place of refuge from calamity; they cannot seek safety in a lower station; they are already so low, that they can fall no lower. On any deficiency of the chief article of their subsistence, there are few substitutes of which they can avail themselves, and dearth to them is attended with almost all the evils of famine.
>
> (I/100–101)

In the countries 'where the labouring classes have the fewest wants, and are contented with the cheapest food', in other words where natural wages are lowest, market wages can never fall below natural wages, but if ever such a situation arises, then the labourer will suffer from 'almost all the evils of famine'. Therefore, Ricardo asserted that it is essential to maintain sufficiently high natural wages in advance, to secure a 'refuge from calamity', in order to protect them from these evils even if market wages should fall below natural wages. We can see from this that for Ricardo: (1) when natural wages are at their lowest, market wages cannot fall below them, and (2) when natural wages are above their lowest level, market wages can fall below them, but this fall means at the most a temporary escape to the 'refuge', and it can never go so far as to cancel out the excess of market wages over natural wages, so as to give rise to an average value named natural wages.

In short, Ricardo's doctrine on the tendency of market wages to fall, i.e., the tenor of the so-called contrary theory of wages, never affirms the fall of market wages below natural wages, but rather the fall of the former to the level of the latter, the former being above the latter in the normal state. In other words, Ricardo never said that natural wages can be obtained as the average of market wages.

VII

The second problem we raised at the beginning of the previous section is: what are the forces that tend to drive market wages to conform to natural wages? Now, considering this problem with reference to the conclusion obtained in the previous section, it is clear that the main point in this problem consists in what drives market wages that are higher than natural wages to fall towards the level of the latter, and that the contrary question about what drives market wages that are below natural wages to rise towards the level of the latter is secondary. However, in considering both of these cases, Ricardo sought the forces behind the convergence of the two sorts of wages in Malthus's principle of population. I will explain how far Ricardo made use of this principle, and then I will examine his view of the effects of population on the evolution of market wages.

We can see from his works and letters how deeply Ricardo was committed to Malthus's *An Essay on the Principle of Population* and how much he respected this principle. But the results he obtained in applying this principle to the theory of wages were not always in keeping with those of Malthus. Before presenting this circumstance, let me recapitulate Malthus's principle of population. It can be reduced to the following points:

1   Food is indispensable to the subsistence of human beings.
2   The (potential) power of population growth is indefinitely higher than the (actual) power of growth in the supply of food.
3   Therefore, population growth is necessarily blocked by the supply of food.

Food here does not necessarily mean only the food physiologically indispensable to the subsistence of human beings, but also the food socially necessary to them (see *An Essay on the Principle of Population*, 1st ed., 1798, p.132).

Now, how far did the results Ricardo obtained in applying this principle differ from those of Malthus? What most attracts our attention on this point is the way each of them interpreted the concept of natural wages and the results they drew from these interpretations. As we have already said, Ricardo's natural wages are an unrealistic concept. In criticizing this, Malthus wrote as follows:

> This price [the natural price of labour, i.e., the natural wages of Ricardo (note by Hori)] I should really be disposed to call a most unnatural price; because in a natural state of things, that is, without great impediments to the progress of wealth and population, such a price could not generally occur for hundreds of years. But if this price be really rare, and, in an ordinary state of things, at so great a distance in point of time, it must evidently lead to great errors to consider the market-prices of labour as only temporary deviations above and below that fixed price to which they will very soon return.
>
> (Malthus, *Principles of Political Economy*, 1820, p. 247)

For Malthus, Ricardo's natural wages are excessively fixed and consequently too unrealistic, and cannot therefore be considered as the central price of market wages, which are real prices. But, as we have seen above, Ricardo never considered natural wages as the central or average price of market wages, he only understood it as the point to which the relatively high actual market wages would ultimately fall 'with the progress of society'. Moreover, this is not an absolutely fixed point. Therefore, in Ricardo's theory, although the relation between the supply and demand of labour influences the determination or variation of market wages, the only influence on natural wages comes mainly from the price of food, the relation between the supply and demand of labour having no direct effect on them. In Malthus' theory, on the contrary, this relation influences not only the determination or variation of market wages but also those of natural wages. He says as follows:

> The natural or necessary price in any country I should define to be, 'that price, which in the natural circumstances of the society, is necessary to occasion an average supply of labourers, sufficient to meet the average demand.' And the market price I should define to be, the actual price in the market, which from temporary causes is sometimes above, and sometimes below, what is necessary to supply this average demand.
>
> (Malthus, *Principles*, pp. 247–8)

Now, how do these differences between Malthus and Ricardo in their respective definitions of these two kinds of wages affect the results they obtain, when considering them in relation to the principle of population mentioned above? The supply of labour means the population of labourers and the demand for labour means the capital. Moreover, since the latter appears in the form of food in a broad sense for both Malthus and Ricardo, the law of supply and demand with regard to the wages in question here expresses an application of the principle of population to the determination of wages. Only we must pay attention to the fact that, while for Ricardo, as is already evident, this principle must naturally be applied solely to market wages and is indeed applied solely to them, for Malthus it must naturally be applied not only to market wages but also to natural wages – the average price of the former – and is indeed applied to both of them. Therefore, while the term wages or price of labour in the passage quoted below can mean both market and natural wages, when the same term is found in the passage by Ricardo it means only market wages.

Let us now compare Malthus's view and Ricardo's view of the relation between wages and the principle of population. First we quote from Malthus. In Section 5 ('On the Conclusions to be drawn from the preceding Review of the Prices of Corn and Labour during the five last Centuries') of Chapter IV ('Of the Wages of Labour') of his *Principles of Political Economy*, he writes as follows:

> It appears then that, making a proper allowance for the varying value of other parts of the wages of labour besides food, the quantity of the customary grain which a labouring family can actually earn, is at once a measure of the encouragement to population and of the condition of the labourer [. . .]. But it is of the utmost importance always to bear in mind that a great command over the necessaries of life may be effected in two ways, either by rapidly increasing resources, or by the prudential habits of the labouring classes; and that as rapidly increasing resources are neither in the power of the poor to effect, nor can in the nature of things be permanent,

the great resource of the labouring classes for their happiness must be in
those prudential habits which, if properly exercised, are capable of securing
to the labourer a fair proportion of the necessaries and convenience of life.

(Malthus, *Principles*, pp. 290–1)

According to the principle of population, the increase in wages – consisting
mainly of food – prompts an increase in the population, which in turn further
deteriorates the condition of the labourer. On the basis of this principle, Malthus
here affirms that the best way to prevent such a process is the limitation of
population by 'the prudential habits of the labouring classes', i.e., 'the moral
restraint' proposed by him after the second edition of *An Essay on the Principle
of Population* (1803).

In opposition to this, Ricardo writes as follows:

When by the encouragement which high wages give to the increase of
population, the number of labourers is increased, wages again fall to their
natural price, and indeed from a re-action sometimes fall below it.

(I/94, see above)

In the natural advance of society, the wages of labour will have a tendency
to fall, as far as they are regulated by supply and demand; [. . .] [as the
rate of increase of capital diminishes] they would fall still lower [. . .] and
would continue to do so until the [increase of] capital became stationary,
when wages also would become stationary, and be only sufficient to keep
up the numbers of the actual population.

(I/101, see above. The words in square brackets are
annotations by Hori)

With a population pressing against the means of subsistence, the only
remedies are either a reduction of people, or a more rapid accumulation
of capital. In rich countries, where all the fertile land is already cultivated,
the latter remedy is neither very practicable nor very desirable, because its
effect would be, if pushed very far, to render all classes equally poor.

(I/99)

Thus, at least for the rich countries, we must attempt a 'diminution of
population'. For this purpose, the friends of humanity cannot but wish that
in all countries the labouring classes should have a taste for comforts and
enjoyments, and that they should be stimulated by all legal means in their
exertions to procure them. There cannot be a better security against a
superabundant population.

(I/100, see above)

Here, in line with Malthus, Ricardo recognizes the growth in population
resulting from the rise in wages, which in turn leads to a fall in wages. But

unlike Malthus, wages here means only market wages. And as the way to prevent market wages from falling to the level of the natural wages, i.e., the wages 'only sufficient to keep up the numbers of the actual population' (I/101), he emphatically recommended an enhancement of the standard of living, i.e., a qualitative rise in natural wages themselves, a more indirect or roundabout means than the 'moral restraint' advocated by Malthus.

Thus, given that Ricardo considered the case of market wages falling below natural wages to be exceptional, together with his recommendation for the qualitative enhancement of natural wages, the tenor of this recommendation is firstly, that the labourer should dispose of a so-called 'refuge' even if market wages fall below natural wages, and secondly, that such an enhancement should encourage the labourer to adopt the 'prudential habits' or 'moral restraint' to prevent the population growth that necessarily leads to a fall in market wages.

Because of their different definitions of natural and market wages, as seen above, it is natural that Malthus and Ricardo should draw different conclusions in applying the principle of population. But, examining in further detail how Ricardo viewed the effects of population on the evolution of market wages, his words on 'friends of humanity' wishing for a qualitative enhancement of natural wages by encouraging in the labourer the taste for comforts and enjoyments turn out to be a policy argument and a simple expectation, naturally different from his interpretation of the actual facts. In other words, according to Ricardo, although

> the increased wages are not always immediately expended on food, but are first made to contribute to the other enjoyments of the labourer [. . .] his improved condition induces, and enables him to marry, and then the demand for food for the support of his family naturally supersedes that of those other enjoyments on which his wages were temporarily expended.
>
> (I/163)

Therefore, even if the rise in market wages in a country appears to encourage a temporary rise in natural wages, the principle of population will necessarily reduce the former finally to 'that rate which nature and habit demand for the support of the labourers' (I/159). This is the actual state of our society. But, unlike other commodities, labour cannot be increased or decreased rapidly.

> You cannot increase [the labourers'] number in one or two years when there is an increase of capital, nor can you rapidly diminish their number when capital is in a retrograde state; and, therefore, the number of hands increasing or diminishing slowly, whilst the funds for the maintenance of labour increase or diminish rapidly, there must be a considerable interval before the [market] price of labour is exactly regulated by the price of corn and necessaries [i.e., natural wages].
>
> (I/165. The words in square brackets
> are annotations by Hori)

In summary, the principle of population plays an important role in Ricardo's theory of wages, not because the rise or fall in market wages brings about an increase or decrease in population, but rather because when market wages are higher than natural wages, they must fall to the level of the latter due to the increase in population.

VIII

The third problem raised at the beginning of Section VI concerns the relation between the iron law of wages and Ricardo's theory of wages. In fact the answer to the second problem (above) shows Ricardo's iron law of wages. However, it does not in itself constitute what is called the iron law of wages, because the essential point of this law consists, in addition to the conformity of the market wages to natural wages, in asserting the limited nature (in a relative sense) of natural wages themselves.

To the question of whether Ricardo actually upheld the limited nature of natural wages, we should reply in the positive despite some anticipated objections. The reason for this is as follows: (1) By natural wages, Ricardo means the wages necessary for purchasing not only the commodities essential to the simple physiological subsistence of the labourer, but also those comforts and conveniences made indispensable by custom for the life of the labourer. However, (2) he discusses the rise and fall of natural wages mainly on the basis of the price of food (corn). Finally, (3) while emphasizing the importance of qualitatively enhancing natural wages in order to counteract the effect of the principle of population on the condition of the labourer, he had to recognize, as a matter of fact, the difficulty of maintaining a high quality of natural wages over a long period due to the inexorable working of this principle. In considering carefully the relation between these three points and the conclusions to be drawn from there, we can reasonably say that Ricardo's natural wages are a comparatively limited concept, because the comforts and conveniences given in the explanation (1) as part of natural wages are virtually ignored in (2) and characterized in (3) as something which can hardly constitute actual natural wages, thus remaining only in their definition, while food is treated as almost the only element in the natural wages to which market wages must necessarily be reduced.

In the first section of Chapter 1 of *Principles*, Ricardo writes that

> In the same country double the quantity of labour may be required to produce a given quantity of food and necessaries at one time, than may be necessary at another, and a distant time; yet the labourer's reward may possibly be very little diminished. If the labourer's wages at the former period, were a certain quantity of food and necessaries, he probably could not have subsisted if that quantity had been reduced.
>
> (I/15)

These words reveal how minimal his natural wages are, i.e., that they do not include any comforts or conveniences. The ultimate conclusion he thus reached is shown in the following passage:

> From the effect of the principle of population on the increase of mankind, wages of the lowest kind [the minimum market wages] never continue much above that rate which nature and habit demand for the support of the labourers [the natural wages].
>
> (I/159. The words in square brackets are annotations by Hori)

This is a passage in Chapter 9 (8 in the first edition) of *Principles* entitled 'On Taxes on Raw Produce', in which we can clearly see his iron law of wages, because this 'rate which nature and habit demand for the support of the labourers', which could be interpreted as containing a considerable range of commodities when natural wages were defined, has now come to indicate a comparatively limited range of commodities like food or corn, in the course of his discussion of natural wages.

As regards the first point above, it is already clear that, according to his parallel theory, natural wages consisting mainly of food will necessarily rise with the progress of society, as the price of corn (food) gradually rises under the effect of the law of diminishing returns, and according to his contrary theory, natural wages governed by the relation between demand and supply will have a tendency to fall as the rate of growth of the population overtakes that of capital with the progress of society. However, as we have said above, the most important point is that Ricardo supposes from the outset that market wages are higher than natural wages. In other words, it is because the former is supposed to be above the latter that it can fall or regress towards this latter. And on the other hand, since natural wages, being constantly below market wages, have a tendency to rise progressively with the natural rise in the price of corn, these two wages, one falling and the other rising, will have to coincide with each other sooner or later. Therefore, in the process prior to this coincidence between them, there exists no contradiction between the parallel and contrary theories.

Then what will happen when market wages pass through this coincident point and fall below natural wages? Again, in such cases, his contrary theory will not be at all contradictory to his parallel theory. If there are any contradictions, they are only reflections of those in the actual facts. Then what do the contradictions in the actual facts mean? To this, Ricardo would respond as follows:

> If, then, the money wages of labour [the market wages] should fall, whilst every commodity on which the wages of labour were expended rose, the labourer would be doubly affected, and would be soon totally deprived of subsistence.
>
> (I/101, see above. The words in square brackets are annotations by Hori)

Next, let us examine the second point, concerning the difference between his policy recommendation for raising natural wages and his parallel theory on natural wages. At first sight these two may appear to be contradictory, but this is not at all the case. When recommending a rise in natural wages to preventing the fall in market wages, he intended that the actual contents of the former should include the comforts and conveniences other than food, i.e., to improve the life of the labourer, but on the contrary, when affirming the tendency of natural wages to rise necessarily with the progress of society, he meant that 'it appears that [. . .] the increasing difficulty of providing an additional quantity of food with the same proportional quantity of labour will also raise [natural (note by Hori)] wages' (I/102). In the first case, he argued for a rise in natural wages in the sense of an enrichment of their contents, and in the second case he affirmed the rise in natural wages due to the gradual rise in the price of food (corn). The former is a policy argument, while the latter is an argument about the real evolution of the economy. Therefore, in view of this difference in the object of study, there can be no contradiction between them, even if Ricardo recognized, for the rise in natural wages in the former sense, that its realization would in fact be temporary and tend to fall sooner or later, while recognizing a rise in natural wages in the latter sense.

IX

With the above, we have accomplished our commentaries on Ricardo's theory of wages – discussions of wages as a fraction of wealth or of wages in the absolute and real sense of the term. In relation to this, we have still to mention his theory of machinery, because it concerns the absolute condition of the labourers in the same way as his theory of wages does. But we must note that here, Ricardo mainly discusses the employment of labourers.

As we have already mentioned how Ricardo abandoned his early view on machinery to adopt a new one, here we will explain the contents of his view on machinery newly added to the third edition of *Principles*. Since John Barton's *Observations on the Circumstances which Influence the Conditions of the Labouring Class of Society* played an important role in Ricardo's change of view, we will briefly review Barton's doctrine. In this work, published in the latter part of the year of publication of Ricardo's *Principles* (1817), Barton has this to say about the relation between the employment of machinery and the demand for labour:

> It does not seem that every accession of capital necessarily sets in motion an additional quantity of labour. Let us suppose a case: A manufacturer possesses a capital of 1000*l.* which he employs in manufacturing twenty weavers, paying them 50*l.* per annum each. His capital is suddenly increased to 2,000*l.* With double means he does not however hire double the number of workmen, but lays out 1,500*l.* in erecting machinery, by the help of which five men are enabled to perform the same quantity of work as twenty

as before. Are there not then fifteen men discharged in consequence of the manufacturer having increased his capital?

But does not the construction and repair of machinery employ a number of hands? Undoubtedly. As in this case a sum of 1,500*l*. was expended, it may be supposed to have given employment to thirty men for a year, at 50*l*. each. If calculated to last fifteen years, (and machinery seldom wears out sooner) then thirty workmen might always supply fifteen manufacturers with these machines: therefore each manufacturer may be said constantly to employ two. Imagine also that one man is always employed in the necessary repairs. We have then five weavers, and three machine makers, where there were before twenty weavers.

(John Barton, *Observations*, p. 15)

Next, supposing that each manufacturer is now able to employ two more domestic servants with the (twofold) increase in his revenue. Instead of the previous twenty weavers, only ten workmen in total (five weavers, three machine makers and two domestic servants) would be employed with twice as much capital and revenue as before (John Barton, *Observations*, pp. 16–17.).

With this example as an illustration, Barton demonstrates that the increase in capital, or rather the use of machinery, diminishes the demand for labour. He continues his explanation with the following passage, which Ricardo quoted in his new chapter on machinery:

The demand for labour depends then on the increase of circulating, and not of fixed capital. Were it true that the proportion between these two sorts of capital is the same at all times, and in all countries, then indeed it follows that the number of labourers employed is in proportion to the wealth of the state. But such a position has not the semblance of probability. As arts are cultivated, and civilization is extended, fixed capital bears a larger and larger proportion to circulating capital. The amount of fixed capital employed in the production of a piece of British muslin is at least a hundred, probably a thousand times greater than that employed in the production of a similar piece of Indian muslin. And the proportion of circulating capital employed is a hundred or a thousand times less. It is easy to conceive that under certain circumstances, the whole of the annual savings of an industrious people might be added to fixed capital, in which case they would have no effect in increasing the demand for labour.

(John Barton, *Observations*, pp. 17–18. I/395)

Now, let us return to Ricardo. In Chapter 31 of *Principles* (in the third edition), he briefly outlines his own previous view of machinery (which he had never published but had advanced in other ways) as follows: he was of the opinion that the adoption of labour-saving machinery would be equally beneficial to the landowner, capitalist and labourer, apart from the temporary inconvenience arising from the transfer of capital and labour from one employment to another, because through the use of machinery the price of commodities would fall, allowing all three classes to buy larger quantities of commodities with the same money income. Moreover, though a certain number of labourers would possibly become superfluous and be discharged in the branches of industry in which the productive power has largely increased through the adoption of machinery, the labourers would not suffer any prejudice, because there would be no change in the quantity of capital existing in the society as a whole, the surplus in some branches being necessarily redeployed to others, thus causing no diminution in the demand for labour (see I/386–8).

Then, on his reconsideration of part of this earlier view on machinery, he writes as follows:

> These were my opinions, and they continue unaltered, as far as regards the landlord and the capitalist; but I am convinced, that the substitution of machinery for human labour, is often very injurious to the interests of the class of labourers.
>
> (I/388)

To illustrate this new conviction, Ricardo used the example of a capitalist and demonstrated that the employment of machinery cannot but cause a diminution in the demand for labour as well as a relative excess of population, since it increases the part of fixed capital and diminishes the part of circulating capital in a country. Thus,

> Although the net produce will not be diminished in value, although its power of purchasing commodities may be greatly increased, the gross produce will have fallen from a value of 15,000*l*. to a value of 7,500*l*., and as the power of supporting a population, and employing labour, depends always on the gross produce of a nation, and not on its net produce, there will necessarily be a diminution in the demand for labour, population will become redundant, and the situation of the labouring classes will be that of distress and poverty.
>
> (I/389–90)

There seem to be some discrepancies between the above example and the subsequent explanation. In any case, Ricardo asserted here that the adoption or increased use of machinery, fixed capital, in order to increase the capitalist's net revenue would be disadvantageous to the labourer, because it would be accompanied by a diminution in gross revenue and hence in the circulating capital, which is the source of the demand for labour. Thus we can see why he wrote as follows, before explaining the above illustrative example:

> My mistake arose from the supposition, that whenever the net income of a society increased, its gross income would also increase; I now, however, see reason to be satisfied that the one fund, from which landlords and capitalists derive their revenue, may increase, while the other, that upon

which the labouring class mainly depend, may diminish, and therefore it follows, if I am right, that the same cause which may increase the net revenue of the country, may at the same time render the population redundant, and deteriorate the condition of the labourer.

(I/388)

And he gives the following four concluding propositions after adding some explanations of the above example:

1st. That the discovery, and useful application of machinery, always leads to the increase of the net produce of the country, although it may not, and will not, after an inconsiderable interval, increase the value of that net produce.

2dly. That an increase of the net produce of a country is compatible with a diminution of the gross produce, and that the motives for employing machinery are always sufficient to insure its employment, if it will increase the net produce, although it may, and frequently must, diminish both the quantity of the gross produce, and its value.

3dly. That the opinion entertained by the labouring class, that the employment of machinery is frequently detrimental to their interests, is not founded on prejudice and error, but is conformable to the correct principles of political economy.

4thly. That if the improved means of production, in consequence of the use of machinery, should increase the net produce of a country in a degree so great as not to diminish the gross produce, (I mean always quantity of commodities and not value, [sic]) then the situation of all classes will be improved. The landlord and capitalist will benefit, not by an increase of rent and profit, but by the advantages resulting from the expenditure of the same rent, and profit, on commodities, very considerably reduced in value, while the situation of the labouring classes will also be considerably improved; 1st, from the increased demand for menial servants; 2dly, from the stimulus to savings from revenue, which such an abundant net produce will afford; and 3dly, from the low price of all articles of consumption on which their wages will be expended.

(I/391–2)

However, at the end of this chapter Ricardo somewhat qualifies the opinion expressed in the passages above, in writing as follows:

The statements which I have made will not, I hope, lead to the inference that machinery should not be encouraged. To elucidate the principle, I have been supposing, that improved machinery is *suddenly* discovered, and extensively used; but the truth is, that these discoveries are gradual, and rather operate in determining the employment of the capital which is saved and accumulated, than in diverting capital from its actual employment.

(I/395, italics in the original)

And he continues that in a country like England, where food is expensive and requires much labour for its production, 'with every augmentation of capital, a greater proportion of it is employed on machinery', since wages rise but the value of machines does not, and 'the demand for labour will continue to increase with an increase of capital, but not in proportion to its increase', only in a diminishing ratio (I/395). And he added a footnote to this last sentence, in which, after quoting a passage from Barton beginning with 'The demand for labour . . .' (see above), he writes that 'it is not easy, I think, to conceive that under any circumstances, an increase of capital should not be followed by an increased demand for labour; the most that can be said is, that the demand will be in a diminishing ratio (I/396, footnote).

Notes

1 In Chapter 26 (24 in the first edition) of *Principles* ('On Gross and Net Revenue'), Ricardo makes clear his point of view on the natural wages rendering them the necessary expenses of production, in saying that 'the whole produce of the land and labour of every country is divided into three portions: of these, one portion is devoted to wages, another to profits, and the other to rent. It is from the two last portions only, that any deductions can be made for taxes, or for savings; the former, if moderate, constituting always the necessary expenses of production' (I/347–8). However he seems to attenuate somewhat the above claim of his in adding a note: 'perhaps this is expressed too strongly, as more is generally allotted to the labourer under the name of wages, than the absolutely necessary expenses of production. In that case a part of the net produce of the country is received by the labourer, and may be saved or expended by him; or it may enable him to contribute to the defence of the country' (I/348, footnote). But if it is possible to interpret the wages mentioned in this note as meaning market wages, his attitude can be considered coherent in regarding 'the quantity of food, necessaries, and conveniences become essential to him from habit' (I/93) as the substantial content of natural wages.
2 As we have seen above, Ricardo makes the natural price of commodities the central value of their market price, arguing that the actual prices of general commodities (i.e., their market prices) are 'accidental and temporary deviations' from 'their primary and natural price' (I/88), and that 'it is then the desire, which every capitalist has, of diverting his funds from a less to a more profitable employment, that prevents the market price of commodities from continuing for any length of time either much above, or much below their natural price' (I/91). Concerning the relation between the natural and market prices of labour, however, he adopted a different view. I conjecture that this may be one of the reasons why he separated the chapter entitled 'On Natural and Market Price' from the chapter entitled 'On Wages' just before publication of the *Principles*.
3 Toward the beginning of the chapter 'On Wages', Ricardo recognizes that in addition to conveniences, the necessaries other than food also tend to fall in price with the progress of society, in writing as follows: 'the natural price of all commodities, excepting raw produce and labour, has a tendency to fall, in the progress of wealth and population; for though, on one hand, they are enhanced in real value, from the rise in the natural price of the raw material of which they are made, this is more than counterbalanced by the improvements in machinery, by the better division and distribution of labour, and by the increasing skill, both in science and art, of the producers' (I/93–4).

5 Essential aspects of Ricardo's theory of value

(From *Studies on Ricardo's theory of value*, Iwanami Shoten, 1926)

Kōjirō Mori

Section 1. Importance of Ricardo's theory of value

In the history of theories of economic value, the two theories of value – the so-called subjective and objective theories of value – have been in opposition to each other since ancient times. Needless to say, it is here in particular that the objective theory of value has occupied the dominant place in the history of economic thought, in the form of the labour theory of value or cost theory. It has exerted various great influences on pure economic theory and practical policies from far back in the past, prior to the establishment of economics as a science, until recent times. Just after the mid-nineteenth century, the subjective theory of value, originally opposed to this objective theory of value, came to take scientific form in the hands of a number of competent scholars and became predominant in the theory of value, threatening to some extent the position of the latter. Nevertheless, the objective theory has substantially maintained its scientific importance up to the present day in many ways, and has not undergone any change.

Prominent in this objective theory of value is of course the labour theory of value. It had already been proposed by Petty, Boisguillebert, Franklin, etc., but it was only after Adam Smith that it took shape as a theory in the science of political economy. But Smith's labour theory of value was impure in its content and its scientific importance remained relatively insignificant, because it confused 'labour-commanded' and 'labour-bestowed' theories of value, in addition to the labour theory of value in its original form. The labour-bestowed theory of value was regarded to be valid only in the primitive society, while in the civilized society, with the accumulation of capital and the appropriation of land, it had to be replaced by a sort of cost-of-production theory of value. Not only did Ricardo eliminate the labour-commanded dimension from this theory of Smith, establishing and developing solely the labour-bestowed theory of value, but he also considered it to be valid for the exchange phenomena in the modern capitalist society. This must be regarded as a great advance in the history of the labour theory of value. In addition, while in Smith the labour theory of value remains only a part of his doctrine, in Ricardo it is treated as the fundamental principle of the whole of his economic theory, which shows that political economy was taking clearer shape as an independent science.

Thus Ricardo's labour theory of value represents a scientific purification and development of the labour theory of value and also forms the fundamental principle of the whole of his economic theory, which is truly of epoch-making significance in the history of economic thought. This is all the more so because his theory of value started from the need to elucidate the practical problems of his time – the bullion controversy, the rise in ground rents and corn prices, the falling rate of profits, the repeal of corn laws etc. – and never from an interest in useless, merely abstract theories. Subsequently, Ricardo's labour theory of value was further extended and developed by Marx, who treated it as the starting point and the fundamental principle for his economic theory. But the labour theory of value in the above sense had already taken almost complete form in Ricardo and can be said to have finished its development in this earlier phase. It is because of this that the theory of value embodied in the political economy of Ricardo is rightly regarded to have been a great advance in the science of political economy in the early stage of development of the capitalist society. In the following, I will enumerate the reasons for the importance of Ricardo's theory of value in the history of economic thought, adding some comments of my own to each of them.

(1) Ricardo's labour theory of value is in its pure form, determining the exchangeable value of commodity by the comparative quantity of labour expended on its production, i.e., the labour-bestowed theory of value, altogether alien from the labour-commanded theory of value, which determines and measures the value of a commodity by the labour it commands or purchases. As we have seen above, Adam Smith did not clearly distinguish between these two theories of value and he put them on an equal footing, so that his labour theory of value remained in an extremely impure form. Malthus followed him in this labour-commanded theory (in his later years), in opposition to Ricardo who adopted the labour-bestowed theory, and they continued discussions throughout their lifetimes about the legitimacy of their respective theories of value. This labour-commanded theory of value ended up with the wage theory of value, which is in turn a kind of cost-of-production theory and hence does not belong to the labour theory of value. Needless to say, it is therefore the labour-bestowed theory that is the labour theory of value in the proper sense of the term. In short, the former is nothing other than the latter in its pure form. Ricardo must be attributed a truly great merit in the history of the labour theory of value, in that he got rid of the labour-commanded theory of value and insisted solely on the labour-bestowed theory.

(2) One important point in Ricardo's theory of value is that he affirmed that the law of labour value could be applied to the phenomena of commodity exchange in the actual capitalist society, in opposition to Adam Smith who only recognized its validity in the phenomena of commodity exchange in the primitive society. Because the value of elucidating the theory of value is not to be found in explaining the economic phenomena in a society far-removed in time, an unreal, hypothetical society, but in making clear the essence of the real economic phenomena taking place in the current society.

(3) In the economists before Ricardo, such as Adam Smith, the theory of value remained only a part of their economic theories. Ricardo was the first for whom the labour theory of value became the fundamental principle of the whole of his economic theory. It was the point of departure for the systematic synthesis of the entire contents of political economy, and every economic phenomenon came to be explained solely on the basis of this theory of value. In Ricardo, the law of value is not merely the principle of commodity exchange, but rather the fundamental principle of every economic phenomenon. Ricardo's attitude in seeking to explain every economic phenomenon with a unified principle – the law of value – shows that political economy had obtained the status of an independent science. However, Ricardo restricted the main problems in economics to those of distribution, so that the economic phenomena he explained with his law of value are only those mainly concerning the distribution of income. Ricardo did not consider the fact that the essence of the phenomena of production, the reverse of those of distribution, or rather the factor that conditions them, cannot be understood without the law of value, that the mechanism of the current capitalist mode of production and the phenomena taking place there cannot be truly explained without elucidating the phenomena of value on both the production side and the distribution side, on the basis of the law of value. Though, of course, when he examined the problems of distribution, he could not avoid mentioning to some extent the problems of production, which actually and naturally conditions the former.

(4) As Ricardo's political economy is developed in an abstract and hypothetical way, his method of research seems to us to be excessively deductive; his doctrine seems at first sight to be altogether alien from the actual situations of the time. But in fact his theory of value, his doctrine are in such intimate relation to the actual phenomena of the time that we can scarcely find other similar examples. The abstract method of explanation does not always entail a deductive method of research. He did not argue his theory of value as such but advanced it as the fundamental explanatory principle to be used to clarify contemporary practical problems. Although *The High Price of Bullion, A Proof of the Depreciation of Bank Notes* and many other pamphlets he published were quite difficult to understand, they attracted the attention of many readers and were repeatedly reprinted. This was because they contained fundamental elucidations of the important practical problems of the time and so obliged those who were interested in these problems to take them into consideration. The unified principle penetrating them is his labour theory of value, which testifies to the fact that his theory of value is not foreign to practical problems. This attitude of Ricardo may have come naturally from his practical career as a stockbroker, far from the academic world. It is one of the vices to which academics are liable that their arguments are not reflections in thought of practical phenomena, but deteriorate to fictitious and useless abstract reasoning. In this sense, I think that Ricardo's attitude in this regard deserves great respect. In all likelihood, his works and his speeches in Parliament exerted a very great influence on the politicians and business people of his time as a guideline for their practical political orientations.

Cannan writes: 'Among all the delusions which prevail as to the history of English political economy, there is none greater than the belief that the economics of the Ricardian school and period were of an almost wholly abstract and unpractical character' (Cannan, *History of Theories of Production and Distribution*, 3rd ed., [P.S. King, 1917,] p. 383). And Patten writes: 'It is a mistake, however, to assume that the deductive reasoning with which we are now so familiar was the work of Ricardo. He was a true economist, working from the concrete facts by which he was surrounded, gradually broadening his generalizations as his study of the facts became more complete' (Patten, *The Development of English Thoughts*, 1899, p. 310. On this point, see the following works: Gide and Rist, *Histoire des doctrines économiques*, p. 169. Dunbar, 'Ricardo's Use of Facts', *Quarterly Journal of Economics*, Vol. I, [Oct. 1886,] pp. 474–6. Lewinski, *Founders of Economics [Political Economy]*, [P.S. King, 1922,] p. 114. Cannan, 'Ricardo in Parliament', [*The*] *Economic Journal*, V. II, [1892,] pp. 247–261). This must be self-evident to those who have ever read Ricardo. Nevertheless, there still seem to be a considerable number of commentators holding an erroneous idea about this point. It must be firmly expunged.

(5) The objects of Ricardo's study are thus the current phenomena of the time, and his method of study can never be said to be wholly deductive. But it is also undeniable that his method of explanation is hypothetical, since the objects of elucidation are themselves of quite an abstract nature. But insofar as economics is an independent science, it is natural that it should 'put these immediate and temporary effects quite aside', and investigate 'the permanent state of things which will result from them' (*Letters of Ricardo to Malthus*, p. 127 [of the 24th January 1817, VII/120]. On this attitude of Ricardo, see also *Letters of Ricardo to Malthus*, pp. 18, 96, 166–7 [of the 22nd October, 1811, VI/64, of the 07th October 1815, VI/294, of the 04th May 1820, VIII/184]). In other words, economics does not only pay attention to the external and temporary phenomena, it also seeks to elucidate their immanent mechanisms and relations. It is natural too that the economic categories and laws obtained in this way should be abstract. The abstraction in this case is abstraction from the facts and never speculative imagination outside the facts. In this sense, the abstract propositions and theories of Ricardo are not to be criticised. It is even said that the shortcomings of his doctrine come rather from his insufficient capacity for abstract thinking (Marx, *Theorien über den Mehrwert [Theories of surplus value]*, II, 1, S. 37, 72. [MEGA^{②}, II/3, S.840–1, 863]). Before him, political economy had gradually been endowed with scientific content through the works of Quesnay and Smith, but in many cases economic doctrine remained within the framework of common-sense explanation and description. Trying to determine the basic laws penetrating every external phenomenon, Ricardo advanced political economy one step further as a science. The fact that the terms 'the science of political economy' and 'the law of political economy' are not found in Smith but in Ricardo is consistent with the essence of his political economy (needless to say, the 'science' mentioned here does not mean a well-organised whole of superficial forms, modalities, classifications,

systems etc.). However, Ricardo failed to consider the historical development of things; he did not see economic phenomena from the historical, evolutionary point of view, as ever-changing. His shortcoming consists in considering them as natural, static and fixed. As a result, it is inevitable that his writings should only include a few historical illustrations and exemplifications, along with his theoretical descriptions for empirically proving them.

(6) Not a few elements in Ricardo's theory of value and economic doctrine have exerted direct and indirect influences on the economists of later times. Apart from the natural differences of opinion among commentators, his theory of differential rent has been adopted on the whole by later economists, and his theory of wages is still considered by some economists as a representative theory founded on the cost of production of wages. His theory of international trade (principle of the comparative cost of production), theory of money (quantitative theory of money), and theory of taxation still maintain direct and indirect dominant positions in today's economics. Not only has Ricardo's economic doctrine thus exerted great influence on the economics of later times, but it has also often been adopted as the foundation for social movements, which have used it in various ways and directions. His theory of rent was used by land socialists as the grounds for their land nationalization policy. His labour theory of value was adopted as a theoretical foundation of utopian socialism by the Ricardian socialists like Thompson, Edmonds and Bray to begin with, but also by all sorts of sentimental, speculative socialists like Proudhon, Rodbertus, etc. And his theory of wages was used by some socialists, represented by Lassalle, as the sole foundation of the movement for the emancipation of labourers through the establishment of productive associations. However, the most important of the influences of Ricardo's doctrine on both economic thinking and social movement is probably that on the economic and socialist theory of Marx. For this reason, Ricardo's doctrine is said to have been dialectically developed and completed in the hands of Marx. Putting aside the possible positive and negative judgments on these various influences, it is undeniable that Ricardo's economic doctrine has exerted, in these respects, an almost incomparably great influence on subsequent economic thinking (in addition, some of the most renowned economists like Marshall, Dietzel, Amonn, Cassel etc. have considered Ricardo as the founder or the most important figure of theoretical economics and sought to establish their own economic theory by adopting and developing Ricardo's economics in various directions).

In spite of the diverse praise and criticism of Ricardo, probably nobody can deny the greatness of the influence that his theory of value and hence his economic theory has exerted on economics in posterity, and the importance credited to him in the history of economic thought. Apart from the eulogy of Ricardo by McCulloch, who recognized and popularised Ricardo's doctrine as it was or rather superficially, we can give other examples of the tributes paid to Ricardo. 'Ricardo is in fact by general consent recognized as the greatest economist of the nineteenth century' (Cossa [L.], *An Introduction to the Study of Political Economy*, [Macmillan,] 1893, p. 311). 'His *Principles of Political Economy* [is] a work of originality and profundity so remarkable that it marks an epoch in the history of our science, though, to be sure, its good points are overstated by such enthusiastic partisans as MacCulloch and De Quincey' (Cossa, *An Introduction to the Study of Political Economy*, p. 313). 'There are many whose reasoning is more perfect, many whose ideas are more clearly expressed, but few have attained the commanding position of Ricardo in economic theory' (Patten, 'The Interpretation of Ricardo', *The Quarterly Journal of Economics*, Vol. VIII, 1893. Included in *Essays in Economic Theory*, 1923, p. 144). And Marx, who seldom praised others, said the following of Ricardo as the greatest economist: 'Although encompassed by this bourgeois horizon, Ricardo analyses bourgeois economy, whose deeper layers differ essentially from its surface appearance, with such theoretical acumen that Lord Brougham could say of him: "Mr. Ricardo seemed as if he had dropped from another planet"' (Marx, *Zur Kritik der politischen Ökonomie [Contribution to a Critique of Political Economy]*, 8 Aufl., 1921, S. 43–4. [MEGA②, II/2, Dietz Verlag, 1980, S.138]). Though each with different intentions, all of these authors are unanimous in emphasizing the merit and importance of Ricardo in political economy.

Since Ricardo's labour theory of value and the whole of his economic theory that it underpins has exerted a great influence on the economic thinking of later times, naturally a considerable number of interpretations and criticisms of this theory of value have appeared up to the present. However, because of its serious, profound and comprehensive nature, Ricardo's doctrine has always left inexhaustible room for later research. Its vast and great influence, along with the considerable difficulty of his text, has given rise to an almost incomparable diversity of criticisms and interpretations of his theory of value, without allowing a consensus to be reached.

Ricardo's theory of value seems to have already been clarified and criticized in considerable detail by the Ricardo scholars like Gonner, Hollander and Diehl to begin with, as well as by such authorities as Marshall, Dietzel, Amonn, etc., and the interpretations of these scholars appear to be recognized as appropriate in academia today. But I am sceptical as to whether these interpretations and criticisms sufficiently communicate the original intention of Ricardo. It is precisely for this reason that I attempt here a study of my own on Ricardo's theory of value. The following words of Bonar and Amonn, made public on the occasion of the centenary commemoration of Ricardo's death, express what I mean to say, though in a somewhat different way: 'The hundredth anniversary of David Ricardo is best commemorated by fresh study of his works' (Bonar, 'Ricardo's Ingot Plan, a centenary tribute', *The Economic Journal*, 1923, Vol. XXXIII, pp. 281–304 [quotation from p. 281]). 'The present task in the field of our science is not to replace Ricardo, as the constructors of the new system have believed, but to *understand* and *further develop* his thoughts' (Amonn, A., *Ricardo als Begründer der theoretischen Nationalökonomie*, 1924, Vorwort [, S.IV., italics in original]).

Section 2. Attitudes of interpretation and criticism of Ricardo's theory of value

As we have seen in the previous chapter, Ricardo's theory of value occupies an extremely important place in the history of economic thought, and its influence on academia and the business world is so great, that it has given rise to number-less criticisms and interpretations. Moreover, the attitudes underlying these criticisms and interpretations are necessarily much diversified and manifold in themselves, because the composition and content of his theory of value are complicated and profound and they are not expressed simply and clearly.[1] Furthermore, the confused conditions of the present day academic world with regard to the problems of economic value continue to aggravate this situation. In fact, it may be said without exaggeration that there is no single important point in Ricardo's theory of value for which different interpretations do not exist.

The main points on which the criticisms of Ricardo's doctrine are directed are: (1) his methods of research and explanation, his attitudes; (2) his theory of value; (3) his general theory of distribution (theories of rent, wages and profits); (4) theories of foreign trade, money and taxation; (5) his practical policy theory and (6) his views on social philosophy, etc. Since these theories are divided parts of a whole, we can best grasp his true intention on these points only by understanding them in the light of a unified principle penetrating and determining the whole. And since this unified principle is nothing other than his labour theory of value, we are to examine in the following mainly the attitudes of interpretation and criticism of his theory of value. The criticisms of other points will be mentioned only insofar as necessary. Besides, in this section as introduction to the study of Ricardo's theory of value, we are to present only a small number of scientifically important and original criticisms with their works. There will be occasions in the later parts of this chapter to examine their detail and other criticisms. In the following, I dare to classify these criticisms into three categories, on the whole in accordance with a small number of conventional streams of the value doctrine. I am not aiming here to explain and describe systematically the relation of these three critical attitudes to Ricardo's theory of value and their reciprocal relations. These three will be presented on the same level, side by side.

1   Fundamental opposition to Ricardo's theory of value understood as a labour theory of value.

Needless to say, those who take this position are theorists of subjective value in a position absolutely opposite to Ricardo's theory. It was Jevons who declared this position very early in England. In *Theory of Political Economy*, he squarely opposed Ricardo's labour theory of value, saying that: 'repeated reflection and inquiry have led me to the somewhat novel opinion, that *value depends entirely upon utility*. Prevailing opinions make labour rather than utility the origin of value; and there are even those who distinctly assert that labour is the *cause* of value. I show, on the contrary, that we have only to trace out carefully the natural laws of the variation of utility, as depending upon the quantity of commodity in our possession, in order to arrive at a satisfactory theory of exchange' (Jevons, W.S., *Theory of Political Economy*, 4th ed., 1911, p. 1 [italics in original]). The incisive criticism of Ricardo by Jevons contained in the second edition of this work – 'When at length a true system of Economics comes to be established, it will be seen that that able but wrong-headed man, David Ricardo, shunted the car of Economic science on to a wrong line' (Jevons, *Theory of Political Economy*, preface to the 2nd ed., p.li.) – has become the subject of many disagreements.

Next, it is self-evident that the theorists of marginal utility on the Continent – Menger, Walras, Böhm-Bawerk, Wieser etc. – stood unanimously in direct opposition to Ricardo's labour theory of value. Böhm, among others, dismisses Ricardo's theory of value simply by saying that his fundamental positions 'are false, as everyone to-day knows' (Böhm-Bawerk, *Annals of the American Academy of Political Science*, 1890, Oct., p. 252).

The economists of the subjective school were right thus to interpret Ricardo's theory of value as a pure labour theory of value, but it cannot be affirmed so easily that Ricardo shunted the car of Economic science on to a wrong line, or that his fundamental attitude to the theory of value was entirely erroneous. However, this kind of critical attitude must be regarded as quite natural from these theorists' own standpoint on the theory of value. The criticisms of Ricardo's theory of value by the scholars who currently adopt the theory of marginal utility are generally of this kind.

2   Those who discern in Ricardo's theory of value both subjective and objective attitudes and therefore mean to approve it.

This applies to the interpretations of Ricardo by Marshall, Dietzel and others – economists adopting the position of a so-called eclectic theory of value. Marshall made clear this critical attitude, in claiming that Jevons' attack on Ricardo in England was not always justifiable, and Dietzel did the same in contradicting the criticisms of Ricardo advanced by Böhm-Bawerk etc. on the Continent.

Marshall writes the following in his *Principles of Economics*: 'Ricardo's theory of cost of production in relation to value occupies so important a place in the history of economics that any misunderstanding as to its real character must necessarily be very mischievous; and unfortunately it is so expressed as almost to invite misunderstanding. In consequence there is a widely spread belief that it has needed to be reconstructed by the present generation of economists. [. . .] the foundations of the theory as they were left by Ricardo remain intact [. . .] much has been added to them, [. . .] very much has been built upon them, but [. . .] little has been taken from them" (Marshall, *Principles of Political Economy* [*Economics*], p. 503), and he explains in detail the reason for this in Appendix I entitled 'Ricardo's theory of value' (Marshall, pp. 813–21).

Ashley published an article refuting this interpretation by Marshall in *The Economic Journal*, Vol. I, no.1, seeking to demonstrate with many arguments that the body of Ricardo's theory of value can never be a labour theory of value (Ashley, 'The Rehabilitation of Ricardo', *The Economic Journal*, Vol. I, [1891,] pp. 477–89). Marshall subsequently inserted a footnote in the above Appendix, replying to this refutation by Ashley.

Dietzel interprets Ricardo's theory of value almost with the same attitude as Marshall, pointing out the error in the criticisms of Ricardo's theory of value by the theorists of marginal utility on the Continent. At the end of the previous [19th] century, they held vehement debates around this problem of interpretation for a time on the pages of *Conrad Jahrbücher* [*Jahrbücher für Nationalökonomie und Statistik*] in Germany. (The following are the main articles concerning these debates: Dietzel, 'Die klassische Werttheorie und die Theorie vom Grenznutzen', *Conrad Jahrbücher*, 1890, Bd. XX; 'Zur klassischen Wert und Preistheorie', 1891, Bd. I, F. III; Böhm-Bawerk, 'Ein Zwischenwort zur Werttheorie', *Conrad Jahrbücher*, 1890, Bd. XXI; 'Wert, Kosten und Grenznutzen', *Conrad Jahrbücher*, 1892, Bd. III, F. III. This article is included in his recently published *Gesammelte Schriften*, 1924.) We will examine Dietzel's position in detail, but his opinion can be summarized as follows: 'the theory of value, although incomplete in some particular points, has on the whole obtained a definitively impeccable answer from Ricardo' (Dietzel, the first article cited above, S. 562). 'After so much turmoil and battle, Ricardo's double formula – here cost, there utility – remains completely intact. The theory of marginal utility has not destroyed the old building, but only extended it' (Dietzel, *Theoretische Socialökonomik*, 1895, S. 296).

It may not be a correct interpretation to find in Ricardo an attitude of subjective estimation along with the objective one, as Marshall and Dietzel do. I am afraid that this interpretation treats Ricardo with too much favour. Ricardo's theory of value must be regarded in essence as a coherently objective labour theory of value. Incidentally, Amonn adopts a critical attitude similar to that of Dietzel (Amonn, *Ricardo als Begründer der theoretischen Nationalökonomie*, 1924).

The following criticism of Ricardo's theory of value, though very similar to those seen above, is slightly different. It affirms that Ricardo invariably held an attitude of objective estimation, whether it was a labour theory of value or a theory of cost of production, but that this position is not capable of truly solving the problem of value. According to this criticism, we should not overlook the other factors – subjective estimation and various other elements – which play a role in the determination of value. A considerable number of scholars have adopted such a critical attitude, starting with economists from the historical school and from the social-legal school, like Diehl (Diehl, *Sozialwissenschaftliche Erläuterungen zu David Ricardo's Grundgesetzen der Volkswirtschaft und Besteuerung*, 2 Bde., 1905) etc. Apart from their interpretation of Ricardo, the author cannot agree with this critical attitude (one can add Cassel, who interprets Ricardo's theory of value as a cost-of-production theory of value and constitutes his own theory of price in developing Ricardo according to his interpretation (Cassel, *Theoretische Sozialökonomie*, 3 Aufl., 1923, ‚Die Produktionskostentheorie Ricardos etc.', *Zeitschrift f. d. ges. Staatswiss.*, 1901).

3   Those who understand Ricardo's theory of value as a labour theory of value and approve it.

Among those who pertain to this category there exist the following two (or three) kinds of attitude.

(A) Those who accept Ricardo's labour theory of value externally and superficially almost as it is. This is the attitude equally adopted by the so-called Ricardians who gathered around him when Ricardo's theory of value was the predominant theory of value of the time. The pure exponents of Ricardo like McCulloch, De Quincey, James Mill etc. all adopted this attitude. We can see from their texts in defence of Ricardo's theory of value and from their own writings how they embraced and recommended it. McCulloch, the vulgarizer, who (superficially) paraphrased almost the whole of Ricardo's doctrine, devoted his whole lifetime to diffusing and promoting it. We can find tributes to Ricardo throughout his writings. For example, when commenting and recommending the first edition of Ricardo's *Principles* in the *Edinburgh Review*, he wrote: 'he [Ricardo] has done more for its [political economy's] improvement than any other writer, with perhaps the single exception of Adam Smith' (McCulloch, 'On Ricardo's Principles of Political Economy and Taxation', *Edinburgh Review*, 1818, June, p. 60). And in McCulloch's work *The Literature of Political Economy*, published more than 20 years after the death of Ricardo, he devoted another hearty eulogy to Ricardo. He wrote as follows:

> This is a most able, original and profound work. Its appearance formed a new era in the history of the science. Exclusive of many valuable correlative discussions, Mr. Ricardo has traced the source and limiting principle of exchangeable value, and has exhibited the laws which determine the distribution of various products of art and industry among the various ranks and orders of society. The powers of mind displayed in these investigations, the dexterity with which the most abstruse and difficult questions are unravelled, the sagacity displayed in tracing the operation of general principles, in disentangling them from such as are of a secondary and accidental nature, and in perceiving and estimating their remotest consequences, have never been surpassed, and will forever secure the name of Ricardo a conspicuous place amongst those who have done most to unfold the mechanism of society, and to perfect this science.
>
> McCulloch, *The Literature of Political Economy*, 1845, p. 16

McCulloch's *Principles of Political Economy*, 1825, and James Mill's *Elements of Political Economy*, 1821, both follow Ricardo's doctrine, and De Quincey's articles and works on political economy (*Dialogues of Three Templars on Political*

Economy, 1824, his own *Works*, Vol. IV, pp. 176–257, Masson's *Works*, pp. 37–112 and *The Logic of Political Economy*, 1844) are based on Ricardo or defend him.

These Ricardians, with McCulloch at their head, thus dedicated the highest approval and respect to Ricardo as one of the greatest economists, leaving no room for any subsequent improvement of political economy. But their interpretations of his theory of value can never be called legitimate. Detecting contradictions between the external phenomena and its immanent essence, Ricardo endeavoured to clarify such contradictions, albeit insufficiently, but for McCulloch and his fellows there existed no such contradictions between phenomena and essence. For them there were only external phenomena. While praising the greatness of Ricardo's theory of value, in fact they failed to understand its essence. It was all the more beyond their reach to identify and remedy its weaknesses. This is why they are called the "vulgar" economists.

Among the so-called Ricardian socialists and humanist socialists who grasped Ricardo's labour theory of value superficially to use as the grounds for their socialist theories, we can name W. Thompson (*An Inquiry into the Principles of the Distribution of Wealth*, 1824), T. Hodgskin (*Labour Defended against the Claims of Capital*, 1825), Bray (*Labour's Wrongs and Labour's Remedy*, 1839), T. R. Edmonds (*Practical, Moral and Political Economy*, 1828), and also Proudhon (*Système des contradictions économiques ou philosophie de la misère*, 1846), Rodbertus (*Zur Erkenntnis unsrer staatswissenschaftlichen Zustände*, 1842) etc. They dreamed of realizing an egalitarian society of free exchange in this actual capitalist society by using Ricardo's labour theory of value for their own purposes. Needless to say, the egalitarian application of his theory of value by such philanthropic, humanitarian and utopian socialists is neither a right interpretation or application of it nor its natural development. It may be a matter of course that no one belonging to this class (A) has ever critically studied Ricardo's theory of value in itself.

(B) Those who think that Ricardo's theory of value is essentially a labour theory of value, but that it includes various defects because of its incompleteness, explaining Ricardo's ambiguous attitude towards the labour theory of value which he had to abandon halfway. For them, the correct interpretation of Ricardo's theory of value consists precisely in extending and developing it as a labour theory of value in its legitimate form, which is also the orientation we should take. Such was Marx's critical attitude towards Ricardo's theory of value. Marx's theory of value is actually an extended and enriched version of Ricardo's. Starting with Ricardo's labour theory of value, Marx derived and developed from it the concepts that Ricardo had not made sufficiently clear from the standpoint of dialectical and historical materialism: abstract human labour, socially necessary labour, hence the veritable value of commodities, money and capital, labour power, surplus value, etc. In so doing, Marx revealed the mechanism of the actual capitalist mode of production to indicate the laws of its historical movement. He thought that many of these ideas could already be found, though in insufficient form and degree, in the classical theory of value, particularly that of Ricardo, which he considered as the precondition for developing his own economic theory, to which he granted the principal position in the history of science. Volume 2 of Marx's *Theories of Surplus-Value* is devoted to his comprehensive and meticulous studies on Ricardo, which are probably the most far-ranging and detailed studies of Ricardo.

Which of the above interpretations and criticisms hits the essence of Ricardo's theory of value? We will examine the details in the following parts of this chapter. In concluding this section I would simply like to assert one point: Ricardo's doctrine on value is a natural product of a consciousness nourished in the economic conditions of England at that time, representing the early stage of development of the capitalist mode of production, where all the ills specific to that mode were already emerging, but the conflict of class interests between capitalist and labourer had not yet risen to consciousness. His doctrine is therefore a faithful reflection in thought of the economic relations of the time and hence it could be qualified as a science.

Section 3. Substance and measure of value – immanent measure of value and external measure of value

In relation to the question of whether Ricardo is considering the relative value or the absolute value when he discusses value, there arises another question: whether he is explaining the cause of value or the measure of value in his labour theory of value. In other words, in the fundamental proposition of Ricardo's labour theory of value, according to which the exchangeable value of a commodity depends on the relative quantity of labour expended on its production, is he explaining the measure of value or its cause, or both of them in confusing them, or both of them correctly? This is a problem which has been discussed after Ricardo and Malthus, along with the same problem in Adam Smith's theory of value, by a number of scholars and critics up to the present time, starting with James Mill, Thomas De Quincey, Samuel Bailey etc., without a consensus ever being reached.

Many of the critics on this problem affirm the need to distinguish between the cause and the measure of value. They attribute the ambiguities and disorders found in Smith's and Ricardo's theories of value mainly to the confusion between these two concepts. For example, Bailey wrote as follows:

> No department of political economy has suffered more from this indefiniteness of purpose, and ambiguity of language, than that which is occupied with investigating the measures and causes of value. It would seem, on a first view, that the ideas of measuring and causing value were sufficiently distinct to escape all danger of being confounded; yet it is remarkable, that both the ideas themselves, and the terms by which they are expressed, have been mixed and interchanged and substituted, with an apparently total unconsciousness of any difference existing between them.
>
> [Bailey], *A Critical Dissertation on the Nature,*
> *Measures, and Causes of Value; chiefly in Reference to*
> *the Writings of Mr. Ricardo and his Followers,*
> London, 1825, pp. 170–1

And John Stuart Mill wrote in his *Principles of Political Economy*:

> The idea of a Measure of Value must not be confounded with the idea of the regulator, or determining principle, of value. When it is said by Ricardo and others, that the value of a thing is regulated by quantity of labour, they do not mean the quantity of labour for which the thing will exchange, but the quantity required for producing it. This, they mean to affirm, determines its value; causes it to be of the value it is, and of no other. But when Adam Smith and Malthus say that labour is a measure of value, they do not mean the labour by which the thing was or can be made, but the quantity of labour which it will exchange for, or purchase; in other words, the value of the thing estimated in labour. And they do not mean that this regulates the general exchange value of the thing, or has any effect in determining what that value shall be, but only ascertains what it is, and whether and how much it varies from time to time and from place to place. *To confound these two ideas would be much the same thing as to overlook the distinction between the thermometer and the fire.*
>
> Mill, J.S., *Principles of Political Economy*,
> ed. by Ashley, p. 568. Italics by Mori

In this section I am going to examine this problem, to see whether these critics really make clear the essence of Ricardo's theory of value. That is to say, I will question the significance of interpreting and criticizing Ricardo's theory of value by distinguishing as they do between the measure and cause of value, to make clear finally that their interpretations do not yet grasp Ricardo's attitude on this problem. First, I will quote some of the passages of Ricardo himself concerning this problem, before considering especially what Ricardo calls the invariable measure of value, and finally concluding this chapter with my own views on this problem.

The passages relative to this problem are to be found for the most part in *Principles*. The following are quotations from the original text [not the Japanese translation. All italics are by Mori].

1 The exchangeable value of these commodities, or the rule which determines how much of one shall be given in exchange for another, *depends* almost exclusively *on* the comparative quantity of labour expended on each.

> Ricardo, *On the Principles of Political Economy and Taxation*,
> p. 7, ed. by Gonner [I/12]

2 If the quantity of labour realized in commodities, *regulate* their exchangeable value, every increase of the quantity of labour must augment the value of that commodity on which it is exercised, as every diminution must lower it.

> Ricardo, *On the Principles of Political Economy and Taxation*,
> p. 8 [I/13]

3   Adam Smith, who so accurately defined *the original source* of exchange-
    able value [. . .] has himself erected another *standard measure of value*.
                    Ricardo, *On the Principles of Political Economy*
                                          and Taxation, p. 8 [I/13–4]

4   [. . .] or in other words, that it is the comparative quantity of commodi-
    ties which labour will produce, that *determines* their present or past rela-
    tive value, and not the comparative quantities of commodities, which are
    given to the labourer in exchange for his labour.
                    Ricardo, *On the Principles of Political Economy*
                                             and Taxation, p. 11 [I/17]

5   In speaking, however, of labour, as being *the foundation of* all value, and
    the relative quantity of labour as almost exclusively *determining* the rela-
    tive value of commodities [. . .].
                    Ricardo, *On the Principles of Political Economy*
                                             and Taxation, p. 15 [I/20]

6   *In making labour the foundation of* the value of commodities, and the
    comparative quantity of labour which is necessary to their production,
    *the rule which determines the respective quantities of goods which shall be
    given in exchange for each other*, we must not be supposed to deny the
    accidental and temporary deviations of the actual or market price of
    commodities from this, their primary and natural price.
                    Ricardo, *On the Principles of Political Economy*
                                             and Taxation, p. 65 [I/88]

7   A franc is not a measure of value for anything, but for a quantity of the
    same metal of which francs are made, unless francs, and the thing to be
    measured, can be referred to some other measure which is common to
    both. This, I think, they can be, for they are both the result of labour;
    and, therefore, labour is *a common measure,* by which their real as well
    as their relative value may be estimated.
                    Ricardo, *On the Principles of Political Economy*
                                      and Taxation, pp. 268–9² [I/284]

We can see clearly from these passages that according to Ricardo, the exchangeable value of a commodity 'depends on' and is 'in proportion [to]' the quantity
of labour expended; that the quantity of labour 'regulates' and 'determines' the
exchangeable value, and that the quantity of labour is the 'source' of exchangeable value and its 'measure', 'standard measure' or 'foundation'. Or again, that
the quantity of labour is the 'only circumstance' in determining the exchangeable
value.

What view of the cause and measure of value did Ricardo have in mind when
he wrote these passages?

The measure of value Ricardo speaks of here means a measure in the sense
that the labour bestowed is the measure of value because it is the component

of value. However, in addition to the measure of value in this sense (what I call the immanent measure of value), Ricardo also brings into play an invariable measure of value (what I call the external measure of value, i.e., the general form of expression of value). He inquired whether there exists a commodity, which, produced with an invariable quantity of labour, can serve to measure accurately the value of other commodities compared with it. And he affirmed that such a commodity does not exist. Whether consciously or not, he can be said to have in fact treated these two measures of value. In this section I am going to examine his views on these measures of value.

Let me now cite some of the main passages on this problem from Ricardo's text.

> When commodities varied in relative value, it would be desirable to have the means of ascertaining which of them fell and which rose in real value, and this could be effected only by comparing them one after another with some invariable standard measure of value, which should itself be subject to none of the fluctuations to which other commodities are exposed. Of such a measure it is impossible to be possessed, because there is no commodity which is not itself exposed to the same variations as the things, the value of which is to be ascertained; that is, there is none which is not subject to require more or less labour for its production.
>
> Ricardo, *Principles* [Gonner's edition], p. 36 [I/43–4]

Hence, according to Ricardo, it is because (1) there is no commodity which does not come to require more or less labour for its production, and (2) the proportion of fixed capital required for the production of money is generally different from that required for the production of many other commodities, that the value of money must undergo relative variations arising from the rise or fall in wages. Moreover, (3) the fixed capital used for the production of money and that used for the production of other commodities to be compared with it differ in their durability, so that their relative values vary with the variations in wages just as in the previous case (Ricardo, *Principles* [Gonner's edition], pp. 36–7 [I/44]).

> That commodity is alone invariable, which at all times requires the same sacrifice of toil and labour to produce it. Of such a commodity we have no knowledge, but we may hypothetically argue and speak about it, as if we had; and may improve our knowledge of the science, by shewing distinctly the absolute inapplicability of all the standards which have been hitherto adopted.[3]
>
> Ricardo, *Principles* [Gonner's edition], p. 260 [I/275]

These arguments of Ricardo on the invariable measure of value were energetically criticised by Bailey, from his well-known position on the theory of value.

According to Bailey, since value is a relative relation between two commodities mutually exchanged at the same time, a comparison between the values of a commodity at two different moments means nothing other than comparing the two different relations it has with another commodity at these two moments. This is a necessary consequence of Bailey's purely relativistic definition of value. However, when Ricardo says that a commodity produced by the same quantity of labour has an invariable value, he means that its value at any given moment is precisely the same as its value at another moment. From Bailey's viewpoint, this is not so in relation to another commodity but in relation to itself. Thus, for Bailey, not only is it physically impossible for such commodity to exist as an invariable measure of value, but thinking about it is already contradictory in itself.

Bailey then continued as follows, asserting that the term 'measure of value' used by Ricardo suffers from some confusion:

> He incessantly identifies constancy in the quantity of producing labour with constancy of value. Hence he maintains, that if we could find any commodity invariable in the circumstances of its production, it would be in the first place invariable in value; and, secondly, it would indicate, or would enable us to ascertain, the variations in value of other commodities.
>
> It is curious enough that he should never have clearly discerned what such a commodity would really serve to indicate: it would not, as he asserts, serve to indicate the variations in the value of commodities, but the variations in the circumstances of their production. It would enable us to ascertain, not any fluctuations in value, but in which commodity those fluctuations had originated. He has in truth confounded two perfectly distinct ideas, namely, *measuring the value of commodities*, and *ascertaining in which commodity, and in what degree, the causes of value have varied*.
>
> Bailey, *A Critical Dissertation*, 1825,
> pp. 121–2 [italics in original]

In other words, Ricardo sought to ascertain, by the invariability in the quantity of labour, not the variations in value existing among two or more commodities, but the variations in the quantity of labour that produced them.

> In this way, according to Bailey, although Mr. Ricardo is professedly speaking of a commodity produced by invariable labour, in the character of a measure of value, he is in reality, without being conscious of the difference, altogether occupied with the consideration of that commodity as capable of indicating variations in the producing labour of other commodities. Instead of a measure of value, such a commodity as he describes would be a measure of labour, or a medium of ascertaining the varying quantities of labour which commodities required to produce them. Before it could be employed in regard to any object, the value of that object, or its relation to the standard commodity, must be given, and then all that could be deduced from the datum would be the quantity of labour bestowed on its production.
>
> (Bailey, *A Critical Dissertation*, 1825, pp. 127–8)

Bailey's criticism of the invariable measure of value proposed by Ricardo is a natural consequence of his definition of value. There are a number of defects in his criticism, but as they relate to the subject of his theory of value in general, we will pass them over. In opposition to Ricardo, he only accepted the measurement of value by simultaneous relative comparison of commodities, excluding the comparison of value at different moments, and for him money was the only possible measure of value (external measure). In this regard he must be considered superior to Ricardo, although he was far from understanding sufficiently the essence of money. It must be said that Marx was right in analysing Bailey's attitude as follows:

> Bailey's book has rendered a good service insofar as the objections he raises help to clear up the confusion between 'measure of value' expressed in money as a commodity along with other commodities, and the immanent measure and substance of value. But if he had analysed money as a 'measure of value', not only as a quantitative measure but as a qualitative transformation of commodities, he would have arrived at a correct analysis of value. Instead of this, he contents himself with a mere superficial consideration of the external 'measure of value' – which already presupposes value – and remains rooted in a purely frivolous approach to the question.
>
> Marx, *Theorien*, III, S.163 [MEGA②, II/3.4,
> Dietz Verlag, [Ost-]Berlin, 1979, S.132–4]

Ricardo defined the quantity of labour expended for the production of a commodity as the (immanent) measure of its value, and in order to measure and express externally the variations in its value, he sought to determine whether there exists any commodity requiring an invariable quantity of labour for its production hence capable of measuring the value of other commodities by comparison with it. He concluded that such a commodity cannot exist, and therefore that money cannot be such an invariable measure of value either. Nevertheless, he still considered it indispensable to ascertain the essence of such a measure, in order to obtain a correct theory.

He then tried to measure, by means of this invariable measure of value, the variations in the value of commodities at different periods in time. But this attitude cannot be said to be based on a legitimate understanding of the problem of the measure of value. In this respect, Bailey's criticism is justified. Marx commented on this point as follows:

> The interest in comparing the value of commodities in different historical periods, is, indeed, not an *economic* interest as such, [but] an academic interest.

According to Marx,

> In order to measure the value of commodities – to establish an *external* measure of value – it is not necessary that the value of the commodity in

terms of which the other commodities are measured, should be invariable. (It must on the contrary be variable, as I have shown in the first part [*Contribution to the Critique of Political Economy*, 1859], because the measure of value is, and must be, a commodity since otherwise it would have no *immanent* measure in common with other commodities.) If, for example, the value of money changes, it changes to an equal degree in relation to all other commodities. Their relative values are therefore expressed in it just as correctly as if the value of money had remained unchanged.

Marx, a. a. O., S.157. [MEGA②, Ebenda, S. 1320,
italics in original]

Therefore, Ricardo's attitude must be fundamentally attributed to his insufficient understanding of the essence of money as the external measure of value, or as the general form of its expression.

To put this in more detail, Ricardo neglected the qualitative consideration of labour as the component content of value. In other words, he did not fully appreciate the fact that in mutually exchangeable commodities, there is a common component of abstract human labour that makes them equal to each other and exchangeable with each other. As a result, he did not recognise the fact that money is the general form of expression of this abstract human labour, and that it is therefore the general, universal measure of value for every commodity. This is a natural consequence of Ricardo's attitude in being occupied exclusively with the quantitative problems of value and failing to take into account its qualitative problems. Marx made clear the nature of Ricardo's invariable measure of value, when he wrote that 'the problem of an "invariable measure of value" was simply a spurious name for the quest for the concept, the nature, of *value* itself' (Marx, a. a. O., S.159, [MEGA②, Ebenda, S.1321, italics in original]).[4]

In the above I believe I have given an overview of what Ricardo says about the cause and measure of value and about the invariable measure of value in his theory of value. In the following I will conclude this section by summarising my interpretation and criticism.

Almost all of the interpretations and criticisms of this problem are founded on an incorrect understanding of the nature of the problem. Hence, they do not sufficiently clarify the matter in question here. To answer this question properly, I believe it is required first and foremost to have a good understanding of the following points:

(1) In Ricardo's theory of value, we find two concepts of the measure of value: the immanent measure of value in the proper sense of the term and the external, general and universal measure of value. The former is a measure of value in the sense that, since labour is value or substance of value, the quantity of labour (labour time) is the measure of value. The latter is a measure of value expressing generally and externally such an amount of value; it is the general and necessary form of expression of the amount of value (although Ricardo did not choose money, but an invariable measure of value, as the measure of value in this sense). Almost all the critics totally confuse these two concepts of

measure. Ricardo himself failed to differentiate them clearly, but he evidently treated these two measures *de facto*.

(2) The problem of the immanent measure of value (expended labour time) and its external measure (money) reduces to the problem of value, real value and relative value, exchangeable value and the 'general' form of expression of value. Therefore the former problem is solved of itself when the latter is elucidated.

Let me take first the immanent measure of value. It hardly comes into question whether Ricardo was considering mainly the cause of value or its measure with the concept of labour expended. Because the quantity of labour (measured by labour time, which in turn is standardized on divisions of time such as days and hours) is the measure of value of itself, since the labour is value or substance forming value, and on the contrary it is because the quantity of labour itself is value or substance forming value that it can be the measure of value. How can a quantity of what is not in itself value be the measure of its value? It is only natural that in Ricardo's theory of value, the substance of value and the measure of value in such a sense are argued in parallel and inseparably.

The immanent measure of value of commodities is thus the quantity of labour expended for their production, but it cannot be expressed externally of itself. There must be something else to express it externally. When the value of a certain quantity of commodity A is expressed by a certain quantity of commodity B, the latter is an external measure of value of the former. And what generally and universally expresses the values of many commodities is money. Other than the immanent measure of value, Ricardo sought to find out an invariable measure of value to express it generally and externally. The measure of value in this case does indeed correspond to the general external measure of value we are speaking of here, which cannot be other than money. But as he could not analyse and elucidate the essence of money, he was incapable of choosing money as such a measure. The general external measure of value is absent in Ricardo. This is an essential defect in his theory of value.

In such a context, debates have continued on the question of whether Ricardo sought to explain the cause of value or its measure. Some assert that he explained mainly the cause, because he affirmed the impossibility of the existence of such a measure, but others argue that he mainly addressed the measure of value, in view of his repeated arguments about such an invariable measure, even if its existence is impossible. But in my view they are all mistaken in examining which of these alternatives Ricardo intended to explain. Because in the labour theory of value in general and hence in Ricardo's theory of value too, such an external measure of value and the value itself are in such close relation to each other, just like the relation between the immanent measure of value and the value itself, that each of them must naturally be discussed inseparably from the other; one cannot be treated without the other. Therefore the fact that Ricardo was incapable of examining the general external measure of value in such a sense, shows at the same time that he could not elucidate sufficiently the substance and essence of value. The correct concept of the universal external measure of value cannot possibly be grasped without analysing fundamentally the substance of value and hence of labour. It is entirely erroneous to argue about the cause and measure of value in separating these two things. In comparing the cause and measure of value to heat and the thermometer, John Stuart Mill affirmed that we should not confuse the two. Superficially, these are of course to be distinguished. But why is heat measured by the thermometer? It is precisely because there exists something common to both of them, i.e. the heat. If a yardstick can measure the length of another object, it is because both of them have a common property of length. Likewise, the measure of value can naturally not measure value without being value itself.

In short, it can only be totally in vain to try to solve the problem of whether Ricardo was considering the cause of value or its measure (immanent and external). Since labour is the substance forming value, its quantity is the measure of value, and money as the necessary and general form of expression of such value measures generally and universally the quantity of value, of labour of every commodity. The substance of value, its immanent measure and its external measure constitute an inseparable unity. It is impossible to think about them one by one. They are in causal relation. Ricardo's study of them remained crude and immature.

Section 4. Natural price and market price

In the various cases of the use of fixed capital, Ricardo admitted the variations in the relative value of commodities caused by the variations in profits and wages. However, in claiming these variations to be quite insignificant, he invariably continued to take his original position, equating the relative value with the labour value. According to him, this law of labour value cannot undergo any alteration with the appearance of ground rent. Moreover, he argued that the market price of a commodity must eventually return to its natural price, despite a temporary deviation from its natural value, because the movement of capital searching for a higher profit from one branch of production to another will prevent such a deviation from lasting long. Thus, Ricardo strove to make clear that the standard of determination of the value of commodities always consists in its natural price, i.e., its labour value (or rather the price of production) and never in the relation between demand and supply, as claimed by some authors. This is the subject I will examine in this section, taken up in Chapter 4 of *Principles* ('On natural and market price') and in its supplement, Chapter 30 ('On the influence of demand and supply on prices'). This attitude of Ricardo, trying to observe the phenomena of value and price independently from the appearance of the movements of demand and supply, is the necessary consequence of his fundamental attitude trying to observe them on the basis of their laws, i.e., in their figures corresponding to their concepts. This must be said to be quite natural.

On the whole, Ricardo's explanation of these points, though somewhat different in its content from Smith's explanation of similar points, follows in the line of Smith's position. In this regard, Ricardo cannot be said to have advanced much from Smith. As we will see in detail below, he treated insufficiently only a small part of Smith's arguments on free competition, capital movement and the influence of average profits on the value and price of commodities.

By the way, since the natural price just mentioned is, as we will see later, the price of production as transformed (or, in Ricardo, 'modified') labour value rather than labour value itself, many scholars cannot be justified in their criticism of Ricardo's theory of value when they first advance his views on these natural and market prices in order to take his natural price as the starting point for his labour theory. It would be more natural to follow the order adopted by Ricardo himself, i.e., to treat this problem after the examination of what he calls the modifications of the labour theory of value (in fact a transformation of value into price of production).

In the following, I first present a brief outline of Ricardo's doctrine on natural and market prices, before seeking to criticize it. I will then examine in particular the significance Ricardo attributed to demand and supply in determining value and price, as well as some interpretations of this position of Ricardo.

At the beginning of Chapter 4 of *Principles* ('On natural and market price'), Ricardo wrote as follows:

> In making labour the foundation of the value of commodities, and the comparative quantity of labour which is necessary to their production, the rule which determines the respective quantities of goods which shall be given in exchange for each other, we must not be supposed to deny the accidental and temporary deviations of the actual or market price of commodities from this, their primary and natural price.
>
> In the ordinary course of events, there is no commodity which continues for any length of time to be supplied precisely in that degree of abundance, which the wants and wishes of mankind require, and therefore there is none which is not subject to accidental and temporary variations of price.
>
> It is only in consequence of such variations, that capital is apportioned precisely, in the requisite abundance and no more, to the production of the different commodities which happen to be in demand. With the rise or fall of price, profits are elevated above, or depressed below their general level, and capital is either encouraged to enter into, or is warned to depart from the particular employment in which the variation has taken place.
>
> Ricardo, *Principles* [Gonner's edition]., p. 65, [I/88]

Thus there arises a tendency to equalize all the rates of profits. This is because, according to Ricardo, every employer of capital invariably seeks to head for a more favourable use of capital, in abandoning a more unfavourable one. But, Ricardo says, it is extremely difficult to see how this capital movement occurs: it is probably realized not by a total change of employment by the manufacturer, but only by diminishing the quantity of capital invested in that employment. According to him, there exists constantly floating capital in society, which the manufacturers use more or less in general. When, for example, the demand for silk rises and that for cotton falls, a cotton producer does not move to the silk industry with his own capital, but discharges some of his hands and ceases his demand for accommodation from bankers or moneyed men. But for a silk manufacturer the contrary is the case. Namely, he tries to employ a greater number of hands, which *raises* his motive for borrowing money, and he will borrow more. Capital can, in this way, move from one employment to another without obliging the manufacturers to interrupt their habitual affairs.

Thus, by the movement of capital from an unfavourable branch of production to a favourable one, every industry comes naturally to obtain a certain average profit. However, according to the nature of different employments, some can be more advantageous than others in security, cleanliness, easiness and other respects, and in regard to these factors the former will have to content themselves with less profit compared with the latter. In consequence of this, said Ricardo, different rates of profit can survive permanently; for example, 20% for the employment of A, 25% for the employment of B and even 30% for the employment of C. This constitutes an exception or obstacle to the average profit.

After talking about the last subject above, Ricardo concluded this chapter by giving a general illustration, in which he supposed the following situation: all commodities are exchanged according to their natural prices. As a result, the profits on capital in every industry are exactly the same, or differ only by a quantity equal to the actual or imaginary benefit the agents would demand or forgo in their estimations. Now, if a change in fashion raises the demand for silk and decreases the demand for wool, the market price of silk will rise and that of wool will fall, although their natural prices, i.e., the quantities of labour necessary for their production, remain unchanged. As a result, the profit of silk manufacturers will rise over and above its general and average rate, while that of wool manufacturers will on the contrary fall below it. In such cases, capital and labour (wages undergoing the same influence as profits) will move from the manufacturing of wool to the more favourable manufacturing of silk, so that the increased demand for silk will be met. In this way, the market prices of these two commodities will again correspond to their natural prices and the general average rate of profits will be restored. In short, according to Ricardo,

> It is then the desire, which every capitalist has, of diverting his funds from a less to a more profitable employment, that prevents the market price of commodities from continuing for any length of time either much above, or much below their natural price. It is this competition which so adjusts the exchangeable value of commodities, that after paying the wages for the labour necessary to their production, and all other expenses required to put the capital employed in its original state of efficiency, the remaining value or overplus will in each trade be in proportion to the value of the capital employed.
>
> Ricardo, *Principles* [Gonner's edition]., pp. 68–9, [I/91]

In the above, I have presented an outline of Ricardo's explanation. In the following, I will examine in detail what he wanted to make clear. In short, he wanted to make clear that the determination of the value of a commodity does not depend on the effects of accidental temporary demand and supply, i.e., on the effects of individual subjective conscious estimations, but on its natural price (labour value or price of production). In other words, value is a socially and objectively regulated social entity. And for this explanation, he naturally presupposed the free inter-sectoral movement of capital and labour, free competition and the existence of an average profit accompanying them.

I will examine in detail in a later part of this chapter the significance of the law of demand and supply that Ricardo recognized in determining the value of a commodity. In the following, I will first examine in more detail Ricardo's doctrine that the market price of a commodity focuses ultimately on its natural price under the effects of capital movement and competition, in its relation to the essence of the labour theory of value. In so doing, we will see how far Ricardo understood the essence of the external, concrete phenomenal forms of the capitalist mode of production – the relation between market price and natural price – in distinguishing and legitimately relating such phenomenal forms and their immanent fundamental relations. It is precisely this point that I intend to make clear in this section.

As we have seen above, Ricardo sought to make clear that, because of the existence of the law of the average rate of profits and the free competition of capital, there exists a mechanism that ultimately restores the market price of a commodity to its natural price, which is in my view one of the influences of competition on the value and price of a commodity.

The competition induced among capitalists (entrepreneurs) by the existence of the law of average profits can exert two kinds of influence on the value and price of a commodity.

(1) The first is the influence of competition within the same branch of production on the value and price of a commodity. In this case, competition regulates the value of commodities in that branch of production to the value of the commodity produced by the quantity of labour socially necessary on average, i.e., produced under the average social conditions of production, bringing about the market value. In this case, the commodities requiring a quantity of labour that deviates from this average quantity, i.e., expending a quantity of labour *less than* the average – commodities produced under *better than average* conditions of production – can acquire a surplus profit equal to the difference between their individual value and the average value (i.e., the market value), which in the agricultural branch of production constitutes the rent. In other words, competition in this case gives rise to plural rates of profits in rendering the commodities of that branch of production saleable uniformly at an average value, the market value. In a word, the market value arises because there are different rates of profits in that branch of production, i.e., because they are not levelled out.

(2) The second is the influence on the value and price of a commodity of the competition among different branches of production. In this case,

competition gives rise to a price of production different from the value in each branch of production, by the law of the general average rate of profits. Competition in this case does not cause the price of production of a commodity to converge towards its value. It acts rather to the contrary. Therefore in such cases, value and the price of production can deviate durably from each other.

Thus, there are two different cases in the influence of competition on the value and price of a commodity. In the first case, we have equal value and price with different rates of profit (in such a case there is no need to distinguish between value and price), while in the second case, we have unequal values with an equal rate of profits or an equal price of production.

Here, Ricardo said nothing about the first case of competition, forming the market value of a commodity within a same branch of production and thus giving rise to surplus profits. What he considers is the second case, i.e., the influence of competition among different branches of production. But he does not argue exhaustively about this case. He treats only one of the two sides of the problem.

In this second case, it is possible to divide into two further cases the influence on the value and price of a commodity of the competition of capital that brings about an average rate of profits.

The first is the influence that tends to transform the value of a commodity into its price of production through the movement of capital from unfavourable to favourable branches of production, bringing about an average rate of profits.

The second is the influence leading to convergence between the actual market price of a commodity and its price of production (natural price), for a similar reason as in the first case, despite their temporary deviations from each other, according to the relation between demand and supply, in other words the mechanism focusing the market price on the price of production.

It is evident from the passages quoted above that it was mainly the latter case that Ricardo explained, including some confusion with the former case.

In the same way, Ricardo only considered the relation between the market price and the price of production (the natural price as he calls it), i.e., only the external movement of value and price, brought about by the movement of capital. However, as this external movement is founded on its inherent movement, it is indispensable to go back to its inherent movement in order to make clear its essence. But Ricardo understood neither this nor the relation between external and internal phenomena. He explained only the former, a datum. This is a shortcoming of his studies on this point.

Ricardo presupposed an average level of price, namely the natural price (in fact the price of production) among different branches of production, and hence an average profit. However, he did not take into consideration how this average price and average profit arise. Since the average price and average profit are transformations of value and surplus value, caused by the competition in social capital bringing about its distribution to different branches of production, we must first understand this movement of transformation in order to make clear the essentials of the problem, just as Marx wrote:

> Once it is assumed that the market-values or average market-prices in the different spheres are reduced to *cost-prices* yielding the same average rate of profit [. . .], persistent deviations of the market-price from the cost-price, when it rises above or falls below it in particular spheres, will bring about new migrations and a new distribution of social capital.
>
> Marx, Theorien, II. 1, S. 61, [MEGA^②, II/3.3,
Dietz Verlag, [Ost-]Berlin, 1978, S.856. Italics in original]

The gist of the above can be illustrated as follows:

1 influence on the value and price of the competition within one branch of production

   individual value ————
   individual value ————→ market value <u>unequal profits</u> ——— surplus
                                              value (rent as its most notable form)
   individual value ————

2 influence on the value and price of the competition among different branches of production

   value → price of production *average profit*
   market price ⇄ price of production (natural price)

In short, Ricardo explained here only the relation between the market price and the price of production, without making clear the route through which they arise (individual value → market value → price of production), because he confused the concept of value with that of the price of production and so could not sufficiently elucidate the inner mechanism of the mode of capitalist production.

Above, we have examined fundamentally the contents of what Ricardo sought to clarify. In the following we will enter into more detail concerning a few particular points among them.

(1) On the movement of capital in competition that Ricardo mentioned here, Adam Smith had already given a similar explanation in the *Wealth of Nations*, as Ricardo himself pointed out in some places: 'in the 7th chap. of the *Wealth of Nations*, all that concerns this question is most ably treated' [I/91]; 'no writer has more satisfactorily and ably shewn than Dr. Smith, the tendency of capital to move from employments in which the goods produced do not repay by their price the whole expenses, including the ordinary profits, of producing and bringing them to market' [I/291]. However, this does not mean that Ricardo added nothing to Smith on this question, because he studied in more detail how capital moves from one branch of production to another. Ricardo

sought in the working of credit the clue to understanding the process of capital movement, believing that this movement would probably be realized by the manufacturers not by entirely changing their employment but only by reducing the amount of capital invested in that employment. He wrote as follows:

> In all rich countries, there is a number of men forming what is called the monied class; these men are engaged in no trade, but live on the interest of their money, which is employed in discounting bills, or in loans to the more industrious part of the community. The bankers too employ a large capital on the same objects. The capital so employed forms a circulating capital of a large amount, and is employed, in larger or smaller proportions, by all the different trades of a country. There is perhaps no manufacturer, however rich, who limits his business to the extent that his own funds alone will allow: he has always some portion of this floating capital, increasing or diminishing according to the activity of the demand for his commodities. When the demand for silks increases, and that for cloth diminishes, the clothier does not remove with his capital to the silk trade, but he dismisses some of his workmen, he discontinues his demand for the loan from bankers and monied men; while the case of the silk manufacturer is the reverse: he wishes to employ more workmen, and thus his motive for borrowing is increased: he borrows more, and thus capital is transferred from one employment to another, without the necessity of a manufacturer discontinuing his usual occupation. When we look to the markets of a large town, and observe how regularly they are supplied both with home and foreign commodities, in the quantity in which they are required, under all the circumstances of varying demand, arising from the caprice of taste, or a change in the amount of population, without often producing either the effects of a glut from a too abundant supply, or an enormously high price from the supply being unequal to the demand, we must confess that the principle which apportions capital to each trade in the precise amount that it is required, is more active than is generally supposed.
>
> Ricardo, *Principles* [Gonner's edition], pp. 66–7, [I/89–90]

It is probably because credit in the economy was more developed in Ricardo's time that he was able to go beyond Smith in this point.

(2) Here Ricardo did not always use the term 'natural price' in a definite sense. In some places, it seems to mean labour value, in others the price of production. For example, in the first paragraph of Chapter 4 – 'in making labour the foundation of the value of commodities, and the comparative quantity of labour which is necessary to their production, the rule which determines the respective quantities of goods which shall be given in exchange for each other, we must not be supposed to deny the accidental and temporary deviations of the actual or market price of commodities from this, their primary and natural price' (*Principles* [Gonner's edition], p. 65 [I/88, see below]) – natural price is understood in the sense of the labour value. But in the following passage – 'let us suppose that all commodities are at their natural price, and consequently

that the profits of capital in all employments are exactly at the same rate, or differ only so much as, in the estimation of the parties, is equivalent to any real or fancied advantage which they possess or forego' [I/90], by 'natural price' Ricardo clearly means the price of production, while he entirely confuses the two concepts in the following phrase, in writing 'their natural price, the quantity of labour necessary to their production [. . .]' [I/90].

But ultimately, it can be said that in Chapter 4 he generally understood natural price in the sense of the price of production. It is only natural that the confusion between these two concepts should persist in his explanation, in view of his attitude: he considered profits and wages as independent component elements of value, though to a slight degree, neglecting the transformation of labour value into the price of production. Here he committed the error of confusing exchangeable value, natural price, (labour) value and price of production. As a result, Ricardo did not perceive possible persistent deviations of the market price or the price of production from the real value, affirming that the market price would ultimately return to the natural value and could not deviate from it for very long, even if it diverged temporarily.[5]

I would like to add one point here: as I have said above, according to Ricardo, the exchangeable value of a commodity, its value, is of purely relative nature: nothing more than a relative, proportional relation between two commodities mutually exchanged. It is therefore strange that here, he considered the natural price as the exchangeable value in his terminology, i.e., the purchasing power over other things (Ricardo, *Principles* [Gonner's edition], p. 69, [I/92]). Because what can exist as an exchangeable value in this sense should rather be only an accidental, temporary market price, and that a general, proper and substantial natural price has no reason to exist, even if it might be labour value or the price of production. This attitude of Ricardo constitutes one of the proofs that his theory of value was actually founded on the real value, absolute value, while he often claimed to talk about the relative value.

As we have seen above, according to Ricardo, the exchangeable value of a commodity is ultimately determined by the cost of production (price of production), and not by the proportional relation between demand and supply, which only exerts a temporary influence on the market price. This is a natural consequence to be drawn from the structure of his theory of value. But subsequent interpretations of this attitude of Ricardo's were either too critical or too favourable to him. In the following, I will examine in more detail Ricardo's position on this point, and at the same time determine whether some of these interpretations are justifiable.

Ricardo gave very detailed explanations of this point in Chapter 30 of *Principles* ('On the influence of demand and supply on prices') and contradicted as far as possible the doctrine which he believed to have become almost an axiom in political economy, according to which the relation between demand and supply determines value.

Let us follow Ricardo's example: if the cost of production of hats diminishes, then their price will ultimately have to fall to its new natural price, even if the demand for them should double, triple or quadruple. Or supposing that the natural prices of the food and clothing comprising the subsistence of the labourers diminish, then their wages will ultimately have to fall to their natural price, whatever the increase in the demand for labour. However, since the view that the price of a commodity is determined exclusively by the proportion of supply to demand or of demand to supply has become something like an axiom in political economy, and so the source of multiple errors in this science, Ricardo contradicted this view upheld by Buchanan, Say, Lauderdale, etc.

He asserted that his position was true independently from the variation in the value of money, and that the determination of the value of a commodity by the relation between demand and supply posited by these economists only applied to monopolized commodities (and actually to the market prices of all other commodities only for determinate periods of time). 'Commodities which are monopolized, either by an individual, or by a company, vary according to the law which Lord Lauderdale has laid down: they fall in proportion as the sellers augment their quantity, and rise in proportion to the eagerness of the buyers to purchase them; their price has no necessary connexion with their natural value' (Ricardo, *Principles* [Gonner's edition], p. 376 [I/385]). But for Ricardo, as we have already said several times, 'the prices of commodities, which are subject to competition, and whose quantity may be increased in any moderate degree, will ultimately depend, not on the state of demand and supply, but on the increased or diminished cost of their production' [Gonner's edition], p. 367 [I/385].

On the other hand, Ricardo stated repeatedly in his letters to friends that the relation between demand and supply is not the final regulator of value. For example, in his letter of the 3rd [30th] January 1818, he wrote: 'at any rate then demand and supply are not the sole regulators of price. I should be glad to understand what Lord King and you mean by supply and demand. However abundant the demand it can never permanently raise the price of a commodity above the expence of its production, including in that expence the profits of the producers. It seems natural therefore to seek for the cause of the variation of permanent price in the expences of production' (*Letters of Ricardo to Malthus*, p. 148 [of the 30th January 1818, VII/250–1]). And he also wrote, in his letter to the same person of the 24th November 1820, that 'I do not dispute either the influence of demand on the price of corn and on the price of all other things, but supply follows close at its heels, and soon takes the power of regulating price in his own hands, and in regulating it he is determined by cost of production' (*Letters of Ricardo to Malthus*, p. 179 [of the 24th November 1820, VIII/302]).[6]

The above explanation by Ricardo of the influence of demand and supply on the value and price of a commodity, although still insufficient from his own point of view, must however be said to be a natural consequence of the nature of his theory of value.

Among those who interpret the attitude of Ricardo in this way, returning to his fundamental position on the theory of value, as in the case of the interpretations of his attitude concerning value in use and value in exchange, some belonging to the subjective school totally reject his position on the theory of value, while others belonging to the objective school generally approve it. In addition to these two interpretations, there exists yet another one, adopted by the so-called eclectic school, according to which Ricardo did not overlook the demand side determinants of value and price to focus solely on the supply side. This has been referred to as Marshall's interpretation (we have already examined a similar eclectic interpretation by Dietzel). In the following, I will examine this interpretation by Marshall, to see how far it can be considered a legitimate interpretation of Ricardo's position. Marshall compared the determinants of value to a pair of scissors. He interpreted Ricardo's position by saying that the value of a thing can only be determined by utility and cost at the same time, just as one can only cut something using both blades of a pair of scissors, not with one blade alone. According to what he wrote in Appendix I of his *Principles of economics*, Ricardo never said that the exchange value of a commodity is only determined by the cost expended on its production, but that its determination also depends on 'the wants and wishes of mankind' [Ricardo, I/88]. Jevons' criticism of Ricardo completely failed to take into account the fact that Ricardo did see the other side of the question – demand and utility. 'He appears to have judged both Ricardo and Mill harshly, and to have attributed to them doctrines narrower and less scientific than those they really held' (Marshall, *Principles of Economics*, p. 817).

Let us continue with Marshall's text. After a quotation from Jevons – 'We have only to trace out carefully the natural laws of variation of utility as depending upon the quantity of commodity in our possession, in order to arrive at a satisfactory theory of exchange, of which the ordinary laws of supply and demand are a necessary consequence. [. . .] Labour is found often to determine value, but only in an indirect manner by varying the degree of utility of the commodity through an increase or limitation of the supply' – he wrote as follows:

> As we shall presently see, the latter of these two statements had been made before in almost the same form, loose and inaccurate as it is, by Ricardo and Mill; but they would not have accepted the former statement. For while they regarded the natural laws of variation of utility as too obvious to require detailed explanation, and while they admitted that cost of production could have no effect upon exchange value if it could have none upon the amount which producers brought forward for sale; their doctrines imply that what is true of supply, is true *mutatis mutandis* of demand, and that the utility of a commodity could have no effect upon its exchange value if it could have none on the amount which purchasers took off the market.
>
> (Marshall, *Principles.*, p. 817)

Marshall affirmed that by inverting the order of Jevons' central proposition ('Cost of production determines supply; supply determines final degree of utility; final degree of utility determines value'), we can make a chain of causation nearer to the truth, as follows: 'Utility determines the amount that has to be supplied; the amount that has to be supplied determines cost of production; cost of production determines value, because it determines the supply price which is required to make the producers keep to their work' (Marshall, *Principles*, p. 819).

Marshall suggested that Ricardo would probably have approved this chain of causation, since he had also taken into consideration the influence of demand, in spite of his particular (but provisional) emphasis on the cost of production as the determinant of value.

Marshall's interpretation, thus detecting in Ricardo's theory of value an ecclesiastical attitude, both subjective and objective, seems to me to overlook the fundamental position of Ricardo's theory of value. Everyone is of course free to adopt such an ecclesiastical attitude, but it is absolutely inadmissible to attribute it to Ricardo. This seems to me to be almost incontrovertible. Marshall's interpretation, to the effect that Ricardo did not adopt the labour theory of value, but the theory of cost of production as the valid theory of value for the actual society, is not to be rejected out of hand, in view of his incoherence in maintaining his value theory in its pure form, although such an interpretation does not well convey the essence of Ricardo's theory of value. However, since Ricardo's attitude totally disclaiming utility as a determinant of value is one of the fundamental characteristics of his theory of value, Marshall's interpretation of this point can be said to rather distort Ricardo's theory of value. For Ricardo, demand is only a temporary, accidental cause of variations in price, and when demand and supply equal each other, they cannot provide any explanation of price determination. Our Professor Koizumi seems to agree with this interpretation by Marshall, when he writes that:

> I share on the whole the same point of view as A. Marshall and Heinrich Dietzel, in thinking that the new doctrines of Jevons, etc. can be useful as materials for supplementing the defects and insufficiencies of the doctrine of Ricardo, and that the latter should be easily integrated into these new doctrines, neither being in an alternative relation. Diehl criticizes these two authors and emphasizes an entire incompatibility between Ricardo's objective doctrine and the subjective doctrine of Jevons, etc., but the grounds for such a claim appear to me to be weak.
> Professor Koizumi, 'On Ricardo's doctrine on value, continuation',
> *Keio Economic Studies*, vol. 16, no.9, [1922] p. 42

An interpretation similar to this reading of Ricardo's theory of value can be found with regard to Marx's theory of value and price, representing one of the types of interpretation of the latter. On the basis of the following passage in Volume 3 of *Capital* – 'for a commodity to be sold at its market-value, i.e., proportionally to the necessary social labour contained in it, the total quantity of social labour used in producing the total mass of this commodity must correspond to the quantity of the social want for it, i.e., the effective social want'

(Marx, *Das Kapital*, III, 1, S.172, [MEGA②, II/15, S.192]) – and other similar passages, the value of a commodity in Marx is said to be determined by two elements: the quantity of labour socially necessary for its production and the social want for it (the social use value or social demand for it). Marx's theory of value is thus also classified as a sort of ecclesiastical theory containing both subjective and objective elements. However, the social want considered here is a condition for realizing value but never a determinant of it. Just as in the case of Ricardo, this sort of interpretation can never be accepted.

The interpretation of Marshall seen above is made from the standpoint that the position adopted by Marshall himself can be found, though insufficiently, in Ricardo's theory of value. There are many who adopt other standpoints than this to criticize Ricardo's view of the influence on price of the relation between demand and supply. They have made various criticisms of this point from the position of the subjective theory of value, and a number of criticisms from the position of the theory of value based on demand and supply. But in fact, these criticisms are accusations rather than interpretations, and since it is the position of each of the critics that is finally more important than their critical arguments, here we refrain from presenting or examining them one by one.

Nevertheless, the attitude of Ricardo examined above concerning the relation between demand and supply and price is, though quite natural from his position, still insufficient, undoubtedly requiring further analysis and development. In Volume 3 of *Capital*, Marx analysed and explained in more detail the relation between this law of demand and supply and value and price, from roughly the same position as Ricardo.

Section 5. Ricardo's theory of value and theory of profit

According to Ricardo, the value of a commodity is determined by the maximum marginal quantity of labour (or cost of production), and the part of value remaining after paying rent (if any), belongs to the labourer and to the capitalist or entrepreneur under the name of wages and profits respectively. And since the final remnant remaining after the payment of wages constitutes the revenue of the capitalist–entrepreneur under the name of profits, he is the residual claimant in Ricardo's theory.

Thus, it seems that his theory of profit depends on his theory of value; that the former is founded on the latter. However, because he considered the existence of profit as something self-evident from the outset and was little interested in elucidating its essence, his views on the essence of profit, the causes of variation in the rate of profits etc. were quite ambiguous or insufficient. Hence, we cannot say that his theory of value and his theory of profits are not adequately related to each other. He was unable to theorize sufficiently the essence of profit and its variation on the basis of his labour theory of value. As a result, his theory lacked a correct explanation of them, and this ended up exerting an incorrigible and fatal influence on the whole of his economic theory and prevented its development.

There appear to be three points to be raised as problems in relation to his theory of value, in other words as fundamental problems in his theory of profits: (1) the essence of profits, the origin of their emergence; (2) the law of the average rate of profits; (3) the general tendency of the rate of profits to fall. As we have already examined generally the second point in the previous Section 4 ('On natural price and market price'), here we will only treat the other two points, which are particularly important for our subject here. But we do not intend to scrutinize secondary, minor points in his theory of profits. We limit ourselves to examining these problems insofar as they relate to his theory of value, i.e., to the essence of his theory of profits. First, we will examine the relation between his explanation of the essence of profits and his theory of value.

Ricardo gave almost no clarification of the essence of profits or how they arise; moreover he was ambiguous and unclear in his explanation. According to Cannan: 'Ricardo, who knew very well what profits meant in the concrete, was little interested in the abstract question of their nature and origin. He gives no definition of the term, and nowhere formally expresses any opinion on the subject' (Cannan, *The Theory of Production and Distribution*, pp. 205–6). His attitude is extremely ambiguous about whether profits are part of the labour value produced by the labourer (i.e., whether his theory of profits is a theory of the exploitation of labour or of surplus value), or whether they arise from certain causes relating to capital or capitalists, independently from such a surplus value or value (i.e., whether he attributes the origin of profits to the productivity of capital or the abstinence of capitalists). Many commentators agree on this point. Böhm-Bawerk may be right to include Ricardo among what he calls the 'farblose Schriftsteller [colourless writers]' (Böhm-Bawerk, *Kapital und Kapitalzins*, I, 4 Aufl., [1921,] S.76). Therefore many interpretations on this point can be distinguished only relatively, according to where each author places the emphasis. But I do not believe that it is impossible to infer and grasp his true intention on this point simply because his attitude on the essence of profits is not clearly stated. I believe that his theory of profits, resulting necessarily from his attitude on the theory of value and the theory of wages, is naturally apparent in his words, without his knowing it. In the following, I present a few important interpretations on this point, and after that I will give my point of view on where to discover Ricardo's true intention on the essence of profits, supported by some proofs.

Rosenberg affirmed, in agreement with Marx, that Ricardo developed a kind of theory of surplus value – without using the term – so that his theory of profits is virtually a theory of surplus value. Here, Rosenberg drew on Ricardo's assertion that the remuneration of the labourer is not the same as his product in terms of quantity of labour, as well as the following passages: 'under different circumstances [. . .], those who furnished an equal value of capital for either one employment or for the other, might have a half, a fourth, or an eighth of the produce obtained, the remainder being paid as wages to those who furnished the labour' (Ricardo, *Principles* [Gonner's edition, p. 18 [I/24]), and 'the comparative value of the fish and the game, would be entirely regulated by the quantity of labour realized in each; whatever might be the quantity of production, or however high or low general wages or profits might be' (Ricardo, *Principles* [Gonner's edition], p. 20 [I/26]) (Rosenberg, *Ricardo und Marx als Werttheoretiker*, [Unionsdruckerei, 1903,] S.18–9).

On this point, Zuckerkandl wrote the following:

> v. Böhm includes Ricardo among the colourless writers on the theory of capital interest. I believe that the doctrine that the quantity of labour determines the proportions of exchange contains in it the doctrine that profits are a subtraction from the yield of labour, and one can find in Ricardo passages in which he draws this conclusion. I rely on Ricardo's assertion to the effect that 'the remuneration of the labourer is in no relation to what he has brought about', and on his doctrine of natural wages. Further, he says clearly that the labour expended for tools, instruments, etc. influences the exchange value of a product only insofar as they are used up in the production, that this does not change at all if these instruments belong to only one class of people.
>
> Zuckerkandl, Zur Theorie des Preises,
[Leipzig, Verlag von Duncker & Humbolt, 1889], S.256, note

However, according to Diehl, it would be erroneous to interpret Ricardo's theory of profit as a theory of surplus value, because:

> generally, Ricardo has never advanced a theory of surplus value, it cannot be found in him even in a rudimentary form. Not only for 'individual exceptional cases', but also for the most important events in economic life, Ricardo recognized the capital factors as an independent determinant of value along with labour. He considered profits as an independent sort of revenue along with the wages of labour. And however poor his theory of profits may be, he allotted an independent role to interest and to the entrepreneur's profit.
>
> Diehl, Erläuterungen, I, S.116 [see above]

Thus, we have diverse interpretations of Ricardo's view on the essence of profits. This is because he did not advance a clear opinion on this point and carelessly used wordings alluding to his apparent adoption of different, contradictory theories of profits. For example, he used the following words in explaining the modifications of his theory of value:

> The difference in value arises in both cases from the profits being accumulated as capital, and is only a just compensation for the time that the profits were withheld.
>
> Ricardo, Principles [Gonner's edition], p. 31 [I/37]

Furthermore, we can find the following passages in other places:

> I have already said, that long before this state of prices was become permanent, there would be no motive for accumulation; for no one accumulates but with a view to make his accumulation productive, and it is only when so employed that it operates on profits. Without a motive there could be no accumulation, and consequently such a state of prices never could take place. The farmer and manufacturer can no more live without profit, than the labourer without wages. Their motive for accumulation will diminish with every diminution of profit, and will cease altogether when their profits are so low as not to afford them an adequate compensation for their trouble, and the risk which they must necessarily encounter in employing their capital productively.
>
> Ricardo, *Principles* [Gonner's edition]., pp. 100–1 [I/122]

> There cannot, then, be accumulated in a country any amount of capital which cannot be employed productively, until wages rise so high in consequence of the rise of necessaries, and so little consequently remains for the profits of stock, that the motive for accumulation ceases.
>
> Ricardo, *Principles* [Gonner's edition]., p. 274 [I/290]

These passages by Ricardo have been quoted in the writings of Diehl (*Erläuterungen*, II, S.153–4), Böhm (a. a. O., S.78) etc., who used them to support their interpretation that Ricardo sought the origin of profits elsewhere than in the exploitation of labour. But I do not think that these sentences serve at all to explain his attitude on the essence of profits. They appear to acknowledge the actual existence of profits and their legitimacy, but they never show what the essence of profits is. Therefore these passages are not necessarily incompatible with his adoption of the theory of surplus value. Even if the origin of profits (i.e., surplus value) lies in part of labour value, profits in their real existence can become a justifiable remuneration for the time during which money is forgone, a compensation for the toil and risk endured by the capitalists, or a stimulus, an incentive to employ their capital productively. However, since Ricardo considered profits as given and did not dare to examine their essence, he could not propose a theory of profits to be drawn naturally from his theory of value, nor could he affirm and support it clearly. Although he was ambiguous about the essence of profits, Ricardo actually sought it in surplus value, but without developing his theory of profits far enough to invest it with what Marx called the theory of the exploitation of labour. This is my own interpretation. In the following I will try to justify this.

In many places in his writings, we can find Ricardo considering labour and profits as opposed to each other, being the two divided parts of a whole, one increasing at the expense of the other. The following are some of the most important of these passages:

> The proportion which might be paid for wages, is of the utmost importance in the question of profits; for it must at once be seen, that profits would be high or low, exactly in proportion as wages were low or high.
>
> Ricardo, *Principles* [Gonner's edition]., p. 21 [I/27]

> Wages might rise twenty per cent., and profits consequently fall in a greater or less proportion, without occasioning the least alteration in the relative value of these commodities.
>
> Ricardo, *Principles* [Gonner's edition], p. 22 [I/28–9]

> There can be no rise in the value of labour without a fall of profits. If the corn is to be divided between the farmer and the labourer, the larger the proportion that is given to the latter, the less will remain for the former.
>
> Ricardo, *Principles* [Gonner's edition], p. 28 [I/35]

> A rise in wages, from an alteration in the value of money, produces a general effect on price, and for that reason it produces no real effect whatever on profits. On the contrary, a rise of wages, from the circumstance of the labourer being more liberally rewarded, or from a difficulty of procuring the necessaries on which wages are expended, does not, except in some instances, produce the effect of raising price, but has a great effect in lowering profits.
>
> Ricardo, *Principles* [Gonner's edition], p. 41 [I/48–9]

> The whole value of their commodities is divided into two portions only: one constitutes the profits of stock, the other the wages of labour. Supposing corn and manufactured goods always to sell at the same price, profits would be high or low in proportion as wages were low or high. But suppose corn to rise in price because more labour is necessary to produce it; that cause will not raise the price of manufactured goods in the production of which no additional quantity of labour is required. If, then, wages continued the same, the profits of manufacturers would remain the same; but if, as is absolutely certain, wages should rise with the rise of corn, then their profits would necessarily fall.
>
> Ricardo, *Principles* [Gonner's edition], pp. 87–8 [I/110–1]

> It has been my endeavour to shew throughout this work, that the rate of profits can never be increased but by a fall in wages, and that there can be no permanent fall of wages but in consequence of a fall of the necessaries on which wages are expended.
>
> Ricardo, *Principles* [Gonner's edition], p. 112 [I/132]

> See page 115, where I have endeavoured to shew, that whatever facility or difficulty there may be in the production of corn; wages and profits together will be of the same value. When wages rise, it is always at the expense of profits, and when they fall, profits always rise.
>
> Ricardo, *Principles* [Gonner's edition], p. 398, note[7] [I/404]

These passages make it clear that for Ricardo, profits and wages are the two divided parts of a certain amount of value, therefore in a mutually opposite relation. But this does not immediately and necessarily lead to a theory of the exploitation of labour in which profit is considered to be the appropriation of part of the value produced by labour, because in Ricardo's theory, indirect labour, just like direct labour, is part of the composition of value, so that both of them are equally the source of value. Therefore there is no clear distinction between constant and variable capital. Though profits and wages are opposed to each other, the ultimate source of profits is not clearly located in labour power. Because of this, he did not clearly affirm the theory of the exploitation of labour, in which profits derive from the so-called surplus value. The reason why he did not pursue this point to its conclusion is that he took as self-evident the existence of profits and was not interested in elucidating their provenance. Theoretically, this may be attributed to his non-distinction between variable and constant capital, his lack of the concept of labour power and his confusion between the price of production and value, and hence between profits and surplus value. However, although Ricardo did not clearly express his view on the essence of profit, the substantial contents of his theory of value and theory of wages took sufficient shape almost to accept the idea of surplus value, so that it would be possible to say without major inconvenience that his theory of profit was de facto a theory of the exploitation of labour or of surplus value.

Ricardo did not directly draw the theory of surplus value from his view on wages and profit as the two divided parts of a certain sum of value. Nevertheless, his theory of profits is substantially a theory of surplus value because, along with this view, he repeatedly asserted that the price of labour, (i.e., wages) are determined by the price of subsistence the labourer receives, and that the value and price of the product he produces is higher than this price of subsistence. In any case, he substantially distinguished between the quantity of labour required for the production of the value of labour power and the quantity of labour produced by the labour power, and considered profit as the difference between these two quantities. Notwithstanding this distinction, he did not examine the reason behind it and hence did not arrive at the concept of surplus value. And this is mainly the result of his failure to comprehend that a part of the labour time of the labourer serves to reproduce the value of his own labour power.

In summary, although Ricardo obtained on the whole a legitimate understanding about the essence of profit, he did not clearly see the source and nature of surplus value; he regarded the total labour time (i.e., the sum of surplus and necessary labour) as a definite magnitude; he overlooked the difference in the magnitudes of surplus value; he did not recognize the compulsion to surplus value (i.e., the compulsion to absolute surplus value on the one hand and the inherent drive to curtail the necessary labour time on the other), and in consequence he did not develop the historical mission of capital (Marx, a. a. O., S.125 [MEGA②, II/3, S.1029]).

If Ricardo can be considered to have supported, though insufficiently, the essential points of the theory of surplus value, this only applies to what Marx calls relative surplus value. In Ricardo's theory, total labour time is supposed to be given, so that surplus value is said to increase or decrease only in accordance with the increase or decrease in the productive power of social labour producing the subsistence of the labourer. Of absolute surplus value, he made no mention.

Let me summarize the above. Since Ricardo could not correctly determine the value of labour power and could not make the distinction between constant and variable capital, regarding indirect and direct labour as equal and indistinct components in the formation of value, he could not perceive the appearance of surplus value and did not come to a clear understanding of the nature of profit as a transformation of surplus value. However, since his economic theory affirms: (1) that the price of labour (i.e., wages) is determined by the price of subsistence – even if, according to him, subsistence here does not mean what is necessary for the reproduction of labour power but simply that received by the labourer – (2) that the value of the product produced by the labourer is higher than the value of labour power and (3) that profits and wages are the two divided parts of a certain amount of value, so that one increases at the expense of the other, or rather since these are the main points in his economic theory, beyond all doubt his theory of value had already taken shape sufficiently to accept substantially the theory of surplus value.

Notes

1 In reading his letters, one can see that Ricardo was impatient at the small number of readers who really understood his doctrine. According to Sismondi, Ricardo said that 'there were not more than twenty-five persons in England who had understood his book' (Hollander, *David Ricardo*, [John Hopkins Press, 1910,] p. 50). This may be because his doctrine is profound, but no doubt also because his style is not clear and fluent. Ricardo himself often confessed that he was a poor master of language (*Letters of Ricardo to Malthus*, pp. 176–7 [of the 9th October 1820, VIII/279–80]; Letters of Ricardo to McCulloch, pp. 47–48 [of the 18th December 1819, VIII/142–3]). Senior and Marshall are right when they say that: 'He is the most incorrect writer who ever attained philosophical eminence' (Senior, *Political Economy*, 2nd ed., 1850, p. 813), or that 'His exposition is as confused as his thought is profound; he uses words in artificial senses which he does not explain, and to which he does not adhere; and he changes from one hypothesis to another without giving notice' (Marshall, *Principles of Political Economy* [*Economics*], 8th ed., 1920, p. 813). And according to Gonner, one of the reasons for the diversity in the criticisms of Ricardo lies in some decisive defects in him, one of which is 'a singularly defective literally style' (Gonner, *Palgrave Dictionary of Political Economy*, 1918, Vol. III, p. 305), and

not only is Ricardo's vocabulary distressingly limited, but he amplifies the difficulties arising from excessive compression in using phrases and words in unusual
senses. It is interesting then to note that McCulloch considers the defects pointed
out by these scholars rather as Ricardo's strong points (McCulloch, *The Literature
of Political Economy*, 1845, p. 17). In any case, it is true that Ricardo was not a
very good writer. This is undoubtedly one of the factors giving rise to various
misunderstandings, but it does not seriously damage the real merit of his
doctrine.

2 In addition to the above quotations, there are also the following passages [italics
by Mori]:

'[. . .] but they are not equal; the first (the quantity of labour bestowed on a
commodity) is under many circumstances an invariable standard, indicating
correctly the variations of other things' (Ricardo, *Principles* [Gonner's edition],
p. 9 [I/14]).

'[. . .] but it is correct to say, as Adam Smith had previously said, "that the
proportion between the quantities of labour necessary for acquiring different
objects seems to be the only circumstance which can afford any rule for
exchanging them for one another"' (Ricardo, *Principles* [Gonner's edition],
p. 11 [I/17]).

'[. . .] yet this division could not affect the relative value of these commodities
[. . .]' (Ricardo, *Principles* [Gonner's edition], p. 18 [I/24]).

'[. . .] still the same principle would hold true, that the exchangeable value
of the commodities produced would be in proportion to the labour bestowed
on their production, not on their immediate production only, but on all
these implements or machines required to give effect to the particular labour
to which they were applied' (Ricardo, *Principles* [Gonner's edition], p. 18
[I/24]).

'The exchangeable value of commodities [. . .] is always regulated not by the
less quantity of labour [. . .] but by the greater quantity of labour [. . .]'
(Ricardo, *Principles* [Gonner's edition], p. 50 [I/73]).

'We have seen that the price of corn is regulated by the quantity of labour
necessary to produce it, with that portion of capital which pays no rent. We
have seen, too, that all manufactured commodities rise and fall in price, in
proportion as more or less labour becomes necessary to their production'
(Ricardo, *Principles* [Gonner's edition], p. 87 [I/110]).

'[. . .] the difficulty or facility of their production will ultimately regulate their
exchangeable value' (Ricardo, 'An Essay of the Influence of Low Price of Corn
on the Profits of Stock', *Works* [ed. by McCulloch, 1846], p. 377 [IV/20]).

3 In the first and second editions of *Principles*, Ricardo discussed the invariable
measure of value in the first section of Chapter 1 (only in the second edition, as
there is no section in the first), but in the third edition he eliminated these passages and added instead a new Section 6 ('On an invariable measure of value')
in Chapter 1 to discuss this problem in detail. In the following, I quote a passage
found only in the first and second editions but deleted from the third (this passage is in particular quoted in Gonner's edition for reference).

'If any one commodity could be found, which now and at all times required precisely the same quantity of labour to produce it, that commodity would be of an unvarying value, and would be eminently useful as a standard by which the variations of other things might be measured. Of such a commodity we have no knowledge, and consequently are unable to fix on any standard of value. It is, however, of considerable use towards attaining a correct theory, to ascertain what the essential qualities of a standard are, that we may know the causes of the variation in the relative value of commodities, and that we may be enabled to calculate the degree in which they are likely to operate' (Ricardo, *Principles* [Gonner's edition], pp. 11–2 [I/17 n3]).

See also the related passages on the invariable measure of value in the third section of Chapter 1 of *Principles* (pp. 21–3 in Gonner's edition [I/27–9]).

4   In the following, we cite yet another passage from Marx, in which he reaffirmed that it is on the grounds of an insufficient understanding of the concept of labour as content and substance of value that Ricardo sought to discover the invariable measure of value:

'Ricardo often gives the impression, and sometimes indeed writes, as if the quantity of labour is the solution to the false, or falsely conceived problem of an "invariable measure of value" in the same way as corn, money, wages, etc., were previously considered and advanced as panaceas of this kind, In Ricardo's work this false impression arises because for him the decisive task is the definition of the magnitude of value. Because of this he does not understand the specific form in which labour is an element of value, and fails in particular to grasp that the labour of the individual must present itself as abstract general labour and, in this form, as social labour. Therefore he has not understand that the development of money is connected with the nature of value and with the determination of this value by labour-time' (Marx, a. a. O., S.163, [MEGA②, Ebenda, S.1324, italics in original]).

5   Whitaker also points out, from the position of his interpretation, the double meanings in Ricardo's natural price. According to Whitaker, 'the term "Natural Price" has, it happens, a "philosophical" and an "empirical" significance. It is at best an inexact pair of words. Its empirical meaning is simply normal value, the excellent term for that value which, under competition, constitutes a centre of oscillation for market values. Its "philosophical" meaning, as suggested a few times by Smith, is the human cost of obtaining goods from outer world' (Whitaker, *History and criticism.*, p. 50 [Albert C. Whitaker, *History and criticism of the labour theory of value in English political economy*, 1904, New York, Columbia University Press. Italics in original]).

6   I quote a passage from Ricardo expressing his view that the relation between demand and supply does not ultimately determine value, from another letter in his correspondence. Letter to Malthus of the 10th [9th] October 1820:

'He [Say] certainly has not a correct notion of what is meant by value, when he contends that a commodity is valuable in proportion to its utility. This would be true if buyers only regulated the value of commodities; then indeed we might expect that all men would be willing to give a price for things in proportion to the estimation in which they held them, but the fact appears to me to be that the buyers have the least in the world to do in regulating price – it is all done by the competition of the sellers, and however the buyers might be really willing to give more for iron, than for gold, they could not, because the supply would be regulated by the cost of production, and therefore gold would inevitably be in the proportion which it now is to iron, altho' it probably is by all mankind considered as the less useful metal. [. . .] You say demand and supply regulates value – this, I think, is saying nothing, and for the reasons I have given in the beginning of this letter – it is supply which regulates value – and supply is itself controlled by comparative cost of production' (*Letters of Ricardo to Malthus*, pp. 173–4, 176 [VIII/276–7, 279]).

7 There exist yet other similar passages:

'In proportion as less is appropriated for wages, more will be appropriated for profits, and vice versa (Ricardo, *Principles* [Gonner's edition], p. 404 [I/411]).

'Whatever increases wages, necessarily reduces profits [. . .] for nothing can affect profits but a rise in wages. [. . .] but the admission of this fact by no means invalidates the theory, that profits depend on high or low wages [. . .]' (Ricardo, *Principles* [Gonner's edition], pp. 96–7 [I/118–9]).

'It will be seen too, that, in all cases, the same sum of 720*l.* must be divided between wages and profits. If the value of the raw produce from the land exceeds this value, it belongs to rent, whatever may be its amount. If there be no excess, there will be no rent. Whether wages or profits rise or fall, it is this sum of 720*l.* from which they must both be provided. On the one hand, profits can never rise so high as to absorb so much of this 720*l.* that enough will not be left to furnish the labourers with absolute necessaries; on the other hand, wages can never rise so high as to leave no portion of this sum for profits' (Ricardo, *Principles* [Gonner's edition], pp. 91–2 [I/115]).

'Thus we again arrive at the same conclusion which we have before attempted to establish: – that in all countries, and all times, profits depend on the quantity of labour requisite to provide necessaries for the labourers, on that land or with that capital which yields no rent' (Ricardo, *Principles* [Gonner's edition], p. 105 [I/126]).

'Thus then I have endeavoured to shew, first, that a rise of wages would not raise the price of commodities, but would invariably lower profits [. . .]' (Ricardo, *Principles* [Gonner's edition], p. 107 [I/127]).

'Profits I think depend on wages, – wages depend on demand and supply of labour, and on the cost of the necessaries on which wages are expended' (*Letters of Ricardo to Malthus*, p. 120 [of the 5th October 1816, VII/72]).

'I know of no cause of the fall of profits but the fall (probably an error for 'rise' [note by Mori; Sraffa also adds the same note in his *Works*]) of labour' (*Letters of Ricardo to Malthus*, p. 197 [of the 28th September 1821, IX/82–3]. See also *Letters of Ricardo to McCulloch*, p. 72 [of the 13th June 1820, VIII/194]).

6 Ricardo's theory of value and distribution

(Chapter 5 'David Ricardo' in *Summary of the History of Economic Thought, Part I*, Iwanami Shoten, 1937)

Chōgorō Maide

1. Introduction

For Ricardo, like Malthus but unlike Smith, developing the theory of distribution was the main task of political economy. He wrote in the preface of his chief work *On the Principles of Political Economy and Taxation*:

> The produce of the earth – all that is derived from its surface by the united application of labour, machinery, and capital, is divided among three classes of the community; namely, the proprietor of the land, the owner of the stock or capital necessary for its cultivation, and the labourers by whose industry it is cultivated.
>
> But in different stages of society, the proportions of the whole produce of the earth which will be allotted to each of these classes, under the names of rent, profit, and wages, will be essentially different; depending mainly on the actual fertility of the soil, on the accumulation of capital and population, and on the skill, ingenuity, and instruments employed in agriculture.
>
> To determine the laws which regulate this distribution, is the principal problem in Political Economy: much as the science has been improved by the writings of Turgot, Stuart, Smith, Say, Sismondi, and others, they afford very little satisfactory information respecting the natural course of rent, profit, and wages.
>
> [Quotation from Gonner's edition published in 1919. I/5]

Ricardo intended to elucidate in this way the laws determining the distribution of the produce of the earth among the three classes participating in its formation, in the form of rent, profit and wages. For this purpose he explained not only the state of the relations of distribution but also their evolution on the basis of the former. It was the study of the mutual relations among these three classes in the process of social evolution that most interested him, and in relation to this study he established the law of diminishing returns. And for this reason he attached particular importance to the theory of rent. This is evident from the following quotation:

> Without a knowledge of which [rent], it is impossible to understand the effect of the progress of wealth on profits and wages, or to trace satisfactorily the influence of taxation on different classes of the community; particularly when the commodities taxed are the productions immediately derived from the surface of the earth.
>
> (Ricardo, *Principles*, I/5–6)

The reason why Ricardo set out to consider the distribution of wealth in society and to elucidate the relative state of the three classes of society at that time and its evolution, focusing particularly on the theory of rent, can be explained by the social situation he observed and the formation of his political economy against the background of this situation.

David Ricardo was born in 1772 in London, the third child of Abraham Israel Ricardo, a Sephardic Jew who emigrated from Holland to England and naturalized there in 1771. His father was a successful stockjobber. Without receiving a formal higher education, he followed practical training first in London and then in Amsterdam, and at the age of 14 he was already working as a stockjobber with his father. In 1793, when he was 21, he married Miss Priscilla Ann Wilkinson, who was from a Quaker family, and converted to Christianity. As a consequence, he was repudiated by his father and started his own business. He was lucky enough to make a fortune in a short time. On the other hand, since the publication of *High Price of Bullion* in 1809, he won renown as economist with a number of writings. In 1819 he became member of the House of Commons, representing Portarlington, but in 1823 he suddenly died of ear disease.

From the moment he ran his own household, Ricardo used his leisure time to study mathematics, chemistry, geology, etc. On one such occasion, while staying in the spa town of Bath in 1799, he discovered by chance the *Wealth of Nations* by Adam Smith, which he found most intriguing. It is said to be this work that inspired him to study political economy. But his first economic publication was *The High Price of Bullion, a Proof of the Depreciation of Bank Notes* [hereinafter *High Price* for short], which first appeared in 1809 as a contribution to the newspaper *Morning Chronicle* and was subsequently published as a pamphlet in 1810. The motivation for writing this text was the sharp rise in prices, particularly of gold bullion, and the fall in the foreign exchange observed since the suspension of cash payment (1797), in 1809 in particular. In this article he argued that when a country's currency is entirely made up of gold and silver coin or convertible paper money, then in the event of devaluation caused by over-issue, it will be exported until it returns to par with the foreign metal currencies or bullion. Inconvertible paper money, on the other hand, will not be exported even in the event of over-issue, and its domestic value and foreign exchange rate will fall. The rising price of bullion then indicates nothing other than the depreciation of the currency, occasioned by the rise in banknote issue due to the suspension of cash payment. This line of reasoning was adopted in the report of the Bullion Committee. When Bosanquet questioned the validity of the report, Ricardo published *Reply to Mr. Bosanquet's Practical Observations on the Report of the Bullion Committee*. In 1816 he published *Proposals for an Economical and Secure Currency; with Observations on the Profits of the Bank of England, as they regard the Public and the Proprietors of Bank Stock*, in which he proposed a plan to replace metallic coin with paper money while maintaining its equivalence with bullion, using an ingot of standard weight and fineness instead of coin for the conversion of the paper money. He thought that such a measure would also make it possible to restrict the currency supply. This plan was recommended by the committee deliberating the resumption of conversion by the Bank of England.

However, it was the debate on the amendment of the Corn Laws that motivated Ricardo to study the theory of distribution, the main subject of *Principles*. This question attracted the attention of both Malthus and Ricardo. However, from the outset they held different views about how the profit of capital would be affected by the rise in food prices caused by the tariff on corn. While Malthus affirmed that the profit of capital can also be increased through the high profits obtained in sectors other than farming by exploiting new markets, as well as through cheaper food prices, Ricardo's view was that the difficulty of corn production, food prices and hence the wage level are almost the sole cause of permanent changes in profit, and the rent is equal to the difference in the rate of profit changing in dependence on these causes. The rent, being 'always withdrawn from the profits of stock' (Letter of Ricardo to Malthus, 6th February 1815 [VI/73]), rises with the fall in profit and to the same degree, but the tariff on corn has the same effect as an increase in the difficulty of corn production, by limiting or prohibiting the importation of cheap food. And in response to Malthus, who defended rent and the tariffs on corn in his pamphlets, Ricardo published in 1815 a pamphlet entitled *An Essay on the Influence of a low Price of Corn on the Profits of Stock, shewing the Inexpediency of Restrictions on Importation: with Remarks on Mr. Malthus's two Last Publications: "An Inquiry etc."; and "The Grounds etc."* [IV/9–41, hereinafter *Essay* for short].

As its title indicates, this pamphlet was written to contradict the opinion of Malthus, by making clear the influence on profits of variations in corn prices and by emphasising the injustice of limiting the importation of corn. Since Ricardo viewed the rent as a surplus arising from the fall of profit, 'in treating on the subject of the profits of capital, it is necessary to consider the principles which regulate the rise and fall of rent' (IV/9). And since the determination of profit can be clarified only after the determination of wages, here they come naturally into question. This pamphlet develops in this way the whole theory of the problems of distribution, besides focusing on the theory of rent. Hence, with this article, Ricardo laid the foundations of his theory of distribution.

However, the *Essay* only laid the foundations of Ricardo's theory of distribution, without developing it sufficiently and in particular without explaining its relation to the theory of value. Then, following the advice of James Mill, one of his close friends, he further organised and elaborated on the explanation and published *On the Principles of Political Economy and Taxation* in 1817. Therefore it was not at all accidental that *Principles* also took the analysis of distribution relations as its main task, and in particular that the theory of rent was central to the accomplishment of this task.

Seeking to develop the theory of distribution with this focus on the theory of rent, Ricardo considered the capitalist economic relation in agriculture as the typical relation in capitalist production. This may be because here, the three main categories of distribution – rent, wages and profit – simultaneously coexist, so that their mutual relations are made more explicit. And herein lies the reason why he says that 'the produce of the earth [. . .] is divided among three classes of the community; namely, the proprietor of the land, the owner of the stock or capital [. . .] and the labourers' [I/5, quoted above]. However, the distribution he considers is of course not limited solely to that of the capitalist production in agriculture, but includes the whole range of the society of capitalist production, as professor Cannan observes:

> He always appears to treat a farm as a kind of type of the industry of the whole country, and to suppose that the division of the whole produce can be easily inferred from the distribution on a farm.
> (Cannan, *Theories of Production and Distribution*, 1917, p. 341)

Moreover, the fact that the theory of rent is given a primary place on the assumption of such relations of production suggests that the real subject of his analysis of capitalism, with the theory of distribution as the main task of political economy, is not the relations between labour and capital, but between land and capital.

Ricardo seeks to discover the laws governing the distribution of such a society. He says that 'to determine the laws which regulate this distribution, is the principal problem in Political Economy' [I/5]. Here he distinguishes the permanent state or effect of things from their temporary state or effect, and examines the former while excluding the latter, believing that the former appear more clearly in the absence of the latter. He says in a letter to Malthus that:

> It appears to me that one great cause of our difference in opinion, on the subjects which we have so often discussed, is that you have always in your mind the immediate and temporary effects of particular changes – whereas I put these immediate and temporary effects quite aside, and fix my whole attention on the permanent state of things which will result from them.
> (Letter of Ricardo to Malthus, 24th January 1817 [VII/120])

These sentences clearly indicate the characteristics of his way of thinking and its difference from that of Malthus. And the permanent and principal state or effect, the subject of his theory, conforms to the natural course, as he mentions in writing that:

> Much as the science has been improved by the writings of Turgot [. . .], they afford very little satisfactory information respecting the natural course of rent, profit, and wages.
>
> [I/5]

The 'natural' mentioned here does not of course mean a regularity given by nature, but only something obeying laws, conforming with them or necessary, in other words adapted to the essence of things, i.e., to the general laws (Amonn, *Ricardo als Begründer der theoretischen Nationalökonomie*, 1924[3], S.3). Incidentally, the essence of things in the social life is the fundamental order or organisation of the society in question, and the society Ricardo is thinking of is that of capitalism, as noted above. Therefore the 'natural course of distribution' he talks of means something adapted to the basic order or organisation of the capitalist society and arising by itself, or conforming to the laws or necessary under their premises. It is precisely such a thing that Ricardo sought to elucidate.

What Ricardo mainly presupposes as the essence or foundation of the capitalist society is, just as it is for Smith, that its member agents are driven entirely by self-interest in a laissez-faire regime, in other words, the dominance of economic self-interest and free competition, with the result that the pursuit of profit becomes the driving force or motive of economic activities. It is the process under such fundamental presuppositions that Ricardo pursued. Naturally, Ricardo did not think that such presuppositions apply to every empirical fact without exception. When, for example, he talked about the pursuit of profit as the driving force in economic activities, he recognised that it could be counteracted by other motives. However, this was for him a question of particular accidental facts but not the question of science relating to the general necessary facts. In saying that 'that is a question of fact not of science, and might be urged against almost every proposition in Political Economy' (Letter of Ricardo to Malthus, 22nd October 1811 [VI/64]), he consciously rejected the factual hindrances occurring by chance and set out to conduct his research under the presupposition that each *homo oeconomicus* is well aware of and driven mainly by his self-interest. In addition to these presuppositions, as will be discussed later, Ricardo takes the law of population and the law of diminishing return on land as the main conditions of distribution, and particularly of its evolution, and these laws influence his laws of capitalist society.

Ricardo thus made a sharp distinction between the question of science and the question of fact, and affirmed that the former should, unlike the latter, address the permanent and principal state and effect, abstracting from the temporary and accidental circumstances. This is the reason why his method is considered abstract and deductive, in affiliation with the 'esoteric' method of Smith, to the contrary of Malthus who adopted an 'exoteric' method [according to Marx's terminology]. However, Ricardo's permanent state or effect, though independent from each temporary and accidental circumstance in itself, is nevertheless the result of their synthesis, and what he presupposes, though accompanied by contrary cases in particular real facts, exists on their basis and dominates them in the last analysis. For this reason, what conformed to law in Ricardo, although independent from temporary and accidental circumstances, and abstract as well as deductive insofar as it was placed under certain presuppositions, was never merely ideal and speculative or far-removed from the facts, but based on the objective reality of the time and realised as its natural and necessary law. His laws could therefore immediately be the foundation for concrete practical policies and applied not only to a certain state of society but also to its development, so that dynamic phenomena, founded on static ones, were comprehended as the necessary development of the latter, and equally natural and necessary. In this way, the law of the falling rate of profit is deduced immediately from his theory of distribution, and the economic policy or theory of taxation was established as its application.

Thus in Ricardo, the analysis of the capitalist society is not a study of the natural order of an ideal society, but led to the discovery of what was realised in objective reality as its necessary law. In this respect he differs from Quesnay, Smith, etc., who were seeking an ideal order on the basis of the natural law or deism, but he is quite similar to Malthus, who tried to rely solely on experience. However, as noted above, although Malthus adopted an inductive and realistic method, he still remained within the metaphysical and theological framework by attributing the empirical laws to providence. Ricardo was the first to emerge completely from the metaphysical and theological framework. With him, political economy obtained autonomy for the first time, as a science analysing the inner mechanisms of capitalism on the basis of its facts.

This certainly corresponds to the actual development of capitalism in England, but it can also be seen as a result of the influence of Bentham's philosophy on Ricardo's doctrine. Of course there are certain objections on this point (Schumpeter, *Dogmen und Methodengeschichte im G. d. S*, I, S. 64), but it is widely held that Bentham's utilitarian philosophy was transmitted to Ricardo via one of his close friends, James Mill. That is why Bentham once described Ricardo as his spiritual grandson. According to Goetz Briefs, the distinguishing characteristic of Bentham's utilitarian thinking is his rejection of metaphysics. He rejected every kind of metaphysics, relying on a purely empirical and experimental method, and beginning with the sentimental life of an individual, he affirmed that the enjoyment of pleasure and the prevention of pain constitute the content of human desire and the objective of human life. For him the predominance of pleasure over pain is the motive for action and the only moral imperative. In social and economic respects, he deduced from this point of view the fundamental theses like those of Smith: self-interest, free competition, etc. However, while for Smith these fundamental theses were metaphysically and theologically founded, for Bentham, as a result of his rejection of metaphysics, the activation of self-interest or free competition were directly justified and allowed per se. Of course, Bentham also thought that the greatest happiness can only achieved when the happiness of an individual is simultaneously connected with the interest of the whole, through the activation of enlightened self-interest, because the interest of an individual is more advanced when obtaining the recognition and sympathy of others. But the activation of this 'enlightened self-interest' was equally based on self-interest itself sacrificing the small benefit for the greater one (Briefs, *Untersuchungen zur Klassischen Nationalökonomie*, [Verlag Gustav Fischer] 1915, S.220–22).

Under the influence of Bentham's thought, Ricardo banished metaphysical and theological aspects from political economy. However, just as Bentham was ahistorical, Ricardo did not see the economic phenomena of his time as developing and changing, but rather as static and fixed. In this respect, he remained unrealistic and unempirical. And if he considered the distribution relations of the capitalist society as the main subject of political economy rather than the production relations, the quantitative aspects of distribution rather than its qualitative aspects, this was not only because of the current situation of his time, as explained above, but also because of this methodological point of view that he adopted.

If Ricardo did not separate distribution from production, considering the question of distribution to concern the sharing-out of the social product among the social classes involved in its formation (unlike Malthus, who considered the same question to concern the shares attributed to land, labour and capital according to their respective contributions), it was probably because of Ricardo's approach, particularly in his theory of value, seeking to determine the influence of distribution on capital accumulation and hence on production.

Of course, the contemporary problem of distribution was first of all that of prices, and the solution of the former appears to have to be based on that of the latter. Incidentally, on prices as on other subjects, Ricardo distinguishes between the temporary and accidental market price and the permanent and principal natural price (Ricardo, *Principles*, Ch. IV). Since the main issue for Ricardo was the latter, he believed that the task of developing the theory of price would be accomplished if the law determining it could be elucidated. He did not distinguish between money and commodity, and so the exchangeable value was the natural price for Ricardo, who wrote:

> In speaking then of the exchangeable value of commodities, or the power of purchasing possessed by any one commodity, I mean always that power which it would possess, if not disturbed by any temporary or accidental cause, and which is its natural price.

[I/92]

Here he placed the problem of determining the exchangeable value or relative value at the very beginning of his study of distribution in the capitalist society, making it the foundation of his study and the main focus of his attention.

He recognised labour as the basis of this exchangeable or relative value, as we will see later. In this position, he approached the viewpoint of absolute value, according to which labour is not only the standard of the exchangeable value of every commodity but also the substance of the value of every commodity, and just because of this it governs the exchangeable value. However, he did not actually arrive at this viewpoint, and labour remained the precondition of the relative value. For this reason, every kind of heterogeneous product became homogeneous for him, and ultimately the question of distribution became the subject of his study of the sharing-out of the value produced by labour among the classes participating in the production. That is why he affirms that:

> It is according to the division of the whole produce of the land of any particular farm, between the three classes of landlord, capitalist, and labourer, that we are to judge of the rise or fall of rent, profit, and wages, and not according to the value at which that produce may be estimated in a medium which is confessedly variable.
>
> [I/49]

Furthermore, as we will see later, Ricardo gives the law of population and the law of diminishing returns on land as the main factors of the variation in the productivity of labour, making little of social and historical factors. But because he adopted (albeit incompletely) the position of the labour theory of value and considered the problem of distribution (in other words the problem of prices) as the problem of how value depends on variations in the productive forces of labour, he also tried to consider the evolution of distribution on the basis of its present state. Of course, in such a point of view, the static state of the economy in itself includes moments of its dynamics, the latter being a necessary development of the former.

In this way, Ricardo sought to develop a theory of economic relations in terms of social and class relations and their evolution, drawing on an unilateral inheritance from Smith: the theory of labour bestowed and the decomposition of value.

2. Theory of value

i) Establishment of the law of labour value

Ricardo's theory of value originates from Smith and represents a more developed form of the latter's theory of labour bestowed.

As we have already seen, Adam Smith distinguished between pre-capitalist and capitalist societies. For the former he proposed the labour theory of value, according to which the relative quantities of labour bestowed in the production of commodities determines their exchangeable value, while for the latter he adopted the production cost theory, according to which it is the sum of wages, profit and rent that determines the value of commodities. But for Ricardo, who almost exclusively considered the capitalist society, there was no essential distinction between pre-capitalist and capitalist societies, the former being simply an earlier stage of capitalist society with relatively little use of fixed capital (machines, etc.), although of course 'even in that early state to which Adam Smith refers, some capital, though possibly made and accumulated by the hunter himself, would be necessary to enable him to kill his game' [I/22–3]. Therefore the capitalist society is the only possible society, from the distant past to the future, and the value of commodities is always determined by the labour directly or indirectly bestowed for its production. Thus, Ricardo considered that wages and profit are the decomposed components of such value, and that the payment of rent has no influence on this law of labour value. However, he subsequently modified the labour theory of value, because he admitted the influence of the differences in the durability of fixed capital and in the composition of capital existing in every state of society, whether in its earlier or later stages.

So Ricardo did not distinguish between pre-capitalist and capitalist societies because he went beyond Smith's point of view, which identified production goods with capital. For Ricardo, 'capital is that part of the wealth of a country which is employed in production, and consists of food, clothing, tools, raw materials, machinery &c. necessary to give effect to labour' [I/95], so that it must exist in every society. As a result of this view, Ricardo continued with his reasoning, ignoring the difficulties Smith saw in the exchange between capital and labour that was unknown to the pre-capitalist society, and assuming from the outset a preliminary formation of the average rate of profit leading to the confusion between the value of commodities and the natural price.

Like Smith, Ricardo began with a distinction between the value in use and the value in exchange, asserting their antinomy and adopting the value in exchange as his subject of consideration: the purchasing power over other things procured by possessing a thing [I/11].

Even in these points he differed somewhat from Smith. While Smith considered that something without any value in use (utility) could still have value in exchange (Smith, *Wealth of Nations*, ed. by Cannan, I. p. 30 [*ditto*, in the Glasgow edition of the works and correspondence of Adam Smith, Vol. I, Oxford, 1976, p. 45–6]), Ricardo held value in use to be a precondition for value in exchange, considering anything without utility to be devoid of any value in exchange [I/11–2]. In this respect, Ricardo's approach is doubtless superior to Smith's. But he only affirmed that value in use is totally different from value in exchange and that the former is a precondition for the existence of the latter, without going one step further and developing the relations between them. In addition, in order to clarify the distinction between value in use and value in exchange, he identified the former with wealth, to contrast this with the value. And from the viewpoint that 'value essentially differs from riches, for value depends not on abundance, but on the difficulty or facility of production', he criticises Smith for being beside the point when the latter says that 'a man must be rich or poor according to the quantity of labour which he can afford to purchase', having correctly determined that 'a man is rich or poor according to the degree in which he can afford to enjoy the necessaries, conveniences, and amusements of human life' (Ricardo, *Principles*, Ch. XX [I/273–8]). Here,

Ricardo's approach falls short of Smith's, because the way that Smith considered the notion of wealth differently in societies with and without division of labour shows that he perceived the historicity of wealth and unconsciously considered value as its particular historical and social form, while for Ricardo, who invariably equated wealth with value in use in every state of society, there existed no such perception.

Then what did determine the exchangeable value of commodities for Ricardo? He wrote: 'possessing utility, commodities derive their exchangeable value from two sources: from their scarcity, and from the quantity of labour required to obtain them' [I/12]. First, he divided commodities into those which can be increased in quantity by bestowing more labour on them and those which cannot. The exchangeable values of the latter are 'wholly independent of the quantity of labour originally necessary to produce them' and 'determined by their scarcity alone'.

> Some rare statues and pictures, scarce books and coins, wines of a particular quality, which can be made only from grapes grown on a particular soil are all of this description. Their value [. . .] varies with the varying wealth and inclinations of those who are desirous to possess them.
>
> [I/12]

This means that the value of a monopolised commodity is determined by the relation between the demand for it and its supply. By contrast, Ricardo considered the exchangeable value of the former (i.e., of the commodity which can be increased in quantity by labour) to be almost entirely determined by the relative quantity of labour needed to produce each commodity. According to Ricardo, 'by far the greatest part of those goods which are the objects of desire, are procured by labour; and they may be multiplied, not in one country alone, but in many, almost without any assignable limit, if we are disposed to bestow the labour necessary to obtain them'. For this reason, 'in speaking then of commodities, of their exchangeable value, and of the laws which regulate their relative prices, we mean always such commodities only as can be increased in quantity by the exertion of human industry, and on the production of which competition operates without restraint'. In this way he disregards the commodities which cannot be increased at will.

What determines the value of a commodity which can be increased in quantity *ad libitum* by spending more labour on it, in other words, the quantity of another commodity given in exchange for it? In answering this question, Ricardo disregarded the means of production used (i.e., the capital in his sense of the term), only taking into account the direct labour used, and answered 'the relative quantity of labour which is necessary for its production' [I/11]. He wrote:

> In the early stages of society, the exchangeable value of these commodities, or the rule which determines how much of one shall be given in exchange

for another, depends almost exclusively on the comparative quantity of labour expended on each.

[I/12]

or again:

In the early stages of society, before much machinery or durable capital is used, the commodities produced by equal capitals will be nearly of equal value, and will rise or fall only relatively to each other on account of more or less labour being required for their production.

[I/42]

And further:

If the quantity of labour realized in commodities regulates their exchangeable value, every increase of the quantity of labour must augment the value of that commodity on which it is exercised, as every diminution must lower it.

This is the fundamental principle of his theory of value. As he himself wrote:

That this is really the foundation of the exchangeable value of all things, excepting those which cannot be increased by human industry, is a doctrine of the utmost importance in political economy.

[I/13]

Here Ricardo criticised Smith for confusing the labour commanded and the labour bestowed as the true measure of value. For Ricardo, the quantity of labour a commodity can command in the market means the value of labour, ultimately the wages. He wrote:

Adam Smith, who so accurately defined the original source of exchangeable value, and who was bound in consistency to maintain, that all things became more or less valuable in proportion as more or less labour was bestowed on their production, has himself erected another standard measure of value, and speaks of things being more or less valuable, in proportion as they will exchange for more or less of this standard measure. Sometimes he speaks of corn, at other times of labour, as a standard measure; not the quantity of labour bestowed on the production of any object, but the quantity which it can command in the market: as if these were two equivalent expressions, and as if because a man's labour had become doubly efficient, and he could therefore produce twice the quantity of a commodity, he would necessarily receive twice the former quantity in exchange for it. If this indeed were true, [. . .] the quantity of labour bestowed on a commodity, and the quantity of labour which that commodity would purchase, would be equal, and either might accurately measure the variations of other things: but they are not equal; the first is under many circumstances an invariable standard, indicating correctly the variations of other things; the latter is subject to as many fluctuations as the commodities compared with it.

[I/13–4]

In this summarising paragraph he refined the labour theory of value, determining the value of commodity not by the level of remuneration paid for the labour but by the relative quantity of labour necessary for its production. But the cause of confusion in Smith goes deeper than the point made by Ricardo. As seen above, it lies in the fact that he started from the pre-capitalist society. As he only ever considered the capitalist society, Ricardo did not understand this.

Incidentally, even if the exchangeable value of a commodity is determined by the quantity of labour spent on its production, as Ricardo says, the products of different kinds of labour cannot be immediately compared with each other in terms of their quantities of labour, because the labour differs in quality according to the different kinds of commodities produced. To compare the values of different products of labour, a standardisation of heterogeneous labours is required, i.e., a unit for converting every kind of labour.

The explanation Ricardo gave on this problem remained practically on the same level as that of Smith. He wrote:

> In speaking, however, of labour, as being the foundation of all value, and the relative quantity of labour as almost exclusively determining the relative value of commodities, I must not be supposed to be inattentive to the different qualities of labour, and the difficulty of comparing an hour's or a day's labour, in one employment, with the same duration of labour in another.

However, he sought the solution to this difficulty merely in the estimation of the various kinds of labour on the market. Thus, he wrote:

> The estimation in which different qualities of labour are held, comes soon to be adjusted in the market with sufficient precision for all practical purposes, and depends much on the comparative skill of the labourer, and intensity of the labour performed. The scale, when once formed, is liable to little variation. If a day's labour of a working jeweller be more valuable than a day's labour of a common labourer, it has long ago been adjusted, and placed in its proper position in the scale of value.

[I/20–1]

The 'estimation in which different qualities of labour are held' of which Ricardo talks here appears to mean the measurement of various kinds of labour executed, but in fact it should be understood as the evaluation of homogeneous labours, i.e., the estimation of their wages, because the title summarising section 2 of the first chapter of *Principles* runs: 'Labour of different qualities differently rewarded.

This no cause of variation in the relative value of commodities' [I/20]. If this is the correct understanding, not only does Ricardo's explanation miss the point, but it also leads to a result contradictory to his fundamental proposition. In any case, what is in question here is the reduction of the qualitative difference in labour to the quantitative difference, but not the differing amounts of wages arising from the qualitative difference. And if he is asserting that labours of different qualities result in different quantities of labour, and hence in different quantities of value because of the different amounts of wages they receive, this stands in contradiction to his proposition criticising Smith, wherein he affirms that the value is determined by the quantity of labour and not by the wages. Moreover, in relying on this proposition, he considers that the proportion of different kinds of labours in the same period is determined on the market, and that once this proportion is determined there it does not easily vary over the course of time [I/20–21].

As regards the values of products of the *same kind* of labour at different periods, on the other hand, he recognised almost no need to take into account the qualitative difference of labour when comparing them, because 'the comparative skill and intensity of labour [. . .] operate equally at both periods' [I/21]. But this is not in question from the outset, since the issue here is about comparing different kinds of labour, not the same kind.

In this way, Ricardo largely failed to solve the problem of reducing the qualitative differences of labour to the quantitative ones, although he did not neglect its existence and difficulties. He tried to justify this fact on the grounds that the subject of his arguments was not the absolute but the relative value [I/21–2].

As we have already seen, when Ricardo wrote about value, he was mainly referring to value in exchange or relative value. Here, this value in exchange or relative value has two different meanings. One is what is determined by the quantity of labour necessary to produce a commodity, which corresponds to what he calls absolute value, real value or positive value. The other is the relation between commodities as an exchange ratio, which he calls the relative value or sometimes the comparative value, in contrast to the absolute value.

Now, the absolute value is determined by the labour bestowed upon the commodity in question, and rises and falls with the quantitative variation in labour. On the contrary, the relative value is the ratio of exchange of one commodity against another, and it is therefore influenced by the variation in the quantity of labour bestowed on both commodities. Therefore these two values are evidently different. However, the absolute value and the relative value are naturally related to each other, the latter presupposing and being determined by the former. Of course, in order to be able to determine the ratio of exchange between two commodities, they must be reduced to a homogeneous entity admitting only quantitative differences, and the ratio is determined by the quantities of this homogeneous entity that each contains. And this homogeneous entity is nothing other than the substance of absolute value. It is therefore understandable that the problem of the standardisation of heterogeneous labours should be considered as a naturally-given fact when talking about the relative value presupposing the absolute value, though important when discussing the latter.

Ricardo also discussed such absolute value. When he wrote, for example, 'if the quantity of labour realized in commodities regulates their exchangeable value, every increase of the quantity of labour must augment the value of that commodity on which it is exercised' [I/13], and that 'value depends not on abundance, but on the difficulty or facility of production' [I/273], the value is absolute value. Moreover, he also talked about the relation between absolute value and relative value. He wrote:

> I do not, I think, say that the labour expended on a commodity is a measure of its exchangeable value, but of its positive value. I then add that exchangeable value is regulated by positive value, and therefore is regulated by the quantity of labour expended.
> (Letter of Ricardo to H. Trower, 4th July 1821 [IX/1–2])

And further:

> The exchangeable value of a commodity cannot alter, I say, unless either its real value, or the real value of the things it is exchanged for alter. This cannot be disputed. If a coat would purchase 4 hats and will afterwards purchase 5, I admit that both the coat and the hats have varied in exchangeable value, but they have done so in consequence of one or other of them varying in real value.
> (Letter of Ricardo to H. Trower, 22nd August 1821, IX/38).

However, Ricardo's main subject in his theory of value was not the absolute but the relative value, and its variation. He wrote:

> I have not said, because one commodity has so much labour bestowed upon it as will cost 1000*l*. and another so much as will cost 2000*l*. that therefore one would be of the value of 1000*l*. and the other of the value of 2000*l*. but I have said that their value will be to each other as two to one, and that in those proportions they will be exchanged.
> [I/46–7]

He also wrote:

> The inquiry to which I wish to draw the reader's attention, relates to the effect of the variations in the relative value of commodities, and not in their absolute value.
> [I/21]

And from this point of view:

> It will be of little importance to examine into the comparative degree of estimation in which the different kinds of human labour are held. We may

fairly conclude, that whatever inequality there might originally have been in them, whatever the ingenuity, skill, or time necessary for the acquirement of one species of manual dexterity more than another, it continues nearly the same from one generation to another; or at least, that the variation is very inconsiderable from year to year, and therefore, can have little effect, for short periods, on the relative value of commodities.

[I/21–2]

We cannot but consider this passage to be his excuse for the incomplete solution to the problem of the quality of labour.

Even if a unit of labour is fixed and in consequence the value of the commodity is determined by the quantity of labour spent on it, there will still remain infinite degrees in the conditions of production of a certain commodity: favourable, unfavourable and intermediary. Hence, the quantities of labour necessary for their production will differ widely. This raises a problematic question. Under what conditions of production does the quantity of labour required to produce a certain commodity correspond to the quantity of labour that determines the value of this commodity? Ricardo's answer to this question can be found in chapter 2 'On Rent' of *Principles*, where he wrote:

The exchangeable value of all commodities, whether they be manufactured, or the produce of the mines, or the produce of land, is always regulated, not by the less quantity of labour that will suffice for their production under circumstances highly favourable, and exclusively enjoyed by those who have peculiar facilities of production; but by the greater quantity of labour necessarily bestowed on their production by those who have no such facilities; by those who continue to produce them under the most unfavourable circumstances; meaning – by the most unfavourable circumstances, the most unfavourable under which the quantity of produce required, renders it necessary to carry on the production.

[I/73]

He continued in the next paragraph as follows:

Thus, in a charitable institution, where the poor are set to work with the funds of benefactors, the general prices of the commodities, which are the produce of such work, will not be governed by the peculiar facilities afforded to these workmen, but by the common, usual, and natural difficulties, which every other manufacturer will have to encounter. The manufacture enjoying none of these facilities might indeed be driven altogether from the market, if the supply afforded by these favoured workmen were equal to all the wants of the community; but if he continued the trade, it would be only on condition that he should derive from it the usual and general rate of profits on stock; and that could only happen when his commodity sold for a price proportioned to the quantity of labour bestowed on its production.

[I/73]

From this passage it is evident that the quantity of labour Ricardo considered to determine the value is not a particular quantity of labour under particular conditions of production, but some general quantity of labour. However, since he says that the prices of commodities will be governed 'by the common, usual, and natural difficulties', and also that the manufacturer should 'derive [from his trade] the usual and general rate of profits on stock', the question arises as to whether the general quantity of labour Ricardo had in mind was the maximum quantity, not only for products of the earth but also for industrial products.

Of course, judging from phrases such as 'the exchangeable value of every commodity' quoted above, he should have considered the maximum quantity of labour to be dominant for every kind of commodity. However, this sentence should be understood as follows: if an additional supply is necessary to satisfy the demand of society, even in the case where the additional supply requires a larger quantity of labour than the other parts, the prices of commodities will generally be determined by the quantity of labour procuring the additional supply, in other words, the maximum quantity of labour that will allow those who produce this additional quantity with unfavourable conditions of production to obtain a general and ordinary profit. This can actually occur temporarily and transitionally for every kind of commodity, but it can only occur permanently and as a rule for the products of the earth. The conditions of production in industry depend for the most part on human and transitional causes, and so the access to more favourable conditions of production and their use to increase production at will are possible there. The commodities thus produced in larger quantities under favourable conditions exert pressure on the commodities produced under unfavourable conditions. The producers under unfavourable conditions of production will then try to improve them, to bring them at least up to the same level as the producers enjoying favourable conditions. Consequently, in industrial production there is a tendency for the conditions of production to level out and so the prices of commodities tend to an average cost of production. In contrast, in primitive productions like agriculture, since the main condition of production is the land, with fertilies and locations that are naturally and permanently different from each other, it is impossible to procure favourable conditions and increase production at will. Therefore, the commodities produced under unfavourable conditions of production are not exposed to pressure from those produced under favourable conditions, and their production is required to satisfy the demand of society. Here the prices of such commodities are governed by the maximum cost of production under the worst conditions of production.

Ricardo does not give sufficient justification for such relations. Following the passage quoted above, 'where the poor are set to work [. . .]', he only says:

It is true, that on the best land, the same produce would still be obtained with the same labour as before, but its value would be enhanced in consequence of the diminished returns obtained by those who employed fresh labour and stock on the less fertile land. Notwithstanding, then, that the advantages of fertile over inferior lands are in no case lost [. . .], since more labour is required on the inferior lands, and since it is from such land only that we are enabled to furnish ourselves with the additional supply of raw produce, the comparative value of that produce will continue permanently above its former level, and make it exchange for more hats, cloth, shoes, &c. &c. in the production of which no such additional quantity of labour is required.

[I/74]

However, in chapter 17 of *Principles*, he affirmed that the prices of products of the earth are determined in the same way as those of industry in their relation to monopolised commodities, but that they differ from each other in their reciprocal relations, as follows:

Raw produce is not at a monopoly price, because the market price of barley and wheat is as much regulated by their cost of production, as the market price of cloth and linen. The only difference is this, that one portion of the capital employed in agriculture regulates the price of corn, namely, that portion which pays no rent; whereas, in the production of manufactured commodities, every portion of capital is employed with the same results; and as no portion pays rent, every portion is equally a regulator of price.

[I/250]

The portion of capital mentioned here which pays no rent in agriculture is, as we will see below, the capital under the most unfavourable conditions, and if every portion of capital in industrial production yields the same result, this is probably because an evenness in the conditions of production is assumed. Thus, Ricardo seems to have recognised the particularity of the price determination of products of the earth, as compared with industrial products. Moreover, the theory of differential rent he proposed is founded on this particularity of price determination, as we will see later.

Therefore, the maximum quantity of labour mentioned in the above quotation should be taken as valid only for the value of products of the earth. For the value of other commodities, particularly industrial products, Ricardo adopted the average quantity of labour as its measure.

Now, the above arguments are based on the hypothesis that only labour is employed for the production of commodities, and there is no capital supporting labour. But if we take into consideration the capital (consisting in instruments, machines, buildings, etc.) that is actually used in every society, how will the value of commodities be determined then? Ricardo considered such capital as realised indirect labour that is transferred into the new product through the production process, and hence that the value of a commodity depends not only on the direct labour spent on its production but also on the indirect labour. He wrote:

> Even in that early state to which Adam Smith refers, some capital, though possibly made and accumulated by the hunter himself, would be necessary to enable him to kill his game. Without some weapon, neither the beaver nor the deer could be destroyed, and therefore the value of these animals would be regulated, not solely by the time and labour necessary to their destruction, but also by the time and labour necessary to provide the hunter's capital, the weapon, by the aid of which their destruction was effected.
>
> [I/22–3]

Furthermore, depending on the instruments, machines and buildings concerned, the quantities of labour required for production may differ, and even if these quantities are equal, their durability may differ. Ricardo thought that the commodities produced with capital requiring more labour for its formation 'would naturally be of more value' than those produced with capital requiring less labour for its formation, and that 'of the durable implement only a small portion of its value would be transferred to the commodity, a much greater portion of the value of the less durable implement would be realized in the commodity which it contributed to produce' [I/23]. He confused the speed of transfer of the value of capital with the physical durability of the capital.

Taking indirect labour into account as a determinant of exchangeable value in addition to direct labour represented a step forward by Ricardo with regard to Smith. This is because Smith did not clearly discuss this point. Moreover, as seen above, when such capital as instruments, machines, etc. belongs to a class of people other than direct labourers, and is offered by the former to the latter – in the capitalist society, that is to say – Smith got into difficulties with regard to the exchange between capital and labour (because he confused labour with wages), and ended up developing the theory of natural price from a viewpoint that denied the validity of the labour theory of value in regarding profit and rent in addition to the labour bestowed (in fact wages) as component parts of the real price. On the other hand, Ricardo distinguished between labour and wages and saw no difficulties in the exchange between capital and labour, since he regarded the capitalist society as the only one possible. He believed that the value of a commodity is determined by the direct and indirect labour necessary for its production, even when the means of production are monopolised by one class. In such a case, the value of a commodity is naturally divided into two kinds of revenue: profit for the capital and wages for the labour. But he thought that the ratio of this division and its evolution would not influence the relative value itself; that wages and profit are of course two different parts of a given value of a commodity but never its component parts, and that therefore the ratio of its division and its proportions certainly influence both profit and wages but have no effect on the value of the product itself. He wrote:

All the implements necessary to kill the beaver and deer might belong to one class of men, and the labour employed in their destruction might be furnished by another class; still, their comparative prices would be in proportion to the actual labour bestowed, both on the formation of the capital, and on the destruction of the animals. Under different circumstances of plenty or scarcity of capital, as compared with labour, under different circumstances of plenty or scarcity of the food and necessaries essential to the support of men, those who furnished an equal value of capital for either one employment or for the other, might have a half, a fourth, or an eighth of the produce obtained, the remainder being paid as wages to those who furnished the labour; yet this division could not affect the relative value of these commodities, since whether the profits of capital were greater or less, whether they were 50, 20, or 10 per cent or whether the wages of labour were high or low, they would operate equally on both employments.

[I/24]

Thus Ricardo kept the labour theory of value better than Smith, but it was at the cost of incomprehension of the latter's problem.

Furthermore, Ricardo confused the value of a commodity with its natural price (because he did not distinguish between pre-capitalist and capitalist societies); he assumed the formation of an average rate of profit, and he took as his subject not the absolute but the relative value. For all these reasons, he also asserted here that a variation in either profit or wages, as equally divided parts of the commodity value, causes not only an opposite variation in the other part, but also a similar influence in every branch of production, which cancels out the variations in relative value. This is why he wrote:

Yet this division could not affect the relative value of these commodities, since whether the profits of capital were greater or less, [. . .] or whether the wages of labour were high or low, they would operate equally on both employments.

[I/24]

The proportion which might be paid for wages, is of the utmost importance in the question of profits; for it must at once be seen, that profits would be high or low, exactly in proportion as wages were low or high; but it could not in the least affect the relative value of fish and game, as wages would be high or low at the same time in both occupations.

[I/27]

or again:

No alteration in the wages of labour could produce any alteration in the relative value of these commodities; for suppose them to rise, no greater quantity of labour would be required in any of these occupations, but it would be paid for at a higher price, and the same reasons which should make the hunter and fisherman endeavour to raise the value of their game and fish, would cause the owner of the mine to raise the value of his gold.

[I/28]

Ricardo's assumption that wages and profit move in opposite directions only holds when the commodity value to be divided is fixed. If, for example, the intensity of labour increases with the rise in wages and the commodity value rises, then the profit will also rise. Even if profit varies in the opposite direction to wages, the rate of profit as a proportion of capital will also depend on the combination between the circulating capital spent on the support of labour and the fixed capital invested on instruments, machines, buildings, etc., and it will also depend on the durability of the fixed capital. This means that the rise in wages exerts an equal influence on the rate of profit in every industry, on the condition that both the combination and the durability are equal. If they differ, on the other hand, each industry will be subject to different degrees of influence. For example, if wages rise, the profit will fall more in an industry where the circulating capital is predominant and a relatively large amount of labour is employed than in other industries where the share of the circulating capital is relatively small, so the former industry will obtain a lower rate of profit, insofar as the commodities are exchanged according to the equivalence in quantities of labour bestowed. Moreover, such a rate of profit will soon contradict the reality of capitalist society, in which it tends to be equalised, whatever the proportions of the two sorts of capital or the speed of rotation.

Here, Ricardo recognised that the division of the commodity value into profit and wages and its variation do not cause variations in the value of the product itself only on the condition that the composition of the fixed and circulating capital employed for the production of commodities and the durability of the fixed capital are equal [I/29]. But if this condition is not satisfied, if the composition of these two capitals and the durability of the fixed capital are unequal, then in addition to the quantity of labour necessary for the production of commodities, variations in the value of labour (i.e., wages) are also introduced as a cause of variations in the relative value of commodities. And Ricardo explained such exceptional cases [I/30]. But in examining his explanations, we can see that he first addressed the contradiction between the law of labour value and the phenomenon of average profit independently from the variations in wages, and after that he considered the influence of the variations in wages on the commodity value.

In short, since Ricardo took the average rate of profit as a given point of departure, he could not solve this contradiction by explaining the phenomenon of the average rate of profit on the basis of the law of labour value, but only by restricting the latter by the former. That is why his explanation is referred to as a modification of the law of labour value.

ii) Modification of the law of labour value

As seen above, Ricardo, just like Smith, considered capital as the material elements necessary to give effect to labour, so that he also recognised the existence of capital in the society that Smith described as primitive. But capital in such a society was limited to the tools for labour. In the civilised society, on the other hand, capital also included the subsistence for labourers. Therefore, for Ricardo too, capital was virtually of a different nature in these two kinds of society, but he was not aware of this point and so did not understand the distinction between them.

He classified these material elements into fixed and circulating capital according to their durability – a physical property of these elements. He wrote:

> According as capital is rapidly perishable, and requires to be frequently reproduced, or is of slow consumption, it is classed under the heads of circulating, or of fixed capital. A brewer, whose buildings and machinery are valuable and durable, is said to employ a large portion of fixed capital: on the contrary, a shoemaker, whose capital is chiefly employed in the payment of wages, which are expended on food and clothing, commodities more perishable than building and machinery, is said to employ a large proportion of his capital as circulating capital.
>
> [I/31]

It is evident from this quotation that the distinction he makes between fixed and circulating capital follows one of the standards Smith gave for this purpose. It is to be noted that there is no raw material in the class of circulating capital defined by Ricardo, because it is in fact reduced to the subsistence on which wages are spent. In this, as seen above, Ricardo went further than Smith, who, following the example of Quesnay, considered the subsistence for labourers as part of the circulating capital distinguished from the fixed capital.

Insofar as physical durability is taken as the standard, the time necessary to recover the value of capital is not brought into question, at least not immediately. But Ricardo sometimes adopted other standards for distinguishing between the two kinds of capital, i.e., the amount of time necessary to recover the value of capital. This is what he was referring to when he wrote:

> The wheat bought by a farmer to sow is comparatively a fixed capital to the wheat purchased by a baker to make into loaves. One leaves it in the ground, and can obtain no return for a year; the other can get it ground into flour, sell it as bread to his customers, and have his capital free to renew the same, or commence any other employment in a week.
>
> [I/31]

Thus, to explain the influence of variations in wages on the relative value when the composition of the two sorts of capital and the durability of the fixed capital differ across different branches of production, Ricardo proposed several illustrations. In the first illustration, he wrote:

> Suppose two men employ one hundred men each for a year in the construction of two machines, and another man employs the same number of men in cultivating corn, each of the machines at the end of the year will be of the same value as the corn, for they will each be produced by the same quantity of labour. Suppose one of the owners of one of the machines to employ it, with the assistance of one hundred men, the following year in making cloth, and the owner of the other machine to employ his also, with the assistance likewise of one hundred men, in making cotton goods, while the farmer continues to employ one hundred men as before in the cultivation of corn. During the second year they will all have employed the same quantity of labour, but the goods and machine together of the clothier, and also of the cotton manufacturer, will be the result of the labour of two hundred men, employed for a year; or, rather, of the labour of one hundred men for two years; whereas the corn will be produced by the labour of one hundred men for one year, consequently if the corn be of the value of 500*l*. the machine and cloth of the clothier together, ought to be of the value of 1000*l*. and the machine and cotton goods of the cotton manufacturer, ought to be also of twice the value of the corn. But they will be of more than twice the value of the corn, for the profit on the clothier's and cotton manufacturer's capital for the first year has been added to their capitals, while that of the farmer has been expended and enjoyed. On account then of the different degrees of durability of their capitals, or, which is the same thing, on account of the time which must elapse before one set of commodities can be brought to market, they will be valuable, not exactly in proportion to the quantity of labour bestowed on them, – they will not be as two to one, but something more, to compensate for the greater length of time which must elapse before the most valuable can be brought to market.
>
> [I/33–4]

He continued with the second illustration, as follows:

> Suppose that for the labour of each workman 50*l*. per annum were paid, or that 5000*l*. capital were employed and profits were 10 per cent., the value of each of the machines as well as of the corn, at the end of the first year, would be 5,500*l*. The second year the manufacturers and farmer will again employ 5000*l*. each in the support of labour, and will therefore again sell their goods for 5,500*l*., but the men using the machines, to be on a par with the farmer, must not only obtain 5,500*l*., for the equal capitals of 5000*l*. employed on labour, but they must obtain a further sum of 550*l*.; for the profit on 5,500*l*. which they have invested in machinery, and consequently their goods must sell for 6,050*l*. Here then are capitalists

employing precisely the same quantity of labour annually on the production of their commodities, and yet the goods they produce differ in value on account of the different quantities of fixed capital, or accumulated labour, employed by each respectively. The cloth and cotton goods are of the same value, because they are the produce of equal quantities of labour, and equal quantities of fixed capital; but corn is not of the same value as these commodities, because it is produced, as far as regards fixed capital, under different circumstances.

[I/34]

In these two illustrations, Ricardo evidently assumed that neither the farmer nor the manufacturer spend anything on raw materials, that the farmer invests nothing on fixed capital, that the fixed capital (machines in this case) does not undergo any wear and tear and that its value is not transferred to the product. For the moment we will not question the absurdity of such an assumption. Now in the first illustration, Ricardo tried to explain that the variation in wages influences the relative value of a commodity 'on account of the different degrees of durability of their capitals'. But in fact he showed the case in which the manufacturer's capital is larger than that of the farmer (the latter being 5,000*l.* and the former 10,500*l.*), only because of the length of the production process and not because of the difference in the durability of capital, and that because of the law of equality of the rate of profit, the commodities are not exchanged for each other according to their labour values independently of variations in wages. If Ricardo affirmed in this explanation that the value of the manufactured goods must be more than twice that of the agricultural product because the profit for the farmer's capital during the first year is consumed and enjoyed, while the profits of the cotton manufacturer and the spinner are added to their capitals, it is because he thought that otherwise, the manufacturer's rate of profit would differ from that of the farmer, which would be contrary to the law of the average rate of profit. Hence, he affirmed that the law of labour value is modified. Consequently, what Ricardo here calls modification only indicates that the value of a commodity transforms itself into the sum of the consumed capital and the average profit (i.e., the natural price), because of the law of the average rate of profit and independently of the variation in wages.

Similarly, in the second illustration Ricardo sought to clarify how the variation in wages influences the relative value of a commodity when the composition of fixed and circulating capital is different, but in fact he only showed that the commodity value must be transformed into the natural price because of the law of the average rate of profit, when differences in the length of the production process lead to differences in the sum of capital employed. This is particularly evident in this illustration, where Ricardo specified 'the men using the machines, to be on a par with the farmer'.

So contrary to Ricardo's intention, both of these illustrations actually describe how the value of a commodity is modified because of the law of the average rate of profit, independently of variations in wages, when there are differences in the length of time which must elapse from the investment of capital in various branches of industry till its recovery or till the commodity is brought to the market. And so when he gave a third illustration, it was similar to the foregoing in both substance and form:

> Suppose I employ twenty men at an expense of 1000*l.* for a year in the production of a commodity, and at the end of the year I employ twenty men again for another year, at a further expense of 1000*l.* in finishing or perfecting the same commodity, and that I bring it to market at the end of two years, if profits be 10 per cent, my commodity must sell for 2,310*l.*; for I have employed 1000*l.* capital for one year, and 2,100*l.* capital for one year more. Another man employs precisely the same quantity of labour, but he employs it all in the first year; he employs forty men at an expense of 2000*l.*, and at the end of the first year he sells it with 10 per cent profit, or for 2,200*l.* Here then are two commodities having precisely the same quantity of labour bestowed on them, one of which sells for 2,310*l.* – the other for 2,200*l.* This case appears to differ from the last, but is, in fact, the same. In both cases the superior price of one commodity is owing to the greater length of time which must elapse before it can be brought to market. [. . .] The difference in value arises in both cases from the profits being accumulated as capital, and is only a just compensation for the time that the profits were withheld.
>
> [I/37]

However, Ricardo gave another illustration showing how the rise or fall in wages really influences the value of a commodity. But what he means by the word 'value' is already modified and transformed into natural price, hence it is not truly the value determined by the quantity of labour, as in the previous illustrations. He wrote:

> There can be no rise in the value of labour without a fall of profits. If the corn is to be divided between the farmer and the labourer, the larger the proportion that is given to the latter, the less will remain for the former. So if cloth or cotton goods be divided between the workman and his employer, the larger the proportion given to the former, the less remains for the latter. Suppose then, that owing to a rise of wages, profits fall from 10 to 9 per cent, instead of adding 550*l.* to the common price of their goods (to 5,500*l.*) for the profits on their fixed capital, the manufacturers would add only 9 per cent on that sum, or 495*l.*, consequently the price would be 5,995*l.* instead of 6,050*l.* As the corn would continue to sell for 5,500*l.*, the manufactured goods in which more fixed capital was employed, would fall relatively to corn or to any other goods in which a less portion of fixed capital entered. The degree of alteration in the relative value of goods, on account of a rise or fall of labour, would depend on the proportion which the fixed capital bore to the whole capital employed. All

commodities which are produced by very valuable machinery, or in very valuable buildings, or which require a great length of time before they can be brought to market, would fall in relative value, while all those which were chiefly produced by labour, or which would be speedily brought to market would rise in relative value.

[I/35]

Incidentally, Ricardo wrote that:

In proportion as fixed capital is less durable, it approaches to the nature of circulating capital. It will be consumed and its value reproduced in a shorter time, in order to preserve the capital of the manufacturer.

And from this point of view he thought that when the durability of fixed capital differs, the influence of the variation in wages on the value of a commodity can be discussed in the same way as when the composition of the fixed and circulating capital differs. Hence, in the same way as 'a rise in the wages of labour would not equally affect commodities produced with machinery quickly consumed, and commodities produced with machinery slowly consumed', a rise in wages would affect differently commodities produced mainly with circulating capital and those produced mainly with fixed capital. The value of the former relative to the latter would rise, and a fall in wages would bring about an opposite result [I/38, 9].

It is to be noticed, in this explanation by Ricardo, that a rise in wages is assumed never to occur without a fall in profit, nor a rise in profit without a fall in wages. This seems to be for the purpose of explaining the influence of variations in wages on the relative value via the preliminary influence of the former on profit, but as seen above this assumption is not always correct in itself. Then he assumed, curiously, that a fall in the rate of profit caused by a rise in wages has no influence on the circulating capital, but only on the fixed capital. In the last place, it is self-evident, if we examine the starting point of the last illustration quoted above (6,050*l.* as the price of manufactured goods and 5,050*l.* as the price of agricultural goods), that when discussing the influence of a variation in wages under such a supposition, his subject was the natural price governed by the phenomenon of the average profit, and not the value itself as determined by the labour bestowed. Yet Ricardo affirmed that this was the influence exerted on the value of a commodity. This is because, far from distinguishing clearly between the value of a commodity and its natural price, he confused the two.

Having thus mistaken the influence of a variation in wages (and hence in profit) on the natural price for its influence on the value, Ricardo explained that the variation in the natural price caused by a variation in wages is very minor compared with the variation in the value caused by a variation in the labour bestowed. He wrote:

The reader, however, should remark, that this cause of the variation of commodities is comparatively slight in its effects. With such a rise of wages as should occasion a fall of one per cent in profits, goods produced under the circumstances I have supposed, vary in relative value only one per cent. [. . .] The greatest effects which could be produced on the relative prices of these goods from a rise of wages, could not exceed 6 or 7 per cent; for profits could not, probably, under any circumstances, admit of a greater general and permanent depression than to that amount. Not so with the other great cause of the variation in the value of commodities, namely, the increase or diminution in the quantity of labour necessary to produce them. If to produce the corn, eighty, instead of one hundred men, should be required, the value of the corn would fall 20 per cent."

[I/36]

For this reason, he concluded as follows:

In estimating, then, the causes of the variations in the value of commodi-ties, although it would be wrong wholly to omit the consideration of the effect produced by a rise or fall of labour, it would be equally incorrect to attach much importance to it; and consequently, in the subsequent part of this work, [. . .] I shall consider all the great variations which take place in the relative value of commodities to be produced by the greater or less quantity of labour.

[I/36–7]

Here, he forgot having explained that the value of a commodity undergoes certain modifications, because of the law of the average rate of profit, when the time necessary for recovery of the capital differs, even if wages remain unchanged. In confusing the value of a commodity and its natural price, he considered the influence of a variation in wages on the latter. And, on the grounds that this influence is actually slight, he argued that the value of a commodity only varies when the quantity of labour bestowed varies, and that the law of labour value applies as a rule also in the capitalist society.

As we have already said, Ricardo's explanation here presupposes an average rate of profit given in advance, and this presupposition is based on confusion between the value of a commodity and its natural price, and more fundamentally on his view of the capitalist society as the only possible form of society, of which the pre-capitalist society is merely an earlier stage. Moreover, it may be for this reason that he took relative value as the subject of his theory of value. And insofar as the subject is the relative value and not the absolute value, the issue will only be about the quantities of value or profit and their variation. Besides, since Ricardo sought to determine the laws governing these quantities or varia-tions, the process of averaging individual profits was presupposed and the average profit became a given magnitude. And with the average profit as a presupposi-tion, the transformation of the value of a commodity into the natural price caused by this phenomenon was interpreted as the limitation and modification of the law of labour value.

In any case, this showed the lack of clear understanding about the relation between individual and average profit, and hence between the value of a commodity and its natural price. For this reason Ricardo raised the question about the variation in wages as an additional cause of variation in value, when the difference between the composition of capital and its durability is admitted, only to end with the following result: explaining how the value of a commodity is in fact modified by the phenomenon of average profit, and then why the value thus modified (the natural price) was influenced by the variation in wages, he immediately neglected the significance of the modification of the former in declaring that the influence of the latter was slight.

If Ricardo presented the problem and drew his conclusions in this way, it was not just for the theoretical reason given above, but also for practical reasons. One motive for Ricardo to develop his theory of value was of course in the Corn Laws controversy, as seen above. In this controversy, in opposition to Malthus, he upheld the position that the difficulty of corn production and consequently the higher or lower wages are almost the only reason for lower or higher profits. In order to defend this position, he had to demonstrate that higher wages are not necessarily the cause of higher prices, since for him, the profit is the residual part remaining after subtracting the wages from the commodity price. When Ricardo wrote that 'Adam Smith, and all the writers who have followed him, have, without one exception that I know of, maintained that a rise in the price of labour would be uniformly followed by a rise in the price of all commodities. I hope I have succeeded in showing, that there are no grounds for such an opinion' [I/46], it is because he supported the theory of the decomposition of value rather than its composition, but it is also grounded on this practical consideration.

In any case, contrary to Smith, who considered that the value depends on the distribution, Ricardo tried to show that the distribution is, on the contrary, based on the value. However, in his efforts to surmount the difficulties posed by the relation between the value of a commodity and the phenomenon of average profit, he finally ended up in a position similar to that of Smith. Because, although he says that 'this cause of the variation of commodities is comparatively slight in its effects' so that the deviation from value is exceptional, this deviation is actually the rule, precisely as Malthus upheld, moreover he presupposed the natural price based on the value composition theory. Indeed, this was one of the principal reasons which led his economic theory to collapse.

iii) Relation between natural price and market price

Above, we set out Ricardo's viewpoint on the relation between individual and average profit, and between the 'value' of a commodity and its natural price. Following this viewpoint, he also attached the meaning of the value of a commodity to the natural price when discussing the distinction and relation between the natural and market price in chapter 4 of the *Principles*. This opens with a sentence discussing the relation between the natural price and a market price that deviates temporarily and accidentally from it. He wrote:

> In making labour the foundation of the value of commodities, and the comparative quantity of labour which is necessary to their production, the rule which determines the respective quantities of goods which shall be given in exchange for each other, we must not be supposed to deny the accidental and temporary deviations of the actual or market price of commodities from this, their primary and natural price.
>
> [I/88]

However, the natural price mentioned here is not in fact the 'value' of a commodity itself, but the 'value' of a commodity already modified by the law of average profit, whose relation with the market price, which varies with the supply and demand of the commodity, is brought into question. Therefore, according to Ricardo,

> In the ordinary course of events, there is no commodity which continues for any length of time to be supplied precisely in that degree of abundance, which the wants and wishes of mankind require, and therefore there is none which is not subject to accidental and temporary variations of price.
>
> [I/88]

For this reason, the actual or market price is sometimes above, sometimes below the natural price, and consequently the rate of profit also moves above or below the general or average level. But, 'whilst every man is free to employ his capital where he pleases, he will naturally seek for it that employment which is most advantageous [. . .]. This restless desire on the part of all the employers of stock, to quit a less profitable for a more advantageous business' naturally attracts or repels capital to or from a given business according to the higher or lower profit which can be obtained by employing it for the production of commodities in that business, with the result that an increase or decrease in the supply of these commodities brings about a fall or rise in their price. As a result, there will be 'a strong tendency to equalize the rate of profits of all, or to fix them in such proportions, as may in the estimation of the parties, compensate for any advantage which one may have, or may appear to have over the other' [I/88–9]. This movement of capital is naturally impeded by many obstacles, but functions as a general tendency, which becomes more tenacious with the development of a credit system and is 'more active than is generally supposed' [I/90].

Then he concluded as follows:

> It is then the desire, which every capitalist has, of diverting his funds from a less to a more profitable employment, that prevents the market price of commodities from continuing for any length of time either much above,

or much below their natural price. It is this competition which so adjusts the exchangeable value of commodities, that after paying the wages for the labour necessary to their production, and all other expenses required to put the capital employed in its original state of efficiency, the remaining value or over-plus will in each trade be in proportion to the value of the capital employed.

[I/91]

It is evident that Ricardo was speaking about the movement of the market prices of various commodities, which tend after all toward their natural prices (governed by the law of average profit) while deviating from them.

However, in the above explanation, Ricardo originally intended to elucidate how the balanced state (the starting point for his explanation of the principle of value) is attained, and by what force the law of value is realised. Of course, his principle of value is based on the reality of capitalistic market exchange, so he recognised that it is also influenced by temporary and accidental causes. But he first tried to clarify its conformity to the natural law, by abstracting away from such temporary and accidental causes (cf. Ricardo, *Principles* [I/91–2]). Therefore his next move was to elucidate the relation between this natural law and the temporary accidentals and thereby return to the real world.

Ricardo's explanation of the relation between natural and market prices cannot be considered as much of an advance of that of Smith, except that Ricardo added the function of credit. But there are some differences between them, because unlike Smith, Ricardo did not consider rent as a component of the natural price. Furthermore, in confusing the value of a commodity and its natural price, he took this as the reason why the payment of rent does not invalidate or modify the law of labour value, contrary to Smith. Ricardo's theory of rent is intended to clarify this point. However, before examining his theory of rent, we must give an overview of his theory of money in relation to the theory of value, insofar as this will be necessary for later explanations.

iv) *Theory of money*

Almost in the same way as Smith, Ricardo recognised the essence of money as a medium of circulation and viewed it as a commodity like any other. Since he took as his subject not the absolute but the relative value, as seen above, it was a matter of course that the process through which the value of a commodity is expressed as a price was not brought into question, value and price often being synonymous and the price and circulation of money presupposed from the outset. Hence, money was not conceived as the general equivalent by which the value of all other commodities can be expressed, but as a medium of circulation.

Thus, according to Ricardo, money is a medium of circulation; not a special commodity but an ordinary one. He therefore considered it to be variable in value like other commodities, and hence not able to serve as the true measure of value [I/44]. And since money is an ordinary commodity, he identified it with its constituent material (i.e., gold or silver), which undergoes no change in its nature as a commodity when it becomes money (*High Price* [III/52–3]).

In any case, considering money as an ordinary commodity, he sought its value in the value of its constituent material, which was to be determined by the quantity of labour necessary for its production. Hence, in *High Price*, he said that gold and silver have their intrinsic value like any other commodity, which 'is dependent on their scarcity, the quantity of labour bestowed in procuring them, and the value of the capital employed in the mines which produce them' (*High Price* [III/52]), but in *Principles* he corrected this definition by applying his labour theory of value and stating that 'gold and silver, like all other commodities, are valuable only in proportion to the quantity of labour necessary to produce them, and bring them to market (*Principles* [I/352]).

Insofar as money is thus a commodity and its value is a material value, hence intrinsic, the quantity of money circulating as a medium of exchange must be determined by this predefined value of money and the total value of the commodities in circulation, if we ignore the velocity of circulation of money. But on the contrary, when it came to the question of the relation between the quantity of money in circulation and the value of money, Ricardo determined the latter by the former and the total value of the commodities in circulation, in other words by the demand and supply of money. Of course, he wrote in *High Price* that 'if a mine of gold were discovered in either of these countries, the currency of that country would be lowered in value in consequence of the increased quantity of the precious metals brought into circulation, and would therefore no longer be of the same value as that of other countries' (*High Price* [III/54]), and a little later: 'The equilibrium between that and other nations would only be restored by the exportation of part of the coin' (*High Price* [III/55]). In this way, the precious metal would be distributed according to the state of commerce and wealth in each country, and hence according to the number of payments to be made using money and their velocity. He continued:

> If instead of a mine being discovered in any country, a bank were established, such as the Bank of England, with the power of issuing its notes for a circulating medium; after a large amount had been issued either by way of loan to merchants, or by advances to government, thereby adding considerably to the sum of the currency, the same effect would follow as in the case of the mine'.
>
> [III/54–5]

In *Principles*, he considered the influence of seigniorage on the value of money, and deduced the value of money equally from the limitation of its quantity. He wrote:

> While the State coins money, and charges no seigniorage, money will be of the same value as any other piece of the same metal of equal weight and

fineness; but if the State charges a seigniorage for coinage, the coined piece of money will generally exceed the value of the uncoined piece of metal by the whole seigniorage charged. [. . .] While the State alone coins, there can be no limit to this charge of seigniorage; for by limiting the quantity of coin, it can be raised to any conceivable value'.

In this way, the value of money becomes altogether independent of the value of its constituent material, and is to be found in its abundance or scarcity. He added that

> It is on this principle that paper money circulates: the whole charge for paper money may be considered as seigniorage. Though it has no intrinsic value, yet, by limiting its quantity, its value in exchange is as great as an equal denomination of coin, or of bullion in that coin'.

> [I/353]

And he considered that the devalued coin could be treated in the same manner.

Ricardo thus determined the value of money in terms of the total value of the commodities in circulation and the quantity of money, without any distinction as to whether it is coin or paper money or even worn and torn money. Needless to say, Ricardo thought in this way because he considered the medium of circulation to be the essence of money. Of course, insofar as money functions as the medium of circulation, its existence as value only represents the value of the commodity to be exchanged for it until the exchange actually takes place, and therefore does not matter in itself. As a result, money can take on an ideal existence, leaving its real existence as value. This is why worn and torn money and in particular inconvertible paper money can circulate on the same footing as full-bodied coin and have value as such. However, if they circulate and have value, it is because they represent the quantity of gold in circulation, as the symbol of its value. Hence, an increase in the issue of paper money reduces the quantity of gold represented by each unit and diminishes its purchasing power. This is caused by changes in the monetary unit, and hence in the price unit, and is not merely a variation in the value of money. As seen above, having neglected to examine the process through which the value is expressed as price, Ricardo considered this immediately as a variation in the value of money, which he thus understood as inversely proportionate to its quantity.

Moreover, just as he was prevented by the confusion during the 'Bank Restriction Period' from recognising the difference between the circulation of paper money as a symbol of value and the circulation of banknotes as bills of credit, Ricardo drew from the phenomenon of the former the law of circulation of metallic money and finally arrived at the quantity theory of money, in which metallic money enters the circulation in the same way as paper money and only obtains its value in circulation, in the form of price.

If Ricardo adopted the quantity theory of money in this way, it was on the theoretical basis of his relative theory of value, which failed to clarify the character of the value shared by both commodities and money (the precondition for their equality), and on the empirical basis of the actual situation of the time, when paper money was depreciating and commodity prices were rising. Indeed, judging from these relations, it appears that Ricardo should be blamed precisely for a lack of abstraction, contrary to the usual criticisms of him.

3. Theory of rent

As we have already said, according to Ricardo, the law of labour value is not refuted by the accumulation of capital and the appearance of profit: it simply undergoes certain modifications in particular cases, without losing its fundamental validity, although

> It remains however to be considered, whether the appropriation of land, and the consequent creation of rent, will occasion any variation in the rela-tive value of commodities, independently of the quantity of labour necessary to production. [. . .] In order to understand this part of the subject, [in chapters 2 and 3 of *Principles* he] enquire[s] into the nature of rent, and the laws by which its rise or fall is regulated.
>
> [I/67]

From this it is evident that, just as the theory of value seen in the previous section presupposes categories of distribution such as wages and profit in order to discuss the relation between these categories and the value of a commodity, while at the same time purporting to give a foundation to the distribution, this theory of rent is also directly and consciously connected with the theory of value. But his scientific contribution is said to consist precisely in the fact that his theory of rent is thus related to the theory of value. That is because except for this point, the doctrine of Ricardo is merely a repetition of what Anderson, West, etc. had already proposed.

As for his theory of distribution, the dynamic part of this theory pivots upon the relation between the value of an agricultural product and the rent, developed in this chapter. And the subsequent theories of wages and of profit presuppose the doctrine in this chapter, simply developing and supplementing them.

According to Ricardo, 'rent is that portion of the produce of the earth, which is paid to the landlord for the use of the original and indestructible powers of the soil [I/67]. 'By rent I always mean the remuneration given to the landlord for the use of the original and inherent power of the land' (*Essay*, footnote [IV/18]). Here the original and indestructible powers of the soil means a power independent of human power and specific to the soil. Ricardo therefore made a strict distinction between rent and the profit and interest paid for capital, which is the result of past labour. 'It is often, however, confounded with the interest and profit of capital, and, in popular language, the term is applied to whatever is annually paid by a farmer to his landlord'. However, 'the rent is that portion which is paid to the landlord for the use of the original and indestructible powers of the soil', which should be clearly distinguished from the interest and profit which is 'paid for the use of the capital which had been employed in ameliorating the quality of the land, and in erecting such buildings as were necessary to secure and preserve the produce' [I/67].

But in practice, the remuneration paid for the use of the power specific to the soil and the remuneration paid for the capital employed in ameliorating the land are not distinguished so clearly, because, as he wrote in another passage, 'a part of this capital, when once expended in the improvement of a farm, is inseparably amalgamated with the land, and tends to increase its productive powers'. So he himself recognised that the remuneration paid for the use of capital of such a nature 'is strictly of the nature of rent, and is subject to all the laws of rent', and he affirmed that only the remuneration for capital not of such a nature, 'bestowed on buildings, and other perishable improvements' which 'require to be constantly renewed' (Ricardo, *Principles*, footnote [I/262]) should be distinguished from the rent and treated as profit.

His recognition of the existence of a sort of capital that 'is inseparably amalgamated with the land, and tends to increase its productive powers', suggests that his concept of the 'original and indestructible powers of the soil' and his definition of the rent founded on this concept are beside the point. This is evident when he himself writes elsewhere that 'rent is always the difference between the produce obtained by the employment of two equal quantities of capital and labour' [I/71]. In fact, if the rent is of such a nature, it is nothing other than a surplus profit for the capital employed in a better-than-average condition of production in whatever branch of production, i.e., whether in manufacture or agriculture. Therefore, it cannot be said to be the remuneration for the use of the power specific to the soil, to be distinguished from the remuneration for capital. Only the differences in the conditions of agricultural production are distinct from those in manufacture, in that this surplus profit is rendered permanent in the former. If Ricardo insisted on the difference between rent and profit, it may be because of his view of their social significance, as we will see below. In particular, when rent is considered as the charge for lending original and indestructible powers, its character as an unearned income is naturally expressed of itself.

Given the essence of rent as described above, how then does it arise? Ricardo divided rent into two different classes: one which arises from differences in the fertility or location of the soil, and the other which arises from the law of diminishing returns from the land, i.e., the fact that successive increases in the capital invested on the same land does not result in proportional increases in yield.

He explained the first class of rent as follows:

> On the first settling of a country, in which there is an abundance of rich and fertile land, a very small proportion of which is required to be cultivated for the support of the actual population, or indeed can be cultivated with the capital which the population can command, there will be no rent; for

no one would pay for the use of land, when there was an abundant quantity not yet appropriated, and, therefore, at the disposal of whosoever might choose to cultivate it.

On the common principles of supply and demand, no rent could be paid for such land, for the reason stated why nothing is given for the use of air and water [. . .]. If all land had the same properties, if it were unlimited in quantity, and uniform in quality, no charge could be made for its use, unless where it possessed peculiar advantages of situation. It is only, then, because land is not unlimited in quantity and uniform in quality, and because in the progress of population, land of an inferior quality, or less advantageously situated, is called into cultivation, that rent is ever paid for the use of it. When in the progress of society, land of the second degree of fertility is taken into cultivation, rent immediately commences on that of the first quality, and the amount of that rent will depend on the difference in the quality of these two portions of land.

[I/69]

Ricardo then proceeded to discuss the rise in rent.

When land of the third quality is taken into cultivation, rent immediately commences on the second, and it is regulated as before, by the difference in their productive powers. At the same time, the rent of the first quality will rise, for that must always be above the rent of the second, by the difference between the produce which they yield with a given quantity of capital and labour. With every step in the progress of population, which shall oblige a country to have recourse to land of a worse quality, to enable it to raise its supply of food, rent, on all the more fertile land, will rise.

[I/69–70]

The first thing that we can see from these quotations, is that Ricardo gave differences in the quality of soil, i.e., differences in their fertility and location, as the condition for rent to arise. He attaches importance only to the differences in fertility; differences in location are treated rather incidentally. Every rent in his theory arises from differences in the quality and productivity of the soil, i.e., differences in the yield obtained from the same quantity of capital and labour invested on lands of the same surface area but of differing qualities. This is the so-called differential rent, which is therefore essentially the same as the surplus profit in general.

Second, he reasoned as if there were no landed property, in writing of the emergence of rent. Of course, since he began with a colony with no landed property, saying that there would be no rent because land is 'not yet appropriated, and, therefore, at the disposal of whosoever might choose to cultivate it', he appeared to be assuming the existence of landed property as the condition of rent, but immediately after that he argued as if there were no landed property and hence no obstacle to investment in the land, writing that: 'it is only because land is not unlimited in quantity and uniform in quality, [. . .] that rent is ever paid for the use of it' under the effect of demand and supply. This explanation must be the result either of applying to the capitalist society the assumption that is valid for the colony without landed property, or of mistaking the social institution of landed property for the natural character of the land. Both are contrary to the reality of capitalism. Naturally, all the land is privately owned here, and capital finds it an obstacle to its investment. In this regard Ricardo differed from Smith, who had recognised landed property.

However, it is not landed property that gives rise to the differential rent itself. The differential rent is, as seen above, the difference between the yields obtained from the application of the same quantity of capital and labour, with no relation to landed property itself. Therefore Ricardo was theoretically right not to require it as a condition for differential rent. In addition, this may have been a historical fact in the English capitalism of the time. Probably the 'Enclosure Acts' that were specific to England and the revolutionary changes wrought on feudal relations by capital since the time of Henry VII gave rise to circumstances seemingly without virtual landed property (K. Marx, *Theorien über den Mehrwert* [in *Zur Kritik der politischen Ökonomie (Manuskript 1861–1863)*, MEGA②, II/3, Teil 3, S.881.])

Next, Ricardo gave the spread of cultivation from better to worse lands, due to the 'increase of population' and 'development of society', as a cause of the rise in rent. This explanation seems to derive from the continual rise of corn prices in his time and his law of the falling rate of profit based on this price movement. But it may also be a historical fact in such a comparatively small country as England, where capital was employed and every kind of agricultural experimentation had been carried out for several hundred years. However, there was technical progress in agriculture too, gradually increasing yields. Therefore the spread of cultivation in the opposite direction, from worse to better lands, is also possible. And in this case too, the extension of cultivation will cause rent to emerge and rise in the better lands, insofar as the additional supply keeps pace with the increase in demand, so that the cultivation of the worse lands remains necessary to satisfy the social demand. Hence the assumption is not only one-sided but also unnecessary for the differential rent. It seems to have been necessary only for Ricardo to establish the law of the falling rate of profit.

Now let us examine the second class of rent. According to Ricardo, other than arising from differences in the fertility of the soil, rent also arises in the following manner:

It often, and, indeed, commonly happens, that before No. 2, 3, 4, or 5, or the inferior lands are cultivated, capital can be employed more productively on those lands which are already in cultivation. It may perhaps be found, that by doubling the original capital employed on No. 1, though the produce will not be doubled, [. . .] this quantity exceeds what could be obtained by employing the same capital, on land No. 3. In such case, capital will be preferably employed on the old land, and will equally create a rent; for rent is always the difference between the produce obtained by the employment of two equal quantities of capital and labour. If, with a capital of 1000*l.*, a tenant obtain 100 quarters of wheat from his land, and by the employment of a second capital of 1000*l.*, he obtain a further return of eighty-five, his landlord would have the power at the expiration of his lease, of obliging him to pay fifteen quarters, or an equivalent value, for additional rent; for there cannot be two rates of profit. If he is satisfied with a diminution of fifteen quarters in the return for his second 1000*l.*, it is because no employment more profitable can be found for it. The common rate of profit would be in that proportion.

[I/71–2]

Evidently, Ricardo here assumed the law of diminishing returns from land. Consequently, the same critical comments can be made as in the case of the first class of rent.

In recapitulating the genesis of these two classes of rent, Ricardo concluded on the process of their emergence and rise as follows:

If, then, good land existed in a quantity much more abundant than the production of food for an increasing population required, or if capital could be indefinitely employed without a diminished return on the old land, there could be no rise of rent; for rent invariably proceeds from the employment of an additional quantity of labour with a proportionally less return.

[I/72]

However, the existence of such a differential rent still presupposes that the price of agricultural products depends necessarily on the highest cost of production paid on the worst land or incurred on the last portion of invested capital. Since this differential rent is the difference between the worst and best lands, or between the capital invested last and that invested earlier, it cannot exist without the cultivation of the worst land or the last investment of capital. On the other hand, the condition for such a cultivation or investment to be implemented is the ordinary and general rate of profit to be obtained from them. And for this condition to be satisfied, the natural price of the agricultural product must be fixed on the basis of the cost paid on the worst land or incurred on the ultimate portion of invested capital. In this sense, Ricardo wrote:

If he [a manufacturer] continued the trade [under unfavourable circumstances], it would be only on condition that he should derive from it the usual and general rate of profits on stock; and that could only happen when his commodity sold for a price proportioned to the quantity of labour bestowed on its production.

[I/73]

Ricardo considered that, if the production under unfavourable circumstances is necessary to satisfy the social demand, the exchangeable value of a commodity is determined by the greatest quantity of labour required under such circumstances. Though his explanation on this point is not complete, it applies to agricultural products, the exchangeable value of which is determined by the greatest quantity of labour required under the most unfavourable conditions of production. And the 'value' of this commodity is the natural price; hence the average profit can also be obtained on the worst land or from the last portion of invested capital. Therefore, the capital invested under better conditions of production will generate a surplus profit over and above the average rate according to the degree of superiority of those conditions. This surplus profit transforms itself into rent, 'for there cannot be two rates of profit' [I/72]. It may be in this sense that Ricardo wrote:

> On the best land, the same produce would still be obtained with the same labour as before, but its value would be enhanced in consequence of the diminished returns obtained by those who employed fresh labour and stock on the less fertile land. Notwithstanding, then, that the advantages of fertile over inferior lands are in no case lost, but only transferred from the cultivator, or consumer, to the landlord.
>
> [I/74]

This same point is explained more succinctly in chapter 3 'On the Rent of Mines':

> There are mines of various qualities, affording very different results, with equal quantities of labour. The metal produced from the poorest mine that is worked, must at least have an exchangeable value, not only sufficient to procure all the clothes, food, and other necessaries consumed by those employed in working it, and bringing the produce to market, but also to afford the common and ordinary profits to him who advances the stock necessary to carry on the undertaking. The return for capital from the poorest mine paying no rent, would regulate the rent of all the other more productive mines. This mine is supposed to yield the usual profits of stock. All that the other mines produce more than this, will necessarily be paid to the owners for rent. This principle is precisely the same as that which we have already laid down respecting land.
>
> [I/85]

As we have already mentioned, the explanation Ricardo gave is based on his confusion between the 'value' of a commodity and its natural price.

In any case, for Ricardo the rent is the difference between the yield on the marginal land or capital and that obtained under better conditions. Hence, the marginal land or capital gives rise to no rent, and yet the price of farm products is regulated by the quantity of labour employed on the land or by the capital yielding no rent. This is because an additional supply of agricultural products can only be made from such land or capital. Thus, Ricardo wrote that:

> The reason then, why raw produce rises in comparative value, is because more labour is employed in the production of the last portion obtained, and not because a rent is paid to the landlord. The value of corn is regulated by the quantity of labour bestowed on its production on that quality of land, or with that portion of capital, which pays no rent. Corn is not high because a rent is paid, but a rent is paid because corn is high; and [. . .] no reduction would take place in the price of corn, although landlords should forego the whole of their rent.
>
> [I/74–5]

and he answered the question raised at the beginning of this chapter, by saying that that corn which is produced by the greatest quantity of labour is the regulator of the price of corn; and rent does not and cannot enter in the least degree as a component part of its price.

> Adam Smith, therefore, cannot be correct in supposing that the original rule which regulated the exchangeable value of commodities, namely, the comparative quantity of labour by which they were produced, can be at all altered by the appropriation of land and the payment of rent.
>
> [I/77–8]

Ricardo's conclusion that 'rent does not enter in the least degree as a component part of its price' is justifiable from his point of view, according to which the rent is differential rent, and he tried in this way to solve the contradiction of Smith, who sometimes considered rent as a component part of price. But Smith's contradiction is rooted in a deeper cause than Ricardo believed it to be. As we have already mentioned, it stems from the fact that Smith perceived, though imperfectly, something like absolute rent, other than differential rent.

However, as for the criticism that rent for Ricardo is limited to the differential rent, an objection has been raised by some commentators. For example, Karl Diehl affirms that Ricardo also recognised the possibility of absolute rent. Indeed, Ricardo wrote that 'until a country is cultivated in every part, and up to the highest degree, there is always a portion of capital employed on the land which yields no rent' [I/252]. He therefore recognised that the price of corn would become a monopoly price when cultivation attained such a degree, which would give rise to a sort of rent different from differential rent. For this reason, he wrote:

> The corn and raw produce of a country may, indeed, for a time sell at a monopoly price; but they can do so permanently only when no more capital can be profitably employed on the lands, and when, therefore, their produce

cannot be increased. At such time, every portion of land in cultivation, and every portion of capital employed on the land will yield a rent.

[I/250–1], cf. K. Diehl, *Sozialwissenschaftliche Erläuterungen zu Ricardos Grundsätzen*, I. S. 169)

But this is a monopoly rent based on the monopoly price of an agricultural product, not the absolute rent as proposed by Rodbertus and Marx and adopted by Diehl.

Ricardo's reasoning excludes from the outset the existence of such an absolute rent. Of course, absolute rent is founded on landed property, whether *de facto* or *de jure*; although the rate of profit is higher in agriculture because the organic composition of agricultural capital is lower than that of industrial capital, absolute rent is obtained by the former because landed property prevents this higher rate of profit from falling to an average level. This naturally presupposes the distinction between the 'value' of a commodity and its natural price or price of production, and the existence of landed property as an obstacle to the investment of capital. But from the outset, the problem of absolute rent could not exist for Ricardo who, as seen above, assumed the formation of an average rate of profit, made no distinction between value and price and did not recognise the monopolised appropriation of land, unlike Smith.

In short, according to Ricardo, rent rises because land of worse quality is drawn into cultivation or capital is invested under worse conditions. Hence, if the social circumstances make such cultivation or capital investment unnecessary, the rent will necessarily fall [I/78]. These social circumstances may be a diminution of capital in a society accompanied by a decrease in population or a great advance in the productive power of agricultural labour. On the latter possibility, Ricardo wrote as follows:

> The same effects may however be produced, when the wealth and population of a country are increased, if that increase is accompanied by such marked improvements in agriculture, as shall have the same effect of diminishing the necessity of cultivating the poorer lands, or of expending the same amount of capital on the cultivation of the more fertile portions.
>
> [I/79]

According to Ricardo, there are two kinds of improvements in agriculture. The first are 'those which increase the productive powers of the land', and the second are 'those which enable us, by improving our machinery, to obtain its produce with less labour. They both lead to a fall in the price of raw produce; they both affect rent, but they do not affect it equally'.

> The improvements which increase the productive powers of the land, are such as the more skilful rotation of crops, or the better choice of manure. These improvements absolutely enable us to obtain the same produce from a smaller quantity of land.
>
> [I/80]

Therefore they make it unnecessary to cultivate unfavourable lands to satisfy the current demand, and thus bring down the price of corn and the rent.

And 'improvements in agricultural implements [. . .], economy in the use of horses employed in husbandry, and a better knowledge of the veterinary art' will reduce the amount of capital invested on land, which is the same as a decrease in labour, and thus decrease the relative value of the product and bring about a decrease in money rent. But,

> Whether improvements of this kind, however, affect corn rent, must depend on the question, whether the difference between the produce obtained by the employment of different portions of capital be increased, stationary, or diminished. If four portions of capital, 50, 60, 70, 80, be employed on the land, giving each the same results, and any improvement in the formation of such capital should enable me to withdraw 5 from each, [. . .] no alteration would take place in the corn rent; but if the improvements were such as to enable me to make the whole saving on that portion of capital, which is least productively employed, corn rent would immediately fall, because the difference between the capital most productive, and the capital least productive, would be diminished.
>
> [I/82–3]

However, according to Ricardo, in the society progressing in wealth and population, the causes of a fall in rent brought about by such ameliorations in agriculture are weak in their effects compared with the causes that make it difficult to produce additional quantities of corn and raise the rent, because 'the causes, which render the acquisition of an additional quantity of corn more difficult are, in progressive countries, in constant operation, whilst marked improvements in agriculture, or in the implements of husbandry are of less frequent occurrence. (*Essay* [IV/19], footnote). Therefore improvements in agriculture can be ignored as secondary elements in the law of rent, like variations in wages in the law of value. For this reason, Ricardo concluded that the general law of rent consists in its rise with the increase in wealth and population.

Lastly, concerning the social effect of rent, Ricardo was opposed to Quesnay, Smith and particularly Malthus and agreed with Buchanan, their opponent. Of course, according to him,

> Mr. Malthus, too, has satisfactorily explained the principles of rent, and shewed that it rises or falls in proportion to the relative advantages, either of fertility or situation, [. . .] has thereby thrown much light on many difficult points connected with the subject of rent, [. . .]; yet he appears to me to have fallen into some errors. [. . .] One of these errors lies in supposing rent to be a clear gain and a new creation of riches.
>
> [I/398]

Because

rent is a creation of value, [. . .] but not a creation of wealth. If the price
of corn, from the difficulty of producing any portion of it, should rise [. . .]
the possessors will have a greater amount of value; and as no one else will,
in consequence, have a less, the society altogether will be possessed of
greater value, and in that sense rent is a creation of value. But this value
is so far nominal, that it adds nothing to the wealth, that is to say, the
necessaries, conveniences, and enjoyments of the society. [. . .] It must then
be admitted that Mr. Sismondi and Mr. Buchanan, [. . .] were correct,
when they considered rent as a value purely nominal, and as forming no
addition to the national wealth, but merely as a transfer of value, advantageous only to the landlords, and proportionably injurious to the
consumer.

[I/399/400]

In the same way,

the rise of rent is always the effect of the increasing wealth of the country,
and of the difficulty of providing food for its augmented population. It is
a symptom, but it is never a cause of wealth; for wealth often increases
most rapidly while rent is either stationary, or even falling. Rent increases
most rapidly, as the disposable land decreases in its productive powers.

[I/77]

Ricardo concluded thus:

Nothing is more common than to hear of the advantages which the land
possesses over every other source of useful produce, on account of the
surplus which it yields in the form of rent. [. . .] It is only when its powers
decay, and less is yielded in return for labour, that a share of the original
produce of the more fertile portions is set apart for rent, and hence if the
surplus produce which land affords in the form of rent be an advantage, it
is desirable that, every year, the machinery newly constructed should be
less efficient than the old.

[I/75]

Insofar as the value of a commodity is considered to be determined by the
quantity of labour bestowed, the society as a whole disposes of a value corresponding to the aggregate quantity of labour bestowed. This value does not
increase, because a proportion of the commodities in a given branch of production has a price superior to the value corresponding to the quantity of labour
bestowed on them. The prices of the other commodities must fall as much as
the relative price of this proportion of the commodities rises. Therefore, from

the viewpoint of Ricardo's labour theory of value, the rent cannot be said to be either a creation of wealth in his sense of the term (i.e., of use value), or of value. In this regard his contention must be criticised. However, this contention has the merit of completely refuting for the first time the feudal remnant still surviving till after Quesnay and concomitant with both Smith and Malthus. And its positive significance becomes clearer when rent is considered in reciprocal relation with wages and profit.

4. Theory of wages

Ricardo regarded labour as a commodity 'like all other things which are purchased and sold, and which may be increased or diminished in quantity', with a market price and a natural price [I/93].

According to him, 'the market price of labour is the price which is really paid for it, from the natural operation of the proportion of the supply to the demand; labour is dear when it is scarce, and cheap when it is plentiful'. However, 'the market price of labour has, like commodities, a tendency to conform to its natural price' [I/94].

> The natural price of labour is that price which is necessary to enable the labourers, one with another, to subsist and to perpetuate their race, without either increase or diminution. And it is determined by the price of the subsistence of the labourers. Of course, the power of the labourer to support himself, and the family which may be necessary to keep up the number of labourers, does not depend on the quantity of money which he may receive for wages, but on the quantity of food, necessaries, and conveniences become essential to him from habit, which that money will purchase. The natural price of labour, therefore, depends on the price of the food, necessaries, and conveniences required for the support of the labourer and his family. With a rise in the price of food and necessaries, the natural price of labour will rise; with the fall in their price, the natural price of labour will fall.
>
> [I/93]

How, then, does the market price of labour tend to its natural price? In the case of general commodities, Ricardo sought the explanation in the law of the general rate of profit, but in the case of labour he found it in Malthus's law of population growth, which states that the population has a tendency to increase to the limit of subsistence. Thus, he wrote:

> It is when the market price of labour exceeds its natural price, that the condition of the labourer is flourishing and happy, that he has it in his power to command a greater proportion of the necessaries and enjoyments of life, and therefore to rear a healthy and numerous family. When, however, by the encouragement which high wages give to the increase of population,

the number of labourers is increased, wages again fall to their natural price, and indeed from a re-action sometimes fall below it. When the market price of labour is below its natural price, the condition of the labourers is most wretched: then poverty deprives them of those comforts which custom renders absolute necessaries. It is only after their privations have reduced their number, or the demand for labour has increased, that the market price of labour will rise to its natural price, and that the labourer will have the moderate comforts which the natural rate of wages will afford.

[I/94]

But Ricardo recognised, in some particular cases, that 'notwithstanding the tendency of wages to conform to their natural rate, their market rate may, in an improving society, for an indefinite period, be constantly above it'. It is in this improving society that the capital increases progressively and constantly. Because in such a society 'no sooner may the impulse, which an increased capital gives to a new demand for labour be obeyed, than another increase of capital may produce the same effect' [I/95]. However, according to him, this is never the natural course of wages, since the accumulation of the means of employing labour (i.e., of capital) depends on the profit, which depends in turn on the productivity of the marginal agricultural labour, as will be seen later. And this productivity gradually diminishes. On the other hand, the population always maintains the same capacity to increase [I/98–9]. Hence 'the wages of labour will have a tendency to fall, as far as they are regulated by supply and demand' [I/101]. And since they are still governed by the price of subsistence, they will naturally tend to their natural price.

In short, the natural price of labour in Ricardo is, in contrast to the market price of labour, nothing other than the price of the subsistence to be obtained in exchange for labour. Such a subsistence must of course be sufficient to reproduce the so-called 'labour power', the price of which is finally determined by the quantity of labour bestowed on its production, according to his theory of value. His natural price of labour may thus be regarded as being virtually reduced to the quantity of labour necessary for the production of 'labour power'. However, for Ricardo, who only perceived the capitalist society, the distinction between labour and wage labour, particularly between labour and labour power, is not clear. Hence, he affirmed that the natural price of labour is the price of subsistence, but did not say that it is the quantity of labour necessary to produce the 'labour power'. But since he stated that 'profits, [. . .] depend on wages; not on nominal, but real wages; not on the number of pounds that may be annually paid to the labourer, but on the number of days' work, necessary to obtain those pounds' [I/143], it appears that he also understood wages to be determined as the value of 'labour power'. But what he wrote here can ultimately be reduced to the view that wages are determined by the quantity of labour necessary to produce the money obtained in exchange for labour, and hence by the quantity of labour the wage labour commands, which must be said to be different from the quantity of labour necessary for producing the labour power. Therefore, wages in Ricardo's theory are not rigorously deduced from the law of labour value, although factually they are treated as such. And in this, his law of value determining the value of a commodity by the quantity of labour bestowed seems to contradict his value of labour determined merely by the subsistence minimum, which led many people, particularly the so-called Ricardian socialists to misuse his theory of value as a tool for attacking the capitalist society.

According to Ricardo, wages are ultimately determined by the price of subsistence for the labourer and his family, and cannot durably remain above this level. This is precisely a natural law of economics. It is because of this that Lassale called later his law of wages the 'iron law' ('*das eherne Gesetz*') (Ferdinand Lassale, *Das offene Antwortschreiben*, 1863). But it is to be noticed here that the natural price of labour in Ricardo does not at all mean the price of subsistence absolutely necessary for physiological subsistence, but of 'those comforts which custom renders absolute necessaries', which vary across different periods and locations with the variation in customs. He himself explained that 'it varies at different times in the same country, and very materially differs in different countries. It essentially depends on the habits and customs of the people' [I/96–7]. And it may be because of this variability in the content of natural wages that he emphasised the enhancement of the labourers' standard of living (i.e., the rise in natural wages) as the antidote for overpopulation, in writing that 'the friends of humanity cannot but wish that in all countries the labouring classes should have a taste for comforts and enjoyments, and that they should be stimulated by all legal means in their exertions to procure them. There cannot be a better security against a superabundant population' [I/100].

Be that as it may, since the natural price of labour is determined by the price of subsistence of the labourers, 'with the progress of society the natural price of labour has always a tendency to rise' [I/93]. Because, while the natural prices of commodities other than foodstuffs naturally fall with the progress in wealth and population, by the improvement of machinery and also by the development of science and art, foodstuffs, the main commodities governing the natural price of labour, become dearer due to the increased difficulty of production. He stated in this context that 'the same cause which raises rent, namely, the increasing difficulty of providing an additional quantity of food with the same proportional quantity of labour, will also raise wages'. But according to Ricardo, 'there is this essential difference between the rise of rent and the rise of wages'. In the former, corn rent and money rent rise in parallel, while in the latter real wages fall with the rise in money wages, because 'with that addition he would be unable to furnish himself with the same quantity of corn and other commodities, which he had before consumed in his family' [I/102]. In addition, such a rise in the natural price of labour is in close relation to profit. We will see this later.

Thus for Ricardo, wages are regulated directly by the relation between demand (capital) and supply (population), but depend in the last analysis on natural and physiological causes such as the productivity of the soil and the capacity of the population to increase. He asserted that 'like all other contracts, wages should be left to the fair and free competition of the market, and should never be controlled by the interference of the legislature' [I/105], and like Malthus, he criticised the Poor Laws in England of that time. In taking this position, he rejected the historical and social character of labour problems and rendered them absolute and natural problems. Incidentally, in the third edition of *Principles* he added a new chapter 'On Machinery', and revised the assumption that an increase in the total amount of capital would bring about a proportional demand for labour [I/95], recognising that it would only generate a demand for labour at a decreasing rate. This involved contradictory elements in the foundations of his doctrinal system, including the theory of wages and the theory of profit that was dependent on it. In the last section, we will discuss how this took place.

5. Theory of profit

Concerning the origin of profit, Ricardo never sought to give any systematic explanation other than that profit consists in the residual remaining after wages and rent have been subtracted from the product of a nation or individual or from the value of that product [I/110, 112]. It is difficult to infer what view he held on this point.

In discussing changes in value he stated that: 'the difference in value arises in both cases from the profits being accumulated as capital, and is only a just compensation for the time that the profits were withheld' [I/37], and in explaining the relation between the fall in profit and accumulation, he wrote:

> Long before this state of prices was become permanent, there would be no motive for accumulation; for no one accumulates but with a view to make his accumulation productive, and it is only when so employed that it operates on profits. [. . .] The farmer and manufacturer can no more live without profit, than the labourer without wages.
>
> [I/122]

We can probably consider these sentences as his explanation of the origin of profit. However, in the first of these quotations, Ricardo explained how the presupposed profit is distributed among various capitals on the basis of their different recovery times, and in the second he only accounted for the psychological motive of capitalists requiring profit. Neither of them can be said to explain the economic origin of profit.

Ricardo considered the price of labour (i.e., wages) to be the price of subsistence of the labourers, and that the value of the product they produce is higher than the value of labour (in fact wages) [I/14]. Furthermore, he stated that profit and wages are the decomposed parts of the value of a product minus rent and in inverse proportions. Therefore, it would be logically justified to consider his theory of profit as a sort of theory of surplus value. But as we saw above, Ricardo's theory of value mainly concerns the relative value and attaches no importance to the absolute value. As a result, the determination of the substance of value lacks clarity and wages are not deduced from the law of labour value. Hence in Ricardo a rigorous thought of surplus value is never clearly expressed.

In short, the creation and existence of profit appeared almost self-evident and given *a priori* for Ricardo, and there was no reason to bother exploring them. This seems to be the reason why Böhm-Bawerk included his theory of profit in the 'grey theories' of similar meaning (Böhm-Bawerk, *Geschichte u. Kritik der Kapitalzinstheorien*, 3te Aufl. S. 104–106, 'farblose Theorien').

Ricardo's position with regard to the origin of profit may be the cause of his positions on both its average and its result. In any case, as seen above, he regarded the phenomenon of average profit as a given and never questioned its formation. However, as for the concept of average profit itself, he distinguished between two states: before and after the emergence of rent. In the former state, he considered it as the average of profit in all branches of production. In the latter state, it was the profit obtained by the agricultural capital invested on the marginal land paying no rent, and the profit of every other capital tended toward this standard profit.

Because of this point of view on the average profit in the state after the emergence of rent, Ricardo had to make two assumptions. First, the profit of agricultural capital is regulated by the profit of capital employed on the worst land, so that the profit cannot rise as long as the capital on the worst land is not withdrawn. This was made clear in his theory of rent. Second, the actual amount of capital invested in agriculture is a necessary condition for procuring the food required by the actual population, and the actual population is a condition necessary for the actual employment of capital, hence it is impossible to reduce the latter. As a result, the state of agricultural capital cannot change even if the commercial and manufacturing profit rises, as long as the actual capital and population subsist. If commercial and manufacturing profit did rise, with only agricultural profit remaining the same, this would evidently contradict the fact of average profit. So the fallacy consists in imagining the change in commercial and manufacturing profit. Ricardo thus rejected Malthus's objection to the effect that commercial and manufacturing profit also influences agricultural profit and therefore regulates the average profit (*Essay* [IV/22]).

Ricardo also considered that this average profit has a natural tendency to fall with the advancement of the wealth and population of society. Thus his explanation in this regard seems to emphasise different points in *Essay* and *Principles*.

According to the explanation in *Essay*,

> In the first settling of a country rich in fertile land, and which may be had by anyone who chooses to take it, the whole produce, after deducting the outgoings belonging to cultivation, will be the profits of capital, and will belong to the owner of such capital, without any deduction whatever for

rent. Thus, if the capital employed by an individual on such land were of the value of two hundred quarters of wheat, of which half consisted of fixed capital, such as buildings, implements, &c. and the other half of circulating capital, – if, after replacing the fixed and circulating capital, the value of the remaining produce were one hundred quarters of wheat, or of equal value with one hundred quarters of wheat, the neat profit to the owner of capital would be fifty per cent or one hundred profit on two hundred capital.

[IV/10]

However,

After all the fertile land in the immediate neighbourhood of the first settlers were cultivated, if capital and population increased, more food would be required, and it could only be procured from land not so advantageously situated. Supposing then the land to be equally fertile, the necessity of employing more labourers, horses, &c. to carry the produce from the place where it was grown, to the place where it was to be consumed, although no alteration were to take place in the wages of labour, would make it necessary that more capital should be permanently employed to obtain the same produce. Suppose this addition to be of the value of ten quarters of wheat, the whole capital employed on the new land would be two hundred and ten, to obtain the same return as on the old; and, consequently the profits of stock would fall from fifty to forty-three per cent or ninety on two hundred and ten.

[IV/13]

Since this rate becomes the average rate for the reason mentioned above, the profit on the first class soil also falls to 43 per cent, and the net revenue of 100 quarters is divided, 86 belonging to capitalists, the rest of 14 to landlords. By the similar process, moreover with the increase of capital on the marginal land, the average profit on capital will fall. He says in conclusion that 'precisely in the same degree profits would fall' [IV/14]. From this it becomes clear that Ricardo was considering the case in which the rate of profit falls when the necessary amount of capital increases while the necessary amount of profit remains the same (Ricardo stated that the profit will become equivalent to the value of 90 quarters of corn when the capital becomes equal to the value of 210, but 90 appears to be a mistake for 100).

He also gave the rise in wages as a cause of the fall in profit. The increase in the difficulty of production mentioned above raises the prices of corn and other agricultural products. Then the money wages naturally rise, since they are largely governed by the price of corn. But the prices of commodities other than raw produce do not rise, since there are no variations in their conditions of production. This pushes the profit further down. Then the agricultural capitalists will benefit from the rise in the price of corn. But, he wrote, it would be more favourable for them to produce more even if the price falls [IV/19–21]. However, Ricardo attached importance to the increase in the amount of capital and only incidentally examined the rise in wages.

In *Principles*, on the contrary, it is the rise in wages that is important, rather than the increase in the amount of capital. Moreover, his critical arguments are directed mainly against the view that the rise in the price of agricultural produce will not reduce agricultural profit, even though it is evident that the rise in money wages reduces non-agricultural profit.

According to Ricardo's explanation, neither the product of the land governing prices nor the manufacturing product pay rent. The value of these products is divided into two parts, one allocated to the profit of capital and the other to the wages of labour [I/110]. However, the amount to be divided between labour and capital always remains the same, independently from the rise in the price of corn. Suppose, for example [I/113–5], that 10 labourers are employed to harvest 180 quarters of corn when the price of corn is 4 pounds per quarter and the annual wage per capita is 6 quarters of corn or 24 pounds, and that, with the increase in population and wealth and the consequent rise in the price of corn, 10 additional labourers are successively employed on the same or other land, yielding successively 170, 160, and then 150 quarters. In this case, the successive quantities of product of land and capital will each be divided between capital and labour. And since the price of corn will rise exactly in proportion to the increase in the quantity of labour producing it on the worst land or with the last portion of capital, it will rise from its original price of 4 pounds a quarter to 4 pounds 4 shillings 8 pence, then 4 pounds 10 shillings, and then 4 pounds 16 shillings. In this way the total price of the corn produced will always remain the same amount of 720 pounds; its price per quarter is 4 pounds when the crop is 180 quarters, 4*l.* 4*s.* 8*p.* when the crop is 170*q.*; 4*l.* 10*s.* when the crop is 160*q.*, and 4*l.* 16*s.* when the crop is 150*q.* But since wages rise with the price of corn, 'it is evident, that if out of these equal values, the farmer is at one time obliged to pay wages regulated by the price of wheat at £4, and at other times at higher prices, the rate of his profits will diminish in proportion to the rise in the price of corn' [I/113]. He continued: 'whatever rise may take place in the price of corn, in consequence of the necessity of employing more labour and capital to obtain a given additional quantity of produce, such rise will always be equalled in value by the additional rent, or additional labour employed' [I/114].

But, as explained above, wages do not rise at exactly the same rate as the price of corn. For example, in the above case of corn prices, the wages of 10 labourers will rise from the original annual amount of 240 pounds only to 247*l.*, 255*l.*, and 264*l.* successively. And since the amount to be divided between labour and capital is constantly 720*l.*, the profit will fall at any rate, at least as far as the rise in wages is concerned. In the above example, it will fall from 580*l.* to 473*l.*, 465*l.*, and then 456*l.* Thus, Ricardo wrote that 'in every case, agricultural, as well as manufacturing profits are lowered by a rise in the price of raw produce, if it be accompanied by a rise of wages' [I/115].

Since the rise in wages accompanying the rise in agricultural prices pushes down the amount of profit, it is self-evident that its ratio to the capital employed (i.e., the rate of profit) will also fall. In Ricardo's example, if the amount of capital is 3000*l.*, then as the amount of profit successively decreases from 480*l.* to 470*l.* and then to 460*l.*, the rate of profit falls from 16% to 15.7% and then 15.5%.

As illustrated by this example, Ricardo affirmed that the rate of profit falls with the rise in wages because the amount of profit falls even when the capital employed remains constant. This is evidently under the supposition that profit and wages are two decomposed parts of a fixed amount of value, so that an increase in one causes an equivalent decrease in the other. And in relation to this explanation, he stated that in such a case, the increase in the value of capital reduces the rate of profit. Therefore, according to him, in the above case, the rate of profit will fall further for agricultural capital because, insofar as it consists of agricultural product, its value increases for example from 3000*l.* to 3,200*l.*, while for manufacturing capital the rate of profit will fall to an even greater degree because, insofar as it consists of agricultural product like the agricultural capital, it will have to increase in value in order to maintain the same scale of production despite the rise in wages, while at the same time being influenced by the rise in its value [I/117]. The increase in capital value due to a rise in wages must take place equally in agricultural capital and manufacturing capital, but he talks of this circumstance only for manufacturing capital.

As already mentioned, his point of view on the causes of the fall in profit differ somewhat in *Essay* and *Principles*. This raises the following question: when, as in *Essay*, an increase in the difficulty of production in agriculture limits the crop to the same quantity despite a greater amount of capital invested and labour employed, will the product of this additional capital and labour not have a greater value? Consequently, will the profit not increase, and as a result will the rate of profit not remain unchanged? To settle this question, it must be demonstrated that the rise in the price of agricultural produce increases the rent by an equal amount, leaving unchanged the amount of value to be divided between profit and wages and also necessitating the payment of higher wages. For this reason, Ricardo may have emphasised the rise in wages in *Principles* for the purpose of supplementing his doctrine in *Essay*, as he himself explained. Further, it is evident that this argument was put forward from the position of the theory of the decomposition of value, in opposition to the theory of the constitution of value of Smith, Malthus, etc., and presupposed rejection of the rise in wages as a cause of price rises. In any case, in *Principles* where we can find his mature thought, he considered the rise in wages as almost the sole cause of the fall in profit. Still, since there remains doubt about his proposition that profit and wages necessarily vary in opposite directions and that cultivation expands from better to worse lands, it may be a matter of course that this theory of the falling rate of profit remains open to doubt.

Be that as it may, according to Ricardo, the increase in the difficulty of food production accompanies the natural development of wealth and population of the society. Therefore, the fall in the rate of profit is also a necessary trend in the development of the society. In this sense, he stated that 'the natural tendency of profit is to fall' and described this as the 'gravitation as it were of profits'. Fortunately, this tendency is repeatedly counteracted by progress and amelioration in the production of necessaries. But it will have ceased to operate before wages are equal to the total sum of value to be shared with profit, which will hence become zero; accumulation will come to an end, there will be no demand for additional labour and population growth will attain its ultimate point [I/120]. But Ricardo denied that profit actually falls to this limit. For him, the sole motive of accumulation is to gain profit, so without this driving force accumulation is impossible. This driving force weakens with the fall in profit, and when profit falls so far as to be incapable of recompensing sufficiently the difficulties and risks that necessarily arise when capital is used productively, it will totally disappear [I/122]. Therefore, he argued, the fall in profit will cease long before attaining zero.

But for Ricardo, the tendency of profit to fall was of most concern, even if it could never attain zero. For him, there is no extension of the production of wealth without accumulation of capital, hence no increase in the demand for labour. Therefore, 'the gains of the stockholder ['capitalist' in Maide's translation] are national gains, and increase, as all other gains do, the real wealth and power of the country' [I/425]. Capital accumulation is not only the aim of the capitalist class but also the national and general aim, because the fall in profit means not only a loss for the capitalist class but also a detriment to the nation as a whole, since it raises an obstacle to accumulation.

The profit invested with such great significance is considered to fall mainly with the rise in money wages. Therefore, in Ricardo, capital and labour are opposing interests. However, in his theory of the relation of distribution, the labourers are placed in an altogether passive position, and their income is fixed as a rule. As the rise in money wages does not keep pace with the rate of rise in the price of corn but rather falls behind the latter, it never substantially promotes the interests of labour but rather brings about loss. In this regard, wages do not differ from profit. And wages or the demand for labour depends on profit or the accumulation of capital. Therefore, it may also be said *to this extent* that labour tends to share a common interest with capital, while being subordinate to it.

For Ricardo, the true opposition of interest exists rather between landed ownership and capital (and labour), because the rent arises and increases at the expense of the value of produce originally divided into profit and wages. Of these two, wages are passive and fixed, as seen above. Therefore the opposition of interest ultimately lies between land and capital. Ricardo made his point of view on the relation between land and capital explicit in writing that: 'by bringing successively land of a worse quality, or less favourably situated into cultivation, rent would rise on the land previously cultivated, and precisely in the same degree would profits fall' (*Essay* [IV/14]). Furthermore: 'Rent then is in all cases a portion of the profits previously obtained on the land. It is never a new creation of revenue, but always part of a revenue already created' [IV/18], and he stated his position adopting profit or accumulation as the social and general objective, in writing that: 'the interest of the landlord is always opposed to the interest of every other class in the community' [IV/21].

In short, the accumulation of capital accompanying the progress of the capitalist society brings about an increase in the demand for labour, which in turn drives an increase in population. The increase in the demand for corn resulting from population growth makes it necessary to cultivate more unfavourable lands or invest capital in worse conditions, which raises the price of corn. The rise in the price of corn causes, on the one hand, a rise in the part of the corn price allotted to rent, and on the other hand, a fall in the part allotted to profit via the increase in money wages. Though decreasing in relative terms, the profit increasing in absolute terms causes the accumulation of capital, thus restarting the same process as before. Thus, in the repetition of this process, the part of the wealth produced in society allotted to labour is fixed, the part going to land is constantly increasing, and the part going to capital is constantly decreasing. Such is Ricardo's picture of the variation in the relation of distribution that takes place with the development of society.

For Ricardo, this picture of the variation in the relation of distribution, in particular the increase in rent and the decrease in profit, was extremely worrisome, even fearful. However, though governed directly by the characteristics of contemporary society (pursuit of profit and capital accumulation), he considered these vicissitudes as being ultimately based on natural, physiological causes like the productive force of land and the capacity of the population to increase. Therefore, while worrying about the decline of profit and the degeneration of capital accumulation, he neither called for the realisation of these general objectives of society by means of positive and artificial devices, nor condemned the landlords for obtaining rent. However, as the decrease in profit and the increase in rent are contrary to the general interest of the nation, he clearly rejected them in the interest of the nation as a whole, when they occurred not as part of the natural process of the economy but through artificial and conscious efforts by landlords, etc. Here we can see the facet of Ricardo as a figure in the foundation of economic liberalism.

It is from this position that Ricardo called for the free importation of corn, in opposition to Malthus. He wrote that insofar as corn importation is prohibited or limited, worse lands must be drawn into cultivation with the progress of wealth and population, whatever improvements and progress there may be in agriculture. Whereas,

> If we were left to ourselves, unfettered by legislative enactments, we should gradually withdraw our capital from the cultivation of such lands, and import the produce which is at present raised upon them. The capital withdrawn would be employed in the manufacture of such commodities as would be exported in return for the corn. Such a distribution of part of the capital of the country, would be more advantageous, or it would not be adopted'

[IV/32]. And he wrote elsewhere that 'if [a small but fertile country] freely permits the importation of food, it may accumulate a large stock of capital without any great diminution in the rate of profits, or any great increase in the rent of land' [I/126]. In this way, the limitation of corn imports prevents the natural distribution of capital and reduces profit. Therefore its maintenance is entirely in the interest of a particular class and detrimental to society as a whole. He wrote:

I shall greatly regret that considerations for any particular class, are allowed to check the progress of the wealth and population of the country. If the interests of the landlord be of sufficient consequence, to determine us not to avail ourselves of all the benefits which would follow from importing corn at a cheap price, they should also influence us in rejecting all improvements in agriculture, and in the implements of husbandry.

(*Essay* [IV/41])

6. Foreign commerce

As shown above, Ricardo named the free importation of corn as an additional factor counteracting the tendency of the rate of profit to fall, along with progress and improvements in agriculture. In what follows we will briefly describe his theory of foreign commerce, because his advocacy of free trade was developed in close relation with his other economic theories, particularly those of value, profit, money, etc., although he based this advocacy on the interest of the international division of labour, as did Smith.

As seen above, Ricardo confused the 'value' of a commodity with its natural price. As a result, he took the free movement of capital and labour among industrial branches and the averaging of profit as a precondition for the law of labour value to prevail, and for commodities to be exchanged according to the labour endowed. However, he considered this precondition to be absent from the international scene, because

the fancied or real insecurity of capital, when not under the immediate control of its owner, together with the natural disinclination which every man has to quit the country of his birth and connexions, and intrust himself with all his habits fixed, to a strange government and new laws, check the emigration of capital. These feelings, which I should be sorry to see weakened, induce most men of property to be satisfied with a low rate of profits in their own country, rather than seek a more advantageous employment for their wealth in foreign nations.

[I/136–7]

Therefore, 'the same rule which regulates the relative value of commodities in one country, does not regulate the relative value of the commodities exchanged between two or more countries' [I/133]. Rather, 'the value of all foreign goods is measured by the quantity of the produce of our land and labour, which is given in exchange for them' [I/128]. For example, the product of the labour of 100 men of England can be exchanged with that of 80 men of Portugal. He continued:

> Under a system of perfectly free commerce, each country [. . .] distributes labour most effectively and most economically: while, by increasing the general mass of productions, it diffuses general benefit, and binds together [. . .] the universal society of nations throughout the civilized world.
>
> [I/133–4]

Ricardo illustrated this relation with the following example.

> England may be so circumstanced, that to produce the cloth may require the labour of 100 men for one year; and if she attempted to make the wine, it might require the labour of 120 men for the same time. England would therefore find it her interest to import wine, and to purchase it by the exportation of cloth. To produce the wine in Portugal, might require only the labour of 80 men for one year, and to produce the cloth in the same country, might require the labour of 90 men for the same time. It would therefore be advantageous for her to export wine in exchange for cloth. This exchange might even take place, notwithstanding that the commodity imported by Portugal could be produced there with less labour than in England. Though she could make the cloth with the labour of 90 men, she would import it from a country where it required the labour of 100 men to produce it, because it would be advantageous to her rather to employ her capital in the production of wine, for which she would obtain more cloth from England, than she could produce by diverting a portion of her capital from the cultivation of vines to the manufacture of cloth.
>
> [I/135]

In this passage, Ricardo assumes international commerce to be a barter exchange. And since 'gold and silver are, by the competition of commerce, distributed in such proportions amongst the different countries of the world, as to accommodate themselves to the natural traffic which would take place if no such metals existed, and the trade between countries were purely a trade of barter. Thus, cloth cannot be imported into Portugal, unless it sell' [I/137], the process of international commerce is ultimately the same as in the trade of barter when gold and silver have become a general medium of circulation, except for the difference in their velocities. He explained the reason for this as follows: in the previous example 'cloth cannot be imported into Portugal, unless it sell there for more gold than it cost in the country from which it was imported; and wine cannot be imported into England, unless it will sell for more there than it cost in Portugal. [. . .] Now suppose England to discover a process for making wine, so that it should become her interest rather to grow it than import it; she would naturally divert a portion of her capital from the foreign trade to the home trade; she would cease to manufacture cloth for exportation, and would grow wine for herself. The money price of these commodities would be regulated accordingly; wine would fall here while cloth continued at its former price, and in Portugal no alteration would take place in the price of either commodity. Cloth would continue for some time to be exported from this country, because its price would continue to be higher in Portugal than here; but money instead of wine would be given in exchange for it, till the accumulation of money here, and its diminution abroad, should so operate on the relative value of cloth in the two countries, that it would cease to be profitable to export it. If the improvement in making wine were of a very important description, it might become profitable for the two countries to exchange employments; for England to make all the wine, and Portugal all the cloth consumed by them; but this could be effected only by a new distribution of the precious metals, which should raise the price of cloth in England, and lower it in Portugal [I/137–8].

Thus, according to Ricardo, while foreign commerce may augment the quantity and variety of commodities and contribute strongly to their enjoyment through abundance and cheapness, 'no extension of foreign trade will immediately increase the amount of value in a country' [I/128] because, as seen above, the value of foreign commodities is measured by the quantity of domestic product of land and labour exchanged with them. Accordingly, 'foreign trade [. . .] has no tendency to raise the profits of stock, unless the commodities imported be of that description on which the wages of labour are expended' [I/133]. So Ricardo opposed the contention of Smith and others to the effect that 'the great profits which are sometimes made by particular merchants in foreign trade, will elevate the general rate of profits in the country [I/128].

The argument put forward by Smith and others was as follows:

> To partake of the new and beneficial foreign commerce, [. . .] less capital being necessarily devoted to the growth of corn, to the manufacture of cloth, hats, shoes, &c. while the demand continues the same, the price of these commodities will be so increased, that the farmer, hatter, clothier, and shoemaker, will have an increase of profits, as well as the foreign merchant'.

But according to Ricardo, 'I deny that less capital will necessarily be devoted to the growth of corn, to the manufacture of cloth, hats, shoes, [. . .] if so, their price will not rise' [I/129].

Then Ricardo distinguishes between three cases: 1. The same part of the national product of land and labour as before is allotted to the purchase of foreign articles. 2. A smaller part is thus allotted. 3. A larger part is thus allotted. If the same part of the national product is allotted to this purpose, there will be the same demand as before for cloth, corn, hats, etc. and so the same part of capital will be allotted to their production. If, as a result of the foreign articles becoming cheaper, a smaller part of the national product is allotted to their purchase, there will be more capital available for the production of the above commodities and greater demand for them, so that neither their prices nor their profits can rise durably. Finally, if a greater part of the national product is so allotted, the demand for the other commodities will diminish, but since the capital necessary for their production and hence their supply will also diminish, their prices will not fall [I/129–30].

Here Ricardo drew the following conclusion: 'in all cases the demand for foreign and home commodities together, as far as regards value, is limited by the revenue and capital of the country. If one increases, the other must diminish' [I/130], and in neither of these cases can the price of domestic commodities or the profit of domestic manufactures possibly rise as a result of foreign trade, except only for the case in which the imported commodities are foodstuffs for labourers or other necessities [I/133].

It is evident that Ricardo's theory of foreign commerce is, as seen above, a prolongation and development of Smith's doctrine. Like the latter, furthermore, it was developed against the backdrop of England's situation at the time – at the forefront of capitalist development – and in keeping with its national interest. The fundamental impossibility of international capital movement which Ricardo took as a basis for his theory of foreign trade only applies to the period of rudimentary international credit organisation. The determination of the value of foreign commodities by the quantity or value of domestic commodities to be exchanged with them is an extreme absurdity, affirming as it does the determination of value by the exchange ratio instead of vice versa. The contention that money is distributed among nations according to the necessity of commercial transactions in such a way as to determine the price level is founded, as we have seen, on the quantity theory of money, and therefore suffers from the drawbacks of that theory. Furthermore, the erroneousness of Ricardo's doctrine about the relation between foreign commerce and profit is evident: one need only consider the importance of the supply of cheap raw materials from India for English industry. These doctrines may ultimately be the result of his attention being wholly focused on the price of corn or wages during the debates of the time about the Corn Laws, etc.

7. Concluding remarks

In applying the above principles of distribution, Ricardo also developed a theory of taxation (*Principles*, Ch. VIII-XVIII, Ch. XXII-XXIII, Ch. XXVI, Ch. XXIX). According to him, 'taxes are ultimately paid, either from the capital, or from the revenue of the country' [I/150]. Therefore the question of the payment of taxes is finally nothing other than an aspect of the theory of distribution, the central subject of his economic theory. He was opposed to the Corn Laws because the fall in profit prevents the accumulation of capital, thus working against national welfare. For precisely the same reason, he rejected the taxation which government policy might impose on capital [I/153].

However, as the outline of his political economy has already been clarified, we will not involve ourselves further with these problems of taxation. In the following, we examine his place in the history of doctrine by reviewing anew his theory of distribution, for Ricardo's importance lies mainly in the fact that his political economy was focused on the problem of distribution, with a view to advancing it farther.

As seen above, in considering the capitalist society, Ricardo presupposed the dominance of self-interest in economic activity and free competition, following the tradition of Smith. Hence, the pursuit of profit or capital accumulation was the be-all and end-all for him. His theory of distribution was intended precisely to clarify the law determining the trend of distribution: more and more of the value produced in the society being allotted to rent to the detriment of profit during repetition of the following concatenated sequence: accumulation of capital – increase in the demand for labour – growth of population – increase in the demand for corn – cultivation of worse lands – rise in corn price – increase in rent – rise in wages – fall in profit. For Smith, economic laws were still considered to belong to the natural order given by nature or Providence, but for Ricardo, such a regular course governed by the law of distribution penetrated society with iron necessity as an essential, permanent law of the capitalist society itself, despite accidental and temporary disturbing circumstances. This may be the result of the difference in their historical environments. Smith, on the eve of the industrial revolution, in the context of a capitalism that was still largely an idea, had to rely largely on metaphysics or theology, though remaining grounded on the reality of this society. Ricardo, on the other hand, in the capitalism that only emerged after the dawn of this revolution, observed solely the reality of this society in his pursuit of its inherent laws. In any event, in Ricardo all the metaphysical and theological elements of Smith were excluded, and it was only with Ricardo that political economy fully became a science treating capitalism as a historical reality.

As can be seen from the above sequence in the process of distribution, the accumulation of capital in Ricardo ultimately depends on the productive power of the land, considered to be governed by the law of diminishing returns, and the increase in the supply of labour responding to the demand for it is based on the power of population growth, which spontaneously attains the limit of subsistence, according to Malthus. Hence, the fundamental determinant of distribution, in the society in which the pursuit of profit or capital accumulation is the be-all and end-all, is ultimately the productive power of land and then the capacity of the population to grow. Of course, Ricardo did not deny that other factors can actually influence distribution, for example the invention of new machines, the extension of new outlets, etc. But according to him, these factors only influence the distribution temporarily and specifically, never generally and permanently. He wrote:

> It is in this enquiry that I am led to believe that the state of the cultivation of the land is almost the only great permanent cause. There are other

circumstances which are attended with temporary effects of more or less duration, and frequently operate partially on particular trades. The state of production from the land compared with the means necessary to make it produce operates on all, and is alone lasting in its effects.

(Letter to Malthus, 16th September 1814 [VI/133])

So for Ricardo, the productive power of land is a fact regulated by the natural laws confirmed by the natural sciences, and the power of population growth is an immutable biological fact. It was in this sense that he affirmed that: 'the land being limited in quantity, and differing in quality, with every increased portion of capital employed on it, there will be a decreased rate of production, whilst the power of population continues always the same' [I/98]. He considered this natural and biological fact, prevailing far beyond his time and country, as the essential determinant of the distribution in his time and country. Here, the relation of distribution, with profit or accumulation as its be-all and end-all, is considered absolute and fixed because it is conditioned by a natural and biological fact; its inherent laws, for example the reduction of wages to the necessary cost of living, are considered iron laws, and the fall in the rate of profit is attributed to a natural and biological cause. He certainly discussed and showed an interest in the variations in distribution occurring with the development of capitalist society. But for him, such variations only raised quantitative questions within a particular relation of distribution, not qualitative questions concerning the relation itself.

As the inherent laws of capitalist society, governed in this way by natural and biological facts, are not social and relative but natural and absolute in character, they cannot be influenced by human endeavour, even if they bring about undesirable results and difficulties. It may therefore be concluded that things must be left to run their natural course. As seen above, it seems to be from this viewpoint that Ricardo did not condemn high rent, while considering its rise as contrary to the interests of the society, and also why he left the determination of wages to fair and free transaction on the market, while recognising their tendency to fall to the minimum necessary for human subsistence.

Ricardo was thus akin to Malthus, the author of population theory, in thinking that economic relations are largely governed by natural and biological facts – and are consequently of a natural, absolute character – and that with the development of society the rate of profit as its prime mover falls and wages are fixed or fall. Adopting a world view governed by deism, he attributed economic relations to human nature, but in contrast to the gay optimism of Smith, who upheld the natural harmony of economic interests, the keynote of Ricardo's theory is extremely dismal and pessimistic. That is why he is described as pessimistic, together with Malthus. We can also see in this point the shift in approach over time. Ricardo searched for the essential and perpetual laws of the society while presupposing a more developed capitalism. However, while in the capitalism that Smith conceived as more of an idea, the free actions of every person pursuing their self-interest could result in a predetermined natural theological harmony, in the already-realised capitalism of Ricardo these individual actions often lacked harmony, and the destinies of different groups appeared to be contradictory to each other. This is particularly manifest in the relation between land and capital. In such circumstances, the liberal tradition since Smith cannot be maintained by metaphysics or theology deducing economic relations from human nature, but rather by their absolutizing in the name of natural and biological causes: the objective is no longer the welfare of all but the greatest happiness of the greatest number.[1] Because in so doing, the economy driven by profit or accumulation becomes absolute and eternal, and the difficulties or contradictions accompanying its development are founded on the iron laws of cruel nature, so that the measures to counteract them are to be found solely in the self-restraint of each individual.

In addition, Ricardo's theory of distribution, based on this view of the economic laws as natural and absolute, elucidated the state and evolution of the social classes of the time and gave a scientific foundation to the call for the abolition of obstacles to the natural development of capitalism. And his theory of distribution explained how the income of the active participants in production diminishes while that of the non-participants increases. In this sense, it became the foundation for the opposition to the tariff on corn as a theoretical expression of the feelings of many people – particularly capitalists – against landed property. His theory of wages exempted capital from its responsibility towards labour and justified the abolition of the poor law, by showing the inevitability of falling wages and poverty just like Malthus's population theory. Therefore, the natural absolutizing of the bleak economic laws of Ricardo served not only passively to maintain the liberal tradition inherited from Smith in the new context that emerged after the industrial revolution, but also as a positive interpretation of newly-developed capitalism in response to capital requiring the further advancement of production in opposition to the strengthening of labour, after the complete refutation of feudalism.

Considered in this way, we can see that Ricardo's doctrine fully reflected the reality of the time and was adapted to its social needs, contrary to what is generally believed. Furthermore, history shows that even the productive power of land or the growth of population, the ultimate conditions of distribution for Ricardo, were in fact only concrete, particular features especially noticed at that time in the development of English capitalism, though Ricardo regarded them to be absolutely fixed as natural and biological fact. He mistook these concrete, particular features for something abstract and general, and was governed by the latter. In this sense too, he is to be criticised for lacking in abstraction rather than for being too abstract.

However, it goes without saying that this view of the economic laws as natural and absolute necessities limited his doctrine and caused many difficulties and contradictions. In particular, because of this viewpoint, his labour theory of value always presupposed the capitalist society without recognising a distinct pre-capitalist society, making it impossible for him to distinguish between the 'value' of a commodity and its natural price, or between individual profit and average profit. This theory therefore contained a contradiction that became increasingly more evident with the development of production and the increase in fixed capital. And for similar reasons, the confusion between labour and wage labour or labour power made it difficult to link the law of labour value and the law of wages, which was condemned and criticised with the increasing difficulty labourers had in earning a livelihood. Accepting with resignation the various difficulties and harmful effects accompanying social development, considering them as something natural, absolute and inevitable, was still not contrary to common sense, insofar as society's productive power was rapidly advancing. But when the productive power stagnates and these difficulties become more serious, such an attitude cannot escape from social criticism.

In such a context, the denial of general crisis in his theory remains to be specifically explained. As seen above, although Ricardo considered profit or accumulation as the fundamental motivation of the economy in contemporary society, he identified this economy with a natural economy directly aiming to satisfy desires, considering the former as natural and absolute. And from this position he denied the possibility of general overproduction or crisis, like Say or Mill. In one passage, he wrote:

> Productions are always bought by productions, or by services; money is only the medium by which the exchange is carried out. Too much of a particular commodity may be produced, of which there may be such a glut in the market, as not to repay the capital expended on it; but this cannot be the case with respect to all commodities; the demand for corn is limited by the mouths which are to eat it, for shoes and coats by the persons who are to wear them; but though a community, or a part of a community, may have as much corn, and as many hats and shoes, as it is able or may wish to consume, the same cannot be said of every commodity produced by nature or by art. [. . .] The wish to do all or some of these is implanted in every man's breast; nothing is required but the means, and nothing can afford the means, but an increase of production.
>
> [I/291–2]

Here we can see clearly that the capitalist, commodity-producing society is altered into an economic society directly aiming solely to satisfy human material desires. It is clear from the above that he divided the branches of production into those producing the necessities of life consumed by labourers and those producing the luxuries consumed by capitalists, and while the former is limited by the population, the latter can be expanded ad infinitum, since human desires are infinite. But according to Ricardo, the former too can be expanded without limit by the accumulation of capital, because it means the capacity to employ more labour. Therefore, production cannot generally exceed desires. The desires in question here are naturally effective ones, i.e., endowed with the ability to pay, which is created by the accumulation of capital and the expansion of production. Thus, for Ricardo, production is equal to consumption, supply to demand, and the accumulation of capital means the accumulation of enjoyment. Therefore, partial overproduction is possible, but not general overproduction. Moreover, it is accidental, never of necessity. Hence the fall in profit he discussed and the limit to the capital accumulation he foresaw were, as seen above, considered to be founded on natural and biological causes, not on social and historical circumstances.

In thus denying the possibility of general crisis, Ricardo maintained the tradition of Smith, according to whom the happiness of both the individual and the society depends only on the development of production and capital, and the infinite development of production and capital contributes of itself to the happiness of both the individual and the society. However, as the first crises occurred in England in 1815 and 1818–1819, and then occurred periodically after 1825, this theory became too contradictory to the reality. For this reason, together with Say, Mill and others who held roughly the same opinion, he became subject to the questioning or objections of Malthus, Owen, Sismondi, etc.

Among these latter, Sismondi (Simonde de, 1773–1842, his chief work: *Les nouveaux principes d'économie politique*, 2 vols. 1819), who initially embraced the thought of classical political economy, came to recognise the inevitability of general crisis after travelling in England and observing its social reality. He examined thus the balance between production and consumption and saw the necessity of its being disturbed by the development of capitalist production, in contrast to Ricardo who affirmed the possibility of an infinite expansion in production and accumulation, in the conviction that consumption is limited solely by production. In other words, according to Sismondi, the income of labourers diminishes with the increase in production (due to the constant effort of capital to economise labour or raw materials), and as a result their consumption also diminishes. On the other hand, although the income of capitalists increases, physical limits render the corresponding expansion of their consumption impossible.

Of course, this questioning and criticism by Sismondi and others still contain many problems in themselves. Nevertheless, in finding the cause of the difficulties represented by overproduction or crisis deep in the profit-seeking process itself, embodied in historical capitalist production, it is not merely directed against the denial of overproduction or crisis, but extends to a criticism of the view that economic laws are natural and absolute. It is because of his view of the crisis that Sismondi became an opponent of industrialism and called on the government to cease encouraging inventions, and on large capital to divert from industry.

However, this questioning of absolute naturalisation was in fact contained and developed in the theory of Ricardo, though in a rudimentary form. This can be said of chapter 31, 'On Machinery', that was added to the third edition of *Principles*.

Discussions about the social and economic influences of machinery only began after the 18th century, when the use of machinery started to play an important role. Thus, Adam Smith affirmed that it would promote the interests of society as a whole, considering that machinery would augment productive power, which would in turn bring about an expansion of capital increasing labour funds. This view was adopted by Ricardo, who was at first 'of opinion, that such an application of machinery to any branch of production, as should have the effect of saving labour, was a general good, accompanied only with that portion of inconvenience which in most cases attends the removal of capital and labour from one employment to another'. However, 'on further reflection' [I/386] his opinion underwent considerable modification as far as the labouring class was concerned, and in the third edition of *Principles* he arrived at the conclusion that 'the opinion entertained by the labouring class, that the employment of machinery is frequently detrimental to their interests, is not founded on prejudice and error, but is conformable to the correct principles of political economy' [I/392].

The reason why he arrived at this conclusion is the following: by the employment of machinery 'the one fund, from which landlords and capitalists derive their revenue, may increase, while the other, that upon which the labouring class mainly depend, may diminish', and therefore 'the same cause which may increase the net revenue of the country, may at the same time render the population redundant' [I/388]. And for this reason, he retracted his former view that the circulating capital to be allotted for paying wages would be separated from the sector in which the machinery is used but would be invested anew in other sectors, and now affirmed that this part of capital is transformed into fixed capital, which does not give employment to every labourer replaced by the machinery [cf., I/389–90]. This point was expressed more clearly in the following passage discussing the process of capital accumulation, where he wrote that machinery

> rather operates in determining the employment of the capital which is saved and accumulated, than in diverting capital from its actual employment. With every increase of capital and population, food will generally rise, on account of its being more difficult to produce. The consequence of a rise of food will be a rise of wages, and every rise of wages will have a tendency to determine the saved capital in a greater proportion than before to the employment of machinery. Machinery and labour are in constant competition, and the former can frequently not be employed until labour rises. [. . .] Therefore, with every augmentation of capital, a greater proportion of it is employed on machinery. The demand for labour will continue to increase with an increase of capital, but not in proportion to its increase; the ratio will necessarily be a diminishing ratio.
>
> [I/395]

Karl Diehl, commentator on Ricardo's political economy, suggested that the motive for his new theory of machinery may have been found in the work of John Barton, *Observations on the Circumstances which influence the Conditions of the labouring Classes of Society*, 1817 (K. Diehl, *Erläuterungen zu Ricardo's*

Grundgesetzen, II, S.425). This may be based on the fact that Ricardo quotes from this work in his note on the above sentence, saying that it 'contains much valuable information' [I/396]. But at the same time, this new view of Ricardo may have been motivated by the actual situation in England at the beginning of the 19th century, particularly during the first 15 years, when the very rapid development of industrial technology gave rise to the Luddite movement (Ludditen Bewegungen), involving the large-scale destruction of machinery in industrial regions, manifesting to an extreme the conflict between machinery and labour.

If this is the case, the chapter 'On Machinery' is surely suggestive of Ricardo's open mind as a researcher, quite prepared to correct frankly the error in his view according to changes in the real situation. However, if he recognised that the same cause which augments the net income comprising profit and rent also gives rise to overpopulation, rendering the position of labourers difficult, this was not only contrary to the tradition following Smith, which considered the progressive production of wealth to contribute immediately to the wellbeing of society as a whole, it was also a confession that the view he originally held was now clearly contradictory to reality and could not possibly be maintained. He could no longer maintain the Smith tradition that attributed difficulties like poverty to the iron laws of nature such as the productive power of the land or the capacity of population growth, since he now not only recognised the existence of such difficulties, but also found their cause in the profit-pursuing process itself in the capitalist society. It is quite natural that McCulloch, one of his disciples who always stuck closely to the traditional line, irrespective of the developments of reality, should send repeated letters to Ricardo, after publication of his new theory of machinery, to point out that it would destroy his work and also inflict serious damage on the science. Furthermore, in his work (J. R. McCulloch, *Principles of Political Economy*, 1825, Part II, Ch. IV.), he mentioned the amelioration of machinery and opposed Ricardo's view.

On the other hand, what Ricardo did as a devotee of the truth was solely to change his opinion according to the requirements of logic and reality, but he was not sufficiently aware of the impact of this change on his doctrinal system to deduce the appropriate conclusion from it. This is the reason why we said above that a questioning of absolute naturalisation was contained and developed in his theory on machinery, though in a rudimentary form. However, from this we can see that the classical political economy developed from Smith completely refuted its feudal character, emerged from its metaphysical and theological aspects and became independent as a science analysing the facts in capitalism, limited to those of the time of Ricardo, but already containing questionable or negative elements in a rudimentary form, which placed it objectively at a turning point.

Note

1 This is the philosophy of Bentham that is considered to have influenced Ricardo. It could certainly be said that in Smith, society is an entity integrating the

individuals by virtue of Providence as a result of his deistic world view, and that in this the society takes precedence over the individuals. But for Bentham, who rejected metaphysics and took the individuals as the sole entities, society could only be conceived as the sum of the individuals. And, while in Smith self-interest was led a priori by an invisible hand to the harmony of social interests, in Bentham there cannot be any practical guarantee that enlightened self-interest also takes into account the interests of all so as to bring about such harmony. Then Ricardo, drawing on Bentham, probably had to carry the banner for the greatest happiness of the greatest number, abandoning the general harmony of Smith (cf. Briefs, *Untersuchungen zur Klassischen Nationalökonomie* [Verlag von Gustav Fischer, 1915]).

Index

For Product Safety Concerns and Information please contact our EU
representative GPSR@taylorandfrancis.com
Taylor & Francis Verlag GmbH, Kaufingerstraße 24, 80331 München, Germany

www.ingramcontent.com/pod-product-compliance
Ingram Content Group UK Ltd.
Pitfield, Milton Keynes, MK11 3LW, UK
UKHW021009180425
457613UK00019B/870